TOURING CHINA

Selected Tour Commentaries

(VOLUME I)
NATIONAL TOURISM ADMINISTRATION
OF THE PEOPLE'S REPUBLIC OF CHINA

CHINA TRAVEL & TOURISM PRESS

Translated by Wang Jun, Liu Lingyan, Chai Jia and Yu Hui

Proofread by Char, Connie Y. Tcheng, Chen Jianmin

Editor in charge: Cheng Weijin, Zhao Xiangxiang

Published by CHINA TRAVEL & TOURISM PRESS
9A Jianguomennei Dajie, Beijing 100005, China
Printed by Beijing 1201 Printing House
Printed in the People's Republic of China

PREFACE

Under the auspices of the National Tourism Administration, a number of veteran guide-interpreters, trainers and administrators from China's tourism industry have collected, compared and chosen from over 100 pieces of sightseeing commentary to compile this publication, entitled "Sightseeing throughout China: Chosen Tourism Commentaries (a comprehensive volume)." The aim of the compilation and publication of 31 model commentaries is to further boost the professional culture of China's tourism, to promote China's rich tourism resources and economic and tourism achievements since China adopted its reform and open-up policy, to enhance the patriotic mentality within tourism employees and to upgrade guide-interpreter's skills through regulating of tourism phraseology and enriching of commentary contents.

"Sightseeing throughout China: Chosen Tourism Commentaries (a comprehensive volume)" contributes to the development of China's tourism in that:

(1) It is unprecedented that China's tourism employees engage themselves in composition and compilation of commentaries on a large scale. Although China in the past saw the publication of a number of tourism books-most of them brief introductions or commentary pieces, they tended not to facilitate the face-to-face interaction between guide-interpreters and their clients. The compilation and publication of this book, though, is a wholly

I

Selected Tour Commentaries

new production that based itself on rich and numerous historical and cultural records as well as skills and orally orientated tourism language on the part of guide-interpreters. In some tourism-developed countries, some kinds of special commentary manuals are on demand in a bid to help guide-interpreters accommodate the different needs of various groups. With the ever deepening of China's reform and open-up policy, the speedy development of the nation's tourism as well as the ever-increasing social needs of standardized services, it is ever imperative to put the commentaries up to standard.

(2) The composition and compilation of model commentaries are done at the demand of many guide-interpreters and sightseers. Over the last few years, there were a few individuals working on some tourist attractions who gave commentaries at will or commented in a ignorant, superstitious and vulgar way. They even went so far as to violate the government's policies. This has not only hampered the upbringing of the public's consciousness, but also inflicted damage to the image of the nation. It is therefore an important mandate in terms of making tourism introductions on the basis of scientific and wholesome commentaries.

(3) The composition and selection of model commentaries serves as a boost to the strengthening of our tourism employees, with guide-interpreters in particular. Most of the authors of the chosen 31 pieces of commentary are on-the-spot guide-interpreters, tourism colleague teachers, students, or administration officials. Their pieces of work serve reflect their long-term experiences and hold attainments and high values. This activity has received positive reaction throughout the industry.

(4) This book, as well as other volumes of soon-to-come model commentary series is a must for tourism employees, especially guide-interpreters who hope to improve their professional

Preface

skills. Past experiences have shown that wherever there was a strengthening in the training and education of tour guides, there was an improvement in guiding skills. All in all, this publication could be good news for tourism practitioners and tourists as well.

The selection and publication of the following 30 pieces of model commentary serves as a good start of systematization of model commentaries which will invigorate the development of China's tourism industry. It is my wish that more books of model commentary series could be accepted for publication in an effort to better serve the tourism and contribute to the society.

He Guangwei
Chairman of the National Tourism Administration

CONTENTS

Preface ··· (I)
Forbidden City ··· (1)
The Palace Museum ·· (17)
Summer Palace ·· (25)
Temple of Heaven ··· (40)
Chengde Mountain Resort ································· (50)
Yungang Grottoes ·· (69)
Hulunbeier Grassland ·· (81)
Water cave of Benxi ·· (87)
Heavenly Lake on Mount Changbai ·················· (94)
Shanghai Museum ··· (105)
Shanghai New Bund ·· (116)
Dr. Sun Yat-sen's Mausoleum ·························· (124)
Zhuozheng (Humble Administrator's)
    Garden in Suzhou ·· (135)
The West Lake in Hangzhou ···························· (150)
Mount Huangshan ··· (161)
Guyao—A Porcelain Factory in Jingdezhen ······· (189)
Qufu ··· (198)
Shaolin Temple (I) ··· (229)
Shaolin Temple (II) ·· (234)
The Three Gorges of the Yangtze River ··········· (242)

V

Selected Tour Commentaries

Temple of The Chen Clan ·········· (262)
Stone Carvings on The Baoding Mountain
In Dazu County ·········· (276)
The Li River ·········· (291)
The Stone Forest ·········· (309)
Huangguoshu Waterfall ·········· (320)
The Potala Palace ·········· (324)
Xi'an Museum of Stele Forest ·········· (334)
History Museum of Shaanxi Province ·········· (342)
Terra—Cotta Army Museum ·········· (356)
Heavenly Lake in Xinjiang ·········· (361)

FORBIDDEN CITY

(In front of the Meridian Gate)
Ladies and Gentlemen,

I am pleased to serve as your guide today.

This is the Palace Museum, also known as the Purple Forbidden City. It is the largest and most well preserved imperial residence in China today. Under Ming Emperor Yongle, construction began in 1406. It took 14 years to build the Forbidden City. The first ruler who actually lived here was Ming Emperor Zhudi. For five centuries thereafter, it continued to be the residence of 23 successive emperors until 1911 when Qing Emperor Puyi was forced to abdicate the throne. In 1987, the United Nations Educational, Scientific and Cultural Organization recognized the Forbidden City as a world cultural legacy.

It is believed that the Palace Museum, or Zi Jin Cheng (Purple Forbidden City), got its name from astronomy and folklore. The ancient astronomers divided the constellations into groups and centered them around the Ziwei Yuan (North Star). The constellation containing the North Star was called the Constellation of Heavenly God and the star itself was called the purple palace. Because the emperor was supposedly the son of the heavenly gods, his central and dominant position would be further highlighted by the use of the word purple in the name of his residence. In folklore, the term "an eastern purple cloud is drifting" became a metaphor for auspicious events

Selected Tour Commentaries

after a purple cloud was seen drifting eastward immediately before the arrival of an ancient philosopher, Lao Zi, to the Hangu Pass. Here, purple is associated with auspicious developments. The word jin (forbidden) is self-explanatory as the imperial palace was heavily guarded and off-limits to ordinary people.

The red and yellow used on the palace walls and roofs are also symbolic. Red represents happiness, good fortune and wealth. Yellow is the color of the earth on the Loess Plateau, the original home of the Chinese people. Yellow became an imperial color during the Tang dynasty, when only members of the royal family were allowed to wear it and use it in their architecture.

The Forbidden City is rectangular in shape. It is 960 meters long from north to south and 750 meters wide from east to west. It has 9,900 rooms under a total roof area 150,000 square meters. A 52—meter-wide-moat encircles a 9. 9-meter—high wall which encloses the complex. Octagon—shaped turrets rest on the four corners of the wall. There are four entrances into the city: the Meridian Gate to the south, the Shenwu Gate (Gate of Military Prowess) to the north, and the Xihua Gate (Western Flowery Gate) to the west, the Donghua (Eastern Flowery Gate) to the east.

Manpower and materials throughout the country were used to build thd Forbidden City. A total of 230,000 artisans and one million laborers were employed. Marble was quarried from Fangshan County on the outskirts of Beijing. Five—colored rocks were cut from Mount Pan in Jixian County in Hebei Province. Granite was quarried in Quyang County in Hebei Province. Paving blocks were fired in kilns in Suzhou in southern China. Bricks and scarlet pigmentation used on the palatial walls came from Linqing in Shandong Province. Timber was cut, processed and hauled from the northwestern and southern regions.

The structure in front of us is the Meridian Gate. It is the main entrance to the Forbidden City. It is also known as Wufenglou (Five—Phoenix Tower). Ming emperors held lavish banquets here

Forbidden City

on the 15th day of the first month of the Chinese lunar year in honor of their courtiers. They also used this place for punishing officials by flogging them with sticks.

Qing emperors used this building to announce the beginning of the new year. Qing Emperor Qianlong changed the original name of this announcement ceremony from ban li (announcement of calendar) to ban shou (announcement of new moon) to avoid coincidental association with another Emperor's name, Hongli, which was considered a taboo at that time. Qing Dynasty emperors also used this place to hold audience and for other important ceremonies. For example, when the imperial army returned victoriously from the battlefield, it was here that the Emperor presided over the ceremony to accept prisoners of war.

(After entering the Meridian Gate and standing in front of the Five Marble Bridges on Golden Water River)

Now we are inside the Forbidden City. Before we start our tour, I would like to briefly introduce you to the architectural patterns before us. To complete this solemn, magnificent and palatial complex, a variety of building patterns were applied. Most important, all of the palaces and their accommodating buildings were arranged on a north-south axis, an 8-kilometer-long invisible line that has become an inseparable part of the City of Beijing. The Forbidden City covers roughly one—third of this central axis. Most of the important buildings in the Forbidden City were arranged along this line. The design and arrangement of the palaces reflect the solemn dignity of the royal court and the rigidly—stratified feudal system.

The Forbidden City is divided into an outer and an inner court. We are now standing on the southernmost part of the outer court. In front of us lies the Gate of Supreme Harmony. The gate is guarded by a pair of bronze lions, symbolizing imperial power and dignity. The lions were the most exquisite and the biggest of its kind. The one on the east playing with a ball is a male, and the ball is said to repre-

3

Selected Tour Commentaries

sent state unity. The other one is a female. Underneath one of its fore claws is a cub that is considered to be a symbol of perpetual imperial succession. The winding brook before us is the Golden Water River. It functions both as decoration and fire control. The five bridges spanning the river represent the five virtues preached by Confucius: benevolence, righteousness, rites, intelligence and fidelity. The river takes the shape of a bow and the north-south axis is its arrow. This was meant to show that the Emperors ruled the country on behalf of God.

(In front of the Gate of Supreme Harmony)

The Forbidden City consists of an outer courtyard and an inner enclosure. The outer courtyard covers a vast space lying between the Meridian Gate and the Gate of Heavenly Purity. The "three big halls"of Supreme Harmony, Complete Harmony and Preserving Harmony constitute the center of this building group. Flanking them in bilateral symmetry are two groups of palaces: Wenhua (Prominent Scholars) and Wuying (Brave Warriors). The three great halls are built on a spacious "H"-shaped, 8-meter-high, triple marble terrace. Each level of the triple terrace is taller than the one below and all are encircled by marble balustrades carved with dragon and phoenix designs. There are three carved stone staircases linking the three architectures. The Hall of Supreme Harmony is also the tallest and most exquisite ancient wooden-structured mansion in all of China. From the Palace of Heavenly Purity northward is what is known as the inner court, which is also built in bilaterally symmetrical patterns. In the center are the Palace of Heavenly Purity, the Hall of Union and Peace and the Palace of Earthly Tranquillity, a place where the Emperors lived with their families and attended to state affairs. Flanking these structures are palaces and halls in which concubines and princes lived. There are also three botanical gardens within the inner court, namely, the Imperial Garden, Cining Garden and Qianlong Garden. An inner Golden Water River flows eastwardly within the

Forbidden City

inner court. The brook winds through three minor halls or palaces and leads out of the Forbidden City. It is spanned by the White Jade Bridge. The river is lined with winding, marble—carved balustrades. Most of the structures within the Forbidden City have yellow glazed tile roofs.

Aside from giving prominence to the north-south axis, other architectural methods were applied to make every group of palatial structures unique in terms of terraces, roofs, mythical monsters perching on the roofs and colored, drawing patterns. With these, the grand contour and different hierarchic spectrum of the complex were strengthened. Folklore has it that there are altogether 9,999 room-units in the Forbidden City. Since Paradise only has 10,000 rooms, the Son of Heaven on earth cut the number by half a room. It is also rumoured that this half-room is located to the west of the Wenyuange Pavilion (imperial library). As a matter of fact, although the Forbidden City has more than 9,000 room-units, this half-room is nonexistent. The Wenyuange Pavilion is a library where "Si Ku Quan Shu"— China's first comprehensive anthology—was stored.

(After walking past the Gate of Supreme Harmony)

Ladies and gentlemen, the great hall we are approaching is the Hall of Supreme Harmony, the biggest and the tallest of its kind in the Forbidden City. This structure covers a total building space of 2,377 square meters, and is known for its upturned, multiple counterpart eaves. The Hall of Supreme Harmony sits on a triple "H"-shaped marble terrace that is 8 meters high and linked by staircases. The staircase on the ground floor has 21 steps while the middle and upper stairways each have 9.

The construction of the Hall of Supreme Harmony began in 1406. It burned down three times and was severely damaged once during a mutiny. The existing architecture was built during the Qing Dynasty. On the corners of the eaves a line of animal-nails were usu-

Selected Tour Commentaries

ally fastened to the tiles. These animal-nails were later replaced with mythical animals to ward off evil spirits. There are altogether 9 such fasteners on top of this hall. The number nine was regarded by the ancients to be the largest numeral accessible to man and to which only the emperors were entitled.

There was a total of 24 successive emperors during the Ming and Qing dynasties who were enthroned here. The ball was also used for ceremonies which marked other great occasions: the Winter Solstice, the Chinese Lunar New Year, the Emperor's birthday, conferral of the title of empress, the announcement of new laws and policies, and dispatches of generals to war. On such occasions, the Emperor would hold audience for his court officials and receive their tributes.

This area is called the Hall of Supreme Harmony Square, which covers a total of 30,000 square meters. Without a single tree or plant growing here, this place inspires visitors to feel its solemnity and grandeur. In the middle of the square there is a carriageway that was reserved for the Emperor. On both sides of the road the ground bricks were laid in a special way: seven layers lengthwise and eight layers crosswise, making up fifteen layers in all. The purpose of this was to prevent anyone from tunneling his way into the palace. In the courtyard there are iron vats for storing water to fight fires. In the whole complex there are altogether 308 water vats. In wintertime, charcoal was burned underneath the vats to keep the water from freezing. Why so vast a square? It was designed to impress people with the hall's grandeur and vastness. Imagine the following scene. Under the clear blue sky, the yellow glazed tiles shimmered as the cloud-like layers of terrace, coupled with the curling veil of burning incense, trarsformed the Hall of Supreme Harmony into a fairyland. Whenever major ceremonies were held, the glazed, crane-shaped candleholders inside the hall would be lit, and incense and pine branches burnt in front of the hall. When the Emperor appeared, drums were beaten and musical instrument played. Civilian officials and generals would kneel down in submission.

Forbidden City

The last Qing emperor Puyi assumed the throne in 1908, at the age of three. His father carried him to the throne. At the start of the coronation, the sudden drum-beating and loud music caught the young emperor unprepared. He was so scared that he kept crying and shouting, "I don't want to stay here. I want to go home." His father tried to soothe him, saying, "It'll soon be finished. It'll soon be finished." The ministers present at the event considered this incident inauspicious. Coincidentally, the Qing Dynasty collapsed three years later and there with concluded China's feudal system that had lasted for more than 2,000 years.

(On the stone terrace of the Hall of Supreme Harmony)

This is a bronze incense burner. In it incense made of sandalwood would be burnt on important occasions. There are altogether 18 incense burners, representing all of the provinces under the rule of the Qing monarchs. On either side of the Hall, 4 bronze water-filled vats were placed in case of fire. Next to the terrace on either side, there is a bronze crane and tortoise, symbols of longevity. This copper-cast grain measure is called "jialiang." It served as the national standard during the Qing Dynasty. It was meant to show that the imperial rulers were just and open to rectification. On the other side there is a stone sundial, an ancient timepiece. The jialiang and the sundial were probably meant to show what the Emperor represented: that he was the only person who should possess the standards of both measure and time.

In the very forefront of the Hall of Supreme Harmony, there are 12 scarlet, round pillars supporting the roof. The hall is 63 meters from east to west and 37 meters from north to south. It is 35 meters in height. In front of this architecture, there stands a triple terrace with five staircases leading up to the main entrance. It has 40 gold doors and 16 gold-key windows with colored drawings on the pillars and beams. In the middle of the hall, a throne carved with 9 dragons sits on a 2-meter-high platform. Behind the throne there is a

Selected Tour Commentaries

golden screen and in front of it, there is an imperial desk. The flanks are decorated with elephants, Luduan (a legendary beast), cranes, and incense barrels. The elephant carries a vase on its back that holds five cereals (i. e. rice, two kinds of millet, wheat and beans), which was considered a symbol of prosperity. As ancient legend has it that Luduan can travel 18,000 li (9,000 kilometers) in one day and knows all languages and dialects. Only to a wise and just monarch will this beast be a guardian.

The Hall of Supreme Harmony is also popularly known as Jinluan Dian (gold bell hall or the throne hall). The floor of the hall is laid with bricks that turn it into a smooth, fine surface as if water has been sprinkled on it. The so-called golden brick, in fact, has nothing to do with gold. Reserved exclusively for the construction of the royal court, it was made in a secretive, and complex way, and, when struck, sounds like the clink of a gold bar. Each brick was worth the market price of one dan (or one hectolitre) of rice.

The hall is supported by a total of 72 thick pillars. Of these, 6 are carved in dragon patterns and painted with gold and surround the throne. Above the very center of this hall there is a zaojing, or covered ceiling, which is one of the Specialities of China's ancient architure. In the middle of the ceiling is a design of a dragon playing with a ball inlaid with pearls. This copper ball, hollow inside and covered with mercury, is known as the Xuanyuan Mirror and is thought to be made by Xuanyuan, a legendary monarch dating back to remote antiquity. The placing of the caisson above the throne is meant to suggest that all of China's successive emperors are Xuanyuan's descendants and hereditary heirs. Now you might have noticed that the Xuanyuan Mirror is not directly above the throne. Why? It is rumored that Yuan Shikai, a self-acclaimed warlord-turned emperor moved the throne further back because he was afraid that the Mirror might fall on him. In 1916 when Yuan Shikai became emperor, he removed the original throne with a Western-style, high-back chair. After the foundation of the People's Republic of China in 1949, the

Forbidden City

throne was found in a shabby furniture warehouse. It was repaired and returned to the hall.

(Leading the tourist to the bronze vats either on the east or the west)

The water vats in front of the palaces or houses were called "menhai," or sea before the door by the ancient Chinese. They believed that with a sea by the door, fire could not wreak havoc. The vats served both as a decoration and as a fire extinguisher. They were kept full of water all year round.

During the Qing Dynasty, there were altogether 308 vats in the palace enclosure. They were made of gilt bronze or iron. Of these, the gilt bronze vats were of the best quality. When the allied forces (Britain, Germany, France, Russia, the United States, Italy, Japan and Austria) invaded Beijing in 1900 under the pretext of suppressing the Boxer Rebellion, the invaders ransacked the imperial compound and scraped the gold off the vats with their bayonets. During the Japanese occupation of Beijing, many vats were trucked away by the Japanese to be made into bullets.

(In front of the Hall of Complete Harmony)

The square architecture before us is called the Hall of Complete Harmony. It served as an antechamber. The Emperor came here to meet with his courtiers and add his final touches to the prayers which would be read at the Ancestral Temple. The seeds, sowers and prayer intended for spring sowing were also examined here. The two Qing sedan chairs here on display were used for travelling within the palace during the reign of Emperor Qianlong.

(In front of the Hall of Preserving Harmony)

This is the Hall of Preserving Harmony. During the Qing Dynasty, banquets were held here on New Year's Eve in honour of Mongolian and Northwestern China's Xinjiang princes and ranking

Selected Tour Commentaries

officials. The Emperor also dined here with his new son-in-law on the wedding day. Imperial examinations were also held here once every three years. During the Ming and Qing dynasties, there were three levels of exams: the county and prefectural level, the provincial level and the national level. The national exam was presided over by the Emperor. The civil service exam in ancient China started during the Han Dynasty. It served the purpose of recruiting Confucian scholars to be ministers and high officials. During the Tang Dynasty, an annual exam system was instituted. The Ming and Qing dynasties reinstituted the ancient system. Once every three years, three hundred scholars from all over the country came to Beijing and took exams for three days and nights. This system was abolished in 1905.

(Behind the Hall of Preserving Harmony)

This is the largest stone carving in the palace. It is 16.73 meters long, 3.07 meters wide and 1.7 meters thick. It weighs about 200 tons. The block was quarried in Fangshan County, roughly 70 kilometers away. To transport such a huge block to Beijing, laborers dug wells along the road side half a kilometer apart, and used the groundwater to make a road of ice in the winter. Rolling blocks were used in the summer. In 1760, Emperor Qianlong of the Qing Dynasty ordered the carving of the existing cloud and dragon design in place of the old one which dated back to the Ming Dynasty.

Note: From here, the tour can be conducted via three different routes: a western route (Route A), a central route (Route B) or an eastern route (Route C). The commentary for each follows.

Route A

Ladies and Gentlemen,

You have seen the three main halls of the Forbidden City. Now I'd like to show you around the Hall of Mental Cultivation and the Imperial Garden. The Hall of Mental Cultivation is situated in the western part of the innermost enclosure and is symmetrical to Fengx-

Forbidden City

ian (enshrinement of forebears) Hall in the east. This hall was built during the Ming Dynasty. It is an H-shaped structure consisting of an antechamber and a main building. The hall is surrounded by corridors. In front of the hall is the Office of the Privy Council.

Before Emperor Kangxi of Qing the Dynasty came to power, the Hall of Heavenly Purity served as the living quarters of the emperors. Emperor Yongzheng chose to live in this hall and attended to everyday state affairs from here. For the sake of protecting cultural relics, this hall is not open to the public. You can have a look at the inside from the door. The central hall was the audience chamber where the emperor read memorials, granted audience to officials and summoned his ministers for consultation. The western chamber of the hall was where the emperor read reports and discussed military and political affairs. The hall consists of many inner rooms and is decorated with images of Buddha and miniature pagodas. On the screen wall there hangs a picture of two emperors in the Han costume. In a southern room there are three rare calligraphic scrolls, hence the name of the room "Sanxitang" (Room of Three Rare Treasures). The room on the eastern side is of historical interest because it was here that Empress Dowager Cixi attended to state affairs behind a bamboo curtain for many years, a political phenomenon which was previously unheard of in the annals of the Qing Dynasty (1644-1911). In 1861, Empress Dowager Cixi usurped power and made decisions on behalf of the young emperor. A bamboo curtain was used to separate them.

Empress Dowager Cixi was born in 1835 in Lu'an Prefecture of Shanxi Province. She's of Manchurian nationality and her father was a provincial governor from South China. When she was 17 years old, she was selected to become a concubine of Emperor Xianfeng and moved into the Forbidden City. She gave birth to a son when she was 21 years old and was made a concubine the following year. When the emperor passed away in the summer of 1861, her son ascended the throne and the title of Cixi, meaning "Holy Mother" was conferred

Selected Tour Commentaries

upon her and she became the Empress Dowager. In that same year Empress Dowager Cixi carried out a court coup d'etat and ruled behind the scenes with another empress dowager, Ci'an, for 48 years. She passed away in 1908 at the age of 73. It was in reference to this situation that the term "attending to state affairs behind a bamboo curtain" developed. In 1912, Empress Dowager Longyu declared the abdication of the last Qing emperor Puyi. They were allowed to remain in the Forbidden City for the next 13 years. The royal family was forced to move out permanently in 1924.

Behind the central hall were the living accommodations of 8 successive Qing emperors. Three of them actually passed away here. The side rooms flanking the hall were reserved for empresses and concubines. Now let's continue with our tour. It will take us to the Hall of Heavenly Purity, the Hall of Union and Peace, the Palace of Earthly Tranquillity, and the Imperial Garden.

Route B
(Inside the Hall of Heavenly Purity)
Ladies and Gentlemen,

We are now entering the inner court. From the Gate of Heavenly Purity northward lies the inner court where the emperors and empresses once lived. The Hall of Heavenly Purity is the central hall of the inner court, and was completed during the Reign of Emperor Yongle of the Ming Dynasty. There are 10 pillars supporting the entire structure and the hall is 20 meters in height. In the center of the hall there is a throne. Above it hangs a plaque with an inscription that reads "Be open and above-board," written by Shunzhi, the first emperor of the Qing Dynasty. Beginning with Qianlong's reign, the name of the successor to the throne was not publicly announced. Instead, it was written on two pieces of paper, one to be kept on the emperor's person throughout his reign, and the other placed in a small strongbox that was stored behind this plaque. The box was opened only after the emperor passed away. Altogether there were 4

Forbidden City

emperors who ascended the throne in this way, namely Qianlong, Jiaqing, Daoguang and Xianfeng.

The Hall of Heavenly Purity was where the emperors lived during the Ming and Qing dynasties. According to tradition, extravagant annual banquets were held here on New Year's Eve in honour of royal family members . Foreign ambassadors were received here during the late-Qing period. Two important "one thousand old men's feasts" of the Qing Dynasty were also held here. All the invitees had to be at least 65 years of age.

This hall was also used for mourning services.

(Inside the Palace of Union and Peace)

This hall sits between the Hall of Heavenly Purity and the Palace of Earthly Tranquillity, symbolizing the union of heaven and earth, as well as national peace. It was first built in 1420 and reconstructed in 1798. The hall is square in shape, and is smaller than the Hall of Complete Harmony. You will see a plaque here inscribed with two Chinese characters, wu wei, which were handwritten by Emperor Qianlong. A throne sits in the middle of the hall with a screen behind it. Above the throne there hangs a caisson, or covered ceiling. The emperor held birthday celebrations and other major events here.

In 1748 during Emperor Qianlong's reign, 25 jade seals representing imperial authority were kept in this hall. No seals were allowed out of the room without the prior consent of the emperor. On each flank there is a water clock and a chiming clock.

(Inside the Palace of Earthly Tranquillity)

This used to be the central hall where successive Ming empresses lived. during the Qing Dynasty, it was converted into a place where sacrifices and wedding ceremonies were held. The room on the western side was used for sacrifices and the room on the east was the wedding chamber.

Selected Tour Commentaries

Route C

Ladies and Gentlemen,

You have seen the three main halls of the Forbidden City. Now I'd like to show you around scenes of interest along the eastern route. The first is the Treasure Hall. This mansion is called the Hall of Imperial Zenith. This is where Qing Emperor Qianlong lived after abdication. Nearly 1,000 artifacts and treasures are on display here, among which the Golden Hair Tower is one of the most famous. This tower is 1.53 meters in height and its base is 0.53 meters in circumference. It was built under the order of Emperor Qianlong to be used to collect fallen hair in commemoration of his mother. There is also a "Dayu Harnessing Water Jade Hill" on display here. Yu was a legendary monarch of the remote Xia Dynasty. Under his leadership, the people learned how to harness the Yellow River. This jade assemblage, 224 centimeters in height and 5 tons in weight, is the largest jade artwork in China. This mat was woven with peeled ivory. These artifacts are among China's rarest treasures.

(In front of the Nine-Dragon Screen)

This is the Nine-Dragon Relief Screen. Erected in 1773, it is 3.5 meters in height and 29.4 meters in width. Underneath is a foundation made of marble. The surface of the screen is laid with a total of 270 colored, glazed tiles in the design of 9 dragons, some rocky mountains, clouds and the sea. It was meant to ward off evil spirits. The ancient Chinese regarded 9 as the largest numeral and the dragon as an auspicious beast. The 9 dragons are different in color and posture and all are made of glazed tiles. Interestingly a piece of the third dragon from the left is made of wood. It is believed that when the Nine-Dragon Screen was almost finished, a piece of glazed tile was damaged. Emperor Qianlong was scheduled to inspect the work the following day. Using quick wits, the craftsman in question molded the missing piece with clay and sailed through the imperial inspection. Later, he asked a carpenter to carve a wooden one to replace

14

Forbidden City

the one made of clay.

(Approaching the Imperial Garden)

Behind the Palace of Earthly Tranquillity and straddling the north- south axis is the Imperial Garden. There are old trees, rare flowers and exotic rock formations in this garden. It covers a space of 11, 700 square meters, or roughly 1. 7 percent of the Forbidden City. Most of the structures in the garden are symmetrically arranged. However, each is different in terms of pattern and decoration. Woods and clumps of bamboo screen off the garden and strengthens its deep and serene atmosphere.

The main structure of the Imperial Garden is the Qin'an Hall. Positioned in the central-northern part of the garden, this hall is flanked by other halls and pavilions on the east and west. The hall sits on a marble pedestal. The Taoist deity of Zhenwu is enshrined here and the emperor would pay homage here on a quarterly basis. Taoist rites were held during the reign of Emperor Jiajing of the Ming Dynasty. In front of the hall there is a cypress that is 400 years old. In all there are a dozen such rare trees in the garden, and most of them are cypresses or pines. To the northwest of the hall, there is the Yanhui (Sustaining Sunshine) Pavilion and to the northeast there lies the Duixiu(Accumulated Refinement) Hill. This Hill was built over the foundation of the long-perished Guanhua (Admiring Flowers) Hall of the Ming Dynasty. It is 14 meters in height and made of all kinds of rocks quarried in Jiangsu Province. At its base stand two stone lions, each carrying a dragon shooting water 10 meters up into the air from its mouth. There are meandering paths leading to the hilltop. At the top of Duixiu Hill sits the Yujing (Imperial Viewing) Pavilion. Traditionally, On the day of the Double Ninth Festival (the ninth day of the ninth lunar month), the emperor, his consort, and his concubines would climb up to Yujing Pavilion to enjoy the scenery.

At the southeastern corner of the Garden is Jiangxue (Crimson

Selected Tour Commentaries

Snowy) Verandah. Nearby to the southwest lies Yangxing Study (Study of the Cultivation of Nature). The Yangxing Study was used as a royal library during the reign of Emperor Qianlong of the Qing Dynasty. The last emperor of the Qing Dynasty, Puyi once studied English there. In front of the Jiangxue Verandah some Chinese flowering crabapples grow. The structure got its name from the crabapples whose blossoms turn from crimson to snowy white. In front of the Verandah, there grows a rare flower that was brought from Henan Province under the order of Empress Dowager Cixi. In the northeast is Chizao Tang (Hall of Using Flowery Language), once used as a library where rare books were stored.

There are aslo specific pavilions symbolizing the four seasons. The halls of Wanchun and Qianqiu, representing spring and autumn respectively, are square in shape and are coupled with multiple eaves and bell-shaped ridges. The halls of Chengrui and Fubi, dedicated to winter and summer, are characterized by two verandahs and bridges at their bases. Paths were paved with colorful pebbles and arranged in 900 different designs.

The Imperial Garden can be accessed through the Qiongyuan (Jade Garden) West Gate or the Qiongyuan East Gate. A third gate, the Shunzhen (Obedience and Fidelity) Gate, opens to the north. Its doors are laid in glazed tiles and it was only used by the empress or concubines.

As our tour of the Forbidden City draws to a close, I hope that I have helped you understand why the Palace is a treasure of China and one of the cultural relics of the world. It is under the strict protection of the Chinese government. Since 1949 when the People's Republic of China was founded, nearly one trillion RMB was spent on its restoration and refurbishment. The Forbidden City has undergone four major facelifts to date. Each year, the governrment earmarks a large sum to gather, sort and study cultural relics. The Palace now contains a total of 930,000 cultural relics. Well, so much for today. Let's go to reboard the coach. Thank you!

THE PALACE MUSEUM

Hello, everyone,

We are now going to pay a visit to a place of special interest. This scenic spot is located at the center of Beijing and is characterized by thousands of palatial architectures and purple walls as well as yellow glazed tile roofs—it is simply a sea of palaces. This is the world-famous wonder—the Palace Museum.

The Palace Museum has served as the royal residence during the Ming and Qing dynasties. It was here that a total of 24 monarchs ascended the throne and wielded power for some 500 years. The Palace Museum, as the most beautiful spot of interest throughout Beijing, is unique for its location: to the northwest is Beihai (North Sea) Park, famous for its white pagoda and rippling lake; to the west is the Zhongnanhai (Central and South Sea); to the east lies the Wangfujing Shopping Street; and to the north is Jingshan Park . Standing in the Wanchun (Everlasting Spring) Pavilion at the top of Jingshan (Charcoal Hill) Park, you overlook the skyline of the Palace Museum. At the southern end of the Palace is Tian'anmen (Gate of Heavenly Peace) and the famous square named after it. This is the symbol of the People's Republic of China.

A world-famous historical site, the Palace Museum is on the World Heritage List of UNESCO and is an embodiment of oriental civilization.

The Palace Museum is rectangular in shape, 960 meters long

Selected Tour Commentaries

from north to south and 750 meters wide from east to west, covering a space of 720,000 square meters, of which 150,000 is building area. It has 9000-strong rooms in it. According to legend there are 9999.5 room-units in all. The whole compound is enclosed by a 10-meter-high wall and is accessed through four entrances, namely, the Meridian Gate in the south, the Gate of Military Prowess in the north, Donghua (Eastern Flowery) Gate in the east and Xihua (Western Flowery) Gate in the west. On each corner there is a turret consisted of 9 roof beams, 18 pillars and 72 ridges. Encircling the compound there is a 3,800-meter-long and 52-meter-wide moat, making the Palace Museum a self-defensive city-within-a city.

The Palace Museum was made a center of rule during the Ming Dynasty by Zhu Di, the fourth son of the founding emperor Zhu Yuanzhang. The whole complex straddles on an 8-kilometers-long central axis that stretches from Yongding (Forever Stable) Gate in the south to Gulou (Drum Tower) in the north. Prominence was given to the royal power by putting the "three main front halls" and "three back halls" on the axis while arrange other subsidiary structures around them. The construction of the Palace Museum involved manpower and resources across China. For example, the bricks laid in the halls, known as "gold brick," underwent complex, two— dozen processes. As the final touch, the fired bricks were dipped in Chinese wood oil. Involving complicated processes and high cost, these brick are called "golden bricks." The Palace Museum serves as a living embodiment of good tradition and styles unique to China's ancient architecture. It reflects to the full the ingenuity and creativity of the Chinese working people. A carefully preserved and complete group of royal residences, the Palace Museum is a prominent historical and tourist site.

What we are now approaching is the main entrance to the Palace Museum—the Meridian Gate, which is characterized by red walls, yellow glazed-tile roofs and upturned eaves. On top of this magnificent building, there stand five lofty halls with a main hall in

The Palace Museum

the center. The main hall is roofed by multiple eaves and covers a space of 9 room-units. It is flanked by two wings on each side. The wings are square in shape, complete with multiple and four-edged eaves and pinnacles. All of these structures are connected by a colonnade. Because these halls resemble a soaring bird, it was also known as Wufenglou (Five-Phoenix Tower). Inside the main hall there is a throne. Drums and bells were stored in the wings. Whenever the emperor presided over grand ceremonies or observed rites in the Hall of Supreme Harmony, drums, bells and gongs would be struck to mark the occasion.

As the legend goes, the Meridian Gate used to be a place where condemned ranking officials would be executed. This is not true. However, flogging was carried out here by the Ming emperors. If a courtier falls afoul of the emperor, he would be stripped of his court dress and flogged with a stick. At one point the punishment became so harsh that a total of 11 people died from fatal wounds on a single occasion. On the other hand, this building was also used to observe important occasions like the traditional Chinese Lantern Festival (15th day of the first lunar month). On these occasions, Chinese lanterns would be hanged and sumptuous banquets would be given in honour of the whole court of ministers and other ranking officials.

Upon entering the Meridian Gate we began our tour of the Palace Museum. The river flowing in front of us is known as Jin Shui He (Golden Water River) and the five marbles bridges spanning it are known as the Inner Golden Water Bridges. The one in the middle was used exclusive by the emperor and its banisters were carved with dragon and phoenix designs. The bridges flanking the imperial one were reserved for princes and other royal members. The rest were used by palatines. Aside from decoration, the Golden Water River was also dug as a precaution against fire. Most of the structures within the Palace Museum are made of wood. What is more, according to ancient Chinese cosmology, the South is the abode of fire, so this brook was dug on the southern tip of the Palace. In this way,

Selected Tour Commentaries

the Palace Museum reflects traditional Chinese culture.

This building is called the Gate of Supreme Harmony. In the foreground stand two bronze lions. Can anybody tell which is male and which is female? The one on the east playing with a ball is male, symbolizing power and universal unity. The other on the west with a cub cuddling underneath its claw is female, representing prosperity and endless succession. A layout of the Palace Museum is posted by the entrance. From it, you can see that the Palace Museum has two main parts: the forecourt and the inner court. The three main halls constitute the mainstay of the forecourt, and it was here that the emperor announced decisions and observed rites. Behind the forecourt, there is the inner court, consisting of major halls and the Imperial Garden. It was where the emperor attended state affairs, lived and enjoyed his luxurious life. The exhibition system of the Palace Museum involves historical court relics and articles of ancient art and culture. The Palace Museum houses nearly one million articles of rare treasure, or one sixth of the total number in all of China's museums. These are the three main halls of the Palace Museum, built on a triple marble terrace. Since most of China's architecture is made of wood, the buildings cannot be too tall. To gain the height of the architecture, ingenious ancient artisans built the hall on a gigantic stone terrace. It is also to this end that not a single plant was grown in the square. On stairways of triple marble terrace there are 18 bronze tripods. The verandah is flanked by bronze tortoises and cranes, which served as symbols of longevity. On the east is a sundial, an ancient timepiece. On the west there is a grain measure suggesting that the emperor was just and equitable.

In the front and on each flank, there is a pair of gilt bronze vats (caldrons) molded during the reign of Emperor Qianlong of the Qing Dynasty. Each of these weights 2 tons and is filled with water as a precaution in the event of a fire. The structure in the very middle is the Hall of Supreme Harmony, also known as the throne hall. It is 64 meters in width and is 38 meters from entrance to rear. With ter-

The Palace Museum

race exclusive, the hall is 26.92 meters in height and is 35.03 meters in all. Covering an area of 2,377 square meters, the Hall of Supreme Harmony is China's largest existing wooden structure. The hall is supported by 6 thick, round pillars carved in a design of coiling dragons. As the holiest place in the hall, the ceiling and colored patterns were made of the finest material available at that time. The throne was placed on a terrace and is flanked by statues of elephants, Luduan (a unicorn which could travel 18,000 Kilometers a day and understand all languages), cranes and incense barrels. Over the throne there is the caisson, or covered ceiling, which consists of a coiling dragon playing with a ball in its mouth. This ball is known as Xuanyuan Mirror, and was supposedly made by a Chinese emperor of remote times to serve as a reminder that the rulers to follow were his hereditary heirs. The throne is made of nanmu and painted in gold. Magnificently built and luxuriously decorated, this hall did not serve as a place in which the emperor attended to daily affairs. He used this hall for major events such as his birthday, conferral of title of empress or dispatch of generals to war.

Behind the Hall of Supreme Harmony, there sits the Hall of Complete Harmony. This structure is square in shape. Each side is 24.15 meters. This was the place where the emperor relaxed and greeted his courtiers before proceeding to the Hall of Supreme Harmony to observe rites. This was also the place where the emperor prepared prayers or examined seeds and sowers before he attended ancestral sacrifices or participated in sowing ceremonies. A grand ceremony was also held here once every 10 years for the emperor to genealogize the royal blood. There are two sedan chairs on display in the hall. Behind the Hall of Complete Harmony, you will see the Hall of Preserving Harmony, which was used as a place where imperial examinations were held. The imperial examination was the highest level of competing for meritorious appointment under the feudal system dating back to the Sui Dynasty. China's last imperial examination was held in 1904 during the reign of Emperor Guangxu of the

Selected Tour Commentaries

Qing Dynasty. To the rear of the hall there is a marble ramp carved with cloud and dragon designs, the largest of its kind in the whole country. It is 16.57 meters in length, 3.07 meters in width, 1.7 meters thick and weighs 250 tons. It was quarried in Fangshan County in suburban Beijing. To bring this giant piece of stone to Beijing, people poured water onto the road and applied rolling blocks during the process.

We are now standing before the square of the Hall of Heavenly Purity. It served as a divide separating the forecourt from the inner court. This building is known as the Gate of Heavenly Purity. Emperor Qianlong held court here. Proceeding further north, you can find three main rear halls, i. e. the Hall of Heavenly Purity, the Hall of Union and Peace and the Palace of Earthly Tranquillity. The Hall of Heavenly Purity is flanked on either side by two gates named after the sun and the moon. Inside the enclosure there are 12 palaces and halls symbolizing constellations. All of the other buildings are centered around the Palace of Heavenly Purity, which was meant to suggest that the monarch's power was endowed by Heaven. The empress and concubines lived in the inner court.

The Hall of Heavenly Purity was where the emperor lived and attended to daily affairs. Later the emperor moved to live in the Palace of Mental Cultivation. Looking up you can see a plaque bearing the Chinese inscription "Be open and above-board," a manifesto to court struggle. Behind the plaque a strongbox was stored containing a will bearing the name of the would-be royal successor. This approach of secretly selecting the next emperor was adopted by Emperor Yongzheng of the Qing Dynasty. Two copies of the will were prepared. One was stashed by the emperor in person, the other was placed inside the strongbox behind the plaque. After the death of the emperor, the two copies would be compared and the successor would be announced. It was in this way that Emperor Qianlong and others have ascended the throne.

Behind the Hall of Heavenly Purity you will see the Hall of U-

The Palace Museum

nion and Peace, which is identical to the Hall of Complete Harmony. It was there that the emperor received congratulations and tributes from imperial officials on major calendar occasions. A total of 25 imperial seals are stored there. In the hall, you will see a plaque with the handwritten inscription of "wu wei," exhorting Taoist doctrines.

Further northward is the Palace of Earthly Tranquillity, which once served as the living room of the empresses'. The hall was later converted into a sacrificial place. Through the windowpanes on the eastern wall you can see the royal bed decorated with dragon and phoenix designs. This hall has also served as the bridal chamber of monarchs.

The Gate of Earthly Tranquillity leads to the Imperial Garden (known to westerners as Qianlong's Garden), which was used by the emperor, the empress, and the concubines. A magnificent structure stands in the middle. It is called the Qin'an (Imperial Peace) Hall. It is the only building in the Palace Museum that was built in Taoist style. It served as a shrine to the Taoist deity. The garden covers a space of 12,000 square meters, and is 130 meters from east to the west and some 90 meters from north to the south. There are a dozen halls, verandahs, pavilions and waterside houses in the garden. On each of the four corners there is a pavilion dedicated to the four seasons which is different in construction style and shape. The garden also features an imperial library that stored rare books and a hilltop pavilion that overlooks the imperial landscape. With rare trees and exotic rockery, the Imperial Garden served as a model for China's imperial parks. In all, a total of 10-strong building styles were applied.

The tall building we are now passing is the Gate of Military Prowess, the back door of the Palace Museum. Our visit is now drawing to a conclusion but the architectures of the Palace are not. On the other side of the road is the 43-meter-high Charcoal Hill, providing natural protection for the Forbidden City. This was also an

Selected Tour Commentaries

embodiment of China's construction style— putting a pool in the front and a hill in the rear. Now let's climb up to Wanchun (Everlasting Springs) Pavilion where we'll have a great view of the Palace Museum.

SUMMER PALACE

The tour will take 4-6 hours. The route is as follows:

Outside the East Gate—inside the East Gate—in front of the Hall of Benevolence and Longevity—in front of Garden of Virtuous Harmony—in front of the Grand Theater Building—a lakeside walk from the Garden of Virtuous Harmony to the Hall of Jade Ripples—by the Kunming Lake—in front of the Hall of Jade Ripples—in front of the Yiyunguan (Chamber of Mortal Beings)-Hall of Happiness and Longevity—in front of the Yaoyue (Inviting the Moon) Gate of the Long Corridor—strolling along the Long Corridor—visiting an exhibition of cultural relics—in front of the Hall of Dispelling Clouds—inside the Hall of Dispelling Clouds—atop the Tower of Buddhist Incense—on a hilltop leading from the back door of the Tower of Buddhist Incense—inside the Garden of Harmonious Interest—outside the south gate to Suzhou Shopping Street—atop the stone bridge inside the Suzhou Shopping Street—on the road from the south gate of Suzhou Shopping Street to the Marble Boat—in front of the ruins of the Garden of Complete Spring-along the lakeside by the Marble Boat-boating on the Kunming Lake—leaving out through the East Gate.

(Outside the East Gate)

Ladies and Gentlemen: Welcome to the Summer Palace. (After the self-introduction of the guide-interpreter) I hope this will be an interesting and enjoyable day for you.

During our tour, you will be introduced to time-honored histori-

Selected Tour Commentaries

cal and cultural traditions, as well as picturesque views and landscapes.

The construction of the Summer Palace first started in 1750. At that time, the Qing Dynasty was in its heyday and China was a powerful Asian country with vast territories. The monarch in power then was Emperor Qianlong. With supreme power and large sums of money, he summoned skillful and ingenious artisans from all over the country to carry out this construction work in honor of his mother's birthday. After 15 years and one seventh of the nation's annual revenue spent, the Garden of Clear Ripples was completed and served as a testimony to China's scientific and technological achievements. In 1860, this vast royal garden was burnt down along with the Yuanming Yuan (Garden of Perfection and Brightness) by Anglo-French allied forces. In 1888, Empress Dowager Cixi reconstructed the garden on the same site and renamed it the Garden of Nurtured Harmony (Summer Palace). Characterized by its vast scope and rich cultural embodiments, the Summer Palace has become one of the most famous tourist sites in the world.

This is the main entrance to the Summer Palace-the East Gate. On top of the eaves of the door there is a plaque bearing a Chinese inscription which means "Garden of Nurtured Harmony," whose calligrapher was Emperor Guangxu. The gate that you are now entering was used exclusively by the emperor, the empress and the queen mother. All others used the side doors.

(Inside the East Gate)

The Summer Palace can be divided into two parts: Longevity Hill and Kunming Lake. The whole garden covers an area of 290 hectares, of which three—fourths consists of a lake and rivers. This imperial garden features 3,000 room-units and covers an expanse of 70,000 square meters, with more than 100 picturesque spots of interest. The layout of the Summer Palace includes three groups of architectures: palaces where the emperor attended to state affairs, resting

Summer Palace

places of the emperor and empress, and sightseeing areas. Entering the East Gate we will come to the office quarters. The annex halls on both sides were used for officials on duty.

This is the Gate of Benevolence and Longevity. Above the door there is a plaque bearing the same name in both Chinese and Manchurian characters. The gigantic rock in the foreground is known as Taihu rock, or eroded limestone, quarried in Jiangsu Province and placed here to decorate the garden.

On the marble terrace sits a bronze mythical beast, known as Qilin or Xuanni. It was said to be one of the nine sons of the Dragon King. A point of peculiar interest is that it has the head of a dragon, antlers of a deer, the tail of a lion and hooves of an ox, and is covered with a unique skin. It was considered an auspicious creature that brought peace and prosperity.

This grand hall is the Hall of Benevolence and Longevity. It was built in 1750, and was known as the Hall of Industrious Government. Emperor Qianlong ruled that the halls where monarchs attended to state affairs would be named after them. After the rebuilding of the Summer Palace, the hall was renamed, suggesting that benevolent rulers would enjoy long lives.

The arrangement of the hall has been left untouched. In the middle of the hall stands a throne made of sandalwood and carved with beautiful designs. In the background there is a screen carved with nine frolicking dragons. On either side of the throne there are two big fans made of peacock feathers, two column-shaped incense burners, crane-shaped lanterns and an incense burner assuming the form of Luduan, a mythological animal which was supposed to have the power to prevent fire. The small chambers on either side were where the Emperor Qianlong and Empress Dowager Cixi rested and met officials on formal occasions.

On the verandah in the foreground of the hall there are bronze statues of dragons and phoenixes, which served as incense burners on major occasions. They are hollow and smoke comes through holes on

Selected Tour Commentaries

their backs. Also on the veranda are Tai Ping (Peace) bronze water vats made during the reign of Emperor Qianlong. As a precaution in case of fire, a fire was lit underneath the vats in the winter to keep the water in them from freezing.

(At the entrance of Garden of Virtuous Harmony)

We are now visiting the Garden of Virtuous Harmony, where Emperor Qianlong and Empress Dowager Cixi were entertained with Beijing Opera performances. It mainly consists of the Dressing House, the Grand Theater Building and the Hall of Pleasure Smiles. The Grand Theater Building known as the "Cradle of Beijing Opera" was uniquely laid out and magnificently decorated. On September 10, 1984, the Garden of Virtuous Harmony opened its doors to visitors. There are also 7 exhibition halls with articles of daily use on display here. The staff here put up court dresses of Qing Dynasty in order to give the visitor a more vivid impression.

(In front of the Grand Theater Building)

This building is 21 meters in height and 17 meters in width and features three tiers of tilted eaves and stages. All of the stages are connected to a raise, and a winch is installed at the top. A well and 5 ponds were sunk under the ground stage. There are trapdoors in the ceiling for fairies to descend, as well as on the floor for demons to surface. The underground passages also served as a means of improving resonance and making the performers' voices more audible. Of the three main theater buildings of the Qing Dynasty, the Grand Theater Building is the tallest and the largest. The other two are Changyin (Fluent Voice) Pavilion in the Palace Museum and Qingyin (Clear Voice) Pavilion in Chengde, an imperial summer resort. The building played a major part in fostering the birth and development of Beijing Opera: since the completion of the Grand Theater Building, many performances were held in it in honor of the Empress Dowager Cixi.

Summer Palace

(A lakeside walk from the Garden of Virtuous Harmony to the Hall of Jade Ripples)

We are now standing in the middle of a rockery behind the Hall of Benevolent and Longevity. It appears that there's nothing special ahead. However, after we clear the rockery, we will reach Kunming Lake. This is an application of a specific style of Chinese gardening.

Not far away in the lake there is an islet. It is filled with peach and weeping willow trees and serves as an ideal place to appreciate the scenery. The pavilion on the islet is called Zhichun (Understanding Spring) Pavilion and is chardcterized by four — edged, multiple — eaved roofs.

(In front of the Hall of Jade Ripples)

This group of special and quiet courtyard dwellings is the Hall of Jade Ripples. It was first used by Emperor Qianlong to attend to state affairs. It was also where Emperor Guangxu of the late Qing dynasty was kept under house arrest.

This hall is a hallmark of the Reform Movement of 1898. Emperor Guangxu was Empress Dowager Cixi's nephew. After Emperor Tongzhi died, Empress Dowager Cixi made her nephew, who was at that time four years old a successor in order to continue her wielding of power behind the scenes. When Emperor Guangxu was 19 years old, Empress Dowager Cixi relinquished power to him but continued to exert considerable influence. In 1898, the Reform Movement took place with the aim of sustaining the core principles of the Qing Dynasty while reforming outdated laws. The movement lasted for 103 days until it was suppressed by Empress Dowager Cixi. The emperor's six earnest reformists were beheaded and Emperor Guangxu was placed under house arrest which lasted for 10 years. All the back doors were sealed and a brick wall was put up behind the wooden partition on each side of the two annexes of the courtyard. Emperor Guangxu was closely watched by eunuchs. The wall remains intact for tourists to see.

Selected Tour Commentaries

[In front of Yiyunguan (Chamber of Mortal Beings)]

This was where Empress Longyu, the wife of Emperor Guangxu, once lived. She was the last empress and empress dowager of China's feudal system. However, Emperor Guangxu was not the last emperor of the Qing Dynasty. The last in the line was Emperor Puyi, who ascended the throne in 1908 at the age of three, too young to be married. In 1912, he was forced to abdicate. During the short reign of Emperor Puyi. Empress Longyu handled state affairs on his behalf in the name of Empress Dowager. In 1911, a revolution led by Dr. Sun Yat-sun succeeded, and the year after, Empress Longyu announced the abdication of the last emperor of China.

(In the Hall of Happiness and Longevity)

The aged Empress Dowager Cixi was so fond of the Summer Palace that she decided to live here from April through October of every year. This group of buildings served as her residence.

This group of courtyard dwellings consists of a forecourt and a backyard with annex courts on each side. The whole compound was basically made of wood, which is ideal for ventilation and lighting. With its quiet and tasteful layout, the Hall of Happiness and Longevity made life very easy and convenient. No wonder one of Empress Dowager Cixi's ladies—in—waiting praised the hall as the best place to live in all of Beijing. On the facade of the courtyard is the main entrance, and not far from it lies a pier reserved for Empress Dowager Cixi's pleasure boat. On the pier there is a tall lantern post. Flanking the staircase leading to the main entrance of the hall, there are bronze cranes, deer and vases, symbolizing universal peace. The interior layout is the same as the imperial court, with throne, a large table and incense burners placed in the middle. At mealtime, eunuchs—in— waiting would make a gigantic table out of this table and Empress Dowager Cixi would dine on 128 courses. Because of this more than 1,800 taels of silver would be spent each month on meals. On the east side of the Living Room is the Cloak

Summer Palace

Room. The bedroom is on its west.

[In front of the Yaoyue (Inviting the Moon) Gate of the Long Corridor]

The famed Long Corridor is ahead. Facing Kunming Lake and in the foreground of Longevity Hill, the Long Corridor stretches from Yaoyue (Inviting the Moon) Gate to Shizhang (Stony Old Man) Pavilion. It is 728 meters in length and consists of 273 sections and connects four octagonal pavilions. In 1990, it was listed in Guinness Book of World Records.

(Strolling along the Long Corridor)

The Long Corridor is one of the major structures of the Summer Palace. Since the corridor was designed to follow the physical features of the southern slope of Longevity Hill, four multiple-eaved, octagonal pavilions (Beauty-Retaining Pavilion, Enjoy-the-Ripples Pavilion, Autumn Water Pavilion and Clarity Distance Pavilion) were placed at bends and undulation. Thus sightseers will hardly notice the rise and fall of the terrain. As a major part of the architectural style of the Summer Palace, the Long Corridor serves as an ingenious connector between the Lake and the Hill. Scattered buildings on the southern slope were linked to create a unified complex.

This corridor can also be called a "corridor of paintings": There are more than 14,000 paintings on its beams. Some of them are of birds, flowers and landscapes of the West Lake in Hangzhou, Zhejiang Province. Others present scenes from literary classics. The majority of the landscape paintings were done under the order of Emperor Qianlong, who preferred the scenery of South China.

(By the door leading to the exhibition of cultural relics)

This group of temple-shaped structures are known as Qinghua (Clarified China) Hall, also known as Arhat Hall during the reign of Emperor Qianlong. The original hall burned down in 1860. After it

Selected Tour Commentaries

was reconstructed, it was renamed.

Qinghua Hall is now used as an exhibition hall displaying rare cultural relics collected in the Summer Palace. The hall consists of 6 exhibition rooms with tens of thousands of articles of treasure on display in turn. Among the exhibits there are bronze ware, porcelain, jade assemblages from the Ming and Qing dynasties, and rare and paintings. There is also a gigantic stone slab, which is more than 3 meters in height and width. It bears the handwritten inscriptions of Emperor Qianlong in commemoration of the suppression of a rebellion in the Xinjiang region. Only this slab survived when the Anglo-French allied forces set fire to the Summer Palace.

(In front of the Gate of Dispelling Clouds)

Now we are approaching the central part of the stuctures on the lakeside slope, the Tower of Buddhist Incense within the Hall of Dispelling Clouds. The Hall of Dispelling Clouds was where numerous palatines kowtowed to Empress Dowager Cixi. It was surrounded by galleries and flanked by annex halls. In the forecourt there is a pool and marble bridges. Starting from the lakeside, there lies in succession a memorial archway, the Gate of Dispelling Clouds, the Hall of Dispelling Clouds and the Tower of Buddhist Incense. All of these structures are built on a central axis and each is taller than its predecessor. This was designed to give prominence to the last structure, the Tower of Buddhist Incense, which was a symbol of imperial power. The layout of this group of architectures was based on scenes described in Buddhist sutras. This group of structures are among the most magnificently constructed here in the Summer Palace.

(Inside the Hall of Dispelling Clouds)

The original buildings on this site were burned down by the Anglo-French allied forces in 1860. A new set of structures was built during the reign of Emperor Guangxu, and was called the Hall of Dispelling Clouds, suggesting that it was a fairyland.

Summer Palace

The hall was built on a high terrace, and has 21 rooms. Inside the hall are a throne, screens, tripods and mandarin fans. On a platform you will see bronze dragons, phoenixes and tripods. At the foot of the platform there are four bronze water vats, the ancient form of fire extinguishers.

The 10th day of lunar October was, Empress Dowager Cixi's birthday. On that day, she sat on the throne here to receive congratulations and gifts.

Now we are going to pay a visit to the highlight of the Summer Palace—the Tower of Buddhist Incense. What we are now standing on is a stone terrace which is 20 meters in height. It has a semi-housed stairway of 100 steps. The elderly of Beijing maintain that if you climb this flight of 100 steps, you will live for 100 years. So, let's go!

(In the front of the Tower of Buddhist Incense)

An octagonal structure with three storeys and quadruple eaves, the Tower of Buddhist Incense is the very center of the Summer Palace, and is one of the masterpieces of ancient Chinese architecture. The tower is 41 meters in height, and is buttressed by 8 solid pillars made of lignumvitae logs. With its complex structure, ingenious layout, towering terrace and convincing grandeur, the Tower of Buddhist Incense was artfully set out by the imperial gardens and beautiful scenery surounding it. The Tower overlooks Kunming Lake and other picturesque spots within an area of tens of kilometers. On the west side of the Tower stands Baoyunge (Precious Cloud Pavilion). It is made of bronze and is 7.5 meters in height and 270 tons in weight. It resembles its wooden counterparts in every detail. It is one of the largest and most exquisite bronze pavilions still in existence in China. Lamas prayed here during the reign of Emperor Qianlong in honor of the monarchs and their families. At the turn of the century 10 bronze windows were spirited abroad. In 1992 an American company bought the windows and returned them intact to China.

Selected Tour Commentaries

(On a hilltop leading from the back door of the Tower of Buddhist Incense)

Now we can see the long and snaking Western Causeway and a shorter dike that divides Kunming Lake into three areas that contain South Lake Island, Seaweed-Viewing Island and Circle City Island. The three islands represent three mountains in ancient Chinese mythology, i. e. Penglai, Fangzhang and Yingzhou. This peculiar method of incorporating a lake and three mountains within a single garden was a brainchild of Emperor Wudi of the Han Dynasty more than 2,000 years ago, bearing testimony to feudal monarchs' longing for longevity. As the legend goes many heavenly elixirs grew on the three mythical islands. Using artificial building techniques, the ancient Chinese built this masterpiece based on the myth to make the mythical one appear to be accessible to humans.

(Inside the Garden of Harmonious Interest)

Setting a garden within a larger garden has been one of China's traditional architectural styles. The Garden of Harmonious Interest serves as a fine example of this.

This Garden was built under the order of Emperor Qianlong and modeled after the Jichang Garden (Garden of Ease of Mind) at the foot of Mount Huishan, Jiangsu Province. It was renamed by his son Emperor Jiaqing in 1811. The existing Garden was rebuilt by Emperor Guangxu. Empress Dowager Cixi used to go fishing here. The Garden features 10 waterfront platforms, pavilions and halls as well as hundreds of galleries.

With all of its structures facing the lake and pools, the Garden of Harmonious Interest is basically a garden of waterscape. Spanning the vast expanse of the lake and pools are five bridges, each quite different from the others. The most famous of them is the bridge known as "Knowing-the-Fishing-Bridge." It is said that more than 2,500 years ago during the Warring States Period, two philosophers named Zhuang Zi and Hui Zi had an interesting argument by the side

Summer Palace

of a pond.

Zhuang said, "Fish swim to and fro in the water. What happy fish!"

Hui asked, "You are not a fish. How do you know they are happy?"

Zhuang replied, "You are not me. How do you know I don't know?"

Hui sighed, "I am not you, therefore, I don't know you. And you are not a fish, so how do you know that fish are happy?"

Zhuang said, "You ask me how I know fish are happy. So long as you know that I understand that fish are happy, why do you keep asking me the same question?"

Although The Garden of Harmonious Interest was designed after Jichang Garden, it not only absorbed the original designs, but exceeded it.

(Outside the south entrance to Suzhou Shopping Street)

Now let's have a look at Longevity Hill. On the back slope of the Hill stands a group of architectures. The centerpiece of structures there are known as the Four Continents and are dedicated to Buddhism. This group was laid out and arranged in accordance with Buddhist cosmology. Aside from a main shrine and structures embodying the Four Continents, there are eight towers representing Minor Continents. The shrine is surrounded by four Lamaist pagodas and between the major and minor continents, there are two platforms representing the sun and the moon.

The Qing authority attached great importance to Buddhism. To further strengthen ties with the ethnic minorities who practiced Buddhism, the monarchs incorporated both Han and Tibetan styles of architecture into this group of temples.

Further north at the foot of the Four Major Continents lies the Suzhou Shopping Street. Built along the Back Lake of the Summer Palace, this street stretches about 300 meters and features more than

Selected Tour Commentaries

60 stores. It includes restaurants, teahouses, pawnshops, banks, drugstores, dyehouses and publishing houses. In order to recreate the atmosphere of ancient times, visitors will have the chance to exchange their money to ancient style Chinese coins for use here. storefronts are trimmed with traditional signboards and ornaments. The commercial culture of the mid-18th century has thus been recreated.

(Atop the stone bridge inside the Suzhou Shopping Street)

Visitors may be surprised to see that this shopping street is almost the same as that in South China. As a matter of fact, this street was designed after the shops along the canals in Suzhou. Originally known as Emperor's Shopping Street, it was built during the reign of Emperor Qianlong. After making several inspection tours to South China and being duly impressed by its commercial prosperity, Emperor Qianlong ordered the construction of this street.

The imperial shopping street was burnt down by Anglo-French allied forces in 1860. The site remained desolate until 1987, when reconstruction began. It was opened to the public in September 1990.

With commercial culture as its hallmark, the Suzhou Shopping Street is a vivid representation of China's traditional cultures.

(On the road from the South Gate of the Suzhou Shopping Street to the Marble Boat)

This is the Hall of Pines. From it to the west we can walk to the Marble Boat. The path we are taking stretches between Longevity Hill and Back Lake. Monarchs and their cohorts used to stroll along it. Hence it was named Central Imperial Path. Along this path you will see lilacs all around. Hence, this road is also known as the Path of Lilac.

(In front of the ruins of the Garden of Complete Spring)

Quite a few unique structures were burnt down during the reign

Summer Palace

of Emperor Qianlong, among which the Garden of Complete Spring was one of the most famous. The ruined and desolate courtyard by the roadside was its original site, it remains to be restored.

This group of structures covers an area of 4,000 square meters and features a number of halls built on three different levels. All of the structures were connected with galleries and stone staircases. With its natural and ingenious combination of pavilions, a hall, galleries and rooms, the Garden of Complete Spring serves as a fine model for other gardens. Emperor Qianlong frequently visited this compound.

(Along the lakeside by the Marble Boat)

Now we have returned from the back of Longevity Hill to the front. There is the famous Marble Boat. This structure is 36 meters in length and its body was made of marble. On top of it is a two-storeyed structure. The floor was paved with colored bricks. All of the windows are inlaid with multi-colored glass and the ceiling was decorated with carved bricks. The drainage system channels rain water down through four hollow concrete pillars and into the lake through the mouths of dragon heads.

According to a book written by Emperor Qianlong, the boat was used for enjoying the scenery and was supposed to be symbolic of the stability of the Qing Dynasty.

Halfway up the slope there stands the Hall for Listening to Orioles. The ancient Chinese liken the warble of an oriole to beautiful songs and melodies, hence the name of the hall which used to be a theater. Now the hall is one of the most famous restaurants in China, featuring imperial dishes and desserts. It is a must for many foreign visitors to have lunch here when then come to Beijing. More than one hundred heads of state worldwide have dined here and the late Premier Zhou Enlai has held banquets here in honor of state guests. (Sightseers who want to try the restaurant can go boating after they eat. Those who do not can go aboard right away. Those who

Selected Tour Commentaries

do not feel like taking the boat can stroll along the Long Corridor to the outside of the East Gate).

(Boating on Kunming Lake)

We are now going to enjoy the lakeside scenery from a pleasure boat.

As a main part of the Summer Palace, Kunming Lake covers an area of 220 hectares, or three fourths of the combined space of this summer resort. This natural lake is more than 3500 years old.

This lake was originally called Wengshan Lake. In 1749 Emperor Qianlong ordered the construction of Qingyi Garden, the predecessor of the Summer Palace. Involving nearly 10,000 laborers, the lake was expanded and turned into a peach-shaped reservoir, the first of its kind for Beijing.

From 1990 to 1991, the Beijing Municipal Government ordered the first dredging of the lake in 240 years. Involving 200,000 men and hundreds of dredgers and other tools, a total of 652,600 cubic meters of sludge was dredged and 205 bombs dropped by the Japanese during the Anti-Japanese War were removed.

The Summer Palace set a precedent for sightseeing by boat. There used to be a large imperial flotilla, of which the "Kunming Merry Dragon" was the most famous. It was destroyed by the Anglo-French allied forces in 1860. To make the tour of the Summer Place a more pleasant one, a large pleasure boat "Tai He" (Supreme Harmony) was built. This double-decked boat is 37.09 meters long, 8.59 meters wide and 10.49 meters high. It can travel at a speed of 9 kilometer per hour. Smaller pleasure boats are also available to tourists.

Another major spot of interest on the Western Causeway is Jingming (Bright View) Hall. Both its front and rear face the lake. This structure also features three two-storeyed halls of varying heights.

Our tour is drawing to a close as we approach the shore. Today we only visited the major scenic areas of the Summer Palace. I have

Summer Palace

left other spots of interest for your next visit.

I will now show you out through the East Gate. I hope you enjoyed today's tour. Thank you. Good-bye and good luck.

Selected Tour Commentaries

TEMPLE OF HEAVEN

(Inside the South Gate of the Temple of Heaven)
Ladies and Gentlemen,

Welcome to the Temple of Heaven. (After self-introduction)

The Temple of Heaven is one of the most strictly protected and preserved cultural heritages of China. There are basically two kinds of visitors who come here: local pensioners who do exercises here in the morning and evening and sightseers both from home and abroad. All in all, there are 12 million visitors every year. Now we are going to go along the route that leads to the altar. It will take roughly one hour. Mind you, the emperor also walked along this route to pay tribute to the God of Heaven.

(Along the Southern Sacred Road leading to the Circular Mound Altar)

The largest group of architectures ever to be dedicated to Heaven, the Temple of Heaven served as an exclusive altar for Chinese monarchs during the Ming and Qing dynasties. It was decreed that rulers of successive dynasties would place altars in their own capitals to worship Heaven and pray for good harvest. But why?

The ancient Chinese believed that Heaven was the supreme ruler of the universe and the fate of mankind, and thus worshiping rites dedicated to Heaven came into being.

The Heaven the ancient Chinese referred to was actually the

40

Temple of Heaven

Universe, or nature. In those days, there were specific rites of worship. This was especially true during the Ming and Qing dynasties when elaborate ceremonies were held.

The Temple of Heaven was built in 1420 during the reign of Emperor Yongle of the Ming Dynasty. Situated in the southern part of the city, this grand set of structures covers an area of 273 hectares. To better symbolize heaven and earth, the northern part of the Temple is circular while the southern part is square. The whole compound is enclosed by two walls, a square wall outside a round one. The outer area is characterized by suburban scenery, while the inner part is used for sacrifices. The inner enclosure consists of the Hall of Prayer for Good Harvest and the Circular Mound Altar.

(Along the Imperial Passage leading from the Southern Lattice Star Gate in front of the Circular Mound Altar)

The Circular Mound Altar is enclosed by two walls, each containing four groups of Southern Lattice Star Gate, each in turn consisting of three doors, with 24 marble doors altogether. Standing on the passage facing north, you will notice that with each pair of doors one is narrower than the other. This reflects the feudal hierarchy: the wider door was reserved for monarchs, while the narrower one was used by courtiers.

On the day of the ceremony, the emperor would don his ritual costume and be ushered in by the official in charge of religious affairs. He ascended the three terraces in the forefront to pay tribute at the altar.

(Atop the Circular Mound Altar)

We are now on the top terrace of the Altar, or the third terrace. Each terrace has a flight of 9 steps. At the center of this terrace lies a round stone surrounded by 9 concentric rings of stone. The number of stones in the first ring is 9, in the second, 18, up to 81 in the 9th ring. Even the number of carved balustrades on these terraces

Selected Tour Commentaries

is a multiplee of 9. But why?

According to ancient Chinese philosophy, yin and yang were two opposing factors. Heaven and the odd numbers belonged to yang while the Earth and even numbers belonged to yin. Nine was the largest heavenly number accessible to man. What is more, the ancient people also believed that heaven consisted of nine layers and that the emperor's abode was on the uppermost tier.

Once more look at the round stone in the center. The upper terrace is nine zhang (a Chinese unit of length, one zhang equals 3.3 meters) in circumference, while the middle is 15 zhang, the lower, 21 zhang. Classified as yang numbers, the sum of these numerals is 45 zhang which was meant to symbolize success. What is more, by applying the concept of odd numbers and strengthening nine and its multiples, the concept of heaven was thus illustrated and realized. The concept of nine will also be mentioned when we visit some other buildings.

Now I will give you a brief account of what happened here annually on the Winter Solstice. The memorial tablet dedicated to Heaven would be set up on the north side of the terrace, while tablets dedicated to the emperor's ancestors would be enshrined on the flanks. The service would begin around 4 o'clock in the morning. All of the lanterns would be lit. In the foreground, a sacrificial calf is being barbecued. On the square in front of the altar, the emperor, under heavy escort of nearly a thousand courtiers, princes of royal blood, musicians, dancers and uniformed soldiers, would slowly ascend the altar to offer sacrifice and pray in honor of Heaven. when the service drew to a close, the sacrifice offered in front of the memorial tablets would be incinerated. All of participants would watch the thick smoke rise upward as if they were seeing God off. Music and dancing would follow. In the end, the emperor would return to the Forbidden City secure in the belief that he would be blessed and protected by Heaven until the next winter Solstice.

It is interesting to note that, the stone in the very middle of the

Temple of Heaven

altar was of major importance, since it was where the emperor used to stand to say his prayer. The stone, which is known as the God's Heart Stone, is peculiar in that it is characterized by a specific acoustic phenomenon: it made the emperor's voice clearer and louder, thus adding to the mystic atmosphere of the service. You can try this out by yourself. (Proceed northward to pass through the Lattice Star Gate)

(In front of the Gate of Glazed Tiles)

This structure is known as Heaven's Storehouse. It is entered through the Gate of Glazed Tiles. The roofing, beams, and brackets are all made of glazed tiles or bricks. This is the only structure of its kind in china today.

The Heaven's Storehouse was where memorial tablets dedicated to the gods were kept. Douglas Hurd, a former British foreign secretary, once said, "God attends to His affairs on the Circular Mound Altar but stays here." Now let's go in to to see it (Go through the left side door)

(In the courtyard of Heaven's Storehouse)

This is the Imperial Vault of Heaven, the main structure of Heaven's Storehouse. It was built in 1530 and is 17 meters in height and 19 meters in diameter. The structure features blue roofs topped by a gilded ball, and carved wooden doors and windows. It is decorated with colored paintings. Founded on a 3-meter-high round marble terrace, the building also features a gigantic carved marble ramp laid in the stone staircase leading up to the front entrance. The ramp is carved in "Two Dragons Playing with a Pearl" design in relief. We will enter the main hall by going up the stone staircase on the eastern side.

(On the marble terrace of the main hall)

The arch of the hall is buttressed by 16 giant pillars on two

Selected Tour Commentaries

rings. On top of the pillars there are gilt brackets supporting a circular caisson, or covered ceiling. The ceiling is characterized by a golden coiling dragon design. The 8 pillars of the inner ring are painted scarlet and decorated with golden lotuses.

To the north of the hall there is a marble pedestal. Atop it, up a wooden flight of 9 steps, is where the major tablet dedicated to Heaven was enshrined. On each flank four tablets are enshrined in honor of the ancestors of the Qing emperors. In the annex halls in the courtyard, there are tablets dedicated to the deities of the sun, moon, constellation, cloud, rain, wind and thunder.

(Echo Wall and Triple-Sound Stones)

Aside from exquisitely laid out architectures, Heaven's Storehouse is also famous for two structures with peculiar acoustic features, i.e. the Echo Wall and the Triple-Sound Stone. A mere whisper at any point close to the wall can be heard clearly on the other side, although the parties may be 40 or 50 meters apart. This is possible because the wall is round and hermetically constructed with smooth, solid bricks.

In front of the steps leading away from the hall is the Triple-Sound Stone. If you stand on the first stone and call out or clap your hands, the sound will echo once; on the second stone, the sound will be heard twice; and on the third stone, the sound will repeat three times. Hence the name. (Go out through the right door and stroll along the circular path northward)

(Nine-Dragon Cypress)

The Temple of Heaven is also famous for its cypress trees — there are more than 60,000 cypress trees in all, among which over 4,000 are more than one hundred years old, adding to the solemn atmosphere of the temple. This tall cypress was planted more than 500 years ago. Its thick branches and twisting trunk resembling nine coiling playful dragons; thus it is known as the Nine-Dragon Cypress. It

44

Temple of Heaven

is said that this tree was here to welcome the monarchs. Now it is here to welcome visitors from all over the world.

(In the south of Chengzhen Gate)

Now we are back again on the Central Axis. This brick-arched gate is known as Chengzhen (Adopting Fidelity) Gate. This gate is the northern gate of the Circular Mound Altar, serving as a line of separation for the Circular Mound Altar and the Hall of Prayer for Good Harvest. The Hall of Prayer for Good Harvest is situated at the extreme end of the axis. It was used by the emperor in the first month of every lunar year for services dedicated to good harvest.

(On the Red Stairway Bridge)

Entering the Hall of Prayer for Good Harvest, we set foot on a raised passage 360 meters long, which the emperor also took to proceed to the hall. This broad north-south walkway, called Danbiqiao (Red Stairway Bridge), connects the two sets of main buildings in the Temple of Heaven and constitutes a single axis.

The passage is divided into left, central and right paths by the cross arrangement of slabs. The central and the widest path is known as Heavenly Thoroughfare, which was reserved exclusively for God; nobody, including the emperor, was allowed to set foot onto it. The emperor used the path on the east, which is known as the Imperial Walk. The ministers and princes used the one on the west. Interesting enough, there is no walkway left for ordinary people. This is because the Temple of Heaven used to be off-limits to them.

Contrary to appearances, this walkway is not a bridge at all. But how so? This road is 4 meters above the ground and there is a cavern underneath that was reserved for sacrificial oxen and sheep. The cattle were slaughtered at a slaughterhouse about 500 meters away and brought here for sacrifice. All in all, it can be said this walkway did serve as bridge and can be looked upon as the first cloverleaf in Beijing.

Selected Tour Commentaries

Looking back at the thoroughfare, you may realize that this walk is gaining height toward its northern end. As people approach the architectural group of the Hall of Prayer for Good Harvest, the flanking groves of cypress recede and perspective widens. Here you are in Heaven.

(Costume-Changing Terrace)

The marble terrace up ahead is called Jufutai, or Costume-Changing Terrace. It is located to the east of the Red Stairway Bridge and covers a space of 25 square meters. It has marble Slab balustrades. The day before the service, officials in charge would put up a yellow satin tent on the terrace for the emperor to change out of his yellow dragon robe into blue ceremonial clothes. After the service, the emperor would return to the tentand change back into his imperial robe before returning to the palace. (Proceed to the South Gate of the Hall of Prayer for Good Harvest)

(At the Gate of Prayer for Good Harvest)

This structure is called the Gate of Prayer for Good Harvest. We can catch a slight glimpse of the central building, the Hall of Prayer for Good Harvest, through the colonnade of the Gate. A gigantic and lofty group of buildings, the complex includcs the Gate of Prayer for Good Harvest, the Hall of Prayer for Good Harvest, eastern and western annex halls, the Huangqian (Imperial Heaven) Long Corridor, Heaven Kitchen, slaughterhouse, etc.

The annex halls were symmetrically built on a 1.5-meter-high brick-and-marble terrace, to set off the loftiness and magnificence of the main hall. This unique building, 38 meters in height, is characterized by a cone-shaped structure with triple eaves and a top that is crowned by a gilt ball. The roofing is made of blue glazed tiles, the color of the sky. Underneath the roof, the beams and brackets are decorated with colored paintings. The base of the structure is a triple-tiered, circular marble terrace. At a distance, the terrace

Temple of Heaven

looks like a gigantic, spiraling cloud with the structure perched on top of it.

Today the Hall of Prayer for Good Harvest is the hallmark of Beijing, which enjoys a prolonged history of civilization.

(At the base of the Hall of Prayer for Good Harvest)

The base of the hall is a triple-tiered, circular marble terrace, which is 90 meters in diameter and 6 meters in height, covering a space of 4,000 square meters. Meticulous accuracy was given to the layout of the structure. In the middle of each three-tiered flight of stairs, there is a giant marble ramp carved in cloud, dragon and phoenix designs. To set off the ramps, the top of the balustrades and downpipes are designed with corresponding floral scrolls. In southern part of each tier, a gigantic bronze incense burner is placed. Sandalwood was burnt in them when rites were observed.

(In front of the Hall of Prayer for Good Harvest)

Climbing up this marble terrace, we see the main hall, a masterpiece of ancient China. Looking up you will see the caisson, or covered ceiling, characterized by complex designs of dragons and phoenixes. In and out, the hall is decorated with colored drawings of dragons and phoenixes.

Without the use of steel, cement and nails, and even without the use of big beams and crossbeams, the entire structure is supported by 28 massive wooden pillars and a number of bars, laths, joints and rafters. The four central pillars, called the Dragon-Well Pillars, are 19.2 meters high and painted with designs of composite flowers, representing the four seasons. There are two rings of 12 scarlet pillars each. The inner ring represents the 12 months and the outer ring the 12 divisions of the day and night. Between the two rings there are 24 partitioned spaces to mark the solar terms of the Chinese lunar year. The pillars, 28 in number, also represent the 28 constellations in the universe — the ancient Chinese believed that there were 28 constella-

Selected Tour Commentaries

tions that made up the sky.

The center of the stone-paved floor is a round marble slab, which is 88.5 centimeters in diameter. Interestingly, the slab features natural black and white veins, corresponding to the dragon-phoenix design on the ceiling. This particular slab is known as the Dragon-Phoenix Stone and is regarded as a treasure inseparable from the hall.

The furnishings within the hall are placed in their original positions dating back to when Emperor Xianfeng ruled. In the forefront and above the throne are enshrined tablets in commemoration of Heaven. On either table on each side tablets of the emperor's ancestors were placed. Each tablet is fronted by an altar. A total of 24 kinds of offerings were made on it, including soup, wine, assorted cereals, and a calf.

The sacrificial rites were observed in the wee hours of the morning, sometime in the first month of the Chinese lunar year. Because it was still dark, candles, lanterns and torches were lit. This lighting coupled with the incense being burnt inside the hall, helped make the ceremony both grand and mystical.

By the time the service began, 207 musicians and dancers would be performing on platforms outside the hall. The emperor, in his blue sacrificial robe and with an air of piety and sincerity, would walk slowly into the hall, kowtow, and offer wine and prayer in honor of the deities and his ancestors. All of the offerings would then be taken to incinerators on the eastern side of the Gate of Prayer for Good Harvest. With this we conclude our visit to the Temple of Heaven. The feudal monarchs and their sacrificial rites have long vanished in history. However, this group of magnificent and lofty structures remain as a fine testament of the ancient Chinese' ingenuity and as one of the cultural heritages of mankind.

(On the Long Corridor)

From the Eastern Gate of the Hall of Prayer for Good Harvest,

Temple of Heaven

we have now entered a 300-meter-long corridor. Consisting of 72 sections, this corridor served as a connecting building between the Slaughterhouse. Heaven Kitchen, and the main hall. It is said that this once served as a sacrificial food production line. Flanking the corridor are shopping stalls. You may find some souvenirs for your family and friends there.

Well, that is all for this tour. Thank you for your attention. I look forward to your next visit. Good luck and bon voyage.

Selected Tour Commentaries

CHENGDE MOUNTAIN RESORT

Ladies and Gentlemen,

Welcome to the Chengde Mountain Resort. Chengde Mountain Resort, the largest remnant imperial garden in China, is located to the north of Chengde City. The residents of Chengde are proud of their city for the following honors it has received:

1. Chengde has been honored by the State Council as one of the top famous cultural cities with splendid heritage;

2. Chengde Mountain Resort is one of the forty-four top scenic spots in China;

3. Chengde Mountain Resort has been selected as one of the top ten historical resorts with scenic spots in China;

4. Chengde Mountain Resort has been chosen as one of the top forty tourist resorts in China;

5. In 1994, UNESCO inscribed Chengde Mountain Resort and its outlying temples on the World Heritage List.

Actually, seldom has a city in China earned so many honors like Chengde.

Chengde Mountain Resort has served as an embodiment of the flourishing ages of Emperor Kangxi and Emperor Qianlong of the Qing Dynasty. The founders of Chengde Mountain Resort, Emperor Kangxi and Emperor Qianlong, each went south of the Yangtze River six times to enjoy the beautiful scenery. With some imagination, you should be able to detect in this resort traces of the original ele-

50

Chengde Mountain Resort

ments found in the gardening masterpieces of South China. Actually you may recognize the adoption of the gardening styles and techniques of the gardens in Suzhou, Hangzhou and some other southern places. Specialists say that the Chengde Mountain Resort is the epitome of the best of China's landscapes. I hope you can tell me why the specialists say so after we finish our whole visiting schedule. I can give you a hint now. The answer is related to the terrain or topography and the features of the Chengde Mountain Resort.

Hi, everybody! we're at the resort. Let's get off the bus. Now I will show you the wonderful sights of Chengde Mountain Resort.

(Outside the main gate—Lizheng Gate)
Ladies and Gentlemen,

This traditional gate is the main gate of Chengde Mountain Resort. It is called Lizheng Gate. This gate was used only by the emperors of the Qing Dynasty. The main gate has two storeys and a 3-room space on each. There are three square gateways on the first floor and a gate tower on the second floor. Above the middle gateway, there is a horizontal board inscribed in Chinese, Tibetan, Mongolian, Manchurian and Uighuran by Emperor Qianlong. The board symbolizes national unity. The two stone lions beside the gateway are symbolic of the power of the emperor. In front of the main gate is a square covered with blue bricks for the emperor's use. Two steles standing in the eastern and western parts of the square are inscribed in Chinese, Tibetan, Mongolian and Manchurian. They read as follows: "All officials dismount here." So we called them the "Dismounting Steles."" A reddish screen wall in the southern area of the square blocks the view of an interior garden from the outside. It is said that a golden cock flew here from Cockscomb Hill and hid in the screen wall. If you knock at the wall at midnight, the golden cock will crow. Anyone who wants to confirm the tale, please come again at midnight. OK! Today, I invite all of you

Selected Tour Commentaries

to experience what an emperor's life was like.

(Inside the main gate)

Everyone, please look to your right . Can you see the huge stone column on top of the mountain? The stone soars into the clouds and becomes thinner and thinner from the top to the bottom. Because of its shape, we call it Wooden Club Rock (Bangchuifeng). The rock is said to resemble a wooden club used to beat laundry in the wash process in the old days. Emperor Kangxi gave it another name "Qingchuifeng," which means "Chime Stone Stick Peak." using the Wooden Club Rock as a part of the scenery of the garden, the designer integrated the inside and outside of the resort and expanded the scenic background with the traditional Chinese gardening art technique called "borrowing scenery."

Almost all visitors to Chengde will make it a point to visit Wooden Club Rock. This is because of an old saying: "You will have long life if you touch the Wooden Club Rock." If you are interested in it, you can go there tomorrow to receive its blessings for a long life. As there is a cableway connecting the Wooden Club Rock and the road terminal at the foot of the mountain, it is very convenient to go up and down.

The buildings in front of us were the interim palace of the emperor of the Qing Dynasty. Now, we know them as the Chengde Mountain Resort Museum.

(In the first exhibition room)

This is a panoramic picture of the Chengde Mountain Resort during the Qing Dynasty. Chengde Mountain Resort has two nicknames, "Jehol Interim Palace" and "Chengde Interim Palace." Construction of this project was started in 1703 and finished in 1792, lasting for 89 years. The emperors in the earlier and middle period of the Qing Dynasty came to the Chengde Mountain Resort almost every year to escape the summer heat of Beijing. The emperors usually

Chengde Mountain Resort

came to Chengde Mountain Resort in the fourth or fifth month of the lunar calendar and went back to Beijing in the ninth or tenth month. During this period of time they handled state affairs from here. Actually, Chengde Mountain Resort became the second political center of that time. The whole garden covers 564 hectares and is surrounded by a 10 kilometers long wall. It is twice as large as the Summer Palace and seven times larger than Beihai Park. The garden resort consists of lakes, hills, woods and flatlands as well as palace buildings but can be divided into two main parts, namely palatial and landscape . The palace can be divided into four parts: the central Hall, "Songhezhai," "Wanhesongfeng" and the East Hall. About 70 percent of the whole resort is hilly. It is said that the mountain resort contains all the elements of Chinese gardens. In it, there are 90 pavilions, 29 bridges and embankments, 25 steles and stone carvings, 70 groups of rookery, and more than 120 groups of buildings such as towers, pavilions, temples, palaces, and pagodas. The total floor space is more than 100,000 square meters. Emperor Kangxi named 36 scenic spots using four Chinese characters for each and Emperor Qianlong named another 36 scenic spots using three Chinese characters for each. Together they are called the"72 beautiful scenic spots of Chengde Mountain Resort." Emperor Kangxi once said that Chengde Mountain Resort was much more beautiful than the West Lake. The local people call the wall surrounding the palatial buildings "the Lesser Great Wall" to show their affection for it. Beyond the wall to the north and northeast, are several former temples and monasteries. All the temples are modeled after temples found throughout China. They form a semi-circle surrounding the Chengde Mountain Resort, which symbolized national unity under the Qing regime. As time passed, Chengde underwent lots of changes. With the founding of P. R. China, Chengde Mountain Resort received full protection of the government. Now Chengde Mountain Resort is known both at home and abroad as the largest remnant imperial garden, as well as a wonderful tourist resort in China.

Selected Tour Commentaries

(In the second exhibition room)

What you will see here are mainly pictures. This picture is called "Mulanqiumi Picture" which means "hunting in autumn." It is the most attractive one of all. "Mulan" means to attract deer by whistling. In the autumn, before dawn, soldiers in deer skins slipped into the woods and whistled to mimic a stag. Because it was mating season the doe would come out of hiding at the sound of the whistle. Then the hunting began. "Mi" means hunting in autumn. This picture shows us a scene of an emperor hunting 200 years ago. It was drawn by Xinglong'e of the Qing Dynasty. You may wonder why an emperor of the Qing Dynasty led his troops such a long distance from Beijing just for hunting. The reason is related to the political situation of that time. Since the founding of the Qing Dynasty, the soldiers' morale at the front declined. In order to escape from the battlefield, some soldiers wounded themselves, just to be taken off the front. Emperor Kangxi was aware that if he wanted to consolidate his position in the north, he needed stronger and more effective soldiers. To this end, Emperor Kangxi, personally headed the troops which patrolled the northern frontier. For this reason, Mulan paddock was built . Mulan paddock also strengthened the relationship between the Qing regime and that of Tibet and Mongolia and helped to consolidate the defensive forces at the frontier and thereby resist the expansion and aggression of Czarist Russia.

Every year, hunting would last for about 20 days. The Emperor himself led Manchurian and Mongolian officials and soldiers in the hunt. In order to meet the requirements of accommodation, prepare an ample supply of food for the the army, and meet the needs of the Emperor to attend to state affairs, more than ten interim palaces were built between Beijing and the paddock. Jehol lies halfway to the north patrol route. It took only one day by courier to send documents to the emperor from it. The temperature, scenery and grassy plain were also ideal there. So Emperor Kangxi decided to build a large interim palace in Jehol, which became the "Jehol Interim Palace." As

Chengde Mountain Resort

to the function of the Jehol Interim Palace, Emperor Qianlong once explained it as follows, "My grandfather Emperor Kangxi built up the Chengde Mountain Resort beyond the Great Wall not for fun during his travel but for the unity and consolidation of the Qing Dynasty." History indicates that Emperor Kangxi achieved his political goal to "let people either for us or against us be united to strengthen the power of the Qing Dynasty." And he did it by building the Chengde Mountain Resort and paddock. Now, let's have a look at this picture. This picture can be divided into two parts, one is the paddock and the other is the imperial Camp, where the Emperors lived and managed government affairs. The paddock was for hunting. Strict rules were set up for hunting. First, soldiers in deer skin whistled to lure the doe out, then soldiers tightened the circle around the area shoulder to shoulder, with the horses joining in ear to ear. The first round of shooting was restricted to the emperor, the second round of shooting was for ministers and generals and the last was for ordinary soldiers. This picture depicts such a hunting scene. Now please follow me. Let's go ahead and visit another part. The second door is called "Yueshe (Watching Archery) Door." The emperor stood here to enjoy the sight of his sons or grandsons' shooting contests. Look over there! An inscribed horizontal board hangs in front of the door with four gilt Chinese characters which read "Chengde Mountain Resorts." It was written by Emperor Kangxi. Maybe you already found the extra stroke in the first character "BI." Did Emperor Kangxi make a mistake or is there some other reason for what be did? (...) (Pointing to a gentleman or a lady for explanation) Yes, exactly, this gentleman/lady gave us the right answer. During the Qing Dynasty, both characters were right. It is a variant form of the Chinese character "BI." Emperor Kangxi wanted his calligraphy to be perfect, so he wrote it in this way.

Let's look at these two bronze lions. There is an interesting story behind them. During the anti-Japanese war, the Japanese invaders came to Chengde and plundered the city. One day, a group of

Selected Tour Commentaries

Japanese soldiers found the priceless bronze lions and thought they were pretty. So they wanted to take them away . But the lions were too heavy to move. The Japanese went away to look for tools to move them. An old keeper of the palace saw the whole thing and couldn't help grieving. He knew the bronze lions were valuable treasures of China and made up his mind to protect them. He went to the village and got some pig blood, which he then applied to the the lions' eyes. When the Japanese came back, they were astonished to see the lions' eyes shedding blood. The Japanese soldiers feared that the spirits protecting the lions would bring them bad luck. As a result they left without the lions. Now the two lions stand for good luck. You can touch the lion and pray for fortune.

(In front of the Hall of Simplicity and Sincerity)

The Simplicity and Sincerity Hall is as spacious as seven rooms put together. It's the main hall in the Chengde Mountain Resort, which was often used for attending to government affairs and holding grand ceremonies. It is built mainly with a kind of aromatic hardwood called nanmu. Nanmu grows in the deep forests of Yunan, Guizhou, Zhejiang and Jiangsu provinces. Because of the lack of advanced means of transportation at that time, Nanmu was often transported from south to north in the following ways: using cargo ships or transporting the wood on an icy surface in the winter using manpower.

According to historical documents, it cost 72,000 taels of silver and took 190,000 laborers to build this hall. The entire hall is simple but elegant. The interior is fully decorated with marble. The throne in the right middle of the hall is surrounded by sculptures of cranes, elephants, etc. Behind the throne, there is a red sandalwood screen named "farmers and happy cultivation." There are 163 different figures carved into the screen. All of them are lifelike. The screen shows us that the emperor was concerned about his people all the time . In the Qing Dynasty, the government sent specialists to survey

Chengde Mountain Resort

the topography of the country. That is the map they drew. It is hung on the east and west walls of the Palace. There are nanmu bookshelves on both sides of the north wall. Ten thousand books called "The Overall Book Collection of Ancient and Present Times" were kept on these bookshelves. You may be curious about what it was like at the grand ceremony. After the announcement of the ceremony, the person who was in charge of the bell would toll it. After 9 strokes, all of the other bells of the inner temples would toll and those of the outer temples would immediately follow. All the bells would toll 81 times. The band standing on the west and east sides of the hall would then play music Civilian and military officials stood at their posts and the emperor sat the throne facing south. Then, another busy day would begin.

Can you imagine the spectacle? Emperor Qianlong met with many officials of the minority nationalities, including Sanceling from Mongol in 1754; "Wobaxi," the king of the Tuerhute tribe from Volga in 1771; and the sixth Panchen Lama from Tibet in 1780. According to historical documents, the rules of that time dictated that when they met, the Panchen would kneel before the emperor. The panchen would then present hata (a piece of silk used as greeting gift) and extend his best wishes to the emperor. The emperor in turn would rise from his throne to help the Panchen to his feet and greet him in Tibetan. He would say, "How are you after the long, tiring and difficult journey?" Panchen would answer, " I am fine. Thanks." And it was not a must for the panchen to kowtow to the emperor to show his obedience and respect. However, the sixth Panchen broke the rule and kowtowed to Emperor Qianlong. It made Emperor Qianlong very happy . On August 13, the grand ceremony was held for Emperor Qianlong's 70th birthday, at which time the Emperor treated the Panchen royally. He invited the Panchen to sit beside him on the throne as he received the congratulations of envoys and officials. After this celebration, Emperor Qianlong held four grand banquets in honor of the Panchen. There were a lot of inter-

Selected Tour Commentaries

esting performances during the banquets, such as sumo, acrobatics, dancing, music, etc. The Panchen's trip to Chengde strengthened the relationship between Tibet and the Qing Dynasty, and prevented the eastward expansion of the British East India Company.

OK ! Let's go along the winding corridor. Now the house in front of us is the "Sizhi Study House." It is as spacious as five rooms. What's the meaning of "Sizhi"? "Sizhi" might mislead you to think about what Yangzheng of the Han Dynasty referred to. He meant that everyone must be aware of his behavior, for the black business he thinks is secret is already known by Heaven and Earth and by you and me. "Sizhi" as used here is credited to Emperor Qianlong, however, and comes from "The Book of Changes." It means that a gentleman should know things either blurred or clear and things either soft or tempered. This "Sizhi" reflects Emperor Qianlong's dominant policy. The emperor used the "Sizhi Study" for a rest or for changing clothes before going to his office. Sometimes the emperor received officials and leaders of minority nationalities here. The side-hall now displays the imperial porcelain, enamel, the royal transport vehicles and stone drum. These unusual treasures will be a feast for your eyes for sure.

(Heading to the north, going inside the "Hall of Refreshment in Mist-Covered Waters")

This is the back part of the palace area and it is called the "Rear Dwelling Quarters of the Palace." It was where the emperor and his wives and concubines lived. The north hall is the "Hall of Refreshment in Mist-Covered Waters." Emperor Kangxi named it so because the surrounding green mountains and lakes brought a freshness to the palace that refreshed the minds of the people therein. The west chamber was the bedroom of the emperor. When the winter came, the chamber would be warmed up by the burning charcoal in the channels beneath the inner floor and some stoves on the floor. Several emperors, including Kangxi, Qianlong, Jiaqing and Xianfeng,

Chengde Mountain Resort

lived here. Leaning against the north wall, the bed made of red sandalwood was the emperor's bed. Emperor Xianfeng died from disease in this bed in 1861. This rectangular courtyard witnessed a series of historical incidents. In 1860, British and French allied forces attacked Beijing. Unwilling to face the fact, Emperor Xianfeng escaped from Beijing to Jehol with his mother and two queens "Ci'an" and "Ci'xi" on the 8th day of the 8th month of the lunar calendar. He sent his younger brother Prince Gong to sign the inequitable"Beijing Treaty" and accepted the Aihui Treaty between China and Russia. These treaties not only brought much humiliation , but also took away large territories from China. After the death of Xianfeng, Queen Ci'xi succeeded in a palace coup and began to hold court from behind a screen. She ruled the Qing Dynasty for 48 years and China suffered even more under her rule. There is one courtyard on each side of the hall. Queen "Ci'an" lived in the east courtyard; now it is where the court clocks of the Qing Dynasty are displayed. Ci'xi lived in the west courtyard. Displayed in it are some articles from Ci'xi's daily life and some of her photos.

The last building of the front palace, also the deepest place, is called "Cloudy Mountain Building ." It's a delicate two-storey building. The interesting feature of the building is that there is no staircase inside of it. The rockery outside the building was used as a staircase. Imperial glassware and hanging screens are displayed in the side rooms.

We are done with visiting the front palace museum, and we are now entering the lake area. Chengde Mountain Resort gets its name from the mountain, but the most attractive part of Chengde Mountain Resort is its lakes. The lakes (including seven lakes) together with eight islands cover an area of 57 hectares. On the lake to the right, you can see that there are three pavilions built on a stone bridge. We call them the "Central waterside pavilions." The embankment in front of us is connected to "Huanbi Islet" on the left side, with Ruyi Islet in the middle and "Moonlight and Water Sounds

Selected Tour Commentaries

Islet" on the right side. Seen from above, the embankment and the three islands look like "glossy ganoderma," a kind of precious herb. So Emperor Kangxi named them "Ganoderma Road and Cloud Embankment." There are two courtyards on Huanbi Island of which the prominent buildings are Chengguang House and Huanbi Courtyard. To the north of Huanbi Hall, there is a grass pavilion near the lake. The pavilion looks like a bamboo hat. During Emperor Kangxi's reign, an annual cymbidium show would be heldon July 15 of the lunar calendar. "Moonlight and Water Sounds" island is wonderful especially when the moon rises. The characters "Moonlight and Water Sounds" on the inscription board hung in the Front Hall on the islet were written by Emperor Kangxi. North of the Front Hall there are several buildings such as "Stone House" and "Yingxin Hall."

Emperor Kangxi and Emperor Qianlong used to do some reading here.

Now, please follow me to the north along "the embankment." The hill on the right across the lake is called Gold Hill Islet. It's a mini-facsimile of the Gold Hill in Jiangsu Province. The main building of the islet is "God Temple." It was used when the emperor offered sacrifices to ancestors and heaven. There are also some other buildings on the islet, such as "Fangzhou Pavilion" and "Pashan Corridor." The emperor usually stepped onto Gold Hill Islet from the dragon boat.

Now, we are standing on the biggest islet of the whole lake area — Ruyi Islet. Out of the 72 beautiful spots named by Emperor Kangxi and Emperor Qianlong, ten are on the Ruyi Islet. The main building of the islet is a palace with an entrance hall called "Cool with No Summer." The name of the main hall is "Yanxunshanguan" and it is as spacious as seven rooms. The hall behind the main hall is called "Shuifangyanxiu." Before the main hall was completed, this hall was used as the office and living quarters of Emperor Kangxi. Now displayed in it are imperial articles of everyday use. The famous "Blue Wave Islet" — a garden in a garden — is in the northwest part

Chengde Mountain Resort

of the island, and is a mini-facsimile of "Blue Wave Pavilion" in Suzhou. Along with winding corridors, all of the buildings here are integrated delicately and form a beautiful spot for the resort.

(Walking over the winding bridge and stepping on to the "Qinglian Islet")

Ladies and gentlemen, the two-storeyed building in front of us is called "Misty Rain Tower." It was built after the "Misty Rain Tower" in Jiaxing of Zhejiang Province. There is a square courtyard between the entrance hall and the main tower with several old pine trees here and there. There is a pair of copper deer on two stone bases. To the east of the tower is the "Blue Sun Study" in which the emperor read in his leisure time. To the southwest of the tower is the "Face Rockery Chamber" which features what its name implies. On the rockery there is a pavilion called Yi (Wing) Pavilion.

(Along the north bank of "Green Lake," passing through the pavilion of "Water Flows But Cloud Stays" and "Orioles Sing on the Arbor" to the east)

Now we have arrived at the famous Jehol spring. The stele beside the spring is engraved with "Jehol." Jehol spring is a hot spring and it never freezes. After snowfalls, the view of the steaming lake surrounded by white snow is really wonderful.

(In the plains of Chengde Mountain Resort)

The open plain in front of us consists of "Grove of Ten Thousand Trees" and "Horse Testing Ground." It covers an area of more than a thousand mu. The topography of the "Grove of Ten Thousand Trees" is quite flat. Sometimes you can see reindeer and hares leap out of the grove or grass. "Horse Testing Ground" lies to the west of the grove. Horses were tested and examined there before the grand hunting.

Selected Tour Commentaries

(At the foot of the hill to the west of front grove)

This building we see is a library called "Wenjin Pavilion." "Jin" means ferry. "Wenjin" means the ferry of knowledge. "Wenjin Pavilion" means: if you want to acquire knowledge, you should seek advice from the library first. The "Wenjin Pavilion" along with the "Wenyuan Pavilion" in the Forbidden City of Beijing, and the "Wenyuan Pavilion" in Yuanmingyuan of Beijing, and the "Wensu Pavilion" in the Shenyang Imperial Palace, were called the " Four Royal Library Pavilions of the Qing Dynasty." Wenjin Pavilion was modeled after the "Tianyi Pavilion" of Ningbo City in Zhejiang Province. If you look at the Pavilion from the outside, it seems to have two storeys with three rooms each. But actually, there is a mezzanine between the two storeys. It was designed for the purpose of protecting the books from damage caused by direct sunlight. In the Wenjin Pavilion a lot of books are stored , including "The Overall Book Collection of Ancient and Present Times" and " The Sikuquanshu," a major anthology of classics, history, philosophy and literature commissioned by Emperor Qianlong.

(In front of the pond before the chamber)

Please stand beside me and look to where I am pointing. There is an inverted reflection of the moon in the water. How could this be? Is it an illusion since we still have bright sunshine right now?

It's not an illusion. It's a wonder of Chengde Mountain Resort called "Sun and Moon Shining Together." Everyone, please go to the rockery to get the answer there. Who knows the answer? Yeah! It is this young lady who discovered the answer first. The optical reflection of a crescent hole in the rockery on the water surface creates it.

(To the entrance of "Hazel Valley")

The Tourism Administration and the Cultural Relics Bureau have jointly developed a tourist program called "touring around the mountain area by bus." Let's follow suit and visit the mountain area

Chengde Mountain Resort

right now. The mountain area lies northwest of the palatial area and it takes up about 80 percent of the whole resort. It would take us several days to travel through the mountain area on foot. (Please get on the bus.) Look at the mountain chains, Hazel Valley, West Valley, Pine Valley, Pear Tree Valley and Pine and Cloud Valley, stretching from south to east, one after the other. Now we have just entered Hazel Valley. Hazel Valley and West Valley are full of hazel trees, as well as other kinds of trees. Pine and Cloud Valley is full of boundless old pine trees. When spring comes, Pear Tree Valley is filled with flowers and sweet smells; and when autumn comes, it is rich in pome. More than 40 different types of gardens, temples and steles are built on the base of the mountains' topographical features. Over time, most of them have collapsed in the course of nature. One exception I must mention is the "Shuyuan Temple." It lies to the west of the West Lake. In the temple, there was a two-storeyed pavilion called ".Zongjing Pavilion" in which bronze Buddhas were enshrined. The pavilion was built of cast bronze parts of excellent workmanship. The pavilion could be easily assembled and disassembled freely. Statues of Sakyamuni and another Buddha in the temple were also made of bronze. So the nickname of the pavilion was "Bronze Hall." But now all that remains is the base of the pavilion. It was plundered by Japanese invaders during the anti-Japanese war. When the Japanese came to Chengde they stole many valuable things. They disassembled the "Zongjing Pavilion" and. except for three bronze boards, carried everything away to Japan. Today, the ruins of "Zongjing Pavilion" has become a venue for patriotism education, just like Yuanmingyuan in Beijing.

(The bus stops at the "Simianyunshan Pavilion" and the guide leads the tourists to the pavilion.)

The pavilion we are now standing in is called "Simianyunshan Pavilion." It's the highest place in the mountain area. The wind comes from all directions. So even in midsummer, you will have the

Selected Tour Commentaries

feeling of being in the cool autumn. Every time Emperor Qianlong came to Chengde Mountain Resort, he would come here and write some poems about the wonderful sights and weather. One of his poems expressed his feelings about this pavilion. It reads as follows: "The pavilion stands as high as the Big Dipper and while seating at the pavilion I get a feeling that all the surrounding mountains are much lower." Today, we can see a more vivid and beautiful view than Emperor Qianlong could — not only the beautiful natural landscape, but also the new look of Chengde City.

(The coach arrives at the northwest gate of the palace. The guide leads the tourists to the top of the wall.)

There is an old Chinese saying: "He who has never reached the Great Wall is not a true man." Now we have climbed the "lesser great wall" in Chengde. It winds on the mountain, rising and falling with the terrain. While walking on the wall, you can see the magnificent palace in the south and the eight splendid outlying temples in the north. Look! This is the Putuozongsheng Temple. It is a mini-facsimile of the Lhasa's Patala Palace. That is Xumifushou Temple, the interim palace of the sixth Panchen Lama. The temple in the distance is called Puning Temple, home of the world's tallest wooden Bodhisattva that has a thousand hands and eyes. Tomorrow, we will visit that temple. You may take as many photos as you like. If you don't, you may later regret not doing so.

(The bus goes down the mountain via the "Qingfenluyu." Visit to the mountain area is over.)

The tower soaring into the sky in front of us a pagoda for Buddhist relics or stupa. It's modeled after the "Pagoda of Six Harmonies" in Hangzhou and the "Bao'en Pagoda" in Nanjing. The octagonal, 9-storey pagoda is 67 meters tall. We call it "Six Harmonies Pagoda." On the south and north sides of the first floor there are arched stone doors. Along the spiral staircase inside the pagoda, we

Chengde Mountain Resort

can climb to the top of it. A statuette of the Buddha was enshrined in the pagoda. While Emperor Qianlong stayed in Chengde Mountain Resort, he sometimes went up to the pagoda in the morning to offer sacrifices to the Buddha .

This is the Mongolian Yurt Holiday Village. The white Mongolian Yurt looks like white swans landing on the green grass. The Qing regime once built yurta in this area. Emperor Kangxi and Emperor Qianlong received and hosted banquets for leaders of the minority nationalities and foreign envoys in the imperial yurt . Now I would like to tell you about a famous event. On September 29, 1792, the first diplomatic delegation of Britain came to visit China. king George II sent a delegation of about 100 people led by Lords Macartney and Stanton. The mission left from Portsmouth on the warship Lion, and sailed directly to Tianjin. On July 26, 1793, the diplomatic mission arrived in Tianjin. Passing through Beijing, they finally arrived at Jehol on September. 8. Emperor Qianlong took the mission seriously and decided to meet them at the Jehol interim palace. On September 14, Macartney accompanied by an envoy and a Chinese interpreter was led by the Minister of Protocol to appear before Emperor Qianlong in the yurt. The special envoy stepped forward, knelt down on one knee, and greeted the emperor on behalf of the delegation. He then presented the gifts and a letter from King George. In his letter , the British king sought the emperor's approval for a resident ambassddor to be stationed in Beijing. This seemingly simple ceremony had been discussed for several days beforehand between representatives of Britain and China. Emperor Qianlong in turn presented Macartney with gifts, including a Ruyi Jade, and requested their presence at a banquet attended by princes, dukes, ministers and Mongol king Taiji. Emperor Qianlong bestowed wine upon the British envoys and invited them to enjoy the performance of acrobatics, opera and wushu . On September. 17, a grand dress parade was held at Chengde Mountain Resort to celebrate Emperor Qianlong's 83rd birthday. Macartney returned to Chengde Mountain Resort and

Selected Tour Commentaries

expressed his best wishes to the emperor. They enjoyed the fireworks together at the grove garden.

After Emperor Qianlong refurned to Beijing, Minister Heshen gave Macartney an edict from Emperor Qianlong addressed "To the King of Britain." On October 7, the envoys returned to Britain with the gifts from Emperor Qianlong for King George II. Macartney sought to open trade with China through negotiations with the Chinese government, but his plan was not put into effect. In the negotiation process, the Qing regime vindicated the prestige and honor of China. During the several months they were in Beijing, the British mission had collected a lot of data on the political, economic and military affairs of China. To a certain extent, Macartney's trip to China paved the way for the coming Opium War. In 1840, Britain broke the gates of China with bombs and guns and started China's semi-colonial, semi-feudal period of history. Now, please follow me to the south along the Mongolian Yurt Holiday Village. We will go out of the resort through the grove.

(Back to the bus)

Ladies and gentlemen, now that you have seen the Mountain Resort, how do you like it? Now I would like to ask someone to answer the question that I had posed at the beginning of our tour — why do garden specialists say that the Chengde Mountain Resort is the epitome of China's landscapes? Before you answer this question, please tell me something about the topography of the Chengde Mountain Resort. ... Great! You've got it! The topography of the southeast area is lowland. The landscapes are just like that of southern China. The topography of the northeast is very smooth with grasslands. The topography of the northwest is that of highlands with gullies. The topography of Chengde Mountain Resort is the work of nature. But it is similar to that of China as a whole. Moreover, the best gardening scenes from all over China have been recreated here. Now you understand why horticulture specialists so highly praise the

Chengde Mountain Resort

Chengde Mountain Resort and see it as the epitome of our beautiful country.

Now let's think about the role the resort has played in Chinese history, culture and gardening. The Chengde Mountain Resort was witness to the consolidation and development of our united country of multi – nationalities. Every year, both Emperor Kangxi and Emperor Qianlong spent six months here enjoying the favorable climate and attending to state affairs . Judging from its rich historical connotations, the Mountain Resort is a history museum of nations and religions and is a book of the Qing Dynasty compiled with special materials. As far as culture is concerned, Chengde Mountain Resort is the end result of Emperor Kangxi and Emperor Qianlong's regimes. The buildings reflect the idea of unity and ethos. The cultures of the Han and some other minorities display not only their own characteristics but also what was adopted from others. The Chengde Mountain Resort shows rich, unified scenes and a pluralistic cultural background. The Chengde Mountain Resort played a very important role during the Qing Dynasty and was once the center of the culture for the whole nation. The Chengde Mountain Resort and its outlying temples belong to not only China, but also to the whole world. Now Chengde has become a world renowned cultural city and it is inscribed on the World Heritage List of UNESCO. UNESCO spaclalists regard Chengde Mountain Resort as a wonderful garden full of eastern philosophical thought. As for its concept of gardening, it is credited to Emperor Kangxi who had the garden built following the natural topography and making the most of hills, rivers, lakes and plains to build pavilions while keeping the natural beauty of the land. The design of the building in the palace area is like an ordinary siheyuan in Beijing. Although it is a palace, the Chengde Mountain Resort is simply furnished, lacking any luxurious materials. It is austere and elegant, harmonizing well with the simplicity of the whole resort. So we can say that the Chengde Mountain Resort is an imperial garden with artistic characteristics and traditional Chinese style. It's a bright

Selected Tour Commentaries

pearl of our classical gardening style and is a wonder of the world. All of us are very proud of it. Ladies and gentlemen, specialists on history, archaeology, geography, aesthetics, religion, gardening and architecture agree unanimously that the Chengde Mountain Resort is not only a big outdoor museum, but also an all – around science. Because time is limited, we have to stop here today. I hope you will return to Chengde. I will be very happy to be your guide again so we can enjoy Chengde Mountain Resort at easier pace. OK! Everyone, see you again and good luck to all of you. Good-bye!

YUNGANG GROTTOES

Ladies and Gentlemen,

The Yungang Grottoes is located on a hill 16 kilometers west of Datong, a city renowned for its cultural relics and coal mines. Now after a 30-minute drive, we have reached the main entrance of this treasure house of oriental grottoes. It is an honor for me to be your tour guide today.

Consisting of a number of honeycomb-shaped grottoes, the Yungang Grottoes was carved into a slope of the Wuzhou Mountain, which stretches for about one kilometer from east to west. This spot of interest was rated by domestic experts as one of the three famous grotto treasure houses in China, the other two being Mogao in Gansu Province in the northwest and Longmen in central China's Henan Province. As the largest grottoes ever dug, the Yungang Grottoes serves as a rare cultural heritage of the Chinese people and provides a large amount of historical information for the research of ancient society, religion and art. In 1961, the State Council listed these grottoes as one of the major places of cultural or historical interest to be placed under the strict protection of local government.

In a courtyard situated in front of the main entrance, there hangs a map of the site. Now I'd like to present a brief history on the development of the grottoes.

As a type of of Buddhist temple, the grottoes first originated in old India. To pay homage to the Buddha who was said to have lived

Selected Tour Commentaries

in a deserted grotto to cultivate himself, Buddhist followers began cutting out caves and modeling Buddhist statues. Since Buddhism was first introduced into China more than 2,000 years ago, construction of grottoes made headway along the world-renowned Silk Road. Beginning with the Wei Dynasty, and ending with the Qing and Ming era, grottoes were constructed during a span of some 1,600 years. As a result, several hundreds of grottoes of different sizes were cut out across the country, along the Silk Road in northwest China's Xinjiang Autonomous Region, Gansu Province and Ninxia Autonomous Region, Shanxi Province, as well as in the central and southwest territory.

These numerous grottoes are different in their styles. The 492 caves of the famous Mogao Grottoes in Dunhuang, Gansu Province, are remembered for their painted Buddhist statues and figurines. In the case of the Maiji Hill Grottoes in Tianshui, Gansu Province, this spot of interest is famous for its clay figurines and statue techniques. The Yungang Grottoes is made special for its stone caves, while the Longmen Grottoes is considered an imitation of Yungang. Last, the Dazu Grottoes serves as a fine model of late China's grotto craftsmanship. All in all, the Yungang Grottoes serves as an important milestone and hence has attained widespread popularity.

Historical documents show that the construction of this site first began in 460 during the reign of the Northern Wei Dynasty, and consisted of 45 caves. It now features more than 51,000 Buddhist statues and figurines and some 1,200 niches. Following the undulation of Wuzhou Mountain, the grottoes can be divided into three major parts. The first or eastern part consists of four caves (No. 1 through No. 4). The second or central part features nine (No. 5 through No. 13) while the third or western division constitutes the rest (No. 14 through No. 45). To begin our tour, we will follow the traditional sightseeing route from Grotto No. 5 in the center. The No. 5 and No. 6 grottoes are a group of caves which connect and serve as one of the most splendid and typical structures of the Yun-

70

Yungang grottoes

gang Grottoes.

On the facade of this two-in-one cave, there is a group of lofty, four-storeyed wooden structures featuring a scarlet colonnade and glazed tile roofing, which is known as grotto pavilions. Under the auspices of a local military commander, this group of architectures was completed in 1651 during the reign of Emperor Shunzhi of the Qing Dynasty. Whenever the structures were shrouded in mist and fog, visitors would feel as if they were in a fairyland. Therefore, it was listed as one of the eight wonders existing in the clouds, and is known as "Grottoes Scraping the Clouds." In 1955, this group of pavilions was renovated by the government.

Now about grotto No. 5. This cave takes the shape of an oval thatched hut and consists of two chambers. In the back chamber there is a lofty Buddhist statue, which is 17 meters in height, the tallest of its kind in the Yungan Grottoes. Sitting cross-legged, its legs are 15. 5 meters in length. It is wearing a loose robe and a kasaya, its hair is worn in a blue bun, and its face is impressively clear. The Buddha is characterized by thin brows, slim eyes, a straight nose and ears with big lobes. Unfortunately, this statue was later covered with gold powder, so we are no longer able to admire the stone statue in its original state. This grotto features three statues. The one in the center is dedicated to Sakyamuni, the founder of Buddhism, while the one standing on its right is known as Future Buddha. The clay on the latter is crumbling so we are lucky we can still admire the original work dating back to the Northern Wei Dynasty. On September 15, 1973, former French President, Georges Jean Raymond Pompidou, accompanied by Chinese Premier Zhou Enlai paid a visit to the Yungang Grottoes and highly admired this statue. This cave is also famous for its eight, exquisite, one-meter-tall statues and a pair of two sitting Buddhas on the ceiling. Behind the main statue there is a tunnel which was used by Buddhist followers .

Cave No. 6 is considered to be the grandest cave of the Yungang

Selected Tour Commentaries

Grottoes. This cave differs from No. 5 in that its back chamber is square with a 15 meters high two-storeyed, square pillar standing in the middle. Almost every inch of its surface is carved with splendid and exquisite designs of Buddha, Bodhisattva, arhats, flying Apsaras, worshipers and exotic animals and flora.

This cave is very famous for two reasons: its carving technique is superb and the content of its carvings is very rich. Now let's take a look at the carving style. On the upper storey of the square pillar is a total of 15 standing statues of Buddha, known as reception Buddhas. In addition to five statues on the lower storey, all were carved in relief to strengthen the 3-D perspective. There are other statues on the pillar which were hollowed out, using a complex, high-level technique that illustrates the ingenuity of the ancient Chinese some 1,500 years ago. In the middle of the pillar, as well as on the walls, there is a total of 33 carvings involving episodes from the life of the Buddha. They involve the following:

(1) Once upon a time there lived in Kapilavastu of ancient India a king, Suddhodana, and his empress, Mahamaya. They are going on 40 years of age and still have no children. Mahamaya conceives on the same night that she dreams that a Bodhisattva riding on the back of a white elephant. pays them a visit. Foreign ambassadors and envoys call upon them in congratulations.

(2) In 454 B. C. , the empress gives birth to the Buddha in a park called Lumbini, on her way to her parent's home. At that time the sky is filled with colorful clouds.

(3) The newborn prince takes seven steps in all directions. wherever he steps, a lotus grows. He points to the sky and the earth and proclaims, "I am supreme to the universe."

(4) The nine dragons bathe the prince with holy water. Till this day, the Festival of Bathing the Buddha is still observed in April in China's temples and monasteries.

(5) Both the father and son return to court and immortals dance in celebration. Even the elephants are very happy.

Yungang grottoes

(6) A famous fortuneteller tells the king, "The prince is a sage by birth. If he stays home, he will succeed the throne. If he goes away, he will become a Buddha."

(7) The king builds luxurious halls for his son and provides him with hundreds of distractions to keep him from practicing Buddhism. However, the prince is unimpressed and unhappy.

(8) The prince marries Yasodhara, daughter of Suprabuddha, at the age of 17. He shoots a single arrow through seven gold drums upon his betrothal.

(9) The prince amuses himself in court after the wedding.

(10) The prince's wife gives birth to a baby. The king grants permission for the prince to travel elsewhere.

(11) to (14) The prince goes out of the four gates in a carriage, meets an old man, a patient, a dead man and a monk, and decides to contemplate ways to relieve people of suffering .

(15) The prince asks his father for permission to become a monk. The king refuses.

(16) The prince leaves the court on a horse, and flies out of the city with the help of four heavenly deities. After his five-year visit and six-year cultivation period, the prince becomes a Buddha under a pipal.

(17) The prince becomes known as Sakyamuni, or sage of the Sakyas. Please take a look at this fine carving depicting the Buddha's first turning of the Dharma wheel in Mrgadava. Sakyamuni is giving a lecture on Buddhism and his disciples listen with respect. Even two deer listen with smiles on their faces.

The layout and construction of cave No. 6 was done by Daozhao, an eminent monk of the Northern Wei Dynasty. This cave is harmonious in overall layout, rich in figure modeling, and combines traditional Chinese architectural style with that of the West.

According to research and investigation done by specialists, the Yungang Grottoes was developed in three phases. The first phase lasted from 460 to 465 and consists mainly of the famous Tanyao

Selected Tour Commentaries

Grottoes, or the caves from No. 16 through No. 20. This phase is characterized by large-scale, grandiose caves, as well as a horseshoe-shaped layout. The majority of the statues are lofty and imposing, taking the center stage of the cave, and resemble statues found in India and Central Asia. The second phase of construction lasted from 465 through 494, during which time five groups of caves were dug. Unlike those of the first phase, the caves of the second phase mainly took the shape of a square. Further, front and back chambers, a central square pillar and carvings on the ceiling were introduced. The themes of the carvings diversified and tended to be more secular and chinese in style. The third phase of construction started in 499 and ended in 524. All the rest of the caves were constructed during this period. Because the Northern Wei court moved the capital away to Luoyang, most of the caves cut out during this time were small to medium in size and the majority of the statues were characterized by Chinese style.

High above the lintel of cave No. 6, there used to hang a gigantic plaque handwritten by Emperor Qianlong of the Qing Dynasty. Unfortunately, this plaque is gone.

' Caves No. 7 and No. 8 are among the first that were built during the second phase. During the Liao Dynasty, these structures became national temples. The pavilions were reconstructed by the government in 1994.

The major statues in cave No. 7 have suffered from severe efflorescence. A two-storeyed niche was dug on the northern wall of the back chamber. On the upper storey threr is a Maityeya, flanked by two leaning Buddhas. On the lower storey there is a carving of two Buddhas preaching face-to-face. This cave is also famous for its exquisite and complex caisson, or covered ceiling . The ceiling features six lattices, each centered around a lotus and flying Apsaras. The flying Apsaras is said to be good at singing and dancing. Whenever the Buddha gave a lecture, she would soar into the sky and scatter auspicious flowers. On the lintel of the southern wall, there are

Yungang grottoes

carvings of six Buddhist followers kneeling and praying. In 1990, the city government of Datong erected a tablet on the east side of this cave, in commemoration of the protection of this site over the last 40 years.

Cave No. 8, like No. 7, also suffers from damage caused by severe efflorescence.

On the western side of the lintel, there is a statue of Kumarajiva, who has three heads and six arms and is riding on a heavenly bird. An eminent monk of the later Qin Dynasty, Kumarajiva was born in 344 and passed away in 413. He was considered one of China's three most prominent translators of Buddhist scriptures. The other two include Xuanzhuang and Paramartha. Many scriptures, including Saddharmapundarikasutra, Amitabhasutra, Vajracchedikaprajnaparamitasurtra, were translated by him into Chinese. He was worshipped as the guardian of Buddhism after his death. The statue, unique and rich in imagination, is considered by scholars and specialists as an ingenious embodiment of the blending of oriental and western art styles, a rare art treasure of the Yungang Grottoes.

On the eastern side is another group of statues. Among them, the docile, heavenly ox and grapes are exceptionally vivid.

In addition, the Yungang Grottoes also features the Wuhua Caves, or caves No. 9 through No. 13. In 1891, these caves were repainted with color , hence the name of Wuhua (Colorful Flowery) Caves.

These caves are divided into two groups. The first group includes caves No. 9 and No. 10, while the second group includes the three caves of No. 11 through No. 13.

Both caves No. 9 and No. 10 consist of two chambers each. Situated in the front chamber of No. 9 is the smallest statue (two centimeters tall) of the Yungang Grottoes. It was made in 484 by a famous eunuch named Wang Yu.

The builders of these caves usde traditional Chinese construction

Selected Tour Commentaries

style with four octagonal pillars in each cave. The back chamber of cave No. 9 features a giant statue of Buddha in the middle and five lace-shaped carvings in relief on the northwestern wall.

cave No. 10 features an exquisitely carved lintel in the front, depicting mountains, dragons, various animals, Asuras and Kumarajiva.

On the ceilings of both No. 9 and No. 10 , there are designs of groups of flying Apsaras in different poses.

Caves No. 11, No. 12 and No. 13 are grouped together with No. 12 serving as the central part.

In the middle of cave No. 11, there is a 13.3 meter-tall, square pillar which is decorated with carved designs. On the upper southeastern wall a tablet was engraved in commemoration of construction on August 30, 483. It serves as the earliest record of events inscribed on the stones of the Yungang Grottoes. Featuring a total of 336 Chinese characters, this inscription serves as a rare piece of calligraphy and as an important historical record for the research of the grottoes.

Cave No. 12 is the most famous cave dedicated to music within the Yungang Grottoes. The theme of the carvings mainly involves the celebration of Sakyamuni's becoming a Buddha. Major events that happened during his lifetime are seen here. The front chamber features group carvings of dancers and musicians as well as a variety of exotic, ancient musical instruments. Standing in this chamber makes us feel as if we are in a music hall. This kind of cave, dedicated to musical themes, is very rare in grottoes throughout the country.

It should be noted that many of the musical instruments depicted in this cave used to be played by the ethnic people of northern China and the musicians' clothes have many characteristic features of those worn by the ethnic nomads. . It serves to provide important and precious historical data for the research of cultural trends of the Northern Wei Dynasty.

Cave No. 13 features a horseshoe-shaped layout topped by an arch. The main statue is 13 meters in height, taking the shape of a

Yungang grottoes

cross-legged Maitreya wearing the costume of a Bodhisattva. He wears a crown and armlets with serpentines on them. His head is held erect. His left hand is on his knee while his right hand is raised high.

This cave is also characterized by three canopies on the southern wall. Underneath the canopies there stand seven, two-meter-high statues with boat-shaped lights and nimbi.

The grottoes constructed in the second phase include caves of No. 5 and No. 6, as well as the Wuhua Caves. Their Buddhist statues served as models for others made during the reign of the Northern Dynasties, as well as for the enshrined statues of the Southern Dynasties. They exerted tremendous influence upon the construction of later grottoes in Northern China. As a matter of fact, their statues became the mainstream style during the reign of the Northern Dynasties.

Proceeding westward we will see caves No. 14 through No. 45 .

Cave No. 14 has collapsed and only some niches and statues remain intact on its western wall.

Cave No. 15 features nearly 1, 000 Buddhist statues, a theme prevalent during the Northern Wei Dynasty. It also features designs in relief of beads, algae and aquatic birds. These are the only carvings involving aquatic flora and fauna.

Now we are going to pay a visit to the famous Tanyao Grottoes. This group consists of five caves, namely, caves No. 16 to No. 20. Now, I will give you a brief history on the construction of these grottoes.

Since ancient time, the northern territory of Shanxi Province has been populated mainly by ethnic, nomadic people. The city of Datong served as a major place where people of the Han nationality and other ethnic groups interacted. In 398, Emperor Daowu of the Northern Wei Dynasty moved from Mongolia southward, and made Datong his capital. In 494, Emperor Xiaowen moved his court to Luoyang in Henan province. During this period, the imperial rulers,

Selected Tour Commentaries

who were devoid of their own languages and culture, turned to Buddhism in an effort to consolidate their kingdoms. With this, a heyday of Buddhism was ushered in during the Northern Wei Dynasty.

In 446, Emperor Taiwu took harsh measures against Buddhism in the belief that Buddhist followers collaborated with rebels. Quite a few Buddhist scriptures were burnt and some monks were buried alive, giving the first blow to Buddhism since its introduction into China. Emperor Wenchen, the grandson of Taiwu, ordered the restoration of Buddhism and reinstated the eminent monk Tanyao. Since 460, with the consent of Emperor Wencheng, Tanyao cut out five grottoes on Wuzhou Mountain to the west of Datong. Tens of thousands of artisans were enlisted over the course of project.

The cutting of Tanyao Grottoes marked the beginning of the large-scale cutting of Yungang Grottoes and implied that North China's Buddhist center had moved from Gansu Province to this capital. It also linked Buddhism with imperial rule in that main Buddhist statues were cut in commemoration of the monarchs of Northern Wei Dynasties.

The lofty statue in cave No. 16 is 13.5 meters tall and is characterized by a felt cloak, knots on the chest and skirt, and a handsome face. This was a symbol of Emperor Daowu. Interestingly his costume is similar to the dress worn by today's Korean woman.

The statue in cave No. 17 is dedicated to Emperor Mingyuan. This statue is even taller, 15.6 meters in height, and looks more imposing than the one in cave No. 16.

In cave No. 18, a 15.5-meter-tall statue was carved for Emperor Taiwu who had ordered the ban on Buddhism. Wearing a kasaya decorated with 1,000 Buddhas and solemnly standing there, he seems to be repentant about what he had done. This cave also has a group of well-preserved carvings of Arhats.

Cave No. 19 features the largest Buddha statue in this group of five grottoes. It is the second largest statue in the Yungang Grottoes. The statue is 16.8 meters in height and is dedicated to Emperor Jing-

Yungang grottoes

mu, the fourth monarch in the line of the Northern Wei Dynasty. He passed away before he ascended the throne. here, you will see two more smaller statues placed outside the main chamber.

The statue of cave No. 20 serves as the hallmark of the Yungang Grottoes. Since the cave collapsed more than 1,000 years ago during the Liao Dynasty, this 13.7-meter-tall Buddha has been laid bare. It was dedicated to Emperor Wencheng, who restored Buddhism and ordered the cutting of the Yungang Grottoes. He sits cross-legged, his face is round, and his right shoulder is exposed. He is also known as the diplomat of the Yungang Grottoes.

The grottoes completed during the third phase include caves No. 21 through No. 45. They were cut with donations from middle or lower level nobles and Buddhist followers after Emperor Xiaowen moved the capital to Luoyang. Cut during the period from 494 to 524, they are characterized by smaller but more complex caves and statues. Of these, caves No. 37 through No. 39 stand out for their slimmer statues and the pronounced characteristics of the Han nationality.

The group of grottoes situated in the east are made up of four caves.

Caves No. 1 and No. 2 are the sole two-in-one structures taking the shape of towers and temples. Statues of Maitreya and Sakyamuni are inside. To the very front of cave No. 2 , there is a running fountain which is rich in minerals.

Cave No. 3 is also noteworthy. It was cut on the largest scale while containing the fewest statues . The cave is 25 meters in height and 50 meters in width, the largest of its kind in the whole grotto. However, anything relating to it was lost in oblivion.

Now more than 1,000 years have passed and the Yungang Grottoes has suffered from severe damage inflicted by weathering, water erosion and earthquakes. Worse still, the Grottoes also suffered from ransacking by imperialists before the founding of the New China. More than 1,400 statues were spirited abroad.

Selected Tour Commentaries

Since the founding of the People's Republic of China, the government has earmarked funds on many occasions for the restoration of the Grottoes. This site has been inscribed on the World Heritage List by UNESCO. During his visit to this site, former French President George Jean Raymond Pompidou remarked, "The Yungang Grottoes are one of the peaks of human arts." It is everybody's responsibility to help preserve this treasure house of stone statues.

HULUNBEIER GRASSLAND

Ladies and Gentlemen:

Welcome to Hulunbeier Grassland! First of all, I'd like to tell you why people call this beautiful grassland Hulunbeier Grassland. There is a moving legend behind it. A long, long time ago there lived a couple of lovers on the grassland. The girl was Hu Lun. The boy was Bei Er. One day a demon chief called Mang Gusi abducted Hu Lun and dried up the grassland. The grass withered and yellowed and domestic animals died one after another. In order to save the grassland and Hu Lun, Bei Er traveled a great distance on foot, chasing after Mang Gasi day and night. Finally, he fainted from exhaustion. In his weakened state, he dreamt that the demon chief had magically turned Hu Lun into a flower which was and suffering from the windy and dusty weather. When Bei Er woke up, he saw the flower of his dream in front of him. He immediately watered the flower and broke the spell. Hu Lun changed back into her former self. But the demon chief would not give up. He seized Hu Lun and took her away again. Hu Lun racked her brain for a way to escape. She succeeded in getting hold of the magic pearl on the demon chief's head. On swallowing the pearl Hu Lun turned into a lake. In the meantime Bei Er had killed all of the other demons, but failed to find Hu Lun. Heartbroken, Bei Er jumped into a lake to kill himself. All of a sudden the earth split open and formed two lakes, Hu Lun Lake and Bei Er Lake, with the Wilson River closely connecting them . Later,

Selected Tour Commentaries

people living on the grassland named the land Hulunbeier Grassland in memory of them.

Hulunbeier covers an area of 250.557 square kilometers, with a total population of 2.66 million. The Mongolian nationality is the dominant ethic group, and 35 other nationalities, such as Dawoer, Ewenke, Elunchun, Han, Manchu, Russian, etc. live in harmony with them on the grassland. Hulunbeier is called "green and clean land" because it is relatively free of pollution.

(Entering the grassland)

Now we're setting foot on Hulunbeier Grassland. All of us have escaped from the city and its clamour and entered a place like a dreamland. Look! The grassland looks like a soft, green carpet. Now you can enjoy the beautiful scenery in the distance; numerous kinds of wild flowers are in bloom, and wisps of smoke are rising continuously from the yurta scattered on the grassland. When the gentle breeze brushes against the grass, herds of horses and cattle and flocks of sheep seem to be drifting from here to there. What a beautiful picture!

(Visiting a yurt)

This is the yurt we saw from the bus just now. Look! The host and his family have come out of the yurt to greet us. Of course, this is not an arranged reception, to be sure. But before we enter the yurt, I'd like to make a brief introduction on the folk customs here. No matter which yurt you happen to visit, you will find that on hearing your footsteps the Mongolian people will extend a warm welcome outside the yurt, to do justice to their reputed hospitality. When greeting you, they will put their right hands against their chests and bow slightly. With a "how do you do," they invite their guests in. Male guests are invited to sit on the left and female on the right, while the host sits in the middle. The moment you take your seats, your host will have milk tea and various kinds of milk products placed

Hulunbeier Grassland

in front of you. After a while, you will most probably be asked to help yourself to a special course called "Shouba lamb." As a way of showing respect to his distinguished guest, your host will present you with a "hada" (a piece of silk used as a greeting gift), together with a cup of local wine. Mongolians are well—known for their talent in singing and dancing. Their beautiful songs are as entertaining and pleasant as the blue sky, white clouds, green grass and fresh flowers. In folk culture, there is a saying that a feast is not a true feast without the company of songs. Every person in the grassland, man or woman, old or young, can sing folk songs. When proposing toasts to their guests, they will show their hospitality by singing folk songs and playing special fiddles. The Mongolian people have lived on the vast grassland for a long time, and they have refined their talent for singing and dancing. You can not only please your eyes with their traditional ethnic dancing but also with their modern ones featuring merry rhythms and vigorous steps. Now let's enter the yurt and take advantage of this opportunity to be guests in a Mongolian herdsman's home.

(Stepping out of the yurt)

Under the blue sky and white clouds, you will see a vivid picture of flocks of sheep and herds of cattle, galloping horses and skillful herdsmen on horseback brandishing horsewhips. Do you want to go for a ride? If you are skilled at riding, why not ride a Mongolian horse for a while or wander about on camelback? If you are afraid of riding horses or camels, never mind. You still can enjoy the nomadic life by taking a special Mongolian vehicle called a "Lele."

(Briefing on the physique of Mongolians)

Now you have had a look at the grassland with your own eyes, but did you noticed that the Mongolian girls are graceful, elegant and vigorous, and the young fellows are robust, heroic and muscular? It is said that this has much to do with their life styles which are con-

Selected Tour Commentaries

nected with horse sports, running and pursuing. Further, the important role played by milk tea and milk products in developing their muscles and bones cannot be underestimated.

(Briefing on the dietary habit of Mongolians)

Let's start with milk tea. The host minces the tea and puts it in a kettle to boil it. When the kettle starts boiling with a gurgling sound, the host pours the fresh milk into it. Thus the herdsman coming in from a snowstorm will warm up immediately after having such a cup of milk tea. A bowl of milk tea, stir-fried rice, several pieces of a dry milk product and some lamb is regarded as a delicious meal by the ordinary Mongolian herdsman. Milk products include the skin of boiled milk, milk curd, milk wine, cheese, butter and so on. The formal meal may be served with meat and a flour-based product.

While you are here on the grassland, it will be a great pity if you do not try "Shouba Lamb" (boiled meat which is eaten using a knife and your hands). The lamb is first cut into big slices and then put into boiling water to cook. When it is half done, you cut it into smaller pieces with the Mongolian knife and eat it. The Mongolian people think that half-done meat contains more nutrients.

(Briefing on Mongolian clothing)

The Mongolian robe is unique to this ethnic group. The robe is often matched with a belt and head decorations. With its high collar and long sleeves, the robe protects people from mosquitoes. The middle part of the robe is made loose for the convenience of riding horses and is long enough to keep the knees warm. You can find all kinds of clothes here today, but the robe is the cultural heritage of the Mongolians and has become a symbol of their national conscience and identity.

(Briefing on Mongolian yurta)

You can see Mongolian yurta here and there on the grassland.

84

Hulunbeier Grassland

But do you know the history and structure of the Mongolian yurta? According to the historical records of the Xiongnu, an ancient ethnic group, their ancestors lived in the Northland long ago. Their living quarters were called yurta. In this sense, Mongolians, as an ethnic group, can date back to 4,000 years ago. So the Mongolian yurta are a symbol of the history of this ethnic group. Now let's talk about the construction of a yurt. Herdsmen first build a round foundation with pieces of stones. Then they set up the structure with wooden rods and beams linked together with woolen or fur ropes, Lastly, they cover the structure with animal skins or felt blankets. The ceiling of the yurt is round. With such a structure, the yurt can withstand snowstorms and heavy rainfalls. The door of the yurt is small and down to the ground. The yurt can be easily moved and this is suitable for nomadic life. This accounts for the reason why the structure of the yurt remains unchanged till today. If the Mongolian yurt is seen as the home of the herdsmen, then the "Lele" carts can be viewed as their mobile homes. "Lele" carts move slowly with big noise. It is hard to tell when the history of "Lele" carts began. All the carts are made of birch, so they will remain in good condition even in wet weather. The wheels of the carts are tall and can easily roll across the uneven roads, lush bushes, thick snow and marshes. "Lele" carts are indispensable for herdsmen when they move across snow-covered areas.

(Briefing on Mongolian festivals)

There are a lot of Mongolian festivals held every year on the grassland, but the most famous one is Nadam, the carnival of the grassland. "Nadam" in the Mongolian language means recreation or entertainment. When it comes, there will be a lot of performances, such as horse racing, wrestling, archery and some other special ethnic performances. The Nadam fair is a time-honored festival and was known worldwide for 700 years. Nowadays the Nadam fair is often held during the harvest season of the grassland, either in June or July

Selected Tour Commentaries

. During that period, herdsmen often take the opportunity to sell domestic animals and livestock products and purchase daily necessities and livelihood – related goods. Actually, the herdsmen have few chances to get together on such a vast grassland, so Nadam also plays the role of a big trade fair for them. When we talk about Nadam, we should also talk about offering sacrifice at "Aobao." "Aobao" in Mongolian means a pile of rocks or earth. On the vast and endless grassland, it is hard to tell directions, so people thought of piling rocks or earth to mark them. In its long historical development, Aobao has become the shrine to offer sacrifices to the God of the Mountain and the God of the Road. During the sacrifice-offering ceremony, people insert tree branches into the Aobao and put pieces of colorful cloth or paper flags with written scripture on the branches. There are four types of memorial ceremonies, namely blood, wine, fire and jade. No matter what type it is, a lama will be invited to burn incenses, chant scriptures and pray for the blessing of the people and their livestock. Participants will walk around the Aobao clockwise three times. After the ceremony, the herdsmen will start to enjoy themselves. The herdsmen will not only enjoy horse races, wrestling and archery, but also singing, dancing and drinking to their heart's content. Around that time, young lovers will probably leave the crowd to be in a world of their own.

Dear, distinguished guests, after this tour of this grassland, I believe you must have a general idea of how the Mongolian people live here and may even feel reluctant to leave the beautiful Hulunbeier Grassland. I believe the grassland and its people enjoyed your visit as much as you did and look forward to your next one.

Ladies and gentlemen, I hope to have another chance to meet you again on this very land, the Hulunbeier Grassland. Goodbye and good luck.

WATER CAVE OF BENXI

Ladies and Gentlemen!
(pointing to the mountain outside the cave)

This mountain is Xiake Mountain. It belongs to the Qianshang Range. The Water Cave of Benxi is hidden inside the mountain and winds with the zigzag of the mountain.

In front of the cave, Prince River flows and the water is very clear and clean. The cave faces north and extends about 3,000 meters to the south inside the mountain. The entrance of the cave is like a half moon, grand and natural. Above the entrance inscribed the four characters of "Water Cave of Benxi" are inscribed. They were made using the handwritten one of Bo Yibo, a senior leader of present China.

The cave is cool in summer and warm in winter because the temperature in the cave is always about 12℃. It's a really good shelter on windy and rainy days. It was once an arsenal of the Northeastern Army when the Japanese invaded Northeast China.

This hall is "Yingke Hall." meaning "the hall to welcome guests" and it can hold several thousand persons. Long ago, people found the cave and lived here. Since the founding of the new China in 1949, our government has organized several explorations and up to now, archaeologists have found relics of the New Stone Age, dating back 10,000 years ago, in the entrance of the cave. The famous archaeologist, Professor Jia Lanpo has been here twice and said that

Selected Tour Commentaries

our ancestors lived in the cave 10,000 or 20,000 years ago so the cave is a very valuable relics site for the research of the ancient people in the North, ancient meteorology and ancient geography. Inside the cave, there are various stalactites, stalagmites, columns and screens. Both Wei Cijun, a poet during the Qing Dynasty, and a contemporary poet Wei Chuantong wrote poems to describe the marvelous scenery of the cave.

The "Yingke Hall" is connected to three other interior caves: Panlong Cave on the right, Yinbo Cave on the left and "Jiuqu Yinhe Cave" straight ahead. Apart from the "Seven Palaces," "Jiuqu Yinhe Cave" has a lot to offer, such as the Three Gorges, the Two Doors, the Nine Turns. Now, let's visit the first palace, "Yinhe Palace."

Look, the spring waters and sprays are greeting the tourists, so it is called "Fei Quan Yingke," meaning "springs welcome the guests."

The Yinhe ferry is the port from which tourists can take boats to visit the cave. Here, the river is wide and calm. Getting on the boat, you may ask, "Where does the water come from?" The water in the cave flows all year round and the flow capacity for one day is 14,000 cubic meters. The average depth is 1.5 meters and the deepest place is 7 meters. Where is so much water coming from? You will know the answer when we get to the source. Now we will board the boat and go against the river flow. We'll go to the first gorge of the cave — Fu Rong Gorge. Although the river is twisting, it's so clear that you can see the bottom. The ceiling of the cave is silvery white.

Look, that's the legendary "Lotus Lamp." It reminds us of the story of Chen Xiang who lifted the lamp and split the mountain to save his mother. The stalactites are all toward the outside, as if they are ready to go out to save all the mothers who are still suffering. You may ask, "Where does the wind come and why does it blow toward the entrance?" This is a secret which will be uncovered later. Now, the boat has brought us to a gloomy but dreamy scene. You may want to ask another question, "How was this cave formed?"

Water Cave of Benxi

I'm going to answer this question first. A long, long time ago this place was part of the ocean. When the earth entered the third period of the Cenozoic Era, the land slowly rose. Then the water above and below the ground mixed together. carbonated water eroded the limestone, and the Karst topography was formed.

My friends, because of water erosion both above and below ground, the cave is still changing.

Now, we have come to "Erxian Palace" which means the "Palace of two immortal persons." Look in front, that's "Ju Yuan Po" which means "the gathering place of monkeys." All the monkeys are lifelike. Some are chasing others, some are running, some are chatting, and some are climbing. But all of them are here to greet you.

Look! Those two stalagmites are just like the two gods of longevity. They stand back — to — back, extending their blessings to you for successful carriers, happy lives and longevity.

The next palace is "Guanghan Palace." You can find the beautiful lady Chang Er dancing with her long gloves and Wu Gang who was punished to cut trees. There are two reefs standing in the river. The left one is like a snake, so it is called Snake Stone and the right one is called Turtle Stone. Here the river is very narrow and it's only four or five meters deep, but only here, can you feast your eyes on the beautiful scenery.

The stone figures on the left are either sitting, looking up the sky or reading their sutras. These different figures are like arhats. On the right before us is the image of "Nuwa Bu Tian." It is said that the God of Water, Gong Gong, fought with the God of Fire, Zhu Rong. Defeated, Gong Gong knocked into the Buzhou Mountain with his head and destroyed the post supporting the sky. Half of the sky collapsed and a big hole appeared in its place. The kind mother of human beings, Nuwa, melted colorful stones and mended the sky. She then cut off a leg of a giant turtle to use as a pillar to support the sky. Now, look up to the right, that's "Bao Ding Shuang Zhong"

Selected Tour Commentaries

meaning "two bells hanging on the ceiling." Now the rope and the bell are almost connected. They are probably only 1 centimeter apart from each other. Scientists say that the stalactite grows 1 centimeter every 100 years. I hope you will live more than 100 years and come back to see it. By then the rope will be connected the bell, I am sure.

According to legend, the Jade Emperor of Heaven sent an immortal old man "Taibai Jinxing" to supervise the production of the two bells. He ordered a man of unusual strength to carry the bells back to the "Lingxiao Palace" using a shoulder-pole. On his way to the palace, the man was attracted by the scenery of Benxi and was reluctant to move on. As he had been standing for a long time, he needed to change shoulders to carry the bells. while doing so, he carelessly dropped the bells. That is the story about how the "Bao Ding Shuang Zhong" came here.

Now, our boat is entering "Shuangjian Gorge" or "Double Swords Gorge." The sword before us is "Zhanyao Sword" of King Yu. It was said that a dragon with single horn often terrorized the people. In order to eliminate the monster, King Yu cut off the dragon's head.

The "sword" is 7 meters long, and the diameter of its base is 1.3 meters. All the stalactites here are like swords. Seen from a distance, they look just like a forest of swords.

Passing the Sword Gate, we come to the Yuhuang Palace or the Palace of the Jade Emperor of Heaven. This is the fourth palace in the cave and it includes more than 20 scenic spots. Look, this is a crocodile. That's "Xiandan Stove." On the left, above us is "Taibai Shenbi" or the "immortal pen of Taibai." Look at the reef before us; it is " Wang Mu," the Queen Mother of Heaven. Looking from a distance, you will see two golden frogs eating something. As you get nearer, you'll see some delicious foods on the islet. It is said that this is the "yaochi" where Wang Mu invited all the immortals to attend her feast.

Water Cave of Benxi

Here is the Earthworm Cave. During the tour, you may have wondered why in this cave some places are high, some are low, some are wide and some are narrow. It is said that the Silver River (Milky Way in English) Cave is also called "Hongjun Laozu Cave." The Hongjun Laozu was formerly an earthworm. Because he was the same age as the earth and heaven, he became an immortal. This cave was his incarnation. So that is why it is twisted and uneven.

Look at the stone screen engraved with flowers. That's the bedroom of "Jiutian Xuannu." She went away to guard the Palace Gate and left only two maids to look after her bed. The white jade bottle on the left bank was left by Hongjun Laozu. Once, all the land was inundated by water that had gushed out of the mouth of a monster. Hearing about this, Hongjun Laozu saved all the living things and placed them in the Zixiao Palace on the Yuquan Mountain, but the monster continued to gush water and wanted to inundate Yu Quan Mountain. Hongjun Laozu used the white jade bottle to absorb the water. 81 days later, the monster was defeated. Now the bottle is here to protect the land from the monster. There is a head on the smooth wall. The wall is called Zhenyao Wall. The single horn dragon was held under the water, and only his head emerged over the water. His horn has been cut off by Jiutian Xuannu. On the upper right wall, there is a stalagmite; it's Laozu's helmet. He put it there to frighten the dragon. OK, in front of us is the source of the Silver River Water Cave. Here is the last palace, Zi Xiao Palace or Source Palace. The round door on the right is Taizhen Gate. The one on the left is Hongjun Door. Both doors are connected to Zixiao Palace. On the right bank, there is a pool called Xiao Tianchi or Little Heavenly Lake. It's there that the Silver River takes a bath.

Now look upwards, That's Yixiantian or Thread Narrow Sky. When Hongjun Laozu fought with the monster, the monster tore the Yu Quan Mountain apart and the Thread Narrow Sky was formed.

Please look downward. This is the source of the river — Zixiao Pond. Although the pond is calm, it's deeper than you imagine. The

Selected Tour Commentaries

end of the cave is still ahead. We will not get there for a while. Scientists estimate that it is at least 3,000 meters deep here. But actual depth is still a secret. I believe that in the future scientists will uncover the secret.

Now, we are going back. Please enjoy the scenery. Ladies and gentlemen, Benxi has a lot of tourist destinations. Dashi Lake is one of them. It is 120 kilometers away from the cave but it is said that the lake is connected to the cave. In ancient times, there was a businessman dealing in timbers. One day, his timbers were washed away into the lake, and he couldn't find them. At last, he found his timbers in the cave. It proved that , there is an underground river between the lake and the cave even if the mouth of the river hasn't been found yet.

Look, that's a scene called "Buddha explains his sutras." On his right is"Amitabba" and on his left is and "Pharmacist Buddha." In the left lower part, there is an iron pagoda. In front of it there is a white crane. On its upper left is a bat hanging upside down. Legend has it that a long, long time ago there was a battle between the birds and beasts. The bat stayed on the sidelines. When the birds appeared to be winning the bat flew to their side and said he was a bird because he had wings. Later, when the beasts seemed to be winning, he flew to them and said he belonged to them because he had teeth. At last, when both sides realized that neither could win, they stopped fighting. But both the birds and the beasts had seen through the bat and neither would accept him as a community member. So the bat has to come out at night.

In this mysterious cave you can find a special kind of fish. Because they lived in darkness for generations upon generations, they have no use for sight and, have become blind or almost blind. But they have very acute hearing. They are called "blind fish."

On the right is "Yinhe Pagoda." It looks like the pagoda in Beihai Park of Beijing. In front of us, the left is "Yinhe Stage," the play is called "Meeting on the Bridge of Magpies." According to the

Water Cave of Benxi

legend of "The Cowherd and the Girl" Wang Mu allowed Niulang, a cowherd, and Zhinu, a weaver to meet every 7 days, but they misheard it as being allowed to meet only once a year on the 7th day of the 7th month of the lunar calendar. Because they met so infrequently, every time they met, they tended to cry. If it rains coincidentally on that very day the raindrops are supposedly their teardrops.

Now let's look upwards. The right is "Yinhe Yang Fan" (sailing on Yin River) and the left is "Zhu Bajie Hui Gu li" or "Zhu Bajie returns to hometown." Look at the head of the crocodile. I will tell you a story about an intelligence contest between a monkey and a crocodile. One day a mother crocodile wanted to eat the heart of the monkey living on the opposite bank. She asked her son to think of a way to catch the monkey . The baby crocodile came up with a good idea. He said to the monkey, "I would like to tell you that there are many banana trees on this bank. Do you want to get some bananas?" The monkey said he couldn't swim. The crocodile promised to help him. The monkey jumped onto the baby crocodile's back. While crossing the river, the baby crocodile told the monkey, "My mother wants to eat your heart." The monkey knew that he was being tricked. He thought quickly and came up with a plan. He told the crocodile, "Sorry, but I left my heart back on the bank. We must go back to get it." The crocodile took him back to the bank. The monkey jumped off its back and climbed a tree. He smiled at the crocodile and said, "Please climb up to get my heart." The crocodile said nothing, but opened his jaws with regret and died right here.

Thanks to the forces of nature, the Water Cave of Benxi has produced beautiful pictures and sets of lifelike sculptures for visitors They are fantastic and marvelous. Look, stone flowers are blooming, forming excellent frescoes on which you can see the images of Wang Mu's "Yaochi," the most beautiful place in heaven. As the water cave has no formal name to date, we would like to invite you to use your imagination and mail us your suggestions.

Thanks!

Selected Tour Commentaries

HEAVENLY LAKE ON MOUNT CHANGBAI

Ladies and Gentlemen:

Good morning! Now we're going to pay a visit to Heavenly Lake on Mount Changbai by bus. But before we begin with today's schedule, please let me give you a brief introduction to the history and tourism development of Mount Changbai.

Mount Changbai lies in the border area between Southeast Jilin Province of China and the Democratic People's Republic of Korea (DPRK). As a mountain right on the borderline, it stretches about 1,000 kilometres. The main peak within China's territory is called White Cloud, 2,691 metres above sea level, and it serves as the highest peak in the northeastern part of China. The highest peak in DPRK's territory on the opposite bank of Heavenly Lake is called Peak General, about 2,750 metres above sea level. Altogether there is a total of 16 mountain peaks that are over 2,500 metres, with a total area of 8,000 square kilometres.

The features or characteristics of Mount Changbai are all natural. The scenery there has never undergone artificial carvings or engravings. Mount Changbai bears an air of mystery much like a newly formed world. Standing firmly between heaven and earth, Mount Changbai has strong appeal with its unique magnificence and sea of forests embracing many rare treasures. It brings a sense of grandeur and extraordinariness. A famous poet of the Qing Dynasty, Wu Zhaoqian, portrayed Mount Changbai as follows:

Heavenly Lake on Mount Changbai

Over looking northeast of China, Mount Changbai
stands far above the great land;
Facing the rising sun from the sea, it stands lonely in
the desolating fall;
With white snow capping thousands of mountain
peaks, the heaven let fall two rivers;
To climb onto the very peak, one is expected to
achieve that goal in the green.

This poem carries an air of bold and unconstrained virtues. With vivid and true-to-life description, the marvelous and magnificent scenery of Mount Changbai is brought to the full and arouses people's imagination one way or another.

Mount Changbai is actually a famous dormant volcano. History witnessed three explosions of this volcano. The first occurred on August 26, 1597, the second in April 1688, and the latest on April 14, 1702.

After three eruptions, grayish pumice rocks cover the top of the mountain. Together with the white snow accumulated through the ages, this mountain is seen from afar as a snow-coated mountain. Hence the name Mount Changbai, or Everlasting White.

The climate on the mountain is changeable: sometimes cloudy, sometimes foggy, sometimes rainy, sometimes snowy. Sometimes it is battered by hailstone. This makes the image of Mount Changbai mysterious, unpredictable, vast and hazy. During the height of summer, wind and rain haunt the mountain frequently; sometimes the weather changes several times within one day or even an hour.

Snow starts falling from late September here, and thaws with the coming of June. So here winter lasts 8 months altogether. The coldest months are December and January, with the temperature falling to over 40 degrees centigrade below zero.

In ancient times, Mount Changbai was called Mount Buxian, meaning not salty. During the Northern Wei Dynasty it was called

Selected Tour Commentaries

Mount Tutai or Taihuang. During the Tang Dynasty it was known as Mount Taibai, and from the Jin Dynasty to date, it is Mount Changbai.

During the Qing Dynasty, Mount Changbai was regarded as the origin site of the ancestors of the Manchus. There is a beautiful legend behind it. In "The True Story about Emperor Wu and the First Emperor of Qing Dynasty" it was written that the first ancestor of the Manchus was born on the banks of a small lake in the shape of a lotus leaf in the inner area of Mount Changbai. The lake was called Buerhuli, but now people call this lake "round pond." The total area of the lake is 40,000 square metres.

As the legend goes, a long, long time ago three colorful clouds drifted over the round pond. The three colorful clouds were actually three fairies who had come to Heavenly Lake on Mount Changbai to invite the little White Dragon to a feast in heaven.

As Heavenly Lake was just ahead, the three fairies wanted to have a bath to refresh themselves after their long journey. It happened that right under the third cloud there was a mirror-like lake with brilliant flowers and luxuriant grass. The youngest fairy, Fu Gulun said to her eldest sister, En Gulun, and her other sister, Zheng Gulun, "Let's take a bath here first, then fulfill our errand at Heavenly Lake." In agreement, the three fairies jumped into the water and played in the lake to their heart's content. Suddenly, a flock of immortal magpies flew overhead. One of them had a flashing red berry in its beak. The red berry accidentally dropped on the fairies' clothes. The fairies quickly went ashore for fear that the immortal magpies would make off with their clothes. To their surprise, the immortal magpies flew away. The red berry looked very much like a ruby. Fu Gulun took a fancy to it and wouldn't let go of it. She put it in her mouth when she dressed herself. However, the red berry was like a living thing and forced its way down to her stomach. At once Fu Gulun felt her stomach swell up and wept to her sisters: "I've gotten pregnant and cannot go back to the heaven with you."

96

Heavenly Lake on Mount Changbai

Her eldest sister comforted her. She said, "Your pregnancy is the will of heaven. After you give birth, you can still go back to the heaven."

Later Fu Gulun gave birth to a boy who could speak from the moment he came into the world. He was handsome and could easily subdue the tiger and the black bear on Mount Changbai. The three fairies then taught him how to deploy troops, administer to state affairs and love the people. Soon the boy became a wise and courageous young man. One day, while sitting togother beside Heavenly Lake, Fu Gulun said to her son, "Beside the Round Pond, I swallowed a red berry and then gave birth to you. Your given name is Bukuliyongshun and your family name is Aixinjueluo. You were born to the world by the will of Heaven and your duty is to wars and rebellions and take care of the people. It is time for me to return to Heaven..."

Aixinjueluo Bukuliyongshun bid farewell to his mother and then used a willow raft to drift along the Songhua River. He later set up the city of Eduoli and named his state Manchu.

In the famous Chinese classical novel the Dream of red Mansion written by Cao Xueqin, there is a beautiful and significant fairy tale at the very beginning. The story goes that Nuwa, a fairy, tried to patch up the sky with 36,501 colorful pieces of stone which were prepared beforehand. Finally, one piece was left at the foot of the Qinggeng Mountain. In the novel, Jia Baoyu, the leading character, became the incarnation of that stubborn stone. The "stone" left the mountain, underwent vicissitudes of life and finally returned to Qinggeng Mountain. Qinggeng shares the same pronunciation as "the origin of the Manchus who established the Qing Dynasty."

Emperors of the Qing Dynasty saw Mount Changbai as admirable and awesome because it was thought to be the birthplace of their ancestors and the living quarters of the immortals. Rulers of various dynasties in history also paid homage to the mountain — "the place to make rulers." Sacrifices were offered to Mount Changbai

Selected Tour Commentaries

throughout the Qing Dynasty .

Mount Changbai has well-kept, primitive forests. From high up, the wind Sweeping through the vast forest sounds like the sea. In the recesses of the forest, the towering old trees block the sky with a thick canopy. During the 1930s and 1940s, that is, the time of the war against Japanese invasion, the forest was a base for the anti-Japanese allied army. Even today you can still find secret barracks made of timbers, anti-Japanese slogans engraved on trees and anti-Japanese posters hanging on the sides of cliffs.. Our invincible soldiers endured all hardships and fought bravely in the face of the Japanese army's crazy, aggressive and "punitive expedition" against our army. Li Zhaolin, an anti-Japanese hero wrote an article which vividly reflected the hard life. He wrote, "The front part of our body is warm with fire while our back is freezing with icy wind; the grass has dried and shriveled and the wind blows so hard; yet the grass can not make fire with frost on it; smoke and fire send heat into the sky while our coats are wet with blood." A good number of national heroes have laid down their lives for China in this forest. There is a popular folk song which reflects the people'feelings about General Yang Jingyu, a national hero of the anti-Japanese war. In it are the following lines: "In the deep winter, the branches and leaves of pine trees and cypresses are still fresh; the people's hero Yang Jingyu will live in the world forever like the trees."

The appealing scenery of Mount Changbai is a resulf of its amazing and marvelous zones from the top of the mountain to its base. Within less than 100 kilometres from the foot of the mountain to its top, you can feast your eyes on plants grown from the temperate zone to the polar region of the European-Asian continent. It makes you feel like you've traveled half the world. With the increase in altitude, the climate, soil, flora and fauna are distributed in obvious belts. The scenery on the top is a far cry from that at the foot of the mountain and thus creates variations of pictures.

In an area less than 1,200 metres above sea level, the terrain is

Heavenly Lake on Mount Changbai

flat and the climate is mild. You will see trees like pines, amur corks and elms. The pine tree is about ten metres tall and has straight branches. Its top is like an umbrella and the branches under the canopy hang downward like welcoming arms. People call it "beauty pine tree." A lot of famous and valuable plants used in Chinese herbal medicine grow in the recesses of these primitive forests. Please keep a sharp eye and if you are lucky enough, you may happen to find a ginseng or the tuber of an elevated gastrodia.

In areas less than 1,800 metres above sea level, the layer of soil is very thin, the temperature is low and the humidity is high. This area is often overcast and misty. This is a coniferous forest belt. Lush pines and cypresses grow here. In the forest, a dark and humid place is the most favorable condition for bryophytes to grow. If you have a chance, do experience the pleasure of strolling on the natural green carpet.

In areas less than 2,000 metres above sea level, the birch forest plays the dominant role. The terrain here is very steep. The soil is barren. The temperature is pretty low. The precipitation is great. The wind is strong, with 200 out of 365 days a year having wind forces above 8 on the Beaufort scale. Therefore, the branches of these birches are often shaped by the wind, looking like flags on top with most of their lower branches and leaves growing on the lee side of their trunks. The trees in these forests have distorted trunks and barks scraped off layer —by —layer by the biting wind. They impress us with their perseverance and indomitable will.

From 2,000 metres up to the very top is the tundra belt. It is treeless, with just green bryophyte and azalea bushes like natural carpets.

Some people say that in spring one comes to Mount Changbai to appreciate cuckoo flowers; in summer, clouds, fog, pine trees and the vast green luxuriance; in autumn, golden white birches, red maple leaves and lush pine and cypress trees and in winter, the snow-coated giant peaks.

Selected Tour Commentaries

Mount Changbai is listed as a state-level natural reserve area with a total area of 2,000 square kilometres. This natural reserve area is situated within three counties of Jilin Province, i.e., Antu, Fusong and Changbai. It stretches 78.5 kilometres from north to south and 53.2 kilometres from east to west. Established in 1961, this natural reserve area was incorporated into the "Man and Biosphere" natural preservation network of UNESCO in 1980 and is now one of the world's biosphere reserves. The primitive forests of Mount Changbai are home to over 50 varieties of wild beasts, 200-odd varieties of birds, and 2,300-odd varieties of reptiles and fishes. Here you will find animals of economic value like sables, otters, lynxes, leopards, manchurian tigers, sika deer, and wisels. So people call Mount Changbai "the garden of all wildlife." Mount Changbai is also a colorful, natural, botanical garden. The primitive forests boast of 2,300 varieties of wild plants and 80-odd varieties of trees of economic value like pine trees, larches, and dragon spruce trees. On top of that, they also have 300-odd varieties of rare and famous medicinal plants like ginseng, dangshen, the root of the membranous milk vetch, and the tuber of the elevated gastrodia.

The well-known, three treasures of Northeast China are produced here. They are ginseng, marten and pilose antler. There ave three types of ginseng: wild mountain ginseng, cultivated ginseng and cultivated wild ginseng. Ginsengs is used for many kinds of illnesses and helps to build up the body. Marten is the fur of sables and is extremely expensive. It can keep you warm in bitter cold and is light in weight. In ancient times marten was a symbol of power and status. Pilose antlers are antlers of the male deer and boast of excellent medical effects.

Heavenly Lake on Mount Changbai lies south of Antu County in Jilin Province and borders the DPRK. The borderline of China and the DPRK is across the center of the lake. The Heavenly Lake is a lake formed in a crater and serves as the source of three rivers, namely, the Songhua River, the Yalu River and the Tumen River.

100

Heavenly Lake on Mount Changbai

The lake is in the shape of an ellipse. It runs 4.85 kilometres long from south to north and 3.35 kilometres wide from east to west. The total area is 9.8 square kilometres. The lake is 2,194 metres above sea level and 373 metres deep at its deepest point, making it the deepest mountain lake in China. Heavenly Lake is surrounded by 16 peaks on four sides. Wind frequently visits the lake and sometimes creates waves over 1 metre high. When there is no wind, the images of the steep cliffs are inverted in the mirror-like lake and create a magnificent natural picture. The beauty of Heavenly Lake lies in the fantastic changes of images, the cloud and mist. The ice will remain frozen for half a year on the lake.

There are a lot of beautiful fairy tales about Heavenly Lake.

In one legend, long ago a fire dragon terrorized Mount Changbai area. Every July 15, the dragon sent a big fire from underground. It burned forests, grass and flowers and brought ruin to the nearby farmlands and villages. A Manchu girl named Rijina decided to subdue the demon and save the villagers. She carried a piece of ice and jumped into the mouth of the demon. When she finally got the ice to the stomach of the demon, an ear-splitting noise rocked heaven and earth and much of the mountain collapsed within a minute. The fire was put out. Over time, the mouth of the demon filled with rainwater and finally became a limpid lake. People named the lake Heavenly Lake in memory of the brave girl.

The giant monster in Heavenly Lake is a widespread and popular topic. On August 22, 1980, someone saw a strange animal in Heavenly Lake at the top of Tianwen Peak. Its head was as big as a human's, its eyes as big as chestnuts, its mouth projected forward, and its neck was between 1.2 to 1.5 metres long and about 10 centimetres in diameter with a white ring around it. Its grayish skin was very smooth, like that of a seal and it was as large as a bull. In 1962, it was reported that someone else caught a glimpse of this water monster and news reports concerning this monster were spread both at home and abroad. Some say that it is not a monster, but probably an

Selected Tour Commentaries

illusive image of a swallow, an otten, a moth, a fancy, a bear or even a pumice stone. Actually sightings of the monster in Heavenly Lake were also recorded in ancient books.

The ancient legends mingled with the latest sightings make Heavenly Lake all the more mysterious. When you stand on top of the mountain, please keep an eye on the lake. Maybe the monster will rise to welcome you. We're assured that the mystery of the monster in Heavenly Lake will be brought to light someday.

The Changbai waterfall is located on the north side of the Heavenly Lake. The water gurgles from the breach year in and year out and flows northward in a narrow stream. The terrain is flat at the beginning and the riverbed is small. You hear nothing. But within one kilometre from , the terrain suddenly turns steep and the river water becomes turbulent. Thanks to the size of the mountain and the steep terrain, the water Turbulently surges and looks like a white ladder towards heaven hence came the name the Ladder to Heaven. The Ladder to Heaven is 1,250 metres long on top of the mountain which is 2,100 metres above sea level. Where the Ladder ends, the water forms the Changbai Waterfall which rumbles down 68 metres to a pool below. Since the drop in elevation is great, the water column violently erodes the rocks at the foot of the cliffs and forms a pool 20-odd metres deep. The running water overflows from the pool and forms two turbulent white rivers. This is the source of the Songhua River.

Mount Changbai has 5 waterfalls altogether. The other four are: Jinjiang Waterfall, lying 10 kilometres south to Guanmian Peak with a drop in elevation of 70 metres; Yuehua Waterfall, located at the source of the three white rivers in the east of Mount Changbai, or the joint point of the mountain tundra and Yuehua Forest Belt, with a drop in elevation of 20 metres; Dongtian Waterfall lying at the entrance of a forest at the bottom of the valley, with a depth of 15 metres into the bottom of a cave; Yinliu Waterfall, located 500 metres north of Longmen Peak and bordering Changbai Waterfall,

Heavenly Lake on Mount Changbai

with a drop in elevation of 20 metres.

Mount Changbai also features hot springs. These hot springs are produced by the heat of the volcano. The hot springs lie 900 metres away from Changbai waterfall and cover an area of 1,000 square meters. The water gushes perennially with steaming heat. The average temperature is 60℃ to 80℃ with the highest at 82℃, which is hot enough to boil eggs . The mouths of the springs vary in size. Some are as big as a bowl; some as small as a ring. The volume of flow each day is 6,455 tons. The spring water contains many minerals and this dyes the nearby rocks and sand with different colors. The Changbai hot spring has dozens of minerals. The water is sweet, mellow and refreshing. If you take a hot spring bath, it can cure some skin diseases and help relieve the pain of some diseases like rheumatism and arthritis.

Another scenic spot of Mount Changbai is a secluded valley forest or "underground forest." The marvelous scene was created by a depression of the earth's crust and covers an area of several square kilometres. Standing on the edge of a cliff, you can only see the tops of the trees. There is a rugged lane leading to the bottom. In the thick of the trees, the waterfall surges out deafening noise.

Mount Changbai has two minor heavenly lakes. They lie to the south of Heavenly Lake and to the north of the White River and are 3 kilometres away from the Changbai waterfall. They were also craters. The circumference of the northern one is 260 metres and the total area is 5,380 square metres with a depth of 10 metres. The southern one lies 200 metres away, is of similar size but has shallower water. In the mountain area to the north of these minor heavenly lakes, there are over 10 springs. These springs gurgle all year round and cultivate the dreamland of the minor heavenly lakes.

The best time to visit Heavenly Lake on Mount Changbai is from June to September. July and August are golden times to enjoy the flowers, birds and beauty of Heavenly Lake. The winter is a good time for skiing. (In terms of sightseeing)

Selected Tour Commentaries

My friends, you may choose different routes for your tour according to your interest, including a vegetation exploration tour of Mount Changbai, skiing on Mount Changbai, trekking on Mount Changbai, climbing Mount Changbai in the winter, a road towards ginseng, folk and local arts of Mount Changbai, a bird watching tour, exploring the mystery of the Heavenly Lake monster, poaching tour on Loushui River, drifting along the White River, traveling from Changchun to Mount Changbai by bicycle or motorcycle, a volcano scenic tour, a spa tour in the primitive forests on Mount Changbai, exploration of the three treasures of Northeast China, etc.

In China people often say, "He who's never been to the Great Wall is not manly." Yet in 1983 the late head of state Ding Xiaoping took pictures here and after seeing all the scenery here said, "You'll regret for life if you've not climbed up Mount Changbai to enjoy the view".

Well, thank you for your attention and I hope to see you again someday on this very land! Good-bye.

SHANGHAI MUSEUM

Ladies and Gentlemen:

Welcome to the Shanghai Museum. The Shanghai Museum, established in December 1952, is a large museum of ancient Chinese art, boasting a collection of 120,000 pieces of culture relics in twenty-one categories, including bronze articles, ceramics, calligraphy, painting, sculpture, furniture, jade and ivory carvings, oracle bones, seals, coins, minority arts, and bamboo, wood and lacquer wares etc. Its collection of bronze articles, ceramics, and painting and calligraphy are the best known in the world. Museums are regarded as windows to show human civilizations. This museum is the window to show the five thousand years of Chinese culture to visitors from home and abroad.

The old Shanghai Museum complex was built in 1952 as one of the first comprehensive art museums in China. The new museum building was erected in September 1994 and most of the facilities were installed in 1995. Occupying a land of 0.8 hectares, the new Shanghai Museum has a construction space of 38,000 square metres with two levels under ground and five storeys above ground in height of 29.5 metres. The new building was constructed with support of the Shanghai Municipality and donations from all trades. With time less than two years, this building rose to tower the People' Square to its north.

As a cultural symbol of Shanghai City, the building of the muse-

Selected Tour Commentaries

um ought to match the image of this mega-metropolitan. For this purpose, the design by Mr. Xing Tonghe, vice chief architectural designer of Shanghai Architecture Institution, was finally chosen. The museum is located on the central axis line of the People's Square, in harmony with the 18-storeyed government building.

The magnificent building is structured with a square base, a circular top, and four arch-shaped handles erected on the top which ingeniously put the traditional feature into a modern architecture. The circular structure at the top with a glass dome in the centre looks like a huge bronze mirror of the Han Dynasty. Viewing it at a distance, the whole building resembles an ancient bronze Ding tripod load with five thousand years' history and civilization.

It was entirely opened on October 12, 1996 with eleven galleries and three exhibition halls in a space of about 12,000 square meters, 3.4 times of the old one. The 11 galleries display separately bronze articles, pottery and porcelain, carvings, jade articles, furniture in the Ming Dynasty, numismatics, paintings, calligraphic works, royal seals, minority handicraft articles and chinaware donated by Hu Huichun.

The total cost of the construction of the Museum amounts to 570 million RMB yuan, 85% of which was collected from home and abroad through efforts by the museum administration itself.

Mr. Woo Po-Shing, Chief Solicitor in Hong Kong, generously donated the funds for the bronze gallery in the Shanghai Museum. Mr. Woo holds a B. A. from the Law School of London University, a Ph. D from Hong Kong University of Technology and is a member of the British Arbitration Committee. He is fond of collecting antiques.

Mr. R. R. Shaw, a very well known entrepreneur and philanthropist, has contributed the funds for the interior decoration of the painting gallery.

The interior decoration of the Chinese Ancient Ceramics Gallery has achieved success with generous support from Mr. T. T. Tsui,

Shanghai Museum

Member of the Eighth Standing Committee of CPCC and Hong Kong and Macao Affairs Office of the State Council, P. R. C. With his profound knowledge and rich collection , Mr. Tsui has established the Tsui Museum of Art in Hong kong and made donations to a number of world-renowned museums in America, Canada and Australia. He is indeed an ardent advocator of Chinese culture.

The museum has three functions: exhibition, scientific study and heritage protection. The new museum is flexible and spacious. The interior decoration of the museum also indicates a perfect combination of traditional culture and modern structure. The floor is covered with gray bricks while the interior wall is covered with yellow granites. In the lobby, there is a carving on the floor with traditional flower design which reminds people of the time-honored ancient culture. The hall banisters are designed with interlocked-dragon patterns and the golden dragon heads at the end of the railings are derived from the Shang bronze design. While stepping into the Shanghai Museum along the stone stairs, you will be overwhelmed by the solemnity and joy of opening the door of history.

The Bronze Gallery

The Shanghai Museum is world-renowned for its rich collection of ancient Chinese bronze articles. The magnificent and solemn Chinese Bronze Gallery displays over 400 exquisite bronze vessels in an exhibition space of 1,200 square metres.

The bronze article is a rare treasure in Chinese ancient culture. The culture of bronze articles is a symbol of the slave society in China. The Palace Museum in Beijing, the Taipei Museum and the Shanghai Museum are the most well known museums for the collection of bronze articles of the Shang, Western Zhou, Spring and Autumn and Warring States periods. As for the bronze articles in the Shanghai Museum they feature long inscribed characters in the vessels. This gallery shows the complete history of the development of the bronze article and the outstanding creativity of the Chinese peo-

107

Selected Tour Commentaries

ple.

It is a special feature that many of the exhibits are important bronze pieces of long-held and heirloom significance, others are valuable vessels of recent acquisitions to the Museum's collection. Ancient Chinese bronzes are the results of the particular social development which characterizes particular times. With its broad range of specimen objects, the Chinese Bronze Gallery chronologically presents the history of bronze art from the 18th to the 3rd centuries BC. The initiation and evolution of the art of Chinese bronzes, spanning one thousand and five hundred years, is embodied in the magnificent shapes, exquisite motifs, profound historical information, delicately inscribed scripts and advanced casting techniques evident in the objects displayed.

A lot of bronze articles were made as arms, instruments, tools, currency as well as sacrificial vessels which include five kinds of articles for daily use (such as cookers, plates, cups, washing articles and decorations).

The bronze decorations are very rich in their styles and reflect the thoughts of the nobles in slavery society.

Here, I'd like to give you a brief introduction to some of the bronze articles in the Museum.

1. These are some bronze cups made between 18 century BC and 16 century BC in the late Xia Dynasty, which belong to the Erlitou Culture in Henan Province.

2. The period from the 16th century BC to the 14th century BC is the period of maturing. The typical article of this period is a cup named as "shou mian wen jia", which is used for memorial ceremony. The cup represents the style of this period - solemn and magic. Besides, there are some other bronze articles made as drinking cups, water cups and plates. The thickness of the bronze article is uniformed. There are lots of pictures of animals on them. From this, we can say that the technology of bronze articles had been quite advanced in the Shang Dynasty.

108

Shanghai Museum

3. The making of bronze articles achieved great success in the period from the 14th century BC to the 10th century BC. Bronze articles made as instruments and sacrificial vessels in this period were regarded as the summit of the evolution procedure. The designs of animals on the bronze articles show ancient people's respect to the nature.

"Yafu" and "Fanglei" are big drinking cups made in the Shang Dynasty.

They are tall and seriously engraved with figures of animals, birds and dragons. On both sides and on the body of the cup, there are three ears. Water for drinking can be easily poured out.

The "Gui Gu Fang Zun" was used to store wine and it was the masterpiece of the early Zhou Dynasty. The shape of the big cup is square. There are designs of animals on it. On the shoulder of the cup are four corners. On each of the corner, there is a figure of animal standing vertically on it made by separate casting. It shows that the technology of casting and carving were at a high level during that period.

The "Gu Fu Ji You" is used for containing wine. The cup is different from the others. It is tube-shaped. On the body of the cup, there is a relief of a cow head protruding, of which the two ears stretch out with the eyes shining.

A bronze pot named "ding" (usually a tripod vessel) is a symbol of social status of that time. According to the rules of the Zhou Dynasty, the emperor could use as many as nine dings and the duke could use seven dings. For the minister he could use five while the officer below could use only three. In the Shang and Zhou dynastic periods, the four-leg ding was popular and often was used together with tripod Ding.

The giant "De Ding" was made in the West Zhou Dynasty and it is one of the few magnificent ones of the West Zhou we can find today. Inscribed in the interior of the De Ding are 11 characters recording a historical fact about the Emperor Zhou's awarding De

Selected Tour Commentaries

with 20 strings of shells.

"Gui" was used as a pot and was made in the early West Zhou Dynasty. Gui has two levels and was used to steam food. Besides, there are also some bronze weapons and farming tools.

4. The period from the middle and late stage of the West Zhou Dynasty to the Spring and Autumn Period (10 century BC- 6 century BC) is the reform period of bronze arts. The process changed and the designs on the vessels are no longer of animal faces and phoenix but of scales and water waves. The bronze articles were not used as cups but cookers or containers. This reflects the cultural difference between the Zhou Dynasty and Shang Dynasty.

The "Dake Ding" is the second biggest of bronze articles. It was unearthed in Fufeng of Shaanxi Province in 1890. It is as heavy as 210. 5 kilograms in weight. The most significant feature is its interior's inscription of 290 characters recording the splendid deeds of aristocrat Ke's ancestors.

"Hugui" is a typical article of the middle and late period of the West Zhou Dynasty. Its bottom is square. The lid is carved with designs. When it is put upside down, it can be used as a container.

"Yi" could be used both as a basin to wash hand and a plate to contain water. The "Qihou Yi" is the biggest Yi among this kind of articles. There are 22 characters carved on the bottom of its bottom recording the history of marriage between the nobles of different families.

The bronze bell is unique in Chinese traditional bronze articles. This one is huge with beautiful sound and reflects the achievement on the bronze casting.

5. From the Spring and Autumn Period to the Warring States period (6 century BC - 3 century BC) the feudal society took the place of the slavery society. The technology of the casting reached a new development stage with a very high standard. Its functions were changed from sacrificial vessels to daily use articles.

The "Xi Zun" is in shape of a buffalo. There are three holes in

Shanghai Museum

the back of the buffalo. The middle hole actually is a pot used to contain wine. Two holes on both sides are used to contain hot water in order to heat the wine. This design is marvelous and practical in use. There is a ring in the nose of the buffalo. It is more valuable in research because it indicates that at that time people knew if you wanted to control the buffalo, you should hold its nose.

At that time, there were many kinds of bronze articles with different functions, designs and materials. Some articles were made with gold and red copper. It indicates that 2500 years ago the technology of casting was very high.

In the Qin and the Han dynasties, the bronze article casting was very advanced. The magic mirror is an excellent example. If you let the light shine on the mirror, the carves on the back of the mirror can be seen through the mirror itself. In recent years, 14 chimes have been unearthed and preserved. The diameter of the biggest one is 52cm and that of the smallest one is 22cm. Historical records are inscribed on these chimes. Some of these records had not been revealed before.

Here, I will especially point out that Mr. Ma, the Head of the Museum, saved and brought back a bronze pot from Hong Kong. On the neck and body of the pot, there are characters inlaid with silver lines. The pot is similar to the one found in the tomb of Liu Sheng, King Jing of Zhongshan in Hebei. But its lid was missing. This pot represents the highest standard of the bronze technology in the West Han Dynasty.

6. In ancient times, the bronze art of the minorities living far away from the central China was an important part of the Chinese bronze art. The minorities had made bronze weapons, articles used on the memorial ceremony, and bell and drum.

7. In order to give people a clear idea of the bronze art, a part of the casting process is shown in the museum.

The Chinese painting Gallery

The Chinese painting Gallery is designed in the flavor of

Selected Tour Commentaries

scholar's studio with traditional Chinese architectural features of long corridor and curved roof, wooden grilled window and low banisters. The auto-motion sensed illumination system has been installed to provide protection of the paintings and convenience of viewing . One hundred and forty exhibits are displayed in an area of 1200 square meters. Masterpieces from the ancient Tang, Song and Yuan dynastic periods and masterpieces of the Zhejiang School, Women School, Songjiang School in the Ming Dynasty, "Four Wangs" of the early Qing, "Four Monks", Yangzhou School and Shanghai School in the late Qing are the best examples of long history of different periods in painting history. This reflects the long history and deep rooted tradition of Chinese painting.

Pottery and Porcelain

Pottery and porcelain are important inventions of the Neolithic Age. They are great Chinese inventions

1. A pottery piece

A pottery piece, found in a Xian Ren Cave in Wan Nian County of Jiangxi Province, has 8800 years of history.

A gray pottery piece found at Hemudu in Yu County of Zhejiang Province has 6800 years of history. Colorful pottery of Banpo in Shanxi represents the prime stage of Yangshao Culture and has 6500 years of history. From these, we can say that the Yangtze River and the Yellow River are the cradles of ancient Chinese culture.

In Shanghai, there are three kinds of ancient culture. One is called Majiabin which has a history of 6000 years. Another is called Songzhe, which dates 5000 years ago. The last one is Liangxu with a history of 4000 years. A pottery pot with a history of 6200 years was found in Qingpu County. This is the earliest pottery found in Shanghai. And that red pottery was used to cook food. It has a history of 5500 years.

The Longshan (Dragon Mountain) Culture has a history of 4000

112

Shanghai Museum

years. Its visible feature is that the black-earth pottery replaced the red-earth pottery. The eggshell pottery is the best product of that period. This white pottery is fine and smooth. Its carving is like that on the bronze article. It reflects the highest standard of the ancient technology. In the Han Dynasty, people made glazed pottery by using lead oxide as flux and by using the ferric oxide and copper oxide as dyes.

In the Tang Dynasty, people used metals such as iron, copper, etc. as dyes and heated them and then the colors of yellow, red, green and purple were made. This type of the pottery is called tri-colored glazed pottery, which was used as burial vessels with the dead. We often see the tri-colored glazed pottery horses. Sometimes, we have chances of seeing glazed camels.

Yixing is famous for making pottery pot and pottery cup. Yixing Pottery pot has different colors such as light color, purple-black and dark red. They are not only functional but also artistic. It was popular in the Song Dynasty and the Ming Dynasty. The pottery teapots exhibited here were been made by masters in the Ming Dynasty and the Qing Dynasty. They are very precious.

2. Porcelain

China is the home of porcelain. The invention of porcelain is a great contribution of Chinese ancient people to human beings.

1. 3000 years ago, in the Shang Dynasty, green porcelain was produced and most of them were. Their designs were buried with the dead. Their designs were similar to the bronze article. This green porcelain is just one of such porcelains that what I mentioned above. Original porcelain is different from pottery in several aspects. (1) Raw material and ferric proportion are different. (2) In process, pottery needs less than 10000c while porcelain needs more than 12000c (3) The pottery was not glazed, but the porcelain was glazed. During the East Han Dynasty, well-developed green porcelains were produced. This is a blue and green celadon made in the

113

Selected Tour Commentaries

East Han Dynasty.

2. In Northern and Southern Dynasty, the skills of making porcelain reached its first peak. Celadon made in Zhejiang and Jiangsu provinces are white and strong. Because people could control the proportion of ferric oxide and the temperature of the fire. So the color of the porcelain was stable. Look, these were some porcelain made in the West Jin Dynasty.

3. In the Tang Dynasty, celadon was made in the south and the white porcelain was made in the north. This bowl is the celadon made in the south. It looks slim with yellow and green colors. This is the white porcelain made in the north. It looks white and elegant.

4. The Song Dynasty is the prime time for pottery and porcelain. The five famous kilns are Ru, Ding, Guan, Ge and Jun appearing with other kilns such as Longquan etc.

Ru Kiln was located in Baofeng County of Henan province. It was the top one among the five. Their green porcelains were made for the imperial palace.

Ding Kiln was located in Quyang County of Hebei Province. White porcelain was made there. Also celadon was made for Palace.

Guan Kiln was located in Kaifeng, Henan Province, and run by the royal family of the Northern Song Dynasty. The accurate site has not been found. Now what we see is the porcelain made by the official cave of the Southern Song Dynasty. It was located in Tortoise Mountain of Hangzhou, Zhejiang province.

Ge Kiln's site has not been found either. The porcelain made in this cave was simple but elegant. It was a representative work of the Ge Kiln.

Jun Kiln was located in Yu County, Henan Province. The process was that the porcelain glazed with copper in high temperature. Before the copper was glazed on porcelain, there was only celadon. That was the symbol of this type of process.

Mei Zi Qing three-leg furnace is made in Longquan cave in Zhejiang Province. The Longquan porcelain reached the top of

Shanghai Museum

celadon. Yao Zhou Kiln produced blue and yellow porcelain. The Chi Zhou Kiln produced white and black porcelain. The Fu Jian Jian yang cave produced porcelain, which looked like rabbits. Jiang Xi Ji Zhou Kiln produced black porcelain.

5. Yuan Dynasty was an important stage for the development of pottery and porcelain. Since Yuan Dynasty, Jinde Town has become the center of porcelain making. Jingdezheng is considered as the capital of porcelain. The new process replaced the old one. The feature of new process is that the color can be quickly put on the article and will not be easily erased.

6. Jingdezheng was thriving during Emperor Yongle and Emperor Juande periods in the Ming Dynasty. Imported material was used. Here are some samples from that period.

7. The Qing Dynast is the last prime period of the Chinese porcelain development. Particularly in the reigns of Emperor Kangxi, Emperor Yongzheng and Emperor Qianlong.

Colorfully glazed porcelain has five different types: Wu Cai, Duo Cai, Feng Cai and Qu Liang Cai. The five-color porcelain was famous in Kangxi's reign with different shapes and carves except for the colors of red, yellow and green. The colors of blue and dark were also used on the porcelain. This dish is the type of products.

Glazing Oil was used in Emperor Kangxi period and was popular in the years of Emperor Yong Zheng and Emperor Qian Long. Feng Cai Porcelain is colorful and soft. People called it Ruan Cai (soft color). The "Emperor Kangxi's Wu Cai" was called Ying Cai (hard color). Enamel Color Porcelain was also called "Ci Tai Hua Fa Lang". It was produced this way: the molded kaolin clay was heated and then drawings were drawn with enamel on it by skillful artists; after heating at low temperature for a while came out the special porcelain exhibited here. At last, there are the prototypes of the working shop and furnace exhibited here. After visiting the gallery you may learn a lot about Chinese porcelain making process.

Selected Tour Commentaries

SHANGHAI NEW BUND

Ladies and Gentlemen, Good afternoon!

Now we are at the Bund of Huangpu River in Shanghai. Welcome to the New Bund and I sincerely hope every one of you will have a good time here.

After about forty years of stagnation, the great metropolis of Shanghai is currently undergoing one of the fastest economic expansions that the world has ever seen. Indeed, the city now seems certain to recapture its position as East Asia's leading commercial centre, a status it last held before World War II. In the early 1990s China's central government decided to push Shanghai once again to the forefront of the country's drive for modernization, thus releasing an explosion of economic activity. The long-suppressed Shanghai ability to combine style and sophistication with a sharp business sense is once again riding high. Not that the old Shanghai is set to disappear overnight. Large parts of the city still resemble a 1920s' vision of the past: a noisy, crowded and grimy metropolis of monolithic, pseudo-classical facades. It is also still possible to make out the former foreign concessions, with their elegant European-style buildings from the early 1900s, while the old city's Chinese heart consists of a bewildering tangle of alleyways. The city's most interesting districts lie to the west of the Huangpu River and its classical colonial waterfront, the Bund.

There are five routes for sightseeing. On your left-hand side are

116

Shanghai New Bund

the wide Zhongshan Road as well as the marvelous buildings with European style which have got a sobriquet "The World Architecture Show". On your right-hand side are the glistening Huangpu River and Lujiazui Finance Trade Area in Pudong. At present, this is a new and special sightseeing area. The buildings, Zhongshan Road, sightseeing area, Huangpu River and Lujiazui are like the staff on a music score and the hard-working people in Shanghai are like the notes in it. All of these compose the new and beautiful welcoming music for every guest.

Shanghai might disappoint if you don't know what to expect. Shanghai used to be a small town on the shore of the Huangpu River. The Bund area in the past used to be the wasteland of old Shanghai covered with reeds. After the first Opium War in 1840, the gate of China was forced to open by the western powers with military forces. Shanghai gradually became a commercial port. Most of the central city was built in the first third of last century. At that time modern buildings were built to replace the factories (warehouses and offices) of the earlier concessions along the shoreline in the area called the Bund. The European colony remained aloof from the culture surrounding it. The European colonialists built the city with all the familiarity of home. There were country clubs, hotels, bars, major banking houses, and stores modeling on the western architecture of the day. Today, the hotels, banks, and office buildings which line the Bund house Chinese banks and businesses and serve the financial and trade needs of one of the busiest ports in Asia.

These buildings in front of us have architectural features of the Renaissance Period in Europe. Though they were not designed by the same designer and not built in the same time, they are matching very well with each other. On the 1.5-km long curvilinear line from Jinling East Road to Waibaidu Bridge stands 52 buildings, some are in British style, and some are in French style while some are in Greek

Selected Tour Commentaries

style. At that time, overseas banks, organizations and consulates were located here. Known as "the Wall Street of the East" then, it was a historical miniature of the Shanghai in the colonial period.

Look, here is the Dongfeng Hotel. Its address is No. 2 New Bund. This is a building in classical British style. In the past it was the British General Assembly. The six-storey building is topped with two pavilions in the north and south. The interior of the building is decorated luxuriously. There used to be a 110. 7 inch-long bar counter on the first floor, the longest one in Asia at that time, which the hotel was very proud of. At present, KFC is located there.

The famous Shanghai & Hong Kong Bank was located at No. 12. The building was built in 1923 with a circular roof in Greek style. The building is square and has five storeys. Plus its dome top, it altogether has 7 storeys. It has a steel-framed structure and the furnishings and decoration are luxurious. It had reception rooms of the American, British, French, Russian and Japanese styles. The British was proud of it and regarded as the best building in the area from the Suez Canal to the Far East. Not long ago it was the office building of Shanghai Municipality.

The building next to the former Shanghai & Hong Kong Bank is Shanghai Customs Building which was built in 1927. The building has a style of " back to the ancient" which was popular in the 19th century, whose remains are rare in the world. On the top of it, there is a big clock. The clock strikes every 15 minutes, giving out a short piece of music, which can be heard within 10 kilometers. You can check you time accordingly because it gives you the standard Beijing time.

The former Shanghai & Hong Kong Bank and the Customs Building were designed by a famous British designer. People in Shanghai called them " Sister Buildings". At present, they remain an important mark of Shanghai.

The two buildings in the eastern end of the Nanjing Road belong to Peace Hotel. The one facing the north built in 1906 in British Re-

118

Shanghai New Bund

naissance style was the earliest hotel in Shanghai called Huizhong Hotel. Seen from a distance, the whole building is elegant and it is really a great work.

The building facing the south was built in 1928. It was originally called Sassoon House. It is steel-framed and has a "A" shape. It is a typical building of Chicago school style. The famous 19-meter tall pyramid on top of the building is covered with copper. The interior of the building was decorated and furnished in different styles of nine countries. The original owner Sassoon of the building intended to show in this way how rich he was. The building was once the paradise for foreign venturers to enjoy themselves. Next to this building is the 17-storeyed China Bank Building. It has four storeys more than the Sassoon. But actually it is 60cm shorter than the Sassoon. How come? Back to 1934, the Kuomintang Government planned to build a 34-storeyed China Bank Building which would be the tallest building in the Far East. But the plan did not succeed because the location area in which the building was going to be built was the rental area of Britain and Sassoon, the owner of the Sassoon House did not allow any building taller to be built next to it so the China Bank Building had to be built with only 17 storeys. When the building was finished, in order to beat the height of the Sassoon two flagpoles were set up on its top, which turned to be much taller than the pyramid.

As the time passes by, the Bund has got different titles. People now in Shanghai would like to call the Bund before 1949 when the Communists took over Shanghai "The Old Bund", the Bund after 1949 "The Bund" and the present day Bund " The New Bund."

With the open policy and the fast development of Pudong, Shanghai has become the pioneer of China's economic reform. The spring wind wakes up the Bund, which has slept for years. Domestic and foreign financial organizations have come to take root in the Bund and some "old residents" returned too. The once deceased Oriental Wall Street seems to be alive again.

The Bund has been the symbol of Shanghai so it has been the

Selected Tour Commentaries

place that the tourists would not miss. But due to the narrow road, it was very crowded. This affected the beauty of the Bund a little bit. In order to change this situation, the government has made great efforts. The widened and newly reorganized street in front of us is named after Mr. Sun Zhongshan. It is one part of the Bund projects. The street is totally 826 meters long and some 45 meters wide. It has 6 to 10 lanes and is a part of the reorganization and expansion project of the Bund. The Bund is not the only one that has benefited from the open policy. From Wujiaochang of Beiwan in the north to the Nanpu Bridge in the south, a 15 kilometers long road has been widened and reconstructed. When completed, it will be the symbol of the fast development of the tourism industry in Shanghai. The reconstruction of the Bund was finished in late September 1992. Atop the dyke is a spacious walkway for sightseeing, paved with colourful tiles and erected with Europeans style garden lights. The embankment is a favourite haunt of the people and a " must " for all visitors to Shanghai. It is from this place that people enjoy the view of the Huangpu River.

The street we are walking on is Jiangbin Road. It is a place full of cultural aura and lined with green grass, trees and flowers. You can see here a lot of people doing exercises in the morning, a great number of tourists pacing with ease in the daytime, quite a few young lovers spotting here and there at night. It is said that a lot of foreigners have been attracted by the fame it has got and are eager to come to experience the aura there.

Ladies and Gentlemen, while walking on the Bund, have you found out that the New Bund not only takes on a new look but also has artistic atmosphere? There is a scene titled "For Tomorrow" on East Yan'an Road. The scene consists of two parts. One part consists of six round posts embracing together; the other part is the Meteorological Tower, which has a history of 80 years. The Customs Building clock and the electronic waterfall clock are another pair of attractions. The electronic waterfall digital clock is 27 meters long and

Shanghai New Bund

3.5 meters tall with 10 stairs. It is totally controlled by a computer. It has more than1000 nozzles and all the water from the nozzles forms the display of the time in digital form. It displays the different times of all the major cities in different countries. This makes Shanghai more close to the world.

Look! A lot of people over there must be attending the Square Concert of the Bund. Just in one year of 1994, almost 50 such concerts were held here with more than one million audience. Some other kinds of activities such as handwriting, drawing etc. are also held here. If you want to know what a real resident's life is like, just participate in these activities.

Mr. Chen Yi's statue standing in the front of the square is something worth seeing. He was the first mayor of Shanghai after liberation. The bronze statue, 5.6 meters tall, is in commemoration of Mr. Chen's great contribution to the development of new Shanghai.

Walking on the beach, we can easily get to the Huangpu Park. This park would often remind people of the humiliating history of the Chinese people in the early decades of 19th century. The Monument to People's Heroes, which consists of three 60-meter high granite obelisks, stands in the center of the descending circular plaza like huge waves bubbling from a long historic river, and serve as an everlasting monument to the history of the people's gallant struggle in Shanghai.

On the opposite is the Mother River of Shanghai, the famous Huangpu River. Its originates from the Taihu Lake of Wuxi. And it is the longest, widest and deepest river in Shanghai, 114 kilometers long and 400 meters wide, 7 meters to 9 meters deep. Its original name was Gong River and had other names such as Chun Shen River and Huang Xie Pu. 2000 years ago, the place of Shanghai belonged to Chu Kingdom. Huang Xie, once a general, was promoted by the king to the position of Prime Minister and titled him "Chun Shen Jun" and asked him to rule Shanghai. He led the people to dig channels and develop agriculture. Later generations, in commemoration

121

Selected Tour Commentaries

of him, named the river as Chunshenjun or Huangxiepu. But ever since the South Song Dynasty, it has been called the Huangpu River.

In the early decades of the 20th century, ordinary people in Shanghai lived a hard life. Quite a number of people lost hope of life and jumped into the river. A lot of changes have taken place since then. Cruising boats can take you along the river and give you a better chance to see the different views of opposite sides of the river—Pudong and Puxi, actually the center and symbol of Shanghai. The Bingjiang Road of "Eastern Bund" is 2,500 meters long linking six squares with special features.

The Broadcasting & Television Tower of Oriental Pearl (shortened as Oriental Pearl TV Tower) is situated beside the Bingjing Road in the tip of Lujiazui of the east foreshore of Huangpu River. Looking from the other side of the river is the New Bund. The 468-meter Orient Pearl TV Tower is the tallest building in Asia and the third tallest TV tower in the world (Toronto TV tower is 553.3 meters high, the tallest; and the TV tower in Moscow is 533.5 meters high, the second tallest.). The high tower is supported by three columns with a diameter of 9 meters and three oblique braces with a diameter of 7 meters intersected in 60' to the ground, piercing straight to the clouds and sky. The 11 steel structured round balls, including space cabin, upper ball, lower ball, 5 ball-like sky hotels in the middle and three decorative small balls at the bottom, are just like 11 shining pearls embedded on the body of the tower, leaving to visitors a poetic conception—big and small pearls dropping down on the Jade plate.

Ladies and Gentlemen, the night is falling. The New Bund will become a vast sea of lights, making the Bund more beautiful. At this time, the night view will remind you of the Chinese history from opium war to the present day. Great changes have taken place in China and in Shanghai within this period of time. It is really pleasant to meet you here when the 21st century has just arrived. Let's strive to make our life happier in this new century. And I believe Shang-

Shanghai New Bund

hai, together with the developing pace of the world, will become more beautiful in the future. Hope you will come back to visit Shanghai before long.

Thank you for your attention. Thanks.

Selected Tour Commentaries

DR. SUN YAT-SEN'S MAUSOLEUM

My dear friends, when you come to a city, you probably want to visit the most famous scenic spots of special interest. Nanjing has many places of historic interests and has been capital for six "dynasties." But if you leave Nanjing without visiting Dr. Sun Yat-sen's Mausoleum, undoubtedly you have missed the most arresting and famous tourist attraction of the city.

Talking about the Mausoleum we should have an idea about Sun Yat-sen, the great pioneer of Chinese democratic revolution. Mr. Sun's original name is Sun Wen and styled himself Yat-sen. So foreign friends would call him "Dr. Sun Yat-sen". Since he took "Woodcutter in Zhongshan" as his alias when he took part in the revolutionary activities, he was respectfully and widely called Mr. Sun Zhongshen in China. On October 12, 1866, Mr. Sun was born in a farmer's family in Caiheng village of Xiangshan County (the present-day Zhongshan City), Guangdong Province. When he was still young, he had great expectations. He studied medicine in Honolulu, Hong Kong and some other places and after graduation he worked as a practitioner in Guangzhou, Macao and other places. Later he gave up medicine as his profession to take part in political activities. In 1905, he set up China Alliance Organization in Japan and he was elected president. He put forward the famous guiding principle-"driving the invaders out, restoring the sovereignty of China, establishing a republic and equalizing the land ownership" and

124

Dr. Sun Yat-sen's Mausoleum

the Three People's Principles—"Nationalism, Democracy and the People's Livelihood." On October 10, 1911, the Wuchang uprising broke out and Dr. Sun was elected Interim President of the Republic of China by representatives from seventeen provinces. On the following New Year's day (January 1, 1912) Mr. Sun took the oath of office in Nanjing. From then on, Mr. Sun experienced Yuan Shikai's usurpation, the Second Revolution, "Campaign Protecting the Republic System" and "Campaign Protecting the Interim Constitution". In 1921, Mr. Sun took the position of President in Unusual Times in Guangzhou. At the first National Congress of Kuomintang held in Quangzhou in 1924, he perfected the original Three People's Principles and put forward Three people's New Principles. He also proposed the policies of "Making an alliance with Russia and the Communist Party of China and helping the farmers and workers." In November 1924, in spite of his illness, Mr. Sun went up to Beijing to discuss state affairs with General Feng Yuxiang. Unfortunately, he broke down from constant overwork and passed away on March 12, 1925.

The location of the Mausoleum was chosen by Mr. Sun himself. Here is exactly a good place to build a mausoleum. You may wonder: Mr. Sun was born in Guangdong but died in Beijing. For his whole life he travelled throughout China for the revolution. Why did he choose Nanjing as the venue of his tomb?

It is said that far before Mr. Sun took office in 1912, the abbot of Lingu Monastery had recommended him that this place is good for fengshui, because it faces the plain and is backed up by green mountains as its protective screen. On March 31, 1912 Mr. Sun resigned as a political compromise for the sake of the union of the North China and the South China. One day of the early April, he went hunting with Hu Hanmin around the Piety Tomb of Ming Dynasty. They took a rest in the place where the Mausoleum is located now. Mr. Sun looked around and said "If possible I would like my countrymen to allow me to have this place to bury my coffin." Surely, the feng-

125

Selected Tour Commentaries

shui of the Zijin Mountain is not the basic reason for the location of Mr. Sun's mausoleum. The basic reason is that, he said on dying "After my death, you can bury me at the foot of the Zijin Mountain in Nanjing in memory of the Revolution of 1911, because Nanjing is where the temporary government was founded." So although Mr. Sun stayed in Nanjing not a long time, it had a special meaning to him. Fundamentally speaking, the reason he chose Zijin Mountain as his permanent resting-place is to commemorate the revolution of 1911 and to encourage the revolutionaries.

In order to respect Mr. Sun's wish, the Preparatory Committee of Sun Yat-sen's Funeral, including his wife Song Qingling and his son Sunke, examined the area and chose the site for the Mausoleum. They delimited 2000 mu and offered a reward in newspaper for the best design of the Mausoleum. Among all the contributions, young architect Lu Yanzhi's design, a design in the shape of a bell, was highly praised and gained the first prize and he himself was invited to supervise the whole project as well.

On March 12, 1926, the first anniversary of Mr. Sun's death, the project got started and 3 years later, it was completed in spring of 1929. It cost 1.5 million silver dollars totally. Unfortunately, Lu Yanzhi, the young architect with great gifts, suffered from liver cancer, the same disease which Dr. Sun suffered when supervising the project, and died at 35, just before the completion of the Mausoleum. The completion ceremony was held on June 1, 1929 and Mr. Sun's remains was transported from Beijing to Nangjing. From then on, Mr. Sun has slept here for nearly 70 years.

The construction of Dr. Sun Yat-sen's Mausoleum was an important event in the history of Nanjing. In order to meet Mr. Sun's coffin, the first asphalt road was built from Zhongshan Port in the west to Zhongshan Gate in the east; it is 12 kilometres in length and also called Zhongshan Road. Up to today, Zhangshan Road is still one of the most important main roads. At the same time, the city gate Chaoyang Gate which was built in Ming Dynasty was renovated

Dr. Sun Yat-sen's Mausoleum

and Changed its name to Zhongshan Gate. Between Zhongshan Gate and Dr. Sun Yat-sen's Mausoleum, a road called the Mausoleum Road was built. Just as the people of Paris take pride of their les Champs-Elysees and the people of New York, the Fifth Avenue, the Nanjing people are proud of their boulevards. And the 3 kilometres long Mausoleum Road is undoubtedly the best representative of these boulevards. Along both sides of the "green corridor" grows the main kind of tree in Nanjing as parasols. Usually Chinese people call them French plane trees, in fact they are Chinese local products. Just because Frenchmen took them from Yunnan Province to France and later they transplanted them in their leased territory in Shanghai, that is why they got such a name.

Now, we are going out of the Zhongshan Gate and driving along the Mausoleum Road. The destination ahead is a square in shape of crescent, According to Lu Yanzhi's design, the place of the Mausoleum is like a "duo", a big wooden bell, which was used to announce a policy, decree or a war in ancient time. Duo's sound is loud and clear, implying to make the whole world peaceful and happy". The design reminds the people of Dr. Sun Yat-sen's well-known saying "The revolution is far from success and we should continue working hard." This saying also serves as an alert to the later generation. The crescent-shaped square is the bottom of the "Bell of Freedom."

Now, please look to the south. There is an octagon platform structured with reinforced concrete but covered with Jinshan stone of Suzhou. The platform is divided into three layers and each layer is enclosed by stone rails. The copper "ding" (an ancient cooking vessel) with two looped handles and two legs weighs 5000 kg. It is 4.25 meters high and its diameter is 1.23 meters. It is one of the constructions for memory of the mausoleum. The "ding" was built in autumn, 1933 with donation of students and teaching staff of the Zhongshan University and Mr. Dai Jitao. One side of the "ding" is engraved with three characters "Intelligence, Humanity and Brevity". These three words are the school instruction of Zhongshan Uni-

127

Selected Tour Commentaries

versity. Inside of the "ding" stands a hexagon copper tablet on which Dai Jitao's mother's handwriting of the "Filial Piety" is engraved. To the bell-shaped mausoleum the "ding" is just like the pendulum. It seems to serve to alarm the whole nation by striking the bell.

Stepping on the steps, we will see a soaring memorial archway with four columns. The archway was built between 1931 and 1933, 12 meters height and 17.3 meters in width. It is made of huge granite from Fujian Province, but its structure is in Chinese traditional wood structure style. Now, look up at the shining words inscribed on the horizontal board. The words in English mean fraternity. They were written by Dr. Sun Yat-sen. The words are taken from a Tang Dynasty poet Han Yu's work "Fraternity is humanity." It is said that Mr. Sun very much liked to write these two words to others. Dr. Sun devoted his whole life to bourgeois democratic revolution with great fraternity and struggled for the national independence and freedom for scores of years. So we can say that "fraternity" is the best generalization of his life.

Further from the Fraternity Archway, there is a road leading to the mausoleum. The road is 480 meters long and dozens of meters wide. The whole design of the mausoleum gives prominence to Chinese traditional style, grand, solemn and specific. In order to embody the greatness of Mr. Sun, the Mausoleum followed the example of ancient mausoleums and was built against mountains and the coffin chamber was placed at the top of the mountain that is 160 meters high. In addition, the plants of the Mausoleum are symmetric, which make it feel more solemn. Now, please look forward to the north, along the hillside, situate the Mausoleum Gate, the Stele Pavilion, the Memorial Hall and the coffin chamber right behind. The pines, cypresses, ginkgoes and maples on the both sides of the road represent Mr. Sun's revolutionary spirit and lofty quality. They take the place of statues and stone beasts which usually flanked the sacred road in ancient times. Among the trees, cedar is one of the "four kinds of tree for appreciation" and has been honored as the

Dr. Sun Yat-sen's Mausoleum

tree of Nanjing City. The grand archway at the end of the Mausoleum Road is the formal beginning of the mausoleum area. It is 16 meters high, 27 meters wide and 8.8 meters deep. It is made of granite from the Fujian Province, too. Inscribed on the horizontal board of the middle passage is Dr. SunYat-sen's handwriting. It means that the state doesn't belong to one family but belongs to the entire nation and the common people. This is the goal for which Mr. Sun struggled for his whole life and it is also the excellent explanation of the Democracy of the Three People's Principles. We have passed the gate of the Mausoleum, then in front of us is the Stele Pavilion. The 9-meter high stele in the middle of the pavilion was engraved with 24 gold- plating characters of Yan Zhenqing style, "Chinese KMT buried Premier Sun here on June 1, 18th year of the Republic of China". These words were written by one of the founder members of KMT, Tan Yankai. When talking about setting up a stele, Wang Jingwei and Hu Hanmin were arranged to write an inscription for Mr. Sun, but two years passed, yet nothing they could write. Because they thought that Mr. Sun's merits couldn't be generated by words, then they chose to use the present form to praise Dr. Sun without engraving an inscription.

Going out of the pavilion, we'll see numerous layers of steps. The people of Nanjing often say that the steps in the Mausoleum are as numerous as the stone lions on Lugou Bridge (known for Westerners as Marco Polo Bridge). So when coming here tourists usually ask, "how many steps on earth are there in the Mausoleum?" My friends, if you are interested you can count them.

Now, we are coming near the top platform. Look, there are two big copper "ding". They were contributed by Shanghai municipal government of that time. Now, please look carefully. There are two holes in the bottom of the left "ding". Why? Just let me tell you. In late 1937, when the Japanese army attacked Nanjing, their shooting left two holes in the left ding. Now, although the circumstances have changed, the two holes always remind Chinese people not to forget

Selected Tour Commentaries

the national humiliation. Not far away, there are two bronze dings in ancient style. They are presented by Mr. Sun's son Sun Ke and his family.

Ascending the steps, now we have reached the top of the platform. Here we can have a bird-view of what it is in the distance. The Memorial Hall is the half way up to the mountain and there are altogether 392 steps covered if you count from the Archway of Fraternity. The vertical distance is 70 meters but the plane distance is 700 meters. If you count the steps from the Stele Pavilion, the number of steps is 290. In order to avoid monotone, the architect divided the 392 steps into 10 parts and every part has a platform and there are totally 10 such platforms. More marvelous, if you look up from the bottom, you can see that the steps extend to the top without stop and you can't see any platform. But if you look down from the top, you only see the platforms. The number of the steps, 392, is not a random number, it implied the number of Chinese population at that time — 392 million.

Now we are in front of the Memorial Hall and the Coffin Chamber. They are the major parts of the Mausoleum. The construction of these two buildings was supervised then by Lu Yanzhi, the gifted young designer. It is when he was doing these two buildings he died of cancer. So when the later generation mention him they would often say, "It is a great pity he died before his complete success." The structure of the Sacrificed Hall is of an ancient wooden palace style. It is 30 meters long, 25 meters wide and 29 meters high, surrounded by smaller constructions of fortress style and two 12.6-miter-high cloud columns. Its roof, with double-eaves and nine ridges, is covered with blue glare tiles. The outside of walls is covered with granite from Hong Kong. The inscription on the horizontal board is engraved with seal characters cut in relief — "Naturalism" "Democracy" and "The people's livelihood". These are the most basic and general guiding principles of Mr. Sun's revolutionary activities. Above "Democracy", there is a horizontal inscription board

Dr. Sun Yat-sen's Mausoleum

with Sun's handwriting on it, "Fill the World with Justice ".

Please follow me into the Memorial Hall. The floor is covered with white and black marble from Yunnan Province. The colors of white and black are among the traditional colors for burial ceremonies in China. There are 12 black stone columns, with 0.8 meter as the diameter for each. You will see that the interiors of the walls around are inset with black marble. Now you can have a look at Mr. Sun Yat-sen's handwriting of "Programme for Founding a State", engraved on the east and west walls. The main colors of the Hall are black, white and blue, which are used to express filial piety in China. The inside windows are inlaid with smaltos. They present western flavors especially with floods of sunshine. The style of the whole structure is a blend of the East and the West, representing the well-blended doctrine of Dr. Sun Yat-sen.

In the middle is the sitting statue of Dr. Sun Yat-sen in a robe. It is 4.6 meters high and the bottom is 2.1 meters wide. It was sculpted by the famous French sculptor Paul Arinsky whose native country is Poland. He was entrusted by the committee of Sun Yat-sen's Funeral for sculpting it. He chose the Italian marble as the material for the statue. In 1930, the sculpture was sent to the Mausoleum from Paris. Its total cost was 1.5 million francs. The six relief below are pictures depicting Mr. Sun's life and revolutionary activities.

Passing through the Hall, we have come to the Coffin Chamber. There are two doors that you need to get through. The outer door consists of two American-made safety door leafs which are made of copper. The nails on them and the mysterious beasts on the copper loops are typical of traditional Chinese. The horizontal inscription board was engraved with "The noble spirit will never perish", which was Sun's handwriting for the 72 martyrs' tomb in Huanghua Mound of Guangzhou. The second door is a single copper leaf engraved with seven characters "Mr. Sun Yat-sen's tomb" which were written by Zhang Jingjiang.

Selected Tour Commentaries

The tomb is a half globe in shape. The design of KMT emblem is mosaicked in the vaulted dome. The floor of the round room is covered with marble. The room's diameter is 18 meters and the height is 11 meters. The walls are covered with pink marbles. The circular marble pit is 1.7 meters deep and 4.35 meters in diameter. It is enclosed with 1-meter-high white marble rails. In the pit lays Dr. Sun's lying statue in Zhongshan Suit. This is sculpted in accordance to Mr. Sun's remains by a Czechoslovakian sculptor. His copper coffin is lying about 5 meters below the sculpture. You may ask why on earth the clothes Dr. Wears for the sitting statue are totally different from those for the lying one? In those years, the leftists and the rightists inside of the KMT had severe conflicts. The rightists, headed by Chang Kai-shek wanted to restore the ancient ways and opposed revolution. They insisted that Mr. Sun should wear long robe, while the leftists insisted he wear Zhongshan Suit. Since they had different opinions thus the two statues have different clothes styles.

My friends, I'm afraid you must be concern about whether Mr. Sun's remains are in the tomb or not. In fact, his remains had an unusual experience. After his death, his remains were dealt with antiseptic and placed in Biyun Monastery in Beijing in March, 1925. When the warlord Zhang Zongchang was defeated by the North Expeditionary Army and withdrew to Beijing in 1926, he ascribed his failure to Mr. Sun's remains and decided to burn them. It is the patriotic general Zhang Xueliang who sent troops to protect the remains. Unfortunately they were once exposed to the air though they were safe again. On May 28, 1929, Mr. Sun's coffin was sent to Pukou from Beijing by Jingpu Railway, and on June 1 it reached the Mausoleum. After the Grand Ceremony of Feng'an, the coffin and the remains were put into the pit and used cement to concrete it. The bottom of the tomb is granite. Under the copper coffin, there is a specially made wooden pad and enclosing the coffin is a well-sealed crystal box. After the breakout of the Resistance War against Japan,

132

Dr. Sun Yat-sen's Mausoleum

KMT government planed to transport the remains to Chongqing and at the end of the Liberation war, Chang Kai-shek planed to transport it to Taiwan this time. Because it was not a easy job to take the coffin out and the work might do damage to the remains as well, this plan was fiercely attacked by the engineering field and the left wing of the KMT. At last Chang gave up the plan. So the remains have stayed here safely up to today.

Passing through the door in the back wall of the square outside you will arrive at the Mausoleum Park. The back wall of the park is a "Exhibition of Construction of Dr. Sun Yat-sen's Mausoleum". The Exhibition contains nearly 200 precious historic materials which show the construction of the Mausoleum and the process of the transportation of Mr. Sun's remains.

Beside the main structure, there are also some constructions around the Mausoleum built in memory of Mr. Sun. Most of the constructions are built after 1929 with the donation of those from both all trades in China and overseas Chinese. The Fraternity Pavilion on top of the Plum Hill is built with the donation of a Taiwanese compatriot. It was completed on November 12, 1993, the 127th anniversary of Mr. Sun's birthday.

Ladies and gentlemen, Mr. Sun struggled for a better China for his whole life and overthrew monarch feudalist system which lasted for more than 2000 years. He carried out the three principal policies of "Making an alliance with Russia and the Communist Party of China and helping the farmers and workers" in his later days. The great feat Mr. Sun has achieved has gained great respect and praise from people from both home and abroad. After liberation, both central and local governments have exerted great efforts in preserving this excellent heritage.

Now, as one of the "Top Forty Tourist Resorts in China," Dr. Sun Yat-sen's Mausoleum receives numerous Chinese and international friends every year. People come here to pay homage to Mr. Sun. Today, the unification has become the main tendency in terms of the

Selected Tour Commentaries

relations between the Chinese on both sides of the Straits. I believe that most Chinese people, from both home and abroad, are expecting from the bottom of heart the coming of the day when our country is united and getting more prosperous. At that time, when hearing this, Dr. Sun would smile and be satisfied for sure in the other world. OK, thank you very much for your cooperation. Goodbye and good luck!

ZHUOZHENG (HUMBLE ADMINISTRATOR'S) GARDEN IN SUZHOU

The Zhuozheng (Humble Administrator's) Garden is one of the four well-known gardens in China. It was listed as one of the most important historical sites to be given special protection by the State Council on March 4, 1961. The four gardens on the list are respectively the Summer Palace in Beijing, the Chengde Mountain Resort in Hebei, the Zhuozheng Garden and the Liuyuan Garden in Suzhou. Two of them are in North China, representing the royal gardens; the other two are in Suzhou, which are the masterpieces of private gardens.

The Zhuozheng Garden has earned its fame mainly for two reasons. One is that it is the treasure of the culture legacy of our nation, an excellent work of classical garden south of the Changjiang River. It was called the Mother of All Gardens for its specifications in architectural models, paintings, sculptures and gardening, etc. The other is that the Zhuozheng Garden had been the stage for many celebrities of great influences in Chinese history. Among them were Qian Muzhai, an eminent writer, and Liu Rushi, his beloved concubine; Wang Xinyi, aid of the Punishment Department of the late Ming Dynasty; Chen Zhilin from Haining, scholar of Hong Wen College and minister of the Rites Department; the daughter and son-

Selected Tour Commentaries

in-law of Wu Sangui, King Pingxi; Li Xiucheng, King Zhong of the Taiping Heavenly Kingdom; Li Hongzhang and Zhang Zhiwan, governors of Jiangsu Province. After the Revolution in 1911, Governor Cheng Dequan issued an announcement to the province and held the Provisional Meeting of Jiangsu Province in the Zhuozheng Garden. After the Anti-Japanese War, Liu Yazi, a patriotic poet, established a social educational college there. It is said that in the reign of the Emperor Kangxi of the Qing Dynasty, Cao Ying, whose son was Cao Xueqin, the author of 'A Dream of Red Mansions', once lived in the garden with his family when he held a post as the officer of textile in Suzhou. Cao Ying recommended Li Xu, his brother-in-law, to take the place of him when he was promoted to be the officer of textile in Nanjing. Then Li Xu's family had lived in Zhuozheng Garden for twenty or thirty years.

Now, we can see on the horizontal board in the upper part of the brick wall the three carved and gilded characters "Zhuo Zheng Yuan", which means "Humble Administrator's Garden". The Garden was built in the fourth year of the reign of Zhengde of the Ming Dynasty (1509). A retired official Wang Xianchen who had once been appointed as minister-level official went back to his hometown Suzhou because of the setback in his official career. He built a garden based on Da Hong Temple and set up pavilions, bridges and planted trees in it. And the name was an abbreviation from a sentence written by Pan Yue in the West Jin Dynasty. According to the materials provided by the Gardening Bureau of Suzhou Government, Wang Xianchen became one of the successful candidates in the highest imperial exams in 1493 and then promoted to a higher position, but his career was not satisfying all the time. He had been taken into custody by Dong Chang (an investigation department for the emperor in Ming Dynasty), put in jail and then relegated to a minor position in Guangdong Province. Later on, he became the magistrate of Yongjia County. He was very depressed with untold sorrows deep in his heart after his relegation. He said to Wen Zhengming, "In the

Zhuozheng (Humble Administrator's) Garden in Suzhou

past Pan Yue was not successful in his official career, so he put up a cottage and planted many trees and vegetables, taking watering them as his daily work. Thus he derided himself by saying 'That is the office work of a humble administrator.' I, a retired old man couldn't do things in politics even as well as Pan Yue, so I decide to go back home to build a garden." That is the reason for his giving the garden such a name, meaning that he wanted to live in seclusion like Pan Yue and Tao Yuanming. The name of the garden reflected his feelings exactly at that time.

Going through the entrance and two side entrances - 'Tongyou' and 'Rusheng', we come to the east of the garden. There is a three-room house in the south, named Orchid Snow Hall, "Orchid Snow" is from a line in Li Bai's poem, "Spring breeze blows orchid buds off like snowfall". It symbolizes that the owner was as natural as spring breeze and as neat as orchid and snow. There is a lacquer painting on the middle screen, which is the panorama of the garden. According to the picture, we can see that the garden could be divided into three parts. The east part, named as Gui Tian Yuan Ju (Return to Nature), mainly consists of idyllic scenery. The middle part Fu Yuan, is the essence of the Zhuozheng Garden, typical of its ponds and rockery. The western part is called Bu Yuan, in which most of its buildings were established in the Qing Dynasty. Its architectural style is obviously different from that of the other two parts. From the map, there's no clear axis line in the garden and no traditionally symmetric structure. It was well organized, spacious and natural, adapted to local topography. The garden could be regarded as the most successful model of all gardens in Suzhou.

Out of the Orchid Snow Hall, we can see rockery in front of us. Green bamboo bushes and ancient trees are surrounding a huge cloud-shaped rock, which stands upright. There are two strange stones in the west, a narrow path running through them. The huge rock is called Zhuiyun Peak, serving as a huge screen for the other scenery of the garden. This kind of construction style is called "Camouflage

Selected Tour Commentaries

View" and has a magnificent importance to the whole scenery. Most of the visitors had a familiar feeling when they come there as if they have been this before. The reason is that most of them have read the great novel in Chinese classical literature, A Dream of Red Mansions. The rockery in the Grand View Garden depicted in that novel is very similar to that of this garden. There is a story in the 17th chapter:

Jia Zheng and his son accompanied guests into the Grand View Garden. When they saw the green rockery standing in front of them, all the visitors said, "Terrific!" "Marvelous!" Jia Zheng said, "It would be less interesting if there were no rockery here and we could see the whole scenery at the first sight, wouldn't it?"

Looking forwards, steep stones stand upright vertically and horizontally like monsters and beasts. They are covered with moss or sheltered by vines. Narrow paths can be seen vaguely. The similarity may be a kind of accidental coincidence, but the description above is very suitable for the situation. Moreover, there are many similarities between the garden in the novel and the garden here.

Passing the rockery, the main scenery of the east part can be seen. During the reign of Chongzhen in the Ming Dynasty, Wang Xinyi, an aid of the Punishment Department, built 'Gui Tian Yuan Ju' after he bought the east part. Look at these islets, lotus ponds, pine hillocks and bamboo bushes, they are gracefully and harmoniously integrated in the garden. What wonderful scenery! The other main buildings in this part are the Shuxiang House, the Tianxiang Pavilion, the Lotus Waterside Pavilion, etc.

Lotus Waterside Pavilion is a pavilion put up beside a lotus pond. Pavilion, a typical style in Suzhou, is a kind of simple building, put up beside the water, under the slope, or built on tilts. There are two kinds of lotus, cotton rose and lotus flower. Cotton rose can change its colors continuously in a day. It is very precious because it is light red in the morning, purplish red at noon and pink at dusk. Lotus flower is the lotus growing in the water. In front of Lotus Wa-

138

Zhuozheng (Humble Administrator's) Garden in Suzhou

terside Pavilion is a lotus pond, with a high wall in the back. The tranquility is appropriately set off by the strong contrast between wideness on one side and the closeness on the other side. The water pavilion of Yiyuan Garden in Vancouver of Canada was modeled on it - with a pond in front, and a high wall in the back - a typical classic garden style in Suzhou. If you stand in front of the pavilion and look to its western side, you will see an engraved round cover on the doorframe. It is like a painting in a round frame when you look at the bridge and the water in front of you through the round frame. If you want to see more clearly, you will find an engraved rectangular floor frame on the doorframe, through which the winding water and the beautiful scenery can lead you to a tranquil, plain and natural circumstance. This is a commonly used perspective style in Suzhou gardens, called "Frame View". The owner of the garden wanted to reach the most satisfying effect by means of leading the visitors to enjoy the scenery at the best angles.

Tian Quan Pavilion is standing in a green lawn, very conspicuous under the blue sky and white clouds. All the eight sides of the pavilion are double-eaved. It is said that, it was once the site of Dahong Temple in the Yuan Dynasty. The pavilion was based on the well of the temple. It seems that the pavilion has two storeys from outside, but it is actually a one-storey structure if you examine it inside. If you look at the Tianqian Pavilion standing under its ledges with the floating clouds in the background, you will feel as if the pavilion were soaring into the sky. That's one of the reasons why most construction in Suzhou has ledges. Except being good for natural lighting and ventilation, these ledges not only add the beauty to the building mainly, but also become one of the typical characteristics of Suzhou buildings.

The Shuxiang House refers to the place where you can see rice fields. The owner of "Gui Tian Yuan Ju" built the house in his garden. "You can look around from the building. The rice in the field would be within your eye's view at the turn of the summer and the

Selected Tour Commentaries

fall." The main part of the current Shuxian House was moved from the Eastern Hill when the Zhuozheng Garden was renovated in 1960's. It is bigger than the former one in size.

It is necessary to mention the rockery in a pond beside the camphor tree in the northwest corner. A big stone is on top of it, which is like a small boat turned upside down waiting for repair. The lake in front has a wide span with luxuriant bushes and a few reeds growing on the waterside, all this makes this scenery resemble a small harbor beside the Taihu Lake. The ancient owners of Suzhou gardens mostly used to be either high-rank civil officials or marshals with illustrious war deeds. They had worked hard for the country for quite a long time, and then came back to their hometowns for a certain reason. They found their own quiet "harbor" in Suzhou, which was far away from the clamorous capital. Those VIPs chose Suzhou as their best solitary place for its beautiful scenery and affluent products. They could not only enjoy a happy life, but also avoid their political enemies. For that reason, they especially appreciated the doctrines of Buddhism, Taoism and Confucianism, hoping to achieve their moral goals in their 'own' world. That is to say, "Roaming lonely all over the world like a small rowboat on the vast ocean with no definite destination, only the place with few people is my home."

The eastern part and the middle part of Zhuozheng Garden are separated by a long corridor. There are 25 carved windows in the wall along the corridor, like elaborate paper-cuts inlaying on a long painting scroll. The surrounding scenes are changing with changes of window designs while walking along the corridor. That is called "Yi Bu Huan Jing" (scenes change with each pace). If you come closer to have a look, you will find that the windows are designed in wave shape and ice shape. The cultural aura of water is exaggerated by the lively ripples reflected on the designs of the windows.

We come to the middle garden when we walk through the black door of the corridor. When we are looking far to the west standing by Yihongxuan, our first impression is the wide water surface and

Zhuozheng (Humble Administrator's) Garden in Suzhou

the beautiful scenery. The careful observers will also find a pagoda standing between the pavilions, over the bridge and brooks, which gives us a feeling of deepness and quietness. The owner actually racked his brains in designing it and he succeeded. Since the space it long and narrow, which would make people feel depressed if the scenery were not elaborately decorated. The owner made use of the low-lying areas to construct ponds and rockery, sheltering the enclosing walls on both sides on purpose. People will feel wide and deep for the enormous space left on the pond surface. All buildings in the garden are of different sizes, shapes and evenly density. Every building has its best view-observing point, and each is one important part of the place. The garden in the middle can be divided into three different scenic areas. Visitors will get more and more excited while travelling around.

The first area consists mainly of islets and rockery, including Bamboo House, Dai Shuang Pavilion and "Xiang Xue Yun Wei" Pavilion on the rockery. The rockery is the main part of the middle garden. "Three Islets on One Pond" is the traditional structure of Suzhou rockery, which is characterized with winding banks and the water flowing around the rockery. This excellently designed rockery is really a masterpiece and was done in accordance with the traditional concepts of Chinese mountain-and-water paintings. From its eastern side you will see one "mountain" is higher than the other; from the south, one is connected with the other; from the west, one is overwhelming the other. In painting terminology, it is called "deep and remote mountains and waters", "horizontally remote mountains and waters" and "high remote mountains and waters". Just like the artistic conceptions described in Su Dongpo's poet "if you look from the front, it is a mountain range; if you look from the side, it is a peak. The mountains are different with the changes of your angles."

Next, we'll come to the Bamboo House first. It is also called Yue Dao Feng Lai Pavilion, located in the far eastern end of the middle garden. It is adjacent to Yihong (Leaning against the Rain-

Selected Tour Commentaries

bow) Pavilion. Here the rainbow refers to the rainbow-like corridor. The house is elaborately built and its four big round doors would make people think of the mid-autumn moon. If you look out from the pavilion you are standing in, the four doors also appear like four huge mirror frames, inlaying the scenery in four seasons in Suzhou's gardens. Located in the north are bamboo and stone pillars; in the west, young and tender shooting lotus; in the south, "parasol trees in autumn rain" and in the east, blooming yulan magnolia. There in the pavilion hangs a horizontal inscription board with the pavilion's name on it. Parasol trees are holy, pure and exalted, and the green bamboo represents things coupling with hardness, softness and loyalty. Beside the board, there was an antithetical couplet, after reading which you mostly probably would have two vivid pictures in your imagination: one is about the beautiful night scene - "With the help of the breeze we have freshness and with the help of the moon we have light in the night"; the other is about the shining sun, singing birds, fragrant flowers and tranquil mountain and rockery. If there is someone who has read The Analects compiled by Confucius, he might have another feeling. Confucius once said, "The wise take delight in water, the benevolent, in mountains. The wise tends to be active while the benevolent tends to be still. The wise would enjoy life while the benevolent would enjoy longevity." Can we say that in the first line of the couplet the breeze and bright moon express the beauty of natural scenery, and in the second line mountains and waters reveal the effect on molding one's spirits by travelling? Now the visitors would have come to understanding that the Suzhou gardens are not simple copies of the natural beauty and landscapes but they are artistic and creative works of horticultural masters. If you realize this you have already understood the beauty.

After we cross a zigzag slabstone bridge we shall climb a hill along a narrow path, then the Daishuang Pavilion greets our eyes. The name originates from a poem by Wei Yingwu, a prefecture governor in Suzhou in the Tang Dynasty, from which a sense of fresh-

Zhuozheng (Humble Administrator's) Garden in Suzhou

ness of the nature gives us the genuine touch the art.

When we pass by the bushes, brooks and mounting steps we come to the 'Xiang Xue Yun Wei' Pavilion. It is located in the central highest point of the islet. The middle garden looks like an old, vigorous and simple painting stretching out before us when we look around. In this painting things high or low, far or near, large or small, wide or narrow, self-effacing or outstanding appears in front of us. The pavilion also has a board inscribed with the words: "Among Mountain Flowers and Wild Birds" and an antithetical couplet "the forest feels more quiet with the only sounds of Cicadas and the mountain feels more still with the only chirp of the birds." If you stay there and have a rest, you will have a feeling as if you have been merged together with the nature. There is a lyric in a film thematic song called The Tale of a Small Town, "Looking like a painting and hearing like a song", which can appropriately describe the Zhuozheng Garden. Can we say that the name inscribed on board is the best and the most popular explanation of the philosophy of "human compliance with the nature".

On the point when visitors might get very excited with the scene in the first part the designer diverts our attention and interest from the rockery to the ponds in the second part. The lotus ponds are the main components of the second part which consists of such interesting places as the Hefengsimian Pavilion, Xiangzhou, Jianshan Pavilion, Xiaofeihong (Little Flying Rainbow), Xiaocanglang, Yiyuxuan and Yuanxiang Hall.

With willows planted on three sides, the Hefengsimian Pavilion is surrounded by water on four sides. There is an antithetical couplet depicting its scenic characteristics of the four seasons of the Zhuozheng Garden. It is very interesting that the ordinal numbers of one, two, three and four are hidden in it. The couplet was copied from two different poems. Although the author changed a little, the atmosphere is quite suitable to the current situation.

A brook flows between Xiangzhou and the pavilion. The Chi-

Selected Tour Commentaries

nese words for "oasis" and "boat" have the same pronunciation as "zhou", and in fact, the oasis here is just a boat-shaped construction. It is called Stone Boat or Land Boat. To tell the truth, the stone boat combines five kinds of architecture styles, i.e. kiosk, terrace, tower, pavilion and waterside pavilion. In fact, almost each garden in Suzhou was built with a stone boat. For geographical reasons, Suzhou is a typical region of water. Boat is the common means of transportation. From the architectural point of view, different architectural styles can make buildings more diversified. From the political point of view, the stone boat can remind people of the truth that the water can not only carry a boat, but can also overthrow it. The former owner wanted to express that although he was far away from the court, he was always concerned about the emperor.

Crossing the zigzag bridge, we come to the Jianshan Pavilion along the corridor, which was once called "Ouxiang Pavilion" in ancient times. With water on three sides, it looks like a dragon playing with water. The pavilion represents the dragon's head, the corridor represents the dragon's body, and the cloudy wall represents the dragon's tail. The door represents the dragon's mouth, and the zigzag bridge represents the dragon's antenna. The structure of the pavilion and the furniture in it are of ancient Chinese style.

Walking southward along the corridor, we come to The Lesser Canglang. The Jianshan Pavilion is the principal building in the north of the second part, and it is wide enough for riding a horse to pass through. As for The Lesser Canglang, Xiao Feihong and the Dezhen Pavilion which are located in the south of the second part, the buildings are relatively smaller. Space in the buildings is narrow. The name Lesser Canglang comes from the poem The Fisherman in The Verse of Chu. In it said, "When the water of Canglang is limpid, I could wash my hat cords with it; When the water of Canglang is turbid, I could wash my twain feet with it." This implies that " If the government is free from corruption, I would be going to assist the ruler; if the government is fatuous, I would live in seclusion." It is a

Zhuozheng (Humble Administrator's) Garden in Suzhou

three-room spacious hall, surrounded by water on two sides. Standing in the front and looking northward, we can see the reflection of Xiao Feihong in the water like a rainbow. This is the best place to see the waterside scenery. All the brooks in front of the Ouxiang Pavilion gather together and are suddenly split up before the Xiangzhou. Only one stream flows windingly through the Lesser Canglang and Xiao Feihong. That is one of the main characteristics of Suzhou classical gardens.

Walking eastward from the Lesser Canglang, we come to the Yuanxiang Hall, in which visitors can have the most excited feelings while going sightseeing around. It is located in the central part of the garden, there is a brook in front and a pond in the rear, both planted with lotus flowers. In summer, the fragrance of lotus flowers can float into the hall. That is the origin of the hall's name. It is decorated with windowpanes, you can sit inside, savoring tea, chatting and enjoying the beautiful sights. You can see the yellow-stone rockery to the south of the hall, an islet rockery to the north, the Xiuqi Pavilion to the east and Yiyuxuan beside a pond to the west. The sight may make you feel that the water is far and low while the rockery is near and high. The name inscribed in the board was first written by Sheng Deqian, a famous scholar in the reign of Qianlong in the Qing Dynasty. Due to the loss of the original, it had to be rewritten by Zhang Xinjia, a modern calligrapher. There is a couplet of 80 words, which is the longest among all the couplets in the gardens of Suzhou. It depicts the luxurious party held by local celebrities. The environment designs play an important role in the garden architectures of Suzhou. Among them, a lot of boards are inscribed with words or verses chosen from poetry of over thousands of years. Most of them have profound meanings, elegant styles and beautiful handwriting, recording the history of those famous gardens, indicating their essentials and expressing the owner's feelings.

The third scenic area of the middle part is called Loquat Garden, located in the southeast of the Yuanxiang Hall. Because a num-

Selected Tour Commentaries

ber of loquat trees have been planted there and thus the name of the garden. The door of the garden is ingeniously designed. A screen wall stands there in front of the visitors when they come here and peonies grow on both sides. It seems that there is no way to walk further. But as you get nearer to the rockery you will find unexpectedly a side door hidden behind the rockery. The view of the door will get gradually full if you get closer and closer. At the entrance, visitors will find the door like a full moon set on the white screen. Through the door, it is sheltered again by rockery. The door also is like a huge precious mirror, and views in the courtyard seem to be the reflection of those outside the courtyard. The former owner properly used the best location of the door to make "Xiang Xue Yun Wei Pavilion", "Moonlike Door" and "Jia Shi Pavilion" abreast in the same line of sight. It shows that the designers paid more attention to the view sights while building doors and windows, in order to create scenic spots everywhere.

Buildings in the courtyard, such as the Linglong Hall, the Jiashi Pavilion, Tingyuxuan and Haitangchunwu, are the main body of the third scenic part of the garden. These buildings divide the place into three different courtyards, which can make the sights of the garden more abundant. The three courtyards make the space and view's setting full of changes. Each courtyard seems to be the same size, but if someone measures them with foot, they will find that they are quite different in size. The reason is that the wall of the Linglong Hall is quite low, so the vision seems to be wider than it is. However, the size of Haitangchunwu is small, but it looks much wider because of its wall windows. The courtyard of Tingyuxuan is quite big, so a pond is built there to set it in a suitable size. The former host of the garden liked sitting there with his family, eating snacks from Suzhou and listening to the rhythm of the falling rain on the roof, tree leaves and ground. The middle garden in a way can be said to be three movements in a symphony. The first movement can be called "The Peak of Mountain"; the second is "The Sea and Its Shore"; the third

Zhuozheng (Humble Administrator's) Garden in Suzhou

is "Family Happiness".

Passing through the middle garden, we come to the western garden. Its main buildings are "36 Mandarin Ducks House" and "18 Daturas House". This building only looks like a roof, in fact it has four rooms. At the first sight you might take it as a hall, in fact it has two parlors. The northern parlor is only used in summer for people to escape the heat, and the southern parlor is used in winter for warming purposes. Four seal characters are inscribed in the bricks above the door. The meaning is that only entering this door you can enjoy the pleasure. The hall was built in the Qing Dynasty and was engraved and equipped exquisitely and extraordinarily. The name of northern parlor was written by Hong Yun and the southern one was by Lu Runyang. Both were brilliant scholars in the Qing Dynasty. This wide and quiet house can lead to all directions so that it is always the meeting place for guests. The mandarin duck represents happy marriage and datura is the mascot of longevity. Because datura and camellia are very similar, 18 camellias are planted here to match the scene. The design of the hall is very unique for its arched room surface and four side rooms in each corner, where the owner watch plays of Kun Opera. It is said in history books that Zhang Luqian, the owner at that time, was very fond of Kun Opera and often discussed the singing techniques with Yu Lilu, the King of Kun Opera at that time. The side rooms were used by actors to do make-up or by servants to wait in. The blue-white panes are very elegant. In the burning sun of summer, the sunshine becomes a bunch of blue-white beam through windows, reflected on floor and making people feel cool. If interested, you can go closer and look out through the blue panes then you'll find that the roof, twigs, stones and lotus leaves seem covered with "snow".

The Liuting Pavilion is located west of the 36 Mandarin Ducks House. Its name originated from Li Shangyin's poem in the Tang Dynasty and was written by Wu Dacheng, provincial governor of Hunan Province in the Qing Dynasty. Its southern hanging dado is

Selected Tour Commentaries

engraved with designs of pines, bamboo, plums and sparrows. Dragon designs were carved in the separating screens. It is said that it was found in the Mansion of Prince Zhong of the Taiping Heavenly Kingdom and had both high artistic and historic values.

The Reflection Pavilion is located north of the 36 Mandarin Ducks House. It is so named because people standing on the other side of the pond can see the building's reflection on the water surface. Its lower floor is called "Memorial Hall for Mr. Wen and Mr. Shen". Wen Zhengming was one of the four most gifted scholars in the Ming Dynasty. Some say that he participated in the planning and designing of Zhuzheng Garden. But some others say that he painted 31 pictures according to the different parts of the garden, and wrote a poem to go with each painting. Besides, he also wrote a prose "Narration of Wang's Zhuozheng Garden" to eulogize the garden, which added luster to the garden's fame. Shen Shitian once was Wen Zhengming's instructor of painting. Both of them made great contributions to the cultural and artistic development of Suzhou. The middle screen door of the Reflection Pavilion was engraved with a painting of bamboo without root painted by Zheng Banqiao, one of the eight bizarre artistic geniuses in Yangzhou. This painting was also matched with a poem, and it was a rare art treasure as well.

There is a zigzag corridor just above the water surface in front of the Reflection Pavilion. Walking up and down in it and looking out at the gleaming ripples visitors would feel just like floating above water. To the west of the water corridor are several buildings, the nearest one is called Yushuitongzuo (With Whom Should I Sit Together) Xuan. Xuan is a carriage-like building. It has doorframes, but no doors; everyone can go in and out freely. There are windows on walls for sightseeing. "With whom shall I sit together? No one but the bright moon and the refreshing breeze." This is Su Dongpo's poem expressing the poet's lofty feeling. The former owner of the garden took Su's poem to express his own loftiness. If you take a closer look at the Yushuitongzuo Xuan you will find it resembles a fan. Its

Zhuozheng (Humble Administrator's) Garden in Suzhou

tile surface looks like a fan leave; the top point of the Li Pavilion in the back is like the fan's handle. The two are flawlessly connected.

An excellent example of Suzhou gardens, the Zhuozheng Garden is typical of fantastic and creative artificial landscape and well designed water space. Besides, it is full of tender family aura as well. The whole garden is the embodiment of what the ancient people had been pursuing all the time as the "Earthly Heaven" because it represents the traditional Chinese philosophical concepts of showing high ideals by simple living.

Selected Tour Commentaries

THE WEST LAKE IN HANGZHOU

Ladies and Gentlemen,

Before you visit Hangzhou, you might have heard of the saying "In the sky, the best is heaven, on the earth, the best are Suzhou and Hangzhou." It means Suzhou and Hangzhou are as beautiful as Heaven. Why has Hangzhou been described as heaven on the earth? Mostly, because Hangzhou has the West Lake. Thousands of years have passed, the West Lake is still as charming as ever and makes people fall in love with it at the first sight. The famous poet Bai Juyi in the Tang Dynast wrote many poems to describe the beauty of the West Lake. He was reluctant to leave Hangzhou just because of the West Lake.

My friends, now I'm going to take you to visit the West Lake from Yue- miao port. Before we start sailing, I would like to give a brief introduction to the West Lake. The West Lake is situated in the west of Hangzhou City with mountains surrounding on three sides. It is to the west of the downtown city. A lake about 15 kilometers in circumference, it is 3.2 kilometers from north to south and 2.8 kilometers from west to east and covers a water area of 5.68 square km. If the isles are included, the area it covers amounts to 6.3 square km. It is 1.55 meters in average depth. The deepest place measures 2.8 meters. The shallowest part is around 1 meter. The quantities of its water are around 8.5 million to 8.7 million cubic meters. The Su Embankment and Bai Embankment separate the lake into several

The West Lake in Hangzhou

small lakes, such as the Outer Lake, the North Li Lake, West Li Lake, Yue Lake and Little South Lake. The West Lake has lots of beautiful scenic spots. In ancient time it was once known for its best ten famous sites. In 1985, the new best ten scenic spots were selected and announced to public. Within 60 square km with the West Lake as the center, there are more than 40 scenic spots. There are more than 30 protected sites of historical value. On November 8th, 1982, the West Lake was listed among the first key scenic resorts. In 1985, the West Lake took the third place during the national competition of beautiful scenic resorts.

The West Lake is rich in beautiful legends. Once upon a time, there lived an immortal boy and an immortal girl in the heaven. The boy was named Yu Long (Jade Dragon) and the girl, Jin Feng (Gold Phoenix). They found a white jade on the island by the Milky Way. They polished the jade for many years until the jade changed into a shining pearl. Wherever it shined, the trees turned green and the flowers bloomed. Later the news was spread in the heaven, and the Queen Mother sent soldiers to rob them of the pearl. Yu Long and Jin Feng fought with Queen Mother and the pearl fell down from the hand of the Queen Mother to earth and became the West Lake. Yu Long and Jin Feng were punished and changed to two mountains, Yulong Mountain and Fenghuang Mountain. They therefore have been here protecting the West Lake from time immemorial.

The Water of the Lake is lucid. Just now, someone asks why is it so lucid? I will give you the answer from the very beginning of story about the Lake. Back to 12000 years ago, the lake was a shallow bay connecting the Qiantang River. To the north and south, there were Wu Mountain and Baoshi (Precious Stone) Mountain. They were capes of the bay. Later the mud and stone brought by the tide piled up and separated the bay and the Qiantang River. In the Western Han Dynasty (206 BC-24AD) the original lake was formed. In the Sui Dynasty, it was basically of the present scale. After five times of large-scale harnessing conducted respectively by Bai Juyi,

Selected Tour Commentaries

Qian Liu, Su Dongpo, Yang Mengying and Ruan Yuan, it finally became a beautiful half-closed lake from a natural lake.

The water in the West Lake is fresh, mainly coming from rainwater and spring water in the mountain. For thousands of years, it has been the water source for people to drink and irrigate. So to keep it from being polluted is very important. During the old time, there was not much pollution. The water is very clear. In the past decades, due to the development of the industry and the building of hotels and restaurants without environmental consideration protection measures, wastewater was once discharged to the lake. And the water of the lake was not as clean and clear as before. The most serious pollution happened from March 1981. At that time, diesel-engined tourist boats were put into use and their leaked oil, together with smoke ashes blown from the nearby factories, turned the lake water brown-red and then brown. The water of the lake became somewhat stinking. The government made efforts to pump the water from the Qian Tang River to change the lake water. Every day 100 thousand tons of water was poured into the lake in this purpose. On May 12th of the same year, the water became clear again. In order to keep the water clean the government has made a lot of efforts to bring water from the Qiantang River. So every 33 days, the water of the West Lake was changed once. Besides, there are two water locks are used to adjust the water level. One is the Shengtang Lock connected with the Shengtang River. The other is the Yongjin Lock connected with the Cheng River by way of underground channels.

In history, the West Lake had different names in different dynasties. In The Han Dynasty (206 BC-220AD) it was called Wulin Water, Golden Ox Lake, and Mingsheng Lake. In the Tang Dynasty (618-907), Shihan Lake, Qiantang Lake and some other names. In the Northern Song Dynasty (960-1127), Su Dongpo was the governor of Hangzhou. He wrote a poet to describe the beauty of the West Lake. He compared it with Xi Shi, one of the four most famous ancient beauties in Chinese culture. So the West Lake has another name

The West Lake in Hangzhou

- Xizi Lake.

Just as Su Dongpo described the West Lake as Xi Shi in ancient time, Guo Moruo, the famous modern scholar described the Lake as a goddess. He composed a poem titled 'Goddess of the West Lake'. According to the poem, there was a Goddess in the Lake. At night, she came out from the lake. If any visitor loves her, he would be attracted to the most beautiful part of the lake. After reading this poem, do you feel wanting to meet the mysterious goddess?

As a famous tourist resort, it is also a favorite place for some famous people. Late Chairman Mao came to visit the Lake for 40 times. Once he stayed here for seven months. He always praised the lake. He considered it his second home. Although he praised the beauty of the West Lake for many times, but he never composed any poems eulogizing the lake. According to the people who have worked with him, Chairman Mao thought that one of Su Dongpo's poems called "Drinking on the lake with sun and then rain" was the best one to describe its beauty. So he was afraid no other poems would be better than it. Chairman Mao had calligraphed a lot of poems by ancient poets and five of them were poems about the lake. The lake was loved not only by Chinese great persons but also by China's foreign friends such as American ex-president, Mr. Nixon. He has been here twice. He said that Beijing is the capital of China, but Hangzhou is the heart of China. And that he would be back again. He also brought to Hangzhou redwood as a gift from his hometown, California.

My dear friends, even great persons loved the West Lake so much, then as for us, I think, we would love the lake all the more. The West Lake is surrounded by mountains on three sides, leaving one side for the city. Taking the West Lake as the center, in the east then is the Hubin Park near to the city; looking in distance, situated in the southwest are the Nangao Peak, the Longjing Mountain, Daci Mountain, Nan Ping Mountain and Phoenix Mountain, etc. These mountains are together called the South Mountains. Looking to the

153

Selected Tour Commentaries

north, you would see Lingyin Mountain, Beigao Peak, Baoshi Mountain, etc. These mountains are together called the North Mountains. In the mountains hide three famous springs, i. e., Hupao, Longjing and Yuquan and seven caves as well — Yanxia, Shuile, Shiwu, Huanglong, Ziyun and Zilai and Ciyun. The lake area consists of three parts according to the topography and region: the North Mountains, the South Mountains and the lake. Located on the North Mountains are the Feilai Peak, Lingyin Temple and Yuewang Temple . On the South Mountains, lie the Liuhe Tower and Hupao springs, etc. On the lake, there are one hill, two dikes and three isles. The West Lake area is so large that we will have to visit the lake along the major routes. I will give you a brief introduction to our route. Firstly, we will visit the scenic spots around the lake, including Gu Hill, Su Embankment and Bai Embankment. Then we will visit the three isles on the lake.

Now we are moving from west to east. The scene here is called Gu Hill. It is connected with the Xileng Bridge in the west and the Bai Embankment in the east. It is 35 meters above sea level and covers 200 thousand square meters. It has been popular since the Tang and Song dynasties. In the Qing Dynasty, Emperor Kangxi took this place as his interim palace. You may ask that since Gu Hill is the biggest isle, why it is called Gu Hill (Lone Hill)? Well, due to its beauty, the emperors of different dynasties took the place as what could be reserved only for them. So it is called Gu Hill (Lone Hill). The Hill was formed by the explosion of a volcano. It is actually a peninsula. So the local interesting saying goes like this, "the Lone Mountain is not lonely, the Broken Bridge is not broken and the Long Bridge is not long." These are the fantastic sights of the West Lake. In the west of the Gu Hill is the Xileng Bridge. The Xileng Bridge together with the Broken Bridge and the Long Bridge are bridges of love. As for this bridge, It reminds people of Su Xiaoxiao's story. Su Xiaoxiao was a beautiful girl good at singing and dancing. Her parents died when she was very young. She lived with

154

The West Lake in Hangzhou

her aunt by the Xileng Bridge. One day, on the bridge, she met a young scholar named Ruan Yu. They fell in love and got married. Ruan Yu's farther, an official in Beijing, ordered him to go back to Beijing. Then Ruan Yu left and never was able to return to Hangzhou. Soon, Su died from sorrow. Bao Ren, who was once financially assisted by Su Xiaoxiao when he fell on evil days, but now was appointed as governor of Huazhou, respected Su Xiaoxiao very much and buried her beside the Xileng Bridge. He also built a pavilion above the tomb in commemoration of her. At present, her tomb doesn't exist any more, but her love story has been still popular.

Passing by the Xileng Bridge we will see a white marble statue of a lady in the back of the Gu Hill. You see, her left hand is in the waist and a sword in her right hand. Her eyes are staring ahead. Who is she? She is Ms. Qiu Jin, the great women liberation pioneer, who has lost life in activities against the Qing Dynasty. The statue is 2.7 meters tall and its holder is 2 meters tall. In the front of the stele, there are four Chinese characters which mean "heroine" written by Mr. Sun Yat-sen. The West Lake has become known not only because of its beautiful sights but also because of tombs of many national heroes such as Yue Fei, Yu Qian and Zhang Cangshui of the ancient time and Ms. Qiu Jin's contemporary revolutionaries Xu Xilin, Tao Chengzhang, etc. Their noble deeds and spirits will always encourage the later generation.

We are heading slowly to the east. Now you can see the white wall. Inside the wall, it is the famous Xileng Press. On the right of the press, there is a building with a combination of the Chinese and the West style. It is the restaurant called Louwailou. This name is taken from a poem. It was built in 1848. This restaurant has received lots of famous people such as Mr. and Mrs. Sun Yat-sen, Mr. and Mrs Lu Xun. In 1952, this restaurant started to receive foreigners. The Prince of Cambodia visited here. Premier Zhou had been here for 9 times with state guests. The famous dish of the restaurant is West Lake vinegar fish. The grass carp in the West Lake is chosen

Selected Tour Commentaries

for the dish. The fish must be left in the clear fresh water for about two days before cooking. In this way the smell of mud can be got rid of. The well-done fish is tender and delicious with a little bit taste of crab. It is the representative dish of Hangzhou. There are 51 kinds of fish in the lake such as silver carp, variegated carp, carp, crucian carp and bream. Now our boat is heading to the Zhongshan Park, we can see the front gate of Gu Hill. Gu Hill is not only known for its beautiful landscape but also for its rich historical heritage.

Beside the Zhongshan Park, we can see lots of new buildings. They are the Zhejiang Province Museum. Inside, there are more than 1700 pieces of cultural relics from Hemudu culture 7000 years ago till modern times. The ancient building at the back of the museum is the Wenlan Pavilion which was the imperial library of the Qing Dynasty. It is one of the seven famous libraries built for storing "The Si Ku Quan Shu (Complete Library in the Four Branches of Literature)".

There is a double-eaved pavilion called "Ping Hu Qiu Yue" by the lake. It is built in the reign of Kangxi of the Qing Dynasty. It is the beginning of the Bai Dike and also is one of the three famous places where you can enjoy the sight of the moon in Hangzhou. In history, Hangzhou people could go to one of the three isles, the lake embankment or the Phoenix Mountain to enjoy the moon.

Now here is the Bai Embankment. On both sides of the dike are lined with different trees. Especially in spring, it is green and red everywhere. Tourists may have the feeling of being in a fairyland. The Bai Embankment's original name is Bai Sha Embankment, popular more than one thousand year ago, in the Tang Dynasty. It is not the one Bai Juyi had directed to construct. People called it Bai Embankment just to memorize him. Su Embankment was built by Su Dongpo. Su Embankment and Bai Embankment are like two satin belts in the lake. In the middle of the Bai Embankment, there is a bridge called Shi Gong Bridge whose original name is Wooden Bridge or Hanbi Bridge. At the end of the Bai Embankment is the ring

The West Lake in Hangzhou

bridge. It is the famous bridge—Duanqiao (Broken) Bridge. The one kilometre long Bai Embankment ends at the Duanqiao (Broken) Bridge.

Duanqiao (Broken) Bridge was so named in Tang Dynasty. In the Song Dynasty, it was called Baoyou Bridge. In the Yuan Dynasty, it was called Duanjia Bridge. It was an old stone arch bridge covered with bryophyte. Now although a common stone arch in appearance, it is the most famous bridge on the West Lake because it is connected with the love story of the White Snake. The story goes like this Lady White is a snake fairy, who met with a young man Xu Xian here. They fell in love and got married soon. Later, Xu Xian was cheated by monk Fahai and became a monk. In order to get her husband back, Lady White Snake fought with Fahai but was defeated and had to return to Hangzhou. Before long, Xu Xian escaped from the monastery and also went back to Hangzhou. This couple finally happily met on the Broken Bridge. One part of the story is called "Meeting at Broken Bridge". This part cloaks the bridge with many romantic auras.

You may ask a question that why it is called Broken Bridge since it is not broken. Let me explain it to you. The bridge is facing the mountain and against the city. It is on the joint point between the North Li Lake and the Outer Lake. It is the best place to enjoy snow in winter. When the sun comes out after snowing the snow on the south side will melt while the other side is still covered with snow. Looking from afar, the bridge is like a broken bridge. Besides, the bridge is the end of the Bai Embankment. In Chinese "duan" also means "ending". Now you've got why the bridge is so named.

On the other side of the bridge is the North Li Lake in which there are lots of lotus plants. When summer comes, fragrance of lotus flowers floats in the air everywhere. The whole lake covers an area of 405 Mu. There are 30 kinds of lotus. You can also find lotus in the Yue Lake and Xiaoyingzhou. The starch made from the lotus root of the West Lake is a very famous local product.

Selected Tour Commentaries

The Baoshi (Precious Stone) Mountain over there is 78 meters above sea level. Precious stones can be actually found in this mountain. Some stones are like diamond shining in the sunlight. That is why the mountain is called Baoshi (Precious Stone) Mountain. There is a tower on top of the mountain. It is called Baoshu Tower. This tower was built in the North Song Dynasty. It is said that when Zhao Kuangyin took over the whole country and became emperor, he asked Qian Hongshu, King of Wuyue, to go up to the capital city of the country to have something discussed. People there thought he might be killed. To bless him, they built the tower on the mountain and named it Baoshu. It means blessing Qian Hongshu. It was rebuilt in 1933. It is 45.3 meters tall and built with bricks. Among the towers in Hangzhou area, it is the most beautiful one and is often compared to a beautiful girl. To its south there used to be another tower Leifeng. People used to liken it to an old monk while to liken the Baoshu to a young beautiful girl. They have different styles resulting in different charms. But unfortunately the Leifeng Tower collapsed long ago.

So much for the lakeside scenery.

Now let's go to visit the three isles on the lake.

First, we will visit the biggest isle on the lake - Santanyinyue. It is also called Xiaoyingzhou. It is actually a park on the lake. Other isles are spread around it. It covers an area of 70 thousand square meters with 60% being water. The isle is in a shape of a square. There are many flowers around the isle such as water lily and small lotus. Red, white and yellow flowers dot everywhere. Water shield of the West Lake has been famous. It is rich in protein and vitamin C and ferrous element. It can be eaten fresh with sugar. West Lake water shield soup is also famous.

The isle of San Tan Yin Yue was formed with the dug bottom-mud of the lake in 1607 in the Ming Dynasty. The essence for its fame lies in the three small pagodas on the lake to the south of the isle. The pagodas are two meters tall. The lower part of the pagoda

158

The West Lake in Hangzhou

is like a ball, on which there are five small holes. The top of the pagoda is like a calabash. In a night with a full moon, especially in the mid-Autumn night, people often light the candle and put thin paper on the holes, then light shone through the paper. At this time, the shadow of the tower, cloud and moon mixed together. The lights from the three pagodas get through the 15 holes then you would see 30 moons in the water. Plus the one in the sky and the one in the water, there are 32 moons altogether. There is a pavilion in the middle of the lake. It is the biggest pavilion in the West Lake. Finished in 1552, it is also the earliest isle built in the West Lake. It has a history of over 440 years. Emperor Qianlong once came here and praised it for its boundless beauty. It is called Huxin Pavilion.

In the northwest of the Huxin Pavilion, there is a small isle called Ruangongdun. It is the smallest isle on the lake, only covering 5561 square meters. It was built in 1800. Ruan Yuan, the official of Zhejiang province in the Qing Dynasty led people to pile the isle by moving the mud from flood protection project. It is a good place to go fishing and for tour at night, when the West Lake is even more beautiful. The performance - "Emperor Qinglong visiting South of the Yangtze" is staged here. If you are interested in that, you can go to watch that performance.

After visiting the three isles, we are heading for the Su Embankment. It is across the lake from the north to the south and it is 2.8 kilometers long. There are 6 stone arch bridges in the embankment. The Su Embankment always reminds us of Su Dongpo, a very well known poet and scholar in the Song Dynasty. He had made great contribution to the local people through his great efforts in controlling the West Lake. The Su Embankment was built under his leadership when he was the local official. In order to commemorate him, the embankment was called Su Embankment. In the south of the embankment, the memorial museum of Su Dongpo is built. People always describe the West Lake and the lake in Geneva as two pearls of the east and west. The great Italian traveler Marco Polo

Selected Tour Commentaries

once described the lake as the most beautiful and gracious place in the world. The West Lake is the famous scene which has been visited by many presidents from different countries. Mr. Sun Yat-sen said that the West Lake was a unique scene of the world. No other lakes could be compared with it. The lake in Geneva is too big to have a full view while the West Lake is neither too big nor too small. So the West Lake is the pearl of Hangzhou, the pearl of the East and the pearl of the world.

Ladies and Gentlemen, so much for our tour today. I hope the West Lake has left you a wonderful impression. See you again.

MOUNT HUANGSHAN

Ladies and Gentlemen, welcome to Mount Huangshan. This is Tangkou. It is regarded as the front gate of Mount Huangshan.

First of all please let me give you a brief introduction to the scenery of Huangshan. Huangshan is located in the south of Anhui Province. It is a part of China's southern ranges. The whole mountain covers an area of 1200 hectares. But the middle part of the mountain is the most significant of all the mountain area. The scenic area covers 154 hectares and belongs to Huangshan City. Huangshan City (formerly Tunxi) is roughly over 60km away from Mount Huangshan. The neighbors of Huangshan in the south are three counties and one district; in the north is "Huangshan District". All the above five areas belong to Huangshan City.

Mount Huangshan has been so named and called since Emperor Li Longji of the Tang Dynasty named it so in the 8th century. Huangshan's former name was "Mount Qian". "Qian" means "black". "Mount Qian" means the mountain is full of black stones. An old tale tells us why the mountain has different names. Legend has it that our ancestor "Huangdi" created the unitary multi-national state and civilized the society. Then he came to Mount Qian to make pills of immortality and take bath in the hot spring. Then he became an immortal. Emperor Li Longji of the Tang Dynasty believed this tale. He changed Mount Qian to Mount Huangshan in commemoration of Huangdi.

Selected Tour Commentaries

For visiting Huangshan, you come from different parts of the world. I would be very glad to say that you have made the right choice. You will find with your own eyes that Huangshan is the most marvelous mountain on earth.

The first attractive scene in Huangshan must be the peaks. The wonderful peaks have unique characteristics and charms. There is no exactly number of the peaks in Huangshan. According to historical documents, there are 36 big peaks and 36 small peaks named. And 10 new peaks that have also been named at present time. Totally 82 named peaks have been chosen to enter the chronicle "Records of Mount Huangshan". Most of the peaks rise more than 1000 meters above sea level. The highest one is Lotus Flower Peak (Lianhuafeng) which is 1864m, followed by Bright Summit Peak (Guangmingding) at 1841m and Heavenly Capital Peak (Tiandufeng) at 1829.5m. The three main peaks with the unique Peak of Starting to Believe (Shixinfeng) at 1683m, are called four famous peaks of Huangshan. You will get something of Huangshan if you climb up any one of the four.

The beauty of Huangshan is not only in its peaks, but also in that it has merged the unique features of all the famous mountains of China; that is to say, Huangshan has the grandeur of Mount Tai, the precipitousness of Mount Hua, the misty clouds of Mount Heng, the beautiful waterfalls of Mount Lu, the exquisite rocks of Mount Yandang and the coolness of Mount Emei. In short, Huangshan epitomized almost all the unique features of mountains on earth. Besides, Hunagshan is also known for its own four unique features — gnarled pines, craggy rocks, rolling seas of clouds and hot springs. Everyone will speak highly of the four unique sights. Mr. Xu Xiake, a famous geographer and traveler of the Ming Dynasty, traveled to every famous mountain of China and climbed up Huangshan twice. His comment on Huangshan was: "No Mountain is better than Huangshan." That means you will realize that no other mountain is better than Huangshan after you have visited Huangshan. To some extent, it is no need for you to visit other mountains if you have once enjoyed the

162

Mount Huangshan

beauty of Huangshan. This is also summarized in the old Chinese saying, no need to visit other mountains after visiting the five famous mountains. No need to visit the five famous mountains after coming back from Huangshan." In May 1990, a UNESCO official came to Huangshan to investigate the natural resources and cultural heritage. He could not help saying, "Huangshan is marvelous. This is the most beautiful mountain I've ever seen." He is the authoritative person in scenic investigation. What he said means that Huangshan can be regarded as the most beautiful mountain in the world.

Huangshan not only has the natural beauty, but also contains rich historical and cultural heritage. The natural beauty in perfect harmony with the historical and cultural heritage creates the beauty of Huangshan.

In 1985, Huangshan was selected as one of the top ten natural and cultural attractions in China. It was the only mountain that earned such honor then. In 1990, UNESCO inscribed it on the World Heritage List and from then on Huangshan, as a tourist resort, has been getting more and more popular among tourists both at home and abroad.

Huangshan symbolizes the spirit of Chinese people just as the Yellow River, the Yangtze River and the Great Wall do.

Now I would like to give you an introduction to the "Four Unique Features" of Huangshan.

The first one is the "gnarled pines". Why are the pines of Huangshan regarded as unusual? Just because of its uncommon vitality. As we know that plants usually can not live without rooting in the soil. The pines of Huangshan can grow up in granite rocks. You can see the pines full of vigor and vitality everywhere in Huangshan, for example at the summits of peaks, on the overhanging rocks, in the deep mountain valleys, etc. For thousands of years, the pines grow out of stones and stem in the chinks, no matter how scarce the soil is and how bad the weather is. Also the fantastic shape and appearance is another characteristic of the pines. The pine needles are short and

Selected Tour Commentaries

thick; and the trunk is gnarled and the top is flat. It shows us the plainness, vigor and firmness. Every pine has a different look, in both posture and style. People named the pines according to their differences, such as Welcome Guest Pine (Yingkesong), Black Tiger Pine (Heihusong), Lying Dragon Pine (Wolongsong), Dragon Claw Pine (Longzhaosong), Tanhai Pine, Solidarity Pine (Tuanjiesong), etc. These names stand for the beauty of those Huangshan pines.

Fantastic rocks lie everywhere in the mountain. When you see the unique style and the great vitality of the unusual pines growing up in the granite rocks, you can associate the phenomenon with the spirit of Chinese nation. The Chinese nation constantly strive to become stronger with a strong will just like the pines. The city of Huangshan has already taken the pine as her symbolic tree for the province and summarized the spirit of pines as follows: striving to become stronger, solidarity is a must; opening to the outside world, supporting and strengthening each other are the core of prosperity. The pine spirit has encouraged the people of Anhui to develop their own province with great efforts.

Rocks of grotesque shapes are another unique feature of Huangshan. You can see such rocks everywhere at Huangshan. The new edition of the chronicle "Records of Huangshan" published in 1988 has listed 121 famous rocks. All the rocks have very interesting shapes. Some look like human beings, some look like articles and some resemble figures in fables or legends. All the rocks are lively and vivid. Among the 121 famous rocks, some rocks such as the "Feilai Rock (which means the rock that flew here from other place)", "Immortals Playing Chess (Xianrenxiaqi)", "Monkey Looking at the sea (Houziguanhai), "Island of Penglai (Penglaixiandao), etc. Some of the rocks are like huge monsters; some are small and exquisite; some can represent individual scenery and some join together to form significant scenery with different styles. Forms of some rocks change when seen from different angles. For instance, at one point, you see a rock like a "Golden Cock Crowing at the Heav-

Mount Huangshan

enly Gate" (Jinjijiaotianmen); if you move your steps further, it gives you an image of "Five Old People Going to Heavenly Capital (Wulaoshangtiandu). Also some will give you different impressions if you look at them at different time. The difference between Monkey Looking at the Sea (Huoziguanhai) and Monkey looking at Peaceful town (Houziwangtaiping) is such an example.

Now, let's talk about the rolling sea of clouds. Although you can see the clouds in other mountains, the unexpected changes and the grand sight of Huangshan clouds are probably the best. Because of the clouds, Huangshan has got a sobriquet Huang Sea of Clouds (Huanghai). In historical records, a famous historian named Pan Zhiheng lived in Huangshan for dozens of years. He wrote a sixty-volume book entitled "Huanghai". Emperor Kangxi bestowed a board to Huangshan with his handwriting "Huanghaitiandu" inscribed on it. Some scenic spots and hotels of Huangshan have been related with "sea". Some spots are more beautiful when seen with clouds together. All of above can prove that "Huanghai" deserves the title.

You can see the rolling sea of clouds every season in Huangshan. The best season is the winter and spring. Especially at the time when sun rises or sets down after snow. The light cloud looks like smoke rising continuously form the ridges and peaks. It's spreading out and the cloud and the sky are merging into one. The tops of the peaks standing above the clouds look like isolated islands on a sea. But in a very short period of time, you will be shocked by the billows of clouds dashing into the sky. While you are blinking your eyes, you will find the clouds melt and the mists disperse. The mountain becomes green again and even more beautiful than before.

Clouds of Huangshan are divided into five parts: the north, the south, the east, the west and the middle. There are also five best places for watching clouds. They are as follows: on the "Qianwenshu Terrace" of Jade Screen Tower (Yupinglou) to see the south cloud; on the Qinglian Terrace of Lion Peak (Shizifeng) to see the north cloud; at the head of White Goose Ridge (Bai'eling) to see the east

165

Selected Tour Commentaries

cloud; in front of the Paiyun Pavilion or at the summit of Lion Peak to see the west cloud. Each of the four places has its own strong points. If you stay on the Bright Summit Peak (Guangmingding) or Heavenly Capital Peak (Tiandufeng) or Lotus Peak (Lianhuafeng) to see the clouds, you can see the grand view of rolling sea of clouds. Therefore, it is said that the best place to see the clouds is in the middle.

Finally, let me give you a briefing about the Hot Springs. What we visit mostly is the hot spring at the south foot of the mountain at Huangshan Hotel. It was called "Tangquan" in the past. The spring comes from Zishi Peak. The hot spring scenic spot is the first spot we will meet with after entering the South Gate of Huangshan. There is plenty of water in the hot spring and the temperature is always 42°C for the whole year. The hot spring contains many kinds of minerals. It is helpful to the treatment of those who have skin disease or rheumatism or disease of digestive system. This hot spring water is used for bath, not for drinking.

This hot spring has been well known for a long time. The stele inscribed "Famous spring under the sun (Tianxiamingquan)" was erected in the Ming Dynasty. On July 11th, 1979 former state leader Mr. Deng Xiaoping came to Huangshan and wrote the same inscription "Famous spring under the sun" again. Huangshan is the only mountain that is famous for both the mountain and the hot spring.

There are several hot springs in Huangshan. A hot spring called "Songgu'an Spring" lies in the north part of Huangshan. It was formerly called "Tin Spring" in old time. It is 7.5km from the hotel hot spring. In addition, the height of the two springs is similar. The two springs stand facing each other in distance and show the beauty of symmetry. The Song Guyan Spring is not developed yet because of the remote location. It will become a new scenic spot after the cable car in the northern mountain has been finished.

Another magical hot spring is called "Shengquan" (Sacred Spring). It lies on the summit of "Nanhaishengquan Peak" with an

Mount Huangshan

elevation of 1574.4m. It is said that pills for immortality could be made from boiling stones with the spring water. So it is called "Shengquan" and the peak called "Shengquan Peak". As the way to "Shengquan" is dangerous what it is about still remains unveiled. However, if you stand on the neighboring peaks on a bright day or moonlit night, you can see the steaming spring water and probably you can smell the sweet smell it gives out.

Besides the four unique features, the waterfalls, the sight of sunrise and sunset are also beautiful scenes of Huangshan.

A brook will become a waterfall when rushing down from the mountain, falling down the steep cliff. The saying that "You can find waterfalls everywhere after a raining night" is very vivid for describing these waterfalls. Huangshan has many waterfalls. The most beautiful ones are "Nine-Dragon Fall" (Jiulongpu), "Renzi Fall" and "Baizhang Fall".

The peaks of Huangshan are quite high and Huangshan is not very far from the East Sea of China. You might be very impressed when you see the sun rise in the far east from the sea.

The sight of sunset is as grand as sunrise but gives visitors different feeling. It might remind you how time flies and it might be better to cherish what you have right now.

The differences between the four seasons in Huangshan are very conspicuous. The mountain is green and flowers can be seen everywhere in spring; there are waterfalls spotted here and there in summer; it is cool in autumn and then the mountain is colorful with red and yellow leaves; the mountain is covered with snow in winter. Whenever you come to Huangshan, you can see the beauty of nature. Huangshan is a very good place to visit.

Huangshan had already opened 8 scenic areas and over 400 scenic spots. There are four main routes to the top. Commonly the visitor will choose two routes; one is the 15km step route starting from the south foot of the mountain. Along this route, the visitor will pass by the Hot Spring and Midway Temple (Banshansi) to Jade

Selected Tour Commentaries

Screen Tower (Yupinglou), then pass the Lotus Peak to Beihai (North Sea). The other way starts from the other side of the mountain. The visitor can walk to Beihai or take the cable car first to White Goose Peak and then walk to Beihai. Now two other cable lines are being built. One is on the north way from "Songgu'an" to "Xihaisonglin Peak". Another is on the south way from "Ciguang Pavilion" to Jade Screen Tower (Yupinglou)". The visitor will feel more convenient after the cables are put into use.

Dear friends, what I have talked about is just a little portion of the real scenery and more will be introduced to you on the way to the top of the mountain. I can see everybody is eager to climb the mountain. Now let's start our tour to the marvelous mountain of China.

(Hot Spring Scenic Area)

This is the gate of Huangshan. There is a horizontal board inscribed with "Huangshan" written by General Chen Yi on the archway over the road. Now we're heading to the hot spring area in the north.

This is the hot spring of Huangshan Hotel. As I mentioned just now, the hot spring is the center of the whole area surrounded by the beautiful peaks. "Taohua (Peach Flower) Stream" and "Xiaoyao Stream" are crossing this area. The scenery contains the rich natural landscape and cultural heritage. About 100 famous tourist spots are in this area.

Please pay attention to the bridge in front of us. It is 25m high and over 100m long. It looks like a rainbow between the "Taohua Peak" and the "Zishi Peak". Let us step on the bridge. You can have a panoramic view of the Hot Spring area when you stand on the bridge. The building in the back of the "Taohua (Peach Flower) Peak" on upper-left side is called "Taoyuan Hotel". Taohua Peak is one of the 36 big peaks. The brook at the foot of the peak is called "Taohua Stream". It is the upper reaches of "Xiaoyao Stream". The oriental cherry is blooming luxuriantly. The stream will turn red

Mount Huangshan

when the oriental cherry and peach petals are floating on the water. That is the reason the peak and the stream are named so. There is a waterfall on Taohua Peak. The waterfall is flying down from the summit like a pearl curtain. The icefall in winter is another aspect of the beauty of the waterfall.

The red three-storey building with stone walls, red columns and upturned eaves in front of us is Huangshan Hotel. It was built in 1965 and is the oldest Hotel in Huangshan. The house in the upper side with green glazed tile is Huangshan Hot Spring Swimming Pool. It was built in 1956.

Now we are arriving at "Ming Stream Bridge". It is a stone bridge crossing the "Taohua Stream". The "Xiaobu Bridge" is over the upper part of the stream. Xiaobu Bridge was built in 1956 and destroyed by flood later. Xiaobu Bridge had a glorious time in history. In 1939, during the Anti-Japanese War, Vice Chairman of Military Commission of the Central Committee Zhou Enlai came to Huangshan to see the injured soldiers after he inspected the headquarters of the New Fourth Army at Maolin. During his stay at Huangshan, he, wearing military uniform, walked onto the Xiaobu Bridge and stood there for some time gazing into the distance. Yeting, the army commander took a photo for him then. Now the bridge is broken and the great man has passed away, but the historical photo left us eternal memory.

Now please pay attention to the characters "Da-hao-he-shan", inscribed on the broken ridges of granite. In English they mean "beautiful country". The characters are two diameters in width. Tang Shizun who was the general of KMT during the Anti-Japanese War wrote it. We can understand what he wanted to express at that historical time.

Across the Famous Spring Bridge, as we walk further we will step onto the Huilong Bridge. Please look to the left. The spring comes from the steer cliffs which are separated by bulgy rocks into two groups. The separated spring looks like a Chinese character

169

Selected Tour Commentaries

"ren" (human being). The right and left lines of water look like two vigorous strokes in Chinese handwriting. This is the "Renzi Waterfall".

Passing through the "Huilong Bridge" and turning to left, we will reach the "White Dragon Bridge". There is a huge stone in shape of a dragon's head on the east bank of the bridge on which Zhuang Wenshu's handwriting "listen to the dragon's chant" is inscribed. Mr. Zhuang wrote it in 1944. What is the meaning of the inscribed characters? Now let me paraphrase these characters: The river has risen up after the big rain. It looks like a white dragon dancing. The roar of the river seems to be the dragon's chant. That is the meaning of the characters. Now we are walking along the "Haohua Stream" to the upper reach. You can see a few strange stones in the stream. The famous Chinese geologist Li Siguang said that the strange stones are things left behind by the fourth glacier period. Look at the two characters "Dan Jing" on the stone. They were written by Wang Daokun, a high-ranking official of Ministry of Defense of the Ming Dynasty.

Let's look at the huge stone by the road. It looks like a tiger crouching forward proudly with glaring eyes. This is the Tiger-head Rock. The three Chinese characters inscribed on the rock were written by Luo Yuan in the South Song Dynasty.

Here is the "Cascade over Three Terraces". You can see the water falling from the top of the mountain and flowing over three bulge rocks. Let go ahead. Look at the rock at the right hand side. It looks like a person sitting on the rock. The rock near it looks like a toad. The combined scenery of the sitting person and the toad resembles a scene of a legendary story of the ancient time. The stream in front of the rock is called "Musical Stream". Why do we give it such a name? You can see the brook rushing down the cliff splashes upon a rock. The rock is hollow inside and it sounds like playing the instrument.

The stone near "Musical Stream" is called "drunken stone". The

Mount Huangshan

spring on the left of "Musical Stream" is called "Cup-Washing Spring". It is said that the famous poet Li Bai of the Tang Dynasty had once stayed here. He drank wine while listening to the rock music. As he washed his cup in this spring, hence the name. "Musical Stream" and "Cup-Washing Spring" are said to be Li Bai's handwriting. It is a precious heritage. Luo Yuanzhang of the Ming Dynasty wrote "drunk stone".

(Passing through the "Musical Stream")

Here is the "Sword-Testing Stone". You can see the rock inscribed with the characters "Sword-Testing Stone" is composed of two parts. It looks like that the rock is cleaved into two by the sword. It seems as if a chivalrous expert swordsman had tested his sword here.

Let's go to visit the "Ciguang Pavilion".

"Ciguang Pavilion" is on the north borderline of the Hot Spring Resort. It is at the foot of "Zhusha Peak" with mountains and bamboo surrounding it. Ciguang Pavilion was a famous nunnery of the south of the Yangtze River. Its original name is "Ciguang Temple. Shi Tao, an outstanding contemporary painter of Chinese traditional painting and the expert of "Xin'an" school of painting of Zhejiang had lived here. Mr. Dong Biwu, a former state leader, wrote the characters Ciguang Pavilion in 1965. Now Ciguang Pavilion has become a museum and exhibition center of Huangshan. The statue of Xu Xiake stands in front of the hall. On the interior walls of the hall there are lots of handwritings by contemporary celebrities of letters.

Now let us go inside and have a look.

[Yungusi (Cloudy Valley Temple) Scenic Area]

Thanks to the cable car it was much easier for us to get here. This is the east part of Huangshan scenic area. What we do here is to enjoy the beautiful lanscape of the Yungusi Scenic Area. The most appealing part of the scenery is from the Yungu Mountain Resort up to the spot of "Immortal Pointing out the Direction (Xianrenzhilu)"

Selected Tour Commentaries

or "Xiquedengmei" in the Chengxiangyuan Valley. The scenery is beautiful and the transportation is convenient. It is the main road up and down the mountain.

Yungusi, namely Cloudy Valley Temple, does not exist any more. When we say it we refer to the place where the temple was once located. The Yungusi site is in an open valley. The valley was formerly called "Zhiboyuan", because it lies at the foot of the Zhibo (Alms Bowl) Peak. A person named Cheng Yuanfeng of the Song Dynasty studied here when he was young. Later he became the Prime Minister. He loved this place so much that when he got old he came here to live a hermit's life. Therefore, the valley's name was changed to "Chengxiangyuan (Prime Minister's Valley). Please look at the huge stone on that peak. It looks like a monk's bowl placed upside down on the peak. It is said that there was an unusual monk throwing a huge bowl on the peak. Therefore, the peak got the name of "Zhibo Peak" or "Alms Bowl Peak". During the Ming dynasty, a senior monk called Yu An built a temple here and named it Zhibo Temple. Later in the same dynasty, a person from She County named Fu Yan wrote two characters "Yun Gu" to describe the cloudy scenery here. And then people began to call it "Yungusi (Cloudy Valley Temple)". But unfortunately the temple was destroyed by fire later. The only thing left was the foundation of the temple. Now the restaurant was built right on the foundation of the temple.

Now please look at the peak in the east. The peak is called "Arhat Peak". The pines on that peak are different from others. They are as giant as arhats. Therefore, we called the pine "podocarpus" and the peak as "Arhat Peak". The peak in the southeast looks like a big incense burner. There are always clouds on the peak like the smoke from the burner. Therefore, we called the peak "Incense Burner Peak".

Look! The huge stone beside the road about 400m away from the Incense Burner Peak is called "Immortal List (Xianrenbang)". The inscription of "Immortal List" is a little faint now. However,

172

the characters below are much clearer. The inscription says if you pass by the Immortal List, you have predestined relationship with the Buddha and your name will be kept on the Immortal List as well. Certainly, it is just a saying of Buddhism.

There are three old trees worth taking a look at.

The tree beside the road is called sago cycas of south China or black sago cycas. It is over 800 years old. It is unusual because there is a mulberry grown inside it. The leaves of the mulberry are like that of yew podocarpus and the fruit of the tree is red. There is another unusual tree which is on the right side behind the restaurant. It is more than 500 years old. It is a rare tree called "East China Douglas fir". The ancient people also called it "yiluo pine". Beside the Douglas fir, there was a ginkgo of more than a thousand years which is a species of the Mesozoic left only in China. It is called "a living plant fossil". These three trees are called "three treasure trees".

The stone road to the Yungu Resort is lined with a lot of stone carvings. The inscriptions are very poetic. The first inscription is "Jianrujiajing" meaning "going forward and gradually seeing the beautiful scenery". The second inscription is "Huishoubaiyundi". It means if you look back here, you will find out the clouds are below. It is the true portrayal of the scenery here on a cloudy day. Besides these two, there are also such inscriptions as "Wonderful Attractions Starting Here" (Miaocongcishi), "A Drunkard's Chant" (Zuiyin), etc. Look at these two characters which means "To the secluded and delightful place (tong yu)". I think it describes exactly what we are doing now.

Yungu Mountain Resort is a hotel with eastern style exterior and western style interior. The outside decorated with blue tiles, white gable, square courtyard, red-lacquered doors and lions in front of the gate. The whole building makes of the momentum, dotted with green pines and cypresses, mixed together with the surroundings. It is the typical style of Anhui province. Now let us enjoy the inscriptions of Huizhou prefecture one by one: A lion stands in front of the

Selected Tour Commentaries

gate. The two columns of the hall are antithetical couplet in bamboo. The front wall inlay with stick "the lucky place in the cloud (yunzhongfudi)". The wood decorates the vertical of the main stages. The inscription skill is terrific.

On the West Side of cloud valley villa, there is a stone monk tower called "baian monk tower". Baian's local name is Xiongkaiyuan. He was a "jinshi" and thrown to prison for his unpleasant suggestion to the emperor. When he got out the prison, the Ming Dynasty had perished. Then he came to cloud valley villa and became a monk. And was buried here after his death. The tower is the monument to him. It is a well-preserved tower of Huangshan.

From cloud valley villa to the summit, you can go there on foot or by cable car. The distance from cloud valley villa to white goose ridge is 2804m. It is the longest double track circled cable car in Asia. It takes 8 minutes for going up and down. Another project of cable car will become the longest one after the whole program have been completed. The length will be 3562m from "songgu nunnery" to "songlin peak". Now let us get on the cable car. It seems that we are standing on a floating view stage. We can enjoy the distance view from the cable car. That is the "fuozhang peak". That is "xiquedengzhi". The "Fairy in boat (xianrenfanzhou)" and "wulaodangchuan" are over there... The eyes are too busy in seeing these things. What do you feel now? I am sure you must feel terrific. I myself feel wonderful.

(Beihai scenic spot)

Reaching the ridge of White Goose, we are arriving at the Beihai scenic spot. Beihai scenic spot lies on the central of Huangshan scenery area. Beihai scenic spot includes Bright Summit Peak (guangmingding) in the south, Cool Stage (qingliangtai) in the north, Start to believe peak (shixinfeng) in the east and flying rock in the west, and the rest between the four areas. Beihai scenic spot is the most attractive place of Huangshan and the tourist will even be

Mount Huangshan

unwilling to return home.

To the west of the white goose ridge, We will have a T-shaped road junction. Looking at the right hand, you will find a small and exquisite peak, which looks firm but gentle. This special characteristic makes it one of the four famous peaks of Huangshan. The name of "shixin feng" has a very interesting story. It is said there was a person coming to visit Huangshan. Passing through the cloud valley villa, he arrived at "shixinfeng". At the first sight of the peak, he thought he was in dreamland. He started to believe that the Huangshang was beautiful. So he wrote an antithetical couplet. The content was as follows: I heard of the beauty of Huangshan. However, I do not believe in. Now I came here myself, I believe that the Huangshan was beautiful. The name of "start to believe peak" started to be used at that time.

Gnarled pines are one of the four unique features of Huangshan. The pines at "start to believe peak" are the most wonderful part. An old saying exactly expressed the attractive features of the pines: You can not see the really Huangshan pines if you do not climb on the start to believe peak. Now let go to the peak to have a look at the beautiful pines.

This is "black tiger pine" (heihusong). It is the one of the nine famous pine of Huangshan. The pine is 15m high with the thick trunk 0. 65m in diameter. Nobody knows the age of the pine or where the name comes from. It is said there was a monk passing through the pine. He found there was a black tiger lying on the top of the pine. Suddenly the tiger disappeared. So the pine got a name "black tiger pine".

Now let us have a look at this pine beside the road. Two meters above the ground, the tree divided itself into two big trunks. This is a silk tree with a lovely name given by local people, i. e. "join together pine". It is a love poem. The pine has grown on the granite for 600 years. Many people in love would like to take photos with the pines to pray for the unchanged love.

Selected Tour Commentaries

This pine is called "dragon claw pine". The main root extends deeply to the earth and the other five-branch root exposed outside. It looks like the claw of the dragon.

"Jieyin pine" leads us to pass the "Duxian Bridge". Now we are arriving at the summit of the "start to believe peak". This is a single peak bulge on the granite, with three sides bordering on the sky. In the east, it is dotted with stalagmite in peaks. Looking to the west, you can see the delighted stone scattering all over the place; Look down at the peak, you can find "wulong pine" on the peak side and "tanhai pine" on the cliff. There are some young pines looking like the down ball hiding on the rift or hanging on the cliff. It is very interesting.

"start to believe peak" has attracted a lot of people through its scenery from Ming Dynasty till now. People wrote many poems to praise the peak. On July 13, 1979, Mr. Deng Xiaoping visited the peak. He could not help saying, "good, good" and lingered there for a long time. This was the highest praise that the peak had ever received. It is the honor for the peak of Huangshan.

Going down the peak to the west, we are arriving at "san-huawu". Beihai is the central scenery of Huangshan. All flowers are waving for beauty in full bloom in spring at "start to believe peak", "xianren peak", and "shangsheng peak" are the source of "san-huawu". In addition, we can see many strange stones here.

Look, there is a stone pillar standing upright on the top of the peak. It is shaped like a writing brush with tip at upside and with a round bottom. This is one of the small peaks of 36 called "pen peak". You can see there is a young pine in the tip of the pen like a flower. Also a stone on the foot of the peak looks like a sleep person in sweet dream. So people give the name to the young pine and the sleep man as "mengbishenghua".

In the past time, the scholar always put the writing brush and the pen-holder together on the desk. Here we also can see the "pen-holder". Let us look at the right of the "menbishenghua". There is a

Mount Huangshan

towering crag with five branches. It shapes like a pen-holder. There were a writing brush and a pen-holder at the same place. It is very interesting.

Let us have a look at the right part between the "start to believe peak" and "stalagmite peak". There is a pine with flat crown. The crown looks like the chessboard. There are two wonderful stones on each side of the pine. The stones look like two elder men. The pine and the stone tell us that two elder men are playing chess. So we give the pine and the stone a name "xianrenxiaqi". On the right side of "xianrenxiaqi", there was a "man" walking slowly with a "basket" on the back. We call the stone "xianrencaiyao". On the right side of "xianrenxiaqi", There is a stone looking like the ancient official. We call it " the Prime Minister looking at the chess game".

Now we are arriving at the first stage of Hunagshan "cool stage" (qingliangtai). This is the best place to see the sunrise and the rolling clouds. Sometimes the visitors can see the "rays of Buddha". Actually, it is the sun's refraction and diffraction. Now we will be back to Beihai hotel to have a good rest. Tomorrow morning we will come here again to see the sunrise. Maybe we can see the rays of the Buddha.

We will continue our tour to other places after the exciting sunrise.

Now we are standing on the "cool top" (qingliangding). Let us look to the north in front of the "lion peak". There is a stone that looks like a monkey squatting on the kneel. It has two names because of the different scenery. When there are a lot of clouds around the peak, the monkey seems to be looking at the rolling clouds. So we call it "monkey looking at the Clouds Sea". The scenery of the bright is totally different. The monkey seems to be gazing at the beauty scenery of "safety town" (taiping xian). This time we call it " monkey looking at the safety town". There is a much moved love story about the monkey. I can not tell you today because of the short time. Let us go forward.

Selected Tour Commentaries

Oh, my friend. Please look at the pine named Unity Pines. Why do we give it this name? Ok, everybody please count the twigs of the pine. How many pines are there? Yes. There are just 56 twigs. China is made up by 56 nationalities. The pine stands for the unity of the nation. Also it reflects the wishes that the whole nation can work together for a better future. Go alone this road; we arrive at the "danxiafeng". The peak is always bathed in the red rays of evening sunshine. It is the ideal place to enjoy the sight of sunset and sunrise.

My friend, we are arriving at the "paiyun pavilion". This pavilion was built in 1935 and sits on the gate of Xihai. The mist of Xihai stops by the pavilion and can never go through the pavilion. So we call it "paiyunting". You can enjoy the sight of setting sun and the scenery in the deep Xihai valley.

There are many peculiar rocks here. Someone call here the museum of the peculiar rocks. Look, the rocks near us look like half-high-rain boots hanging on the cliff upside down. The rock called "xianrenshaixue". Let us see the stone column on gully of the right, two rocks like the slope shoes are called "xianrenshaixie". Sometimes visitors are kidding that the fairy is fastidious about his shoes.

Let us see the rocks and pines on the side of "stone bed peak". It looks like a woman doing embroidery. So we called the rock "fairy embroider the flower". Beside "fairy embroider the flower ", there are two rocks on the top of the right peak. It looks like two fairy playing the instrument. So we called the rock "fairy playing the instrument". On the right down side, there are two rocks. It looks like two person are listening to the music. One is sitting and the other is standing. We called the rocks "two immortal listen to the music". On the side of "immortal playing the music", another rock looks like a dog facing the immortal. The "dog" seems to be listening to the music as well. So we called the rock " the dog from the heaven listen to the music". It seems that the immortal is holding a show with a lot of audience. The embroidery fairy lady must be one of the audi-

Mount Huangshan

ences.

There are too much peculiar rocks here. We can not introduce them one by one. Let us go forward for some other wonderful sight.

Now we are arriving at the famous rock "flying rock". You can come near the rock and touch it. The flying rock is in rectangular parallelepiped column shape. It stands tall and upright on the East Side of "tianhaipingtiangang". If you look at its north side from upper side of south from far away, you will find that the rock looks like a huge peach. The peak has a pointed end and a round bottom. So someone calls it "peach rock" or "peach peak". It is 7m width, 1.5-2.5m thick, 15m high and 544 tons in weight. The link surface is very small between the flying rock and the foundation. It seems that the rock flies here from somewhere else. So we called it "flying rock". There is a tourist of Ming Dynasty named Chenyuheng. He was astonished by the flying rock and left a poem like these. Oh. Flying rock. I come to visit the peak. But I dare not to climb to the summit. Because I know, you are flying from somewhere else. I am afraid to startle you. You will fly to somewhere again. It is really a very interesting poem. Where the rock comes from has confused many people for years.

I think some of you may see TV play ＜Dream of the Red Mansion＞. The huge stone of the stage photo for the title is this rock. Why did the director choose the flying rock? It has a very long story. Long time ago, the sky was destroyed. There were some holes on the sky. Nuwa, a female immortal, melt the stone to mend the sky. There was two stones left after the sky was mended. One of the stone fell into the barren mountain named "qinggeng peak". The other fell into Huangshan. It was the flying rock. The stone at the barren mountain reincarnated to Jia family and became Jia Baoyu. You may still remember when Jia Baoyu was born, there was a jade in his mouth. And the stone accompanied Jiaboyu for a whole life. Mr. Cao Xueqin changed part of the tale and wrote in his story and published a famous book with the "true and false" as a main idea.

179

Selected Tour Commentaries

Maybe the director did not find the stone in the barren mountain. So he used the flying stone instead. It is not a big matter because the two stones are twins. And the flying stone gets more popular in the world because of the TV play. Actually, the flying mountain is formed because of the influence of climate, wind, rain and gravitational collapse. Some rocks peel off from the stone. The link between the foundation and the flying rock became thinner. Now its looks like an independent rock from the foundation.

There was two Chinese characters "picturesque scene (huajing)" written on the flying rock. Let us stand beside the flying rock. You can find the pines dotted with peculiar rocks surrounded with clouds. It's really like a fairyland.

My friend, the peak in front of us is Bright Summit Mountaintop. This friend asks me, " The Bright Summit Mountaintop is the second top peak of Huangshan. Why you called it mountaintop not peak." Let me explain it to you at length. Bright Summit Mountain is the neighbor to the "liandan peak". It is one part of the "liandan peak". < Huangshan direction > was published in 1929 and separated Bright Summit from "liandan peak". At that time, 36 big peaks and 36 small peaks had already been named. So the Bright Summit Mountain top was isolated from the other 72 peaks. The name of mountaintop is from a temple. A monk of Ming Dynasty built a temple named "dabei courtyard" or "dabei mountaintop". Also the top of the mountain is very smooth covering 6 hectares. The mountaintop is fully bathed in sunshine. So it was named "Bright Summit Mountaintop". Now the "dabei courtyard" has already disappeared. A weather station had been built there. This is the highest station of East China.

Now everybody has known the reasons of Bright Summit Mountaintop. Let us go to the top to have a look.

Now we are on the top of the Bright Summit Mountaintop. It is a place with sunshine and a wide field to have a pleasant sight. Please look at the right side, the farthest peak is Heavenly Capital Peak. It is the most dangerous peak of Huangshan. The ancient people thought it was the capital of the fairy. So they called it Heavenly Capital Peak. The peak is a little bit nearer to us than the Heavenly Capital Peak, which is called Lotus Flower Peak. It was the highest peak of Huangshan. It is surrounded by many peaks. It seems like a bloom lotus surrounded by leaves. Another peak between the Heavenly Capital Peak and the Lotus Flower Peak is called "yuping Peak". The building with yellow wall red roof is yuping building. We will visit that peak after a while. Now let us have a look at that peak. It looks like huge soft-shelled turtle facing to the left and tale pointing to the right. There is a stone on the peak. It looks like a tortoise. It is the scenery combined by the rock and the peak. We call it " soft-shelled turtle backing the tortoise". The scenery on our foot belongs to tianhai. It is a developing area.

(Jade Screen Tower scenic spot (Yupinglou))

Jade Screen Tower is the center of the Jade Screen tower scenic spot. It starts from Mid-level temple in the south to the lotus flower peak in the north and runs from Heavenly Capital Peak in the east to Rongchen Peak in the west. Commonly the peaks rise above 1700m of the scenic area. Depth of the valley reaches 1000m. Beside Bright Summit Peak, the other two peaks; Lotus Flower Peak and Heavenly Capital Peak are in this area. The marshal Mr. Chenyi had ever given a brilliant summarized of Huangshan. His common was "the front mountain is grand and the back mountain is pretty." Jade Screen tower shows the grand.

There are two roads to Jade screen tower. One leads to the front mountain, and visitors can enter tower directly after visiting hot spring; the other leads to the back mountain, visitors can visit the cloud valley temple and beihai scenic spot, then to tower. We will go along the road of Back Mountain.

Now we have come down the Bright Summit Mountaintop and arrived at the foot of soft-shelled turtle peak. There is a triangle

Selected Tour Commentaries

grotto with 10m long in front of us. This is soft-shelled turtle hole. Pass through the hole, we are arriving at the bottom of the valley. The scaling ladder with over 100 stone steps in front of us. Let us climb the step in a hurry to see the tortoise and the snake. It is not the really thing but two stones on each side of the end of the steps. This is "tortoise and snake guard the entrance". Let us say hello to them.

After passing the scaling ladder, we are arriving at the highest peak of Huangshan. There is a distance of 1km or 2km from Lotus Flower range to the peak. The road is called Lotus Flower stalk. There are a lot of pines and azalea on both sides of the road. There are four holes to the peak. Now we are arriving at the peak. The peak is 5m in diameter and is round in shape. People call it "stone ship". It has enclosed by stone column and iron fence. There is a concave in the surface of the stage full of water. It is called "xiangsha pool". Now let us look at the distance far away from us. You can feel that every thing is small and you are a man of gigantic stature.

Going down from Lotus Flower Peak, we arrive at Yama cliff. Why do we call it Yama cliff? Because in the past, people feared climbing the mountain. Now things have changed, there are new ways for climbing the mountain. Several meters far from the end of the steps, we can find an unordinary old pine. Nobody knows its ages. It always keeps one meter high. The twig spread all around. The crown is flat. It looks like cattail hassock. So we call it Cattail Hassock Pine. Also it looks like a round table. It can provide enough space for ten people have lunch together. There is a stone behind the pine. It looks like a hawk. The combined scenery of the "hawk" and "cattail hassock" are called "hawk guard the cattail hassock". Passing through the pine, we are arriving at the Jade Screen Tower.

Jade Screen Tower Hotel is a famous mountain hotel. It was built in front of Jade Screen peak at 1716m high. The former name of Jade Screen Tower is "wenshu study". It is a famous temple of Huangshan. It was built on Ming Dynasty. It is rebuild several times

182

Mount Huangshan

because of the fire. Now let us have a look around the tower. On the cliff of Jade Screen peak behind the tower inscribe the handwriting of Chairmen Mao: "the land is so rich in beauty". On the cliff of East tower inscribe the handwriting of Zhude, the commander in chief: "the landscape like the beautiful painting." There is a lion stele inscribes a poem to memorize the anti-Japanese war by the general Liu Bocheng.

I know you must be familiar with the pine on the left side of Jade Screen tower. Yes, it is the Welcome Guest pine. The pine is thousands of years old. However, it is still energetic to welcome the guest from all over the world.

Now we are standing in front of the Jade Screen Tower. You can see Heavenly Capital Peak on your left side and the Lotus Flower Peak on your right side. You are surrounding by the beautiful pine and peculiar rock. That is terrific. It is very easy to understand why the famous traveler praised this place as " the best place of Huangshan".

Now we are going down from Jade Screen Tower and will arrive at "wenshu hole" in few minutes. The hole is in the intersection of the two peaks. It seems that we are at the end of the road. After entering the hole, we go along with the spiral steps and arrive at "penglai three island". The three peaks with different height look like the remote island of the sea especially when the rolling sea of clouds comes.

The thrilling scenery in front of us is called "a ray of sky". This place is 50m deep, 25m high. The widest place is 2.2m in width. The narrowest place is less than half a meter. A people can go through sideways. The road has many bends. Now let us go inside to have a try. Now we are arriving at the bottom of the gully. We can not see the sun but a ray of sky. A poet of the Qing Dynasty wrote down a poem like this: A stone in the sky has a little rift. The sun can never be seen in the rift.

Passing through the ray of sky, crossing the Duxian Bridge, go-

Selected Tour Commentaries

ing through the wosong gully, we are in front of the cattail hassock rock. There is a big valley on the right side of us and a cliff on the left. The peak in front of us is Heavenly Capital Peak. On each side of the air ladder, there are two peculiar rocks. One looks like ancient maid. The other looks like a groveling boy. These two rocks called "boy Kowtow to Guanyin".

Now we will take a walk by "Heaven ladder (Tianti)". Heaven ladder means the steps to the heaven. It is a very dangerous road. Everyone must place one hand carefully on the chain railing or the stone column. We are going up step by step. Now the most dangerous part has been finished. We are arriving at the Jade Screen on Heaven. Let us go forward. There is a huge stone overhead on the two mountains. That is "Hunchback".

Hunchback is the most dangerous steep to Heavenly Capital Peak. It is 20m long and 1-2m wide. The narrowest part is less than 1m. There is no earth on the road. There is an abyss under it. And there is a rift about 0.3m in width in the middle of the road. A manmade bridge connects it. The stone column and the iron link were installed on the side of the road. So it is safe for you to go through the road. If the rolling clouds cover the road, another scenery will appear. It seems that you are standing on the back of the hunch and the hunch is swimming on the surface of the sea. You can see many locks on the chain railings by lovers, symbolizing that they are locked together. Usually they throw the key into the abyss.

Passing through the Hunchback and crossing three stone holes, you will be on the summit of Heavenly Capital Peak. It is dangerous to climb the Heavenly Capital Peak. But how can you enjoy the limitless wonderful sight if you can not reach the right place. The monk of Tang Dynasty was the first one in historical data who climbed on the summit of the peak. He left a poem to praise the wonderful sight and the dangerous road of the peak. Also the poem expresses his excitement. I think everyone must be very excited now.

Let us go down the peak through the new way to the Mid-level

Mount Huangshan

temple. Mid-level temple lies in the middle of the hot spring to Jade Screen Tower. The tourist who climbs or goes down the mountain can have a rest here and enjoy the sight. Let us look at the peculiar rock on the half way up to the Heavenly Capital Peak. It looks like a cock. The "cock" holds his head high to "Heaven Gate " and flap the wings singing. This is " golden cock call at the Heaven Gate". The cliff is inscribed with " cock sing on air".

Now we've come to "Lima Bridge" from Mid-level temple. Let us look at the north from the end of the bridge. There is a huge stone inscription on the cliff " li makongdonghai, denggaowang-taiping." General Tang wrote this Ten Chinese characters in 1939 during the anti-Japanese war. It took six months to stone inscription the ten characters on the cliff by six artisans. Each character is 6m in length. There is a distance of 5m between each character. The depth of the stone inscription character is 8cm. The whole length of the ten characters is over 100m and the width is over 30m. The vertical length of last character is 9.4m. The handwriting is beautiful with a tremendous momentum. This is the biggest, longest and powerful stone inscription of Huangshan.

The stone inscription has its profound implication. " lima " means "lima peak", but the connotative meaning is resisting to force; "donghai" means the East Sea, but the connotative meaning stands for the Japanese militarist; "taiping" means "taiping town", the connotative meaning is the peaceful world; "Kong" shows the determination of defeating the enemy; "Wang" shows all the people looking forward to peace. This huge stone inscriptiond cliff is not only a beautiful sight, but also shows the heroic spirit of Chinese. It shows the awe-inspiring righteousness.

My friend, we have visited Hot Spring Scenic Spot, Cloud Valley Scenic Spot, Beihai Scenic Spot and Jade Screen Scenic Spot. These are the four main spots of Huangshan. We climbed up the four famous peaks and saw a lot of peculiar rock and pines. We took the bath on the Hot Spring. Especially we saw the sun rise on "cool

185

Selected Tour Commentaries

stage". All of us are very excited about the whole visiting. One thing we feel regretful is the clouds. The past two days were sunny and we had no chance to enjoy the rolling sea of clouds. Do not worry, we have some other programs to finish, maybe we will have chance later. Some friends told me that it is not enough to visit here just once. It is true. If you come here again, you have more chances to enjoy the beautiful scenes. Tomorrow I will accompany you to visit "Fishing bridge nunnery", " White cloud brook" and "Pine valley nunnery". Now I will give you a brief introduction about the spot.

The picture hanging on the wall is the scenic spot of Huangshan. This part is "Fishing Bridge nunnery". It lies in the southwest of the Huangshan scenic spot. The area starts from "Xuguo Bridge" in the south to "Funu Ridge" in the north, and from "Yunmen peak" in the east and "Shuanghei" in the west. The fishing bridge nunnery is the center of the spot. Yunmen brook of east nunnery and Yuhua brook of the east nunnery are on the way of the spot. Fishing bridge nunnery lies at the foot of the "Stone person peak" and the intersection of the "White cloud brook" and "Cloud gate brook". The former name is "White cloud nunnery". There was a bridge near the nunnery. Some tourists and monk in ancient times always fished there while enjoying the sight seeing on the bridge. Therefore, the name was changed to "Fishing Bridge nunnery". There are tier upon tier of green bamboo, ample in old and strong pines. The road from the West connects a bridge and there is a limpid river under it. The scenery is beautiful.

There is a tea garden here. The famous tea here is called "Huangshan maofeng". It grows up in the deep high mountain and has the best quality. It is popular both at home and abroad.

Now let us have a look at the gorge on the West Side of Huangshan. It starts from the east Tianhaihaixin pavilion to west Diaoqiao nunnery. It's called west sea gorge. The pavilion lies at the altitude of 1600m and the Diaoqiao nunnery at 600m. There is a distance of 1000m between them and the cloud rivulet fills the whole abyss be-

186

Mount Huangshan

tween them. This area is known as cloud rivulet area opened in 1988. The roads on it conform to the appearance of the mountain and there are 10 view stages on it. You can see many scenery here, such as "Fairy party (Qunxianjunhui)", "go west for Bible (Xitianquejing)", "Penglai mountain", "Juxian bridge", "Dongpo make poem (dongpoyinshi)" and "the fall on the end of river (Hekoufeipu)" etc and the beautiful scenery of the west sea peak. People call here "beauty in heaven (Yaotaishengdi)".

Let us have a look at the upper part of the scenery map. This is the north part of Huangshan where the Cloud valley nunnery is located. There are two major scenes in this area. One is the peculiar rock of north at the South Sea. The other is waterscape along cloud valley brook around the cloud valley nunnery.

The difference in the height between cool stage and the cloud valley nunnery is more than 1000m. Walking along the gorge of Lion hill, Camel hill, Bookcase hill and Pagoda hill, you can see many wonderful scenes. For example, "swan incubation", "xiaomengbishenghua", "three god statues", "Guangong defeating Mr. Cao", "Fairy seeing the list" and "Taibai getting drunk" and so on.

Songgu Nunnery lies on the bottom of the Diezhangfeng and near Songgu Rivulet. It was built in Song Dynasty, and there were many scenic spots around it.

From the south of "pine valley nunnery" to go down the mountain, we can see pines, brooks, "five dragon pond" and "jadeite pool". Standing on the Lotus ridge to look at the north area, you can see the open grassland, small villages and a high building of "gantang" town in distance.

Pine valley nunnery holds a collection of all the beauty of the back mountain, such as the graceful peak, the peculiar of the pond and the luxuriant grass, etc. It is an attractive place for tourists....

Jadeite valley lies in the east of Huangshan scenic spot. It is the spot of the new scenery called "donghai new scenic spot". It lies at the foot of "fairy capital peak". You can see the direction from the

Selected Tour Commentaries

map. This is a deep gorge. " green jade brook" is rushing through the gorge. There are many colorful ponds spread on the brook. The color of the riverbed, the brook and the granite on the cliff add radiance and beauty to each other. The visitors who has ever come here will praised the place as the No. one brook under the sun. This area has become a new scenic spot. Maybe we can go to see the new spot right now to make our trip perfect.

GUYAO — A PORCELAIN FACTORY IN JINGDEZHEN

Ladies and gentlemen,

as you know, porcelain is a daily necessity of our life. I am sure you have seen various kinds of porcelain. Then do you know how it is made? Since we are already here in Jingdezhen, it is convenient for us to get the answer. Today we are going to visit Guyao (meaning an old porcelain kiln) porcelain factory. Where was the name Guyao derived from? I will explain this to you when we arrive there. Now I will give you a brief introduction to porcelain while we are on our way to the factory.

An old Chinese saying goes like this: "People regard food as important as the heaven." As we need containers to hold food, the making of porcelain is closely linked to the subsistence of human beings. In primitive society, lightening often caused big forest fires. The soil became hardened when burned by the fire. Enlightened by this phenomenon, people mixed clay with water and applied this mixture to the basket. This waterproof utensil was the earliest pottery. These utensils were used to hold water, rice and food. The invention of pottery was a major step forward in the history of human civilization. It was realized as early as five to six thousand years ago in China. Later, porcelain was gradually invented on the basis of pottery. Compared with pottery, porcelain is smoother, finer and harder. Porcelain is made of porcelain ore at a heating of 1300 de-

Selected Tour Commentaries

grees centigrade, while pottery is generally made of clay at a heating of lower than 1000 degrees centigrade.

Porcelain is one of the great inventions of the Chinese people as early as in the mid-Shang Dynasty (16th century B.C). While making white pottery and decorative pottery, the Chinese working people improved the quality of the raw materials and the craft, intensified the heating temperature, and invented the earliest porcelain. It is said that when Chinese porcelain wares were first exported to Europe, people marveled at this fantastic and hard ware. They did not know what they were and what they were called. The only thing they know was that they came from China. So they were named "CHINA" That is why "China" has dual meanings in English.

While visiting Jingdezhen in 1965, Mr. Guo Moruo wrote down a poem. The first two lines of which read, "China is a country of porcelain, Jingdezhen represents the zenith of porcelain craft." Jingdezhen is world famous for producing porcelain and has thus won the name of "the Capital of Porcelain." This city was called Xinping in ancient times. According to historical documents, the makings of pottery began in the Han Dynasty in Xinping, which was over 1,700 years from now. Actually the name Jingdezhen was also derived from the trade of Porcelain-making. Toward the Song Dynasty, the porcelain industry in Jingdezhen had become rather prosperous. Yingqing Porcelain (a kind of porcelain) was a major invention of that time and was of great significance. During the Jingde Period (1004-1007) of the Northern Song Dynasty, Emperor Zhao Hen took a fancy to this porcelain-making place and ordered the craftsmen here to make porcelain for the imperial court. These skillful craftsmen worked very carefully and presented the chinaware to the court. Written on these utensils were "Made in Jingde Period". Since then, people all over the country called these porcelains "Jingde porcelain". Following this, the court named the city "Jingdezhen." Of course today the city is much larger as it has become a medium-sized city with a population of over a million. In 1953, Jingdezhen became a city directly

Guyao — A Porcelain Factory in Jingdezhen

under the administration of the province. While discussing the name of the city, some people suggested the name "Jingde city" (Because "zhen" in Chinese means "town"); however, as the name "Jingdezhen" was historically known and had gained worldwide fame, it was hard to separate it apart. At last, "Jingdezhen" was adopted.

Over more than 1,000 years, the craft of porcelain making was handed down from one generation to another and new inventions emerged one after another as well. For example, a new formula for making porcelain was initiated in the late Southern Song Dynasty. This formula mixed porcelain ore and Kaolin. There were other representative porcelain products in the dynasties of Yuan, Ming, and Qing respectively. After years of perfection, Jingdezhen porcelain has established itself with unique features. Now we have come to the Guyao Porcelain Factory. Please allow me to give further introduction to Jingdezhen porcelain during our visits later.

Ladies and gentlemen, we are now coming to the Panlonggang (Dragon Hill) of the Western District. Look at these ancient buildings in the shades of trees, it is the Guyao Porcelain Factory that we are going to visit. Porcelain factories, especially modern ones, are not rarely seen in China and even in the world. However, this porcelain factory in our view is absolutely unique. This factory adopts the craft of the Ming and Qing Dynasties. Everything, including the craft, tools, workshops and kilns are all in ancient style and the products also imitate the ancient style. That's why it is called "An old Porcelain Kiln" (Guyao Porcelain Factory). Now let's visit the factory.

Maybe you have found that there are no noises from machines, no electric wires, even the road is paved by slabstone. Do you feel refreshed and far away from the clamor of modern cities? This factory was built in the early 1980s and occupies an area of over 40 hectares. The factory was built to preserve the traditional craft of porcelain making of the Ming and Qin dynasties and reproduce the

Selected Tour Commentaries

whole process of producing porcelain for the imperial court. At the same time the scattered mills and kilns of the Ming and Qing Dynasties could be protected. Following rigorous procedures, they were moved and rebuilt to set up this factory. Thus the important heritage of porcelain culture was preserved. After the factory was set up, production was carried out in an ancient pattern. It is also open to Chinese and foreign tourists and now it has become an attractive tourist sight. Now you can see four workshops in old style, they are called base shops. Each base shop occupies an area of about 600 square meters. They are almost the same in exterior and general layout. However, each produces different products and the craft and equipment are different, too. Now, please come into this base shop. The workers are busy working. You see it is the same as what it should be in ancient time. It is made up of four parts: the main shop, the warehouse, the clay shop and the interior yard. The main shop and the warehouse paralleled each other in the south and north; the clay shop is in the west and the rectangular interior yard is in the middle. Each part opens its door to the yard and they become a closed courtyard. There is enough sunshine and the building and the workers are integrated harmoniously with nature.

The main shop faces south and gets enough sunshine. The different procedures of making porcelain base are finished here. This is a winch, important equipment in making base. Look, they are put in clear order so that workers at different posts can cooperate very well. Look upward, and you can see the base framework. This wooden framework is for holding rows of semi-finished porcelain products. Thus the space of the main shop is fully utilized.

The warehouse is used to store raw materials. It is near the east door and it is convenient to bring in the materials. Now look at the clay shop. It is very cool here. The clay is exquisitely made and it feels even better than wheat dough. The workers are stamping on it. After that, it should be left there for a while before being made into base. Now who can tell me the reason for this? Yes, sir, you are

Guyao — A Porcelain Factory in Jingdezhen

right. This is to eradicate the air and organism in the clay, as they will affect the quality of the porcelain. The longer the clay remains, the better it is stamped, and the better quality the porcelain will have.

Now let's have a look at the interior yard. This place is used to dry the base. You can see a rectangular pool in the middle with the width and depth of about 2 meters. Above the pool there is a wooden framework. Together they are called sunning pond. As an important facility of the ancient porcelain factories, it is ingeniously designed. Any lady or gentleman can tell me why I say so? Yes, this lady, please. Thank you. As the pond is below and the frame above, it saves room. The water in pond is accumulated rainwater, which is necessary for washing the clay. Besides, behind this there is a further reason for it. We know that water can evaporate. The amount of e-vaporation varies with temperature and humidity. When the weather is hot and dry, the water in the pond evaporates quickly and thus making the area around the wooden frame more humid. This, to certain degree, can help to control how fast the base is dried. It is dries slowly, it shrinks evenly so that when it is finished after heat-ing, there should be no cracks in it. Most of the bases are finished by the winch. Look! That worker is sitting on it, rolling the winch quickly. The bases are made on it. During the course the rolling winch gradually slows down when it is too slow to work, the worker rolls it again. Thus the winch keeps on rolling with inertia and there is no trouble of machines' noises. This young worker is putting a ball of clay onto the winch. He cups his hands and a base of a bowl comes out. This is how a base is made. Bowls, vases, pots and jars are all made in the same way. We can see how skillful these workers are.

Look, this worker is rolling the winch carefully to make a base. When the base is dried to a certain degree, the worker will use knife and the winch to produce the required base. The base is put on the wood stake in the middle and the worker uses different knives to cut

Selected Tour Commentaries

the base according to the requirements. He seldom uses any measuring instruments to meet the requirements for exterior, height and width of the base. He only uses his eyes to observe, his hands to feel and his ears to listen. Then how to listen to the base? The worker flicks the base and judges the thickness of the base. At different places of the base the worker decides how to cut by judging the thickness through sound of the flick. With the excellent skill and the attentive work of the worker, a semi-finished perfect base comes into being. Of course, judging the thickness of the base by the sound of the flick is by no means a skill to be mastered overnight. Instead, it is out of years of accumulated experience. Tang Ying, a famous official in the Qing Dynasty in charge of porcelain production, once said, "The thickness of the base is controlled only by the skillful base-makers. So it is a crucial job".

Now these workers are painting pictures on the base with blue pigment. Cobalt oxide is the main material for the pigment. After the pictures are done the workers paint glaze onto the base. The bases can be heated in the kiln. The young women workers paint pictures with a special brush, thin and pointing. We can see their hands moving quickly and in about 10 seconds the base is covered with a colorful camellia flower.

From raw material to porcelain bases, the whole process is finished in a single base shop. What do you think of this unique way of porcelain making in Jingdezhen? Generally speaking, it is efficiently arranged and distributed. It is both practical and economical and easy to manage. It presents one of the best examples of processing assembly which combines function, structure and style harmoniously.

Then how does the base become porcelain? To find the answer, let's go to the kiln. The base is sent to the kiln to be fired under a temperature of over 1,300 degree Celsius.

Now in this unsophisticated room is the kiln. Please look at the chimney. It's not round in the top, but looks like the tip of a pen. Experts say that it is designed in this way so that the wind will not af-

Guyao — A Porcelain Factory in Jingdezhen

fect the normal function of the chimney.

The firewood kiln is also called (Jingde) Zhen kiln and it is the crucial equipment. It is fueled by pinewood. The kiln has been listed as one of the cultural relics. Here only the unique traditional porcelains are fired, it is especially suitable to fire colored and glazed porcelain. The length of the firewood kiln is around 18 meters; it is conical and looks like a half egg lying there. At the end of the kiln is a chimney with a height of 21 meters and a thickness of 80 to 90 millimeters. It is fairly strange that there is an angle of about 8 degrees between the chimney and the concrete. Yes, it helps to consolidate the chimney. As the crystallization of Jingdezhen's porcelain craft, the firewood kiln combines the technology of heat, mechanics and mechanics of materials. Besides, it is highly practical. It has a huge containing capacity of 8 to 15 tons of daily porcelain and can fire porcelain of various kinds. Taking colored and glazed porcelain for example, over 100 pieces with different colors can be fired at each time. It has high heating efficiency—for firing 1 kilogram of porcelain only 2 to 2.4 kilograms of pinewood is used.

Look at this peculiar kiln. The craftsmen skillfully use the bended wooden frame in order to make the kiln stronger. The second floor is used to store pinewood. Every square metre can hold a weight of one ton. It is said that a strong earthquake took place in the Ming Dynasty, causing a lot of houses collapsed. However, this one remained intact.

Now the kiln workers are about to fill the kiln with the containers of the porcelain base into the kiln according to certain order. About 20 workers are needed for each time to work with good order. It takes about 8 hours to fill the whole kiln. Then the door is shut closely and workers start firing for about 24 hours. Then they put out the fire to wait for another 24 hours to cool. Then a miscellaneous "collection" of porcelain is taken out of the kiln. It is a really exciting moment. Before firing the base is of one color, but after firing it becomes fairly colorful porcelain. It is a product of intelligence and

Selected Tour Commentaries

hard work. As we don't have enough time, it's a pity that we can not see this with our own eyes. I hope you can make up this next time when you have the opportunity to come again.

Since as much as 10 tons of porcelain can be fired in a single kiln, we can imagine how sophisticated the craft can be. However, since ancient times, no measuring instruments have been used. Till early 1960s, oil lamps were used to give out light. Experience, rational division of labor and skills are the only things to rely on to fire porcelain. There is a general director of technician called "Master of Bazhuang" who is the person in charge of the whole kiln. He is responsible for tackling all the difficult technical problems. When the baking process is about to end, it is of crucial importance to decide when to stop the fire. Overheating will result in the breaking of the base container and the porcelains will turn yellow. But if the duration and degree of heating are not enough it is no good either. Now everything depends on the eye of "Master of Bazhuang". He would look carefully at the color of the fire and spit on the fire to judge the right time. The instant change of the saliva helps him to make the judgement. There is something mysterious in terms of the firing work of the ancient kiln and there is no lacking in the legendary stories about the "Master of Bazhuang". Among the stories, the following one is the most widely spread.

This story tells about Tong Bin (a famous "Master of Bazhuang") in the reign of Wanli of the Ming Dynasty. He was not only versed in making porcelain but also wins respect for his personality. He was ordered by the imperial court to make a king-sized blue and white jar with the picture of a dragon on it. The difficulty lay not only in the size, but also in the high requirement. Not one stain could be allowed to appear on the surface, which could hardly be achieved. Tong Bin and his followers racked their brains but never succeeded. The deadline was impending and the imperial requirements should be satisfied otherwise the craftsmen and their family were endangered. Shouldering heaven responsibilities, Tong Bin

Guyao — A Porcelain Factory in Jingdezhen

sought for the last resort to save the lives of the craftsmen. At the crucial moment of firing, Tong Bin suddenly jumped into the fire as a sacrifice. Strange enough, this time they succeeded. People ascribed this success to Tong Bin. Later Tong Bin has been regarded as the guardian deity of the kiln. Later on, this deity is worshipped all the time in Jingdezhen.

I mentioned that this factory mainly produces traditional porcelain and imitations of ancient porcelain. Finally, let's have a look at the exhibits to get a general idea about Jingezhen porcelain.

What do you think of them? Isn't it a feast for the eye to see them? Coming to the features of Jingdezhen porcelain, people make a generalization like this, "white as jade, bright as mirror, thin as paper and sounds like bell." There are several kinds of porcelain that the natives here are most proud of.

Ladies and gentlemen, that's the end of our visit to the Guyao Porcelain Factory. A British expert who was specialized in the history of technology gave me his comments after his visit that "It made me feel as if I were back to the 16th century Jingdezhen. The workshops, firewood kilns, and the equipment all have cultural value. What's more significant, they follow an ancient procedure to make porcelain. So we can say that Guyao Porcelain Factory is a live porcelain museum in its true sense."

QUFU

My dear friends:

First of all, welcome to Qufu, the hometown of Confucius. Confucius had a famous remark: "Isn't it a pleasure to have friends from afar?" Today I am very glad to have an opportunity of making new friends and to be at your service as a tour guide. I'll be much obliged to you for your cooperation, and I am ready to take your timely advice on my service.

Before we start visiting the major scenic spots, I'd like to give you a brief introduction to Qufu and tell you something about Confucius.

Look at the inscribed stone tablet erected on the Southern bank of the moat outside the southern gate of the old city of the Ming Dynasty. Inscribed on it was "one of China's top historical and cultural cities". In the middle you will see "Qufu". These two characters were written by the late great leader Mao Zedong. His calligraphy is bold and vigorous, as we can see from here. Mao paid two visits to Qufu in his lifetime. The first visit was in March 1919 when he left Beijing for Shanghai and stopped at Qufu for an inspection. The second was on Oct. 28, 1952. During that tour, Mao visited the Temple of Confucius, Graveyard of Kong Family and some other cultural relics. As early as in 1938, Mao proposed that "we should summarize the history of cultural development from Confucius to Sun Yat-sen and inherit and carry on this valuable cultural heritage." You can al-

Qufu

so find a lot of quotations of Confucius's remarks and viewpoints in Mao's works and speeches.

Qufu lies in Southwest of Shandong Province. It has a total population of 620,000, including 100,000 urban residents. It covers an area of 890 km. "Qufu" made its first appearance in an ancient book "Er Ya". Ying Shao, a scholar in the Eastern Han Dynasty, explained in this way: there was a mound in the city of Lu. This mound wound its way for seven or eight li (some four km), and thus came the name "Qufu (Winding Mound)". In the fifth year of Emperor Songzhen, i. e., in 1012, Qufu was renamed "Xianyuan" county in memory of the ancestor of the Chinese nation Huangdi who was thought to be born in Qufu. In the 7th year of Emperor Jintai, that is, in 1129, it regained the current name to this day.

Small-sized as it is, Qufu is an old cultural city with a history of 5000-year civilization. It was on this sacred and old land that we could find the traces of four of the Three Emperors and the Five Sovereigns, legendary rulers of remote antiquity. As recorded in Records of the Historian and History of Emperors, "Huangdi was born in Shouqiu", "Shao Hao ascended the throne in Jiusang and made Qufu the capital; after his death, he was buried in Yunyang Mountain." There is a famous Chinese saying that goes like this: "Gifted Scholars are to be found in South of the River while Saints are to be found in North of the River." (north of the River—a region including parts of Jiangsu and Anhui which are north of the Yangtze; south of the River—a region in the lower Yangtze valley, including southern Jiangsu and Anhui and northern Zhejiang). Actually, nearly all saints in north of the River are from Qufu. During the feudal period, there were 6 saints who enjoyed favours bestowed by the emperors. They were Confucius, Mencius, Yanzi, Zisi, Zengzi and Zhougong. The first four of them were born in Qufu. One of the latter two was Confucius' disciple, and the manor of the other was also in Qufu. 33 descendants of Zhougong were once the Kings of the State of Lu. That is why standing Province is still called

199

Selected Tour Commentaries

Lu for short today. At present there are a multitude of cultural relics under and on the ground. It has 4 cultural sites listed at national level, 11 listed as provincial level and over 100 listed at municipal level. The year 1982 saw Qufu listed by the State Council as one of the first 24 famous historical and cultural cities, and in 1994 the "Three Kongs" (i. e., the Temple of Confucius, the Graveyard of Kong Family and the Living Quarters of Kong Family) were officially inscribed on the World Heritage List by the UNESCO. Thanks to its great contributions to the oriental culture, Qufu is regarded as one of the three sacred cities in the world— known as the "Eastern Mecca." Standing on this land, you cannot help pondering and feeling excited because the Chinese nation and China's traditional culture have taken root deep into this land. My dear friends, in China and on the very land with a long history of 5000-year civilization, you probably can not understand the inscriptions on bronze wares and what the monsters with human's head and animal's body express or symbolize, but once you approach the life of the Chinese people and walk on the old land where the Chinese people have been living, working, creating and prospering, you can sense the aura of the culture of the Confucianism in daily life of the Chinese people. And thus you will observe and understand all the differences of the Chinese people from the other nations in terms of living style, local conditions and customs and ideal ethics. Suppose you investigate into the personality and characters of the Chinese nation, no matter what angle and what level you search from, it is no difficult job to find out the influence of the culture of the Confucianism. During the long evolution of history, the culture of the Confucianism has almost been the synonym of China's traditional culture. And the originator of the culture is nobody other than Confucius.

Confucius was born in the State of Lu during the Spring and Autumn Period. His given name was Qiu, his courtesy name Zhongni. Born in 551BC, he died in 479BC at the age of 73. He was bereaved of his father Shu Liangge at the age of 3 and lost his mother Yan

Qufu

Zheng at the age of 16. Orphaned at such young age, Confucius started to make a living by himself, studying and struggling through his own efforts in the rigidly stratified feudal society. Young as he was, Confucius was fond of learning, and through self-teaching diligently and consulting others frequently, he soon had a good command over the six arts which were musts to be familiar with if one wanted to participate in aristocratic politics. The six arts are rites, music, archery, charioteering, reading and writing and arithmetic. After that, he went further to get versed in the Five classics, namely, The Book of Songs, The Book of History, The Book of Changes, The Book of Rites and The Spring and Autumn Annals. All this laid a solid foundation for the creation of the culture of the Confucianism. At the age of 30, Confucius started his life as a lecturer by setting up a school to teach his followers. This was the first private school in China and was open to the masses. He advocated the method of "teaching without distinction between subjects." Confucius was the first great educator in China and in the world as well.

Not until at the age of 51 was Confucius appointed County Magistrate of Zhongdu. Later on, he acted for the Prime Minister, but he resigned the post soon and began his trip of touring various states in the following 14 years.

Confucius returned to the State of Lu at the age of 68. He dedicated himself to teaching and document systematization to his last breath. In his life, Confucius drifted from place to place and endured all kinds of hardships. He braved extreme hardship and difficulty and exerted himself to cultivate persons of superior talents. He wrote a lot of scholarly works to rescue the times and the world. Now his body is no longer to be found, but his thoughts have penetrated into the mind of almost everyone in the east. It is he who forged the personality and characters of the Chinese culture. The thoughts of the Confucianism are the representative of the Chinese culture and are an unparalleled national cohesive force. The Dictionary of World Celebrities published in America and People's Annals

Selected Tour Commentaries

Manual published in Britain spontaneously listed Confucius as one of the ten greatest thinkers in the world and the top of historical celebrities. In January 1998 when the meeting held in Paris was concluded, more than 70 Nobel Prize organizers and winners issued a declaration all of a sudden: "If human beings are to survive in the 21 century, we have to look back on 2500 years ago and pump wisdom from Confucius." It is not unique, but has its counterpart. In August 1995 the People's Daily of China and East Asia's Daily of South Korea jointly held an International Symposium on the Confucian School in Qufu. At the end of the symposium, scholars of both countries also drew a conclusion; that is, Confucius will usher mankind into the 21 Century.

Confucius's thoughts pool the cream of the Chinese culture and are the common spiritual wealth of human society. His theory is all embracing, from cultivating one's moral character and managing family affairs to ruling the nation and unifying the whole country. Politics, economy, military, ethics, education and catering are all included in his theory. Over the past years numerous renowned figures at home and abroad conferred a good number of supreme titles on Confucius, such as "the teacher of all times" and "the Saint of all ages". A lot of visitors form home and abroad pay a visit to Qufu not only for sightseeing, but for paying tribute and respect to Confucius with reverence. Besides, the 192nd issue of China's Tourism published in Hong Kong outlined Qufu with four "greatest things under the sun", that is, "Confucius, the greatest person", "the Temple of Confucius, the greatest temple", "the Living Quarters of Kong Family, the greatest family", and "the Graveyard of Kong Family, the greatest graveyard." Now let's start our visit to have a close look at these major scenic spots.

(10,000 Ren Palace Wall)

This is the southern gate of Qufu City, which was built in the Ming Dynasty. On it hangs an inscribed board of four characters "10,000 Ren Palace Wall" which was Emperor Qianlong's handwriting. It stemmed from Confucius's disciple Zi Gong. When the State of Lu received its dukes, someone argued that Zi Gong's knowledge was extensive and profound and could match that of Confucius's. Zi Gong was on the spot and refuted immediately. "How dare I compare with my teacher Confucius? The knowledge of one is like a wall. Mine is only 1 ren (1 ren = 2.6 metres) high and can be seen through at first sight; while that of my teacher's is several rens high and you can not measure its profundity without entering into it." In order to describe the profundity of Confucius's learning, later generations inscribed these four characters onto the gate tower.

(The Temple of Confucius)

What we are visiting now is one of the "Three Kongs"— the Temple of Confucius. Also called the Temple of the Supreme Saint, this temple is where to offer sacrifices to Confucius. The Temple of Confucius, together with the Forbidden City in Beijing and the Summer Mountain Resort in Chengde City of Hebei Province are called China's three great ancient building complexes. Among these three, the construction of the Temple of Confucius enjoys the longest history. There are a lot of temples for Confucius all over the world, especially in Japan, South Korea and Vietnam, but the one in Qufu is the greatest of all. The construction first began in 478BC and became the Temple of Confucius the second year after Confucius's death. At that time, three rooms were built in front of the residence of Confucius to exhibit Confucius's clothes, carriage and books. And every year sacrifices were offered there. Later on with the spread of Confucius's influence, rulers of many dynasties admired and revered Confucius, and the Temple of Confucius has been constantly expanded to the present scale. Over the past 2000 years the Temple of Confucius has undergone 15 big renovations, 31 medium ones and hundreds of small ones. After liberation in 1949 and since the reform of opening up to the outside world, the central and local governments have earmarked special allowances on many occasions to renovate the Temple of Confucius on a large scale. Therefore, the Temple of Confucius still re-

Selected Tour Commentaries

mains intact after having been exposed to the nature for more than 2000 years. This is rarely seen in the world.

The Temple of Confucius imitates the construction of the imperial palace. The layout is like this: it has 3 roads, 9 courtyards, 466 buildings, halls, palaces and workshops, 54 gates and pavilions and over 1000 stone tablets and steles. It covers an area of 327.5 mu and is over 1 km long from North to South. No matter from what angle you enjoy the sight of the Temple of Confucius, it is all the same: magnificent and resplendent. It is commensurate to the influence and renown of Confucius in this sense.

(Golden Sound and Jade Vibration Gateway)

The first gateway of the Temple of Confucius is called Golden Sound and Jade Vibration Gateway. Mencius once evaluated Confucius in this way: "Confucius synthesized all previous teachings and brought them to their culmination. The voice of such a great thinker is golden and can make jade vibrate." "Golden Sound" and "Jade Vibration" symbolize the whole process of playing music. The music starts by beating a drum and ends by striking an inverted bell. This means that the Confucius's thoughts are a comprehensive expression of all previous saints.

On the stone gateway and on the lotus throne are engraved unicorns called "avoiding evil spirits" or "growling towards the sky". They are decorations used only for the mansions of dukes in feudal society.

(Stele of Dismounting)

There is one stone stele on either of the wall of the temple. On the steles writes "officials should dismount here." In the past civil and military officials and people in the street should dismount horses or sedan chairs and walk on foot when they passed by to show their reverence for Confucius and his temple.

(Two Cypress Trees Supporting One-Arch Stone Bridge)

When Crossing "Jade Vibration Gateway", we come to a one-

Qufu

arch stone bridge. On either side there is an old cypress tree, seemingly trying to carry the bridge, thus the name " Two Cypress Trees Supporting One-Arch Stone Bridge. " The name of the bridge is "Dissolving Water Bridge". The water under it is supposed to be connected with that in the pool of dissolving water in imperial palaces, and thus came the name. In the past one read works of Confucius and Mencius and if one could be admitted to institutions of higher learning, it was called "entering Pan". (In Chinese, "pan" has two characters. The "pan" here means the institution of higher learning) while "pan" for "dissolving water" shares the same pronunciation.)

(Ling Star Gate)

This gate was erected in Ming Dynasty and was rebuilt in 1754. The three characters were written by Emperor Qianlong. The legend has it that there are 28 constellations in the galaxy. The star in charge of culture is called "Ling Star" or "Wenqu Star", "Tianzhen Star". The ancient Chinese offered sacrifices to Ling Star before they did to Heaven because it was believed that their reverence to Confucius was same important as that to Heaven.

(The Gateway of Great Combination of Vigour)

This gateway was built in 1544. It symbolizes that Confucius's thoughts are like the universe which feeds thousands of things of creation. The great combination of vigor means the combination of heaven and earth, yin and yang and the four directions. The combination of the universe brings about the vigor of human beings. These four characters were the handwriting of Zeng Xian, the governor of Shandong Province in ancient time.

(The Gateway of the Temple of Supreme Saint)

It was erected in Ming Dynasty and was made of white marble. On eastern and western sides of the courtyard there are two unique memorial gateways. These two gateways are surrounded by wooden

Selected Tour Commentaries

corner towers and below them are eight beasts called "Heaven Dragons and Immortal Lions". According to the legend, it could expel the evil spirits and rectify the wrong. The eastern memorial gateway writes "morality matches heaven and earth". That is, the contributions of Confucius's thoughts to human beings can equal heaven and earth; the western one writes "learning outwits all others in the past and at present". It means that Confucius and his thoughts are the best throughout the ages.

(Shengshi Gate)

"Shengshi" comes from Mencius: Ten Thousand Chapters, "Confucius goes with the times." It means that among all the saints, Confucius is best adaptable to the times. In the past when emperors came to offer sacrifices they must observe the ritual of "kneeling down three times and kowtowing nine times" before they went through the gate. Whenever descendants of Confucius were born, this gate would be open. This gate keeps closed except on special occasions.

(Kuaidu Gate and Yanggao Gate)

There is one gate on both sides of the courtyard. The eastern gate is "Kuaidu Gate". It means one considers it a pleasure to be among the first to learn Confucius's works. The earlier to learn, the more knowledge to have. This reflects that people emulate each other in reading Confucius's works. The western gate is "Yanggao Gate". It comes from Yan Zi's compliment to Confucius: "If you look upward, you will find my teacher's thoughts are still higher; if you dig into them, you will find my teacher's thoughts are still harder to understand." This means that Confucius's thoughts are very profound.

(Stone Statues in Han Dynasty)

The pavilion on our left is called the pavilion for stone statues in

Qufu

Han Dynasty. These two stone statues have a history of 1800 years and were originally placed in front of the tomb of King of Western Lu in Zhangqu Village, Southeast of Qufu City. In the 59th year under the reign of Emperor Qianlong, a famous scholar of epigraphy Ruan Yuan moved them to the Juexiang Garden to the west of the Temple of Confucius. In 1953, they were moved into the Temple of Confucius and a pavilion was erected for preserving them.

(Green Water Bridge)

Green Water Bridge is similar to Golden Water Bridge in front of the Forbidden City. Three arch bridges span the water, and stone railings with exquisite carvings surround the water. In the past people described the bridge as "a round flat piece of jade with a hole in its center", therefore, it gained this name afterwards.

[Hongdao (Carrying Virtues) Gate]

The name is taken from a remark in Lunyu "Man can carry forward virtues, but virtues can not carry forward man." It implies that Confucius elucidated virtues of Yao, Shun, Yu and Tang as well as Zhou Wengong and Zhou Wugong who were considered virtuous rulers. This gate also served as the gate to the Temple of Confucius in 1377. In the early Qing Dynasty it was called The Gate to Heaven, and in the 8th year under the reign of Emperor Yongzheng it was renamed as Hongdao Gate, that is, carrying forward virtues. "Man can carry forward virtues" demonstrates man's subjective initiative in the development and creation of history. At the foot of the gate there are two stone tablets: the eastern one records the development of Qufu through dynasties; the western one writes Grave Inscriptions for Mr. Chu Shi. It boasts of high calligraphic value.

(The Big Middle Gate)

The Great Middle Gate is the gate to the Temple of Confucius in Song Dynasty. It is also called " Middle Gate". This copies

Selected Tour Commentaries

Confucius's thought of mediocrity. "Impartial is the kingly way, and mediocrity is the theorem of the world." Justice can not be done without being impartial and mediocre. One must be unbiased in one's words and action. "Mediocrity" is the highest norm of dealing with people actually, and it is hard for commoners to do so. It is absolutely different from "trying to mediate differences at the sacrifice of principle" in modern society.

(Chenghua Stele)

This stele is a famous one in the Temple of Confucius. It was erected under the reign of Ming Emperor Xianzong Zhu Jianshen. The Stele has two characteristics: one is that the regular script is standard and exquisite; the other is that the inscription sang highest praise for Confucius. The whole text was written off in the pattern of argument and is very persuasive. Please look at these sentences on the stele: "We think the whole world can not live without Confucius's thoughts even for a day. With them the three cardinal guides and the five constant virtues will keep on right track and the ethics will be standing out, and the ten thousand things of creation will find their own roles to play." Then he added: "Confucius's thoughts are like clothing and food to the world and people can not live without them in daily life." This has brought the role of Confucius's thoughts played in society to the extreme urgency. I'd like to ask you a question here. There is an animal similar to a tortoise under the stele. I wonder if any one of you can tell me its exact name. All right. No one? Let me tell you then. The animal carrying the stele is not a tortoise but a dragon called Bixi. According to the legend, the dragon king has 9 sons and every one of them has its own hobbies. Bixi is the 8th son of the dragon and it is fond of literature and can carry something very heavy. Therefore, it is assigned to carry the imperial stele. It can also prove that none of the 9 sons of the dragon king becomes the dragon, the symbol of the winner of honors and success according to China's culture.

Qufu

(Tongwen Pavilion)

It takes from the saying "man should be of the same mind and words should be of the same text." This is an important screen for Kuiwen Pavilion.

(Kuiwen Pavilion)

This was originally a building to preserve books and store books given by the emperors. It was built in 1018 and has stood here for more than 900 years. This unique and grand construction is one of the famous wooden pavilions in China. It remains undestroyed through many earthquakes. In the 5th year under the reign of Emperor Kangxi of the Qing dynasties, "nine out of ten collapsed in the earthquake", and the Kuiwen Pavilion stood rock-solid there. At present, there are wooden carvings of Confucius's tour on display inside the pavilion.

(Eastern and Western Abstinence Rooms)

These two courtyards in front of Kuiwen Pavilion are called Abstinence Rooms. The staff members offering sacrifices abstained from food and wine and took bath here. In the western Abstinence Room, the offspring of Confucius embedded more than 130 stele engravings through Song, Yuan, Ming and Qing dynasties. So it is also called "Stele Room". The eastern Abstinence Room offers an exhibition of Confucius's life story. You may go and have a look.

(Thirteen Stele Pavilions)

This is the 6th courtyard of the Temple of Confucius. There are 13 stele pavilions, with 8 in the south and 5 in the north. 55 stone steles were erected in Tang, Song, Jin, Yuan, Ming and Qing dynasties. The inscriptions are all in commemoration and evaluation of Confucius, given by emperors and imperial envoys when they came to pay tribute or offered sacrifices to Confucius. The third pavilion from east in the north was a stele erected by Emperor Kangxi. The

Selected Tour Commentaries

stele was made of a block of stone quarried from Western Mountain of Beijing and was carried all the way down the Grand Canal to Qufu. It weighs 65,000 kg. The ancient people transported the stone on iced road and they could only move forward metres long each day. We can see from this that how much Emperor Kangxi revered Confucius and how hardworking and great the laboring people were.

(Donghua Gate and Xihua Gate)

There are two gates in the east and west of the courtyard. The eastern gate is "Yucui Gate", and the western one is "Guande Gate". They are also called "Donghua Gate" and "Xihua Gate". Go through the Donghua Gate and you will see the Kong Family Mansion.

(Dacheng Gate)

The Temple of Confucius is divided into three layouts from here. There are one road and five gates. The middle gate is Dacheng Gate, the two beside Dacheng Gate are Golden Sound Gate on the left and Jade Vibration Gate on the right. The one on farther western side is Qisheng Gate and the one on farther eastern side is Chengsheng Gate. If you raise your head and look upward, you will find the two eaves of Dacheng Gate and the centers of two stele pavilions are criss-crossed. In architecture, this is termed as "hooking the hearts and fighting the eaves", and later on the term was employed to refer to the situation that people were not in harmony with each other and resorted to all sorts of schemes and intrigues to fight against each other. The characters "Dacheng Gate" were written by Emperor Yongzheng to imply that Confucius gathered all the best of the previous teachings and reached the culmination of the time.

(The Tree Planted by the Saint)

This tall and straight old tree inside the Dacheng Gate was said to be planted by Confucius. During the reign of Emperor Wanli in

Qufu

Ming Dynasty a talented scholar Yang Guangxun inscribed these five characters.

(Eastern and Western Shrines)

The two rows of corridors on eastern and western sides of the courtyard are called Eastern and Western Shrines of the Temple of Confucius. They are used for preserving the tablets of 72 saints. Tablets for those who were regarded as extremely virtuous, scholarly and faithful to their rulers in later generations were also placed here, such as that for Dong Zhongshu, a great scholar, Han Yu, a Tang poet, Zhuge Liang, a great master-mind, and Yue Fei, the famous general loyal to his country and emperor. 156 tablets were housed here during the years of Republic of China, and the last and the latest tablet was that for Mr. Liang Qichao, who organized and started 1898 Revolution. The preserved spirit tablets were destroyed in the Cultural Revolution, and the things on display instead are famous stone carvings and stele inscriptions of Qufu. The most valuable ones are 22 stele inscriptions of Han and Wei Dynasties. They are listed as national treasure and boast of high reputation in the field of calligraphy both at home and abroad. The rare inscriptions, such as Liqi Stele, Yiying Stele, Shichen Stele, Five-phoenix Carving Stone, Zhang Menglong Stele, are priceless today. In the northern part exhibit 584 Yuhong Building handwriting stone inscriptions collected by Jisu, the 69th generation descendant of Confucius. These inscriptions and rubbings are a gathering of the calligraphy of ancient celebrities and have a high value in this regard. If any one of you is fond of calligraphy, you are expected to go there on special tour and I am sure you cannot tear yourself away but gasp with admiration.

(Apricot Platform)

This pavilion is called Apricot Platform and was specially built in memory of Confucius for his lecturing at the right place. It was said that at that time Confucius set up a platform to teach his disciples.

Selected Tour Commentaries

He taught the six arts, that is, rites, music, archery, charioteering, reading and writing and arithmetic. There were many apricot trees outside the platform and the late generations also planted apricot trees and erected a platform to commemorate Confucius. Dang Huaiying, a great calligrapher in Jin Dynasty wrote the two characters "Apricot platform", Emperor Qianlong inscribed Ode to Apricot Platform on a stele inside the platform. Confucius is the first educator with the greatest attainment. He initiated the teaching concept of educating people with no regard to their social status and summarized a lot of teaching method, which is still in practice to this day. Under his instruction and education, a number of talented students came to the fore one after another and he was reputed as "having 3000 disciples and among which 72 were sages." Confucius made tremendous contributions to the education both of China and the world at large.

(Dacheng Hall)

This is the main hall of the Temple of Confucius. Dacheng Hall, together with Supreme Harmony Hall in Beijing and Tiankuang Hall at Daimiao Temple in Tai'an City are called the three greatest halls in China or "the Three Greatest Halls in the East". This hall is 4.8 metres high, 45.7 metres wide and 24.89 metres deep. It has double eaves and 9 ridges and stands solemn and magnificent. It is surrounded by 28 dragon columns carved out of whole blocks of stone. The 10 columns in front are deep relief sculptures and the others are shallow ones. They are made with exquisite technique and are treasure of the whole world. The 10 dragon columns in front are outstanding. Carved on each column are two dragons twisting and flying. They are made true to life and three is no similarity between each other. In the past when the emperor came, the Kong family assigned someone to cover them up in case the emperor would be enraged after seeing them: even the emperor who was thought to be the son of Heaven or "the real dragon" did not have this special honor to have his palace columns carved with such vivid dragons. Tablets

Qufu

preserved in the hall are those for the five Saints and those for 12 Sages. The one in the middle is Confucius, the two in the east are two sages Yan Zi and Zi Si, and the two in the west are Zeng Zi and Mencius who has held a position next to Confucius. The twelve sages are equally placed on both sides. Eleven of them are disciples of Confucius, including Zigong, Zilu and Ranqiu, and the rest is Zhuxi who lived in Song Dynasty. He made achievements in interpreting the Four Books, namely, The Great Learning, The Doctrine of the Mean, The Analects of Confucius and the Mencius, and the Five Classics as I mentioned, and thus he was conferred the title "sage" for his noble deed. On the inscribed board outside the palace writes "There is no such great person since time immemorial" which means that since the appearance of human beings, no one could have been greater than Confucius. On the inscribed board inside the hall writes "teacher of all times" which was the handwriting of Emperor Kangxi. This means that Confucius is the teacher of emperors of all dynasties and the person of exemplary virtue of all ages. The four characters written by Emperor Guangxu mean that all knowledge under the sun is gathered here. Since 1984, Qufu has been holding International Confucian Culture Festival each year. On September 26, the opening ceremony will be held in front of the Dacheng Palace. The birthday of Confucius fell upon 28th September when grand commemoration activities will be held here to show people's respect to Confucius. During the festival, music and dancing are performed and visitors from home and abroad swarm into Qufu. Various cultural and tour activities are rich and colorful and have a high cultural grade. You're welcome to come to attend this festival and enjoy yourselves in this world-famous cultural and travel ceremony.

(Bedroom Hall)

This memorial temple is designed to enshrine Confucius's wife Qiguan. It is the third largest in Confucius Temple. Qiguan came from Shangqiu of Henan Province and married Confucius at the age

Selected Tour Commentaries

of 19. Later, she gave birth to Kongli. Good mother and virtuous wife, she died 7 years before Confucius. There are also 28 stone columns outside the palace. Carved on each column are 72 phoenixes. The number equals that of dragons and this is so-called "the dragon and the phoenix bringing prosperity."

(Hall of Traces of Confucius)

This is the first picture storybook made of 120 stones. It has high historical and artistic value for recording Confucius's life stories in this way. The image of Confucius in the middle was the work by a great painter Wu Daozi in the Tang Dynasty. Emperor Kangxi wrote "Teacher of all times" in praise of Confucius. In the west you can see the ode to Confucius written by a great calligrapher Mi Shi of the Song Dynasty: "Confucius, the great master-mind; since no one greater than him was born before him, no one would be born to be greater than him in the future. Confucius, the great master-mind."

The influence of Confucius is unprecedented in a sense.

(On the West Road of the Temple of Confucius)

Sacrifices are offered here to Confucius's Parents. Qishengwang Hall, Bedroom Hall and Jinsi Hall were built here. Confucius's father was Shu Liangge and his mother Yan Zhengzai. There are many wonderful stories about the birth of Confucius. I'll tell you in detail next time when you come to visit Nishan Hill, the birthplace of Confucius in Southeast of Qufu.

(The East Road of the Temple of Confucius)

This memorial hall is to enshrine and worship the five generations following Confucius. The hall in the foreground is called "Poem and Rite Hall". In front of the hall are locust trees planted in the Tang Dynasty and ginkgo trees dating from the Song Dynasty. This hall is where Confucius taught his sons and grandsons to learn poems and rites. At the back are the well in the old residence of Confucius

Qufu

and The Wall of State of Lu. When the First Emperor of Qin burned books and buried Confucian scholars alive, all the scripts of Confucian schools were getting drowned. The 9th generation descendant Kong Fu hid works like Analects of Confucius and Spring and Autumn Annals in the wall. 200 years later, the wall fell in, and these works came to light again and made it possible for many Confucius's works to be passed down to the following generations. Chongsheng Memorial Hall and Five Generations Memorial Hall are at the farther back.

My friends, the Temple of Confucius is not only a grand and large history museum, but a sacred art temple hall. You get a general idea of China's history, traditional culture and magnificent architecture here. No matter from what aspect you try to appreciate its connotation, you will never exhaust your eyes and your thoughts. As a tour guide, I stroll along this temple hall every day. I have been thinking, I have been communicating and I have been delving but I still fail to get to the root of the connotation. I'm trying to compliment it with the most beautiful language and I always find myself at the end of the rope and my words always fail to convey my thought. From this respect we can see how great and profound Confucius and the Temple of Confucius are, and this also reminds us that there is still much to learn. Yet our life is too short compared with the long, long history. Confucius died at 73, but he left us with ever-lasting spiritual wealth. No matter who you are, easterners or westerners, we all have a resounding name in our mind — Confucius. This is the pride of the Chinese nation and the world as well. Premier Li Peng inscribed a few words when he inspected Qufu: "Draw on the essence of Confucius's thoughts and carry forward the fine culture of our nation." Well, that is all about the temple, and now let's move on and visit the "First Family under the Sun" - the living Quarters of Kong Family.

The Living Quarters of Kong Family is "Duke Yansheng's Mansion," also called "Shengfu Manshion". The first son or grandson of

Selected Tour Commentaries

Confucius's descendants attended to family affairs and lived here. The title "Duke Yansheng" was bestowed on the 46th descendant Kong Zongyuan by Emperor Songrenzong in 1055. This title has been inherited for 32 generations or more than 900 years.

As early as in the Qin and Han dynasties, emperors conferred titles one after another on Confucius and his offspring. Emperor Liu Bang, i.e., the first emperor of the Han Dynasty, Emperor Yuandi of the Han Dynasty, Emperor Xuanzong of the Tang Dynasty and Emperor Renzong of the Song Dynasty Conferred titles respectively on the 9th, 13th, and 46th generation descendants of Confucius. "Yansheng" means this title will be inherited from generation to generation. "Duke Yansheng" of Kong Family was third-rank official in the Yuan Dynasty and in the Ming Dynasty it was "first-rank civil official". In the Qing Dynasty, the rank was above all ministers and was granted the privilege to ride horses in the Forbidden City and walk on the "imperial road" in the palace. Besides, a lot of privileges and "land to offer sacrifices" were granted and taxes and errands were also exempt from. In feudal society, dynasties changed with time but the principal descendants of the Kong Family became unchangeable "dukes" thanks to Confucius, and this is the unique case even in the history of the whole world. The Kong Family Mansion was called "the First Family Mansion under the Sun" and it really deserves the reputation it enjoys.

Similar to the Temple of Confucius, the Kong Family Mansion was also divided into 3 layouts with 9 courtyards. It covers an area of 240 mu and has 463 halls, buildings and houses.

(At the Gate to the Kong Family Mansion)

A couple of stone lions are guarding the gate on both sides to show the dignity. Mounting stone and Dismounting stone are in front and at the back respectively. In the middle of the gate hangs an inscribed board with "Shengfu" on it. There is a pair of antithetical couplet on both sides of the gate, and people call it" the best antithetical couplet under the sun". All the characters are written in golden color with blue background. This antithetical couplet eulogizes the Kong Family for it went through thick and thin with the nation and would survive to the last day of the earth. Two characters are written wrong on purpose. One is "fu". It lacks a dot and this implies there is no end of wealth; the other is "zhang". You can see there is a vertical stroke through the character and this means that the articles reflect the universe.

(The East Wing and The West Wing)

Entering the gate, you will find there are 5 wing rooms on either side. The East Wing is where the Kong Family attended to cases, urged land rent and delivered official documents. The errands were as many as 224 sometimes. The West Wing is a special place to attend to affairs concerning the state. Usually officials under the sixth rank had to wait here before they were permitted to enter the second gate.

(The Second Gate)

Above the gate are characters "Gate of Saints" which were written by Li Dongyang, a scholar in the Ming Dynasty. Entering the second gate you will find a gate which does not connect walls and has four wood columns to prop up the roof. Eight weeping flower buds carved out of wood are decorated on the gate, and hence the gate gained the name "Weeping Flower Gate". Usually it was closed and was open only on grand occasions such as when the emperors held grand ceremonies, when Kong Family received the imperial edicts and when grand activities were held to offer sacrifices to Confucius.

(The Six Halls)

In this courtyard there are six halls which imitated the six ministerial mansions of the emperors: one hall was in charge of collecting taxes and rent; one in charge of doing corvee; one in charge of rites,

Selected Tour Commentaries

scripts and codes and records; one in charge of music study, music players, dancers and musical instruments; one in charge of seals, letters and official documents; the other in charge of documents and archives. The ranks of officials were sixth and seventh and they administered various affairs of the Kong Family.

(The Major Hall)

This is where "Duke Yansheng" read imperial edicts, received officials, heard cases and held grand ceremonies.

(The Second Hall)

The second hall is also called the "back hall". Duke Yansheng used to receive officials above 4th rank here. The stone steles and inscribed boards inside were bestowed on Dukes of Yansheng and their wives by Emperor Guangxu and Empress Dowager Cixi in the Qing Dynasty. It is said that in the past when officials made obeisance to the emperors, they were only allowed to be accompanied by two servants, but Duke Yansheng enjoyed the privilege to have four servants.

(The Third Hall)

The Third Hall is where Duke Yansheng tackled internal affairs of the family. The above-mentioned three halls demonstrate the rigid stratification and the dignity and influence of the Kong Family.

(Interior Residence)

After the three halls, we now come to the "Interior Residence". In the past, people were not allowed to go inside without special permit. Dozens of guards were on watch in turns and if anyone disobeyed the order, the guards would have the right to beat him to death. The water storage in the west of the gate to the Interior Residence is called Shiliu. In the past, the water carriers were also not allowed to enter, so they poured the water into Shiliu and the

Qufu

water would flow into the Interior Residence.

On the wall of the Interior Residence there was an animal painted like unicorn. It is called "Tan". It is an avaricious animal and could swallow down treasure. Legend has it that it swallowed down the treasure of the Eight Immortals and was attempting to eat the Sun. It is said that whenever Duke Yansheng went out on business, he would stop and gaze at this picture and someone would cry "cross the Tan gate". Thus it was a warning to Duke Yansheng and he was expected to have clean hands and never take bribes or bend the law. Is it instructive to today's officials and "public servants"?

(Qianshangfang Hall)

Qianshangfang Hall has 7 rooms and the owners of the Kong Mansion used to receive close relatives and friends here. At that time the opera troupe performed plays here. In the east there was a bed made of vitex root. It was a gift from Emperor Qianlong. On the table there were original imperial edicts by Emperor Tongzhi and in the middle there is a whole set of tableware. Dishes were as many as 196 and the tableware was 404 pieces. The western inner room was where Duke Yansheng examined files.

(Qiantang Building)

Qiantang building is a two-storey building with 7 rooms. You can see it is just as magnificent. The things set out inside are what they were at that time. Rare calligraphic works, paintings, treasure and clothes are also on display inside. The inner bedroom was for Madam Tao, wife of Kong Lingyi. The western room is the bedroom for Madam Wang, a concubine of Kong Lingyi. Madam Wang was the mother of Mr. Kong Decheng and her pictures can still be found. She was first a maid in the Kong Family and later married Kong Lingyi as a concubine. Unfortunately, she was killed by Madam Tao. The western inner room was Madam Feng's bedroom. Madam Feng was another concubine of Kong Lingyi, but she lived

Selected Tour Commentaries

silently and died at 27.

(Houtang Building)

Houtang building has two supplementary buildings. This is where Mr. Kong Decheng held his wedding ceremony. Inside the necessities for wedding gifts and inscriptions given by celebrities are on display. When Mr. Kong Decheng got married, the marriage coincided with the Xi'an Incident. As planned, Chang Kaishek decided to attend this wedding in person, but he was under arrest by anti-Japanese generals Zhang Xueliang and Yang Hucheng. As a result, he failed to attend the grand wedding held for the last Duke Yansheng.

(Back Garden of the Kong Mansion)

The Back Garden was built in 1503 and it was designed by Li Dongyang, Minister of the Board of Civil Office, also father of Kong Wenshao's daughter-in-law. Kong Wenshao was the 62nd generation descendant, by the way. During the reign of Emperor Jiaqing of the Ming Dynasty, another powerful minister Yansong helped renovate the garden. The granddaughter of Yansong married the 64th Duke Yansheng Kong Shangxian. In the Qing Dynasty, Emperor Qiaolong married his daughter to Kong Xianpei, the 72th Duke Yansheng, and much new construction was conducted to rebuild the garden. The garden has turned out to be such after three big renovations and the garden is larger than that of the Forbidden City. There are various rare flowers and plants as well as ancient trees and famous rocks either planted or placed in the garden. Please feast your eyes while we move on.

There are a good number of priceless cultural relics in the Kong Mansion. Ten thousand volumes of archives of the Kong Family are particularly treasurable. In a bid to protect these cultural relics, allowances were earmarked to build the Archives Hall of the Kong Family with the special approval of Li Ruihuan, a senior official in

220

Qufu

the central government. Accordingly, these cultural relics and archives are well preserved.

Just now we have visited the temples where sacrifices were offered to Confucius and the Kong Family Mansion. Next we will visit the Graveyard of the Kong Family where Confucius and his offspring were buried.

After his death, Confucius was buried here, south of Sishui and north of Zhushui. During the Qin and Han dynasties, the area of the graveyard was less than one hectare, but with the enhancement of Confucius's fame, the scale of the graveyard had become larger and larger. After the Han Dynasty, the graveyard underwent 13 renovations, 5 afforestations and 3 expansions. Now the total area is 3000 mu, and the circumference is 7.5 km long. The Graveyard of the Kong Family is a family graveyard with the longest history and the largest area in the world. It has been listed as a cultural relic under the state protection and one of the world's cultural heritage places. It is said that when Confucius passed away, his disciples transplanted rare trees and plants here from everywhere. Now there are some 100,000 trees in the graveyard, including old and famous trees. As one of the three largest stele forests in China, stone steles in Qufu feature the largest number. Among the 5000 steles, 3000 are placed in the graveyard. There are stele inscriptions of many famous calligraphers in the graveyard.

There are many old buildings in the graveyard. The two gates we passed just now are "First Gate" and "Guanlou" (also called "Second Gate"). Guanlou is also the northern city gate of the old city of the State of Lu, and on the gate are inscribed "Zhishenglin".

As we are now walking along the 5-km-long Huanlin Road, it is better for us to get a main idea of the graveyard. The people buried in the graveyard are all Confucius's descendants. According to the customs of the Kong Family, there were 4 kinds of family members who were not allowed to be buried in the graveyard: the first refers to those who died before 18; the second refers to who violated the

221

Selected Tour Commentaries

state law and were sentenced to death; the third refers to daughters who got married; the last refers to those who became monks.

The grave in front of us is that for Kong Lingyi, the 76th generation descendant and the father of Kong Decheng, the 77th generation descendant. He was buried with his three wives. The stone tablet near the roadside with the inscription of "Tomb of Mr. Dongtang" is the grave of Kong Shangren, the great writer and the author for the famous play Peach Flower Fan. When he was young, Kong Shangren was very diligent and intelligent. In the 23rd year under the reign of Emperor Kangxi, Xuanye came to pay homage to Confucius and intended to choose some from Confucius's descendants to interpret Confucian classics. Kong Shangren and his cousin Kong Shangli were chosen to explain Confucian Classics to the emperor. The two's work won the favor of the emperor and 13 days later they were appointed to be the Doctor of the Imperial College and sixth-rank officials. This memorial gateway is called "Yushifang", and in the tomb right in the north were buried Qianlong's daughter and Kong Xianpei, the 72nd generation descendant. It is said that Qianong's daughter was very ugly and there was a big black spot on her face. Fortune-tellers told her she would encounter a misfortune in life and must marry a man of fortune. The officials in court came to a conclusion that the descendants of saints had good fortune. But at that time the Manchus could not marry Han people, so Qianlong let his daughter take Han minister Yu Min as her adoptive father and employ his family name Yu. Then, she married Kong Xianpei with the family name Yu.

We're now walking towards the Confucius's tomb. This stream is called "Zhushui River", and the bridge is called "Zhushui Bridge." Since the stream is in front of the Confucius's tomb it is believed to flow to the last day of the earth. The stone columns on both sides of the lane are called "Watching Columns", and they are the symbol of entering the gate to heaven. The animal is called "Wenbao" i. e., civilized leopard. It is very gentle and kind-hearted and is assigned to

Qufu

guard the tomb. This stone-carved animal is thought to travel 18,000 li a day and is versed in all languages. This house is called "xiaodian palace", and it is where to enshrine and worship the wooden image of Confucius.

This is the tomb of Confucius. It is surrounded with red enclosure about half a km long. The house to the west of the tomb is where Zi Gong guarded the tomb. After Confucius's death, his disciples guarded the tomb for 3 years and left one after another except Zi Gong who stayed there for another 3 years. To the right of the Confucius's tomb is Kong Li's tomb, the one in front of the Confucius's tomb is Confucius's grandson Kong Ji's tomb. The three graves are in the shape of "carrying the son and the grandson." These pavilions are called "Zhubiti Pavilion" and used to be the resting-place for the emperors when they came to pay homage to Confucius.

My friends, we finished visiting the "three Kongs" of Qufu, i. e., the Temple of Confucius, the Kong Family Mansion and the Graveyard of the Kong Family. They are cultural heritage places of the world. And now for sure you have got some idea about Qufu and Confucius. You can see the sacred, steady and developing status of the Confucian thoughts from the development of the Temple of Confucius, the continuity of the Kong Family and the Graveyard of the Kong Family with an area of 3700 mu and a long history of 2540 years. And you must give a thought to the fact that the Confucius's thoughts are in combination with today's society and world. It is beneficial for you to buy some books about Confucius from the book-stalls, cultural relic store and book stores. Now let me give you a brief introduction of other major scenic spots so that you can visit them at your convenience. There are many scenic spots in Qufu and they can be divided into several types: one refers to cultural sites concerning Confucius; second, theme parks or scenic spots created and built by modern people according to the theme of Confucius and Confucius's thoughts; and the third, scenic spots combined with

Selected Tour Commentaries

beautiful natural scenery and local customs. In a word, Qufu City is a unique scenic spot. The local customs and festivals, the delicious food of the Kong Family, the rich and colorful tourism commodities with Confucian characteristics, the hospitable and frank people, the simple, graceful and antique outlook of an old city, the institutions and places to learn and study Confucius's thoughts, are all what the city can offer for tourists.

Apart form "the three Kongs," several other major scenic spots of cultural sites are as follows.

(Shouqiu, Tomb of Shaohao)

According to "Shiji" (Records of History) compiled by Sima Qian this is where Huangdi was born. Emperor Songzhenzong in Song Dynasty renamed Qufu County as Xiaoyuan County to mark the birthplace of Huangdi, the ancestor of the Chinese nation. Jingling Palace was built in Shouqiu in memory of Huangdi. Jingling Palace covered an area of 1800 mu and had 1340 halls, palaces and pavilions. That was 3 or 4 times as large as the Temple of Confucius. Recently we excavated two huge stone steles of that time and re-erected them. They are 18 metres high and weigh 300 tons. To the north of Shouqiu, there was a graveyard for Shaohao, one of the Five Lords. It is made of 10000 blocks of stone and is in the shape of pyramid, thus gaining the name "China's Pyramid".

(Nishan Temple of Confucius, Confucius's Cave)

Confucius's name was Qiu and his courtesy name was Zhongni. "Zhong" in Chinese means the second child in a family and "ni" means he was born in Nishan, Nishan lies in the Southeast of Qufu. The construction complex includes the Temple of Confucius and Nishan academy of classical learning. The cave where Confucius was born is called "Fuzi Cave". Guanchuan Pavilion is where Confucius wrote the famous remark: "I said on the bank of the river: everything passes by like the current in the river." Besides, you may go to

Qufu

the Shengshui Lake to enjoy the sight there.

(The Temple of Yan Hui)

This is the temple to offer sacrifices to Yan Hui, a disciple of Confucius. When you get out of the back gate of the Temple of Confucius and turn right, you will find yourself in the Temple of Yan Hui. This temple covers an area of 85 mu and has 159 palaces, halls and workshops. Yan Hui was Confucius's favorite disciple and was a good example of learners who were born to poor families. Confucius commended Yan Hui "is fond of learning. He never vents his anger on others and never makes the same mistake." Yan Hui died before Confucius and this rended Confucius's heart. He once cried bitterly and said, "The death of Yan Zi is not different from that Heaven killed me".

(The Temple of Zhougong)

The Temple of Duke Zhou lies in the east of Qufu City. Duke Zhou's full name was Zhou Gongdan who was conferred the title "Yuan Sheng" by emperors. This temple covers an area of 75 mu and has 57 palaces, pavilions, stations and halls. It was first built during the rule of the State of Lu. Duke Zhou helped King Wu defeat King Zhou, the famous tyranny in Chinese history and King Wu bestowed Qufu to him. Since Duke Zhou served in court and could not enjoy the bestowal, his son Bo Qin and the later offspring received manors and titles in the State of Lu, i.e., Qufu.

(Graveyard of Lianggong)

This is the graveyard for Confucius's parents. It is 13 km east of Qufu City. After his parents' death, Confucius had no idea where to bury them. Someone suggested he bury them near Fangshan Mountain of Qufu and he did so. He ordered a big grave mound to be built and then buried his parents. Confucius was the first to bury the couple together in the Chinese history, and this practice has been popu-

225

Selected Tour Commentaries

lar to this day. This graveyard covers an area of 63 mu and has numerous old and famous trees.

(In the Graveyard of Mencius's Mother, the Residence of Mencius)

This is the place where Mencius's parents were buried together. It covers an area of 578 mu and has towering old cypress trees inside. To the west of this graveyard is the birthplace and old residence of Mencius. The old halls and courtyard still exist now. As the most important successor of Confucian thoughts, he won the title of "Second to the Saint Confucius" and the Confucian thoughts are also called the learning of Confucius and mencius. We can see that Mencius played a pivotal role in Confucian thoughts system. Born in Qufu, Mencius was brought up in present-day Zoucheng City. His mother moved three times for the sake of his education. It is said that Mencius's mother chose good neighbours to live with for the better influence on her son and she once cut her weaving just because Mencius learned bad things from her neighbour. The famous saying "he who stays near vermilion gets stained red, and he who stays near ink gets stained black" is originated from this story. In Zoucheng (about 20 kms from Qufu) there are also many cultural sites such as the Temple of Mencius, the Meng Family Mansion and the Graveyard of Meng Family. They are just second to the "three Kongs" in Qufu. The second type of scenic spots includes the following places. They are mostly built recently but the scale is pretty large. Young visitors probably prefer to visit these places, I think.

(The City of six Arts of Confucius)

It lies in the new area in the south of Qufu and covers an area of 200 mu and the total floor space is 35,000 sq. m. It was built according to the Six Arts as we mentioned before and 60,000,000 RMB was invested in the project. The bronze statue of Confucius's tour of various states, the journey of Confucius to various states and Confucius's

Qufu

Lecturing on the Apricot Platform are all impressive. You will have chances to enjoy the graceful music and dancing, with special flavour of Spring and Autumn Period.

(Confucian Analects Stele Park)

It is located on the western side of Dacheng Road in South of Qufu. It covers an area of 100 mu and Confucius's Analects were engraved on the wall and pieces of stone in various forms. Accompanied by buildings, halls, palaces, pavilions and long corridors, this park is of noble taste.

(Confucius's Essence Centre)

It is on one side of the moat to the south of the old Qufu City, I mean, it lies in the centre of the present city. Glass carvings record the life stories of Confucius and it is for the first time that paintings or portraits of descendants of Confucius, their wives and celebrities of Qufu have been on display.

The third type of scenic spots refers to those of integration of natural beauty and human customs and traces.

(Stone-Gate Mountain)

Stone-Gate Mountain is on the way from Qufu to Mount Tai. It is a national forest park and boasts of hills of various kinds. In spring and summer everywhere is covered with lush green and in autumn the whole mountain is a world of colorful leaves. This is where Confucius's 64th descendant Kong Shangren led a life of a recluse. Two great poets of the Tang Dynasty Li Bai and Du Fu made an appointment to say good-bye to each other at Stone-Gate Mountain as well. And they parted with each other here and never met again.

(Jiuxian Mountain)

It lies 20 km north of Qufu City. The mountain winds its way across the plain and various flowers and plants can be found here and

Selected Tour Commentaries

there. This was the battlefield for Changshao Battle during the Spring-Autumn and Warring States periods. Even today you can still come across numerous bones exposed on the ground with wounds by knife and arrow. There is a stone called Confucius stone on the mountain. It is true to life and looks as if Confucius were lecturing his disciples.

Qufu enjoys convenient transportation. The state lines No. 104 and No. 327 criss-cross Qufu. It is only 150 km from Qufu to the International Airport of Jinan, 60 km to Jining airport and 15 km to the railway station of Yanzhou City.

If you want to go shopping, a good number of souvenirs are to choose from, such as Kong Mansion wine, Kong Mansion Sesame Oil, Nishan Inkstone and classics and works of Confucian School.

Qufu also provides you with good service and cuisine in a number of star-rated hotels. The three-star hotel Queli Hotel lies on one side of the Temple of Confucius; and Apricot Platform Hotel, Distinguished Guests Hotel are two-star ones; Three-Kong Hotel, Kong Mansion Hotel, Qufu Hotel and other ones also provide good facilities and first-class service.

Qufu is the hometown of loyalty, and rites. The local customs, hospitable people, and the simple and old city will make you feel at home. If you want to see, buy, eat or inquire something, just feel free to tell me and I'll try my best to satisfy your demand.

Thank you all for your cooperation.

SHAOLIN TEMPLE (I)

Ladies and gentlemen,

Welcome to the world-famous Shaolin Temple in Henan Province. It is my honor to be your tour guide. This spot of interest became famous with the showing of Chinese feature film "Shaolin Temple" during the 80s. A great number of tourists from home and abroad have visited this place.

We are now standing at the foot of Mount Wuru (Five Breasts), which is situated on the northern slope of Mount Shaoshi, an offshoot of the Songshan Mountains. It is 13 kilometers northwest of Dengfeng City. A huge and lofty memorial archway over there serves as its hallmark. The main entrance to the Shaolin Temple is about one kilometer's away. Now I'd like to make a brief introduction to this scenic place which has a worldwide fame.

The Shaolin Temple was first completed more than 1,500 years ago. In 495 during the Northern Wei Dynasty, Emperor Xiaowen ordered the construction of this temple, to help with the settling down of a famous Indian monk. Then another eminent monk came here from India to introduce the Zen doctrine. At the turn of Sui and Tang dynasties, the temple was made ever famous by the founding monarch of Tang Dynasty, as 13 monks who were good at martial arts had provided protection for him at a critical time. In March 1928, a warlord burnt down the major buildings that caused severe damage to the temple. After the founding of the People's Republic of China, this derelict temple was renovated on many occasions un-

Selected Tour Commentaries

der the auspices of the government. It was listed as one of the major areas of historical and scenic interest in China.

Broadly speaking, the Shaolin Temple consists of residence compound, pagodas as well as two temples dedicated to the above-mentioned founding monks. In a narrow sense, the temple mainly refers to the residence compound, to which we are paying a visit today. Covering a space of more than 30,000 square meters, this area is a place where abbots and ordinary monks live and observe Buddhist rites.

Look, this is the main entrance leading to the residence compound. This is a three-section architecture with single eaves. Leading up to the gate is a stone staircase that is flanked by a pair of marble lion statues. On the lintel of the gate there hangs a plaque bearing Shaolin Temple in Chinese characters. This was the handwritten work by Emperor Kangxi of the Qing Dynasty.

Entering the gate you will be greeted by the statue of the smiling pot-bellied Maitreya. Flanking the main path are a dozen of stone tablets that are erected by foreign monks who have completed their studies in the temple. Among these one is dedicated by the daughter of a famous Japanese boxer who studied martial arts here from 1936-46. By its side there grow a 1,000-year-old gingko tree and cypress.

The majority of China's temples and monasteries are characterized by a group of architecture facing the south. The main buildings usually consist of a gate, a hall of Heavenly God, a Mahavira Hall, depositary of Buddhist sutras, the abbots' room, etc. All the structures are positioned along a central axis in symmetry and flanked by annex halls. This also applies to the construction of Shaolin Temple. In addition, there are also halls that house rare tablets and martial arts illustrations.

In the forefront of the Hall of Heavenly God, there are two sculptured fierce looking gods, known as Generals Heng and Ha. As the legend has it that whenever they entered a war, they would win by shouting the sounds of "heng" and "ha". Later, the Shaolin

Shaolin Temple (I)

monks adopted this practice while mastering martial arts.

In the hall erect four statues of Heavenly Kings, which serve both as guardians of the temple and well-wishers on behalf of local people. Their missions were evident in the musical instruments they hold in their hands.

The Belfry and the Drum Tower were restored only recently, owning to the contribution and help offered by people of all walks of life.

In front of the Belfry, there is a line of three stone tablets. The first tablet deals with conferrals upon Shaolin monks of ranking titles, high pays, fertile farmlands and farm tools offered by Li Shimin, the emperor of the Tang Dynasty for their assistance. It bears the autograph handwritten by the monarch.

The second tablet is known as the Trinity Tablet. The figure depicted by it is an embodiment of Buddhism, Taoism and the Confucian School. Given the fact that the three schools fought with each other time and again in other parts of China, this harmonious coexistence of the three is admirable.

The third tablet bears a poem written by Emperor Qianlong in September 1750. This poem deals with the scene when he paid an imperial visit to the Temple.

Now we are approaching the lofty Mahavira Hall, a structure rebuilt in 1988. Enshrined in the middle of the hall are a group of statues including that of Satyamuni. As China adopts a policy of religious freedom, quite a few pilgrims have paid their homage here.

After turning around the Mahavira Hall and proceeding further northward, there is the brand-new Depositary of Buddhist sutras. At the foot of the staircase leading up to the gate, there places a big iron pot, which was cast in the Ming Dynasty and weighs 1,300 jin (one jin equals half a kilogramme). This pot is said to be used to cook meal for as many as 2,000 monks. In the heyday of the Shaolin Temple, the temple boasted possessing a total of more than 14,000 mu (one mu equals 1/15 hectare) farmland, and more than 5,000 room-

Selected Tour Commentaries

units of halls and pavilions.

Proceeding further northward, we come to the Abbots' Room, or the fifth group of buildings of the temple. A bronze statue dedicated to Bodhidharma, or the founder of the Zen sect, is enshrined in the center of the room. On the advice of his master, this eminent monk went to China to practice Buddhism. He first came to Guangzhou, then proceeded to Jinling (Nanjing) and eventually settled down at Shaolin Temple. It is said that to cross the Yangtze River, he borrowed a reed from an old laundrywoman, and crossed the river on it. In the back of the statue hangs a piece of painting depicting this scene. This is worshipped and cherished by monks of the Temple.

Bodhidharma reached the Shaolin Temple in 527 and settled down. With his face against the wall, he sat alone in meditation for nine years in a natural stone cave in the back of the temple. At a result, the shadow of his face and body was imprinted on the wall, hence the Stone for Facing the Wall.

This founder of the Zen sect developed a set of "Arhat boxing" in an effort to relax himself after prolonged sitting in meditation. Later, his disciples perfected this school of Chinese boxing and made it a must for every monk. In this sense, the Shaolin Temple is also known as a place famous for its martial arts, in addition to the Cradle of Zen Sect.

The tradition has it that in the end, Bodhidharma retired and left the temple. It is said that he died from poison on the bank of Luo River and buried by the Mount Xionger (in today's Yiyang County, Henan Province). Another legend has it that he returned to hometown in India with his shoes in his hands.

The sixth group of architectures consists mainly of Lixue (Standing in the Snow) Pavilion, which was dedicated to Bodhidharma and Huike, his pious follower and the second founder of Zen. It is said that in a snowy winter, Huike who was deep in snow standing outside asked his master Bodhidharma to pass on teachings to him.

232

Shaolin Temple (I)

But he was refused by his master. At last, Bodhidharma replied that unless it snowed in scarlet flakes, he would not meet his demand. When hearing this, Huike cut off his left arm with the sword and went round the courtyard, his blood dripping into white snow. Deeply moved by this, Bodhidharma gave grand ceremony and passed his mantle and alms bowl as well as teachings to him. Later, Huike became the first prominent Chinese abbot of the Shaolin Temple.

The last and the rearmost buildings include Pilu (Vairocana) Hall. This used to be where the monks practice Shaolin School of Chinese boxing, a kind of boxing that is famous for its leg movement. Ages of hard work left 48 deep hollows on the brick ground. Today, an annual international festival concerning martial arts is observed here.

Aside from martial arts practice, the Pilu Hall is also known for Buddhist treasures it houses. Enshrined in the middle of the hall are two statues of Buddha. The one in the rear is a bronze one cast during the reign of Emperor Jiajing of the Ming Dynasty. A Burmese lay Buddhist, Yang Guangfo, donated the other one placed in the front in 1989. It was made of marble and inlaid with jams and gold.

On the wall in the north there is a mural that was painted during the Ming Dynasty. Featuring 500 Arhats who were received by Vairocana, this piece of mural is seven meters tall and covers a space of over 300 square meters. The Arhats are different from each other in complexion, pose and costume. The skin colors are also different as a varying result of oxidation of pigment.

This concludes our visit to the Shaolin Temple. To sum up it may be said that this temple is famous for four reasons: it is the cradle of Zen sect and the Shaolin School of Chinese Boxing; it is also a treasure house full of cultural and religious relics; at last, this temple serves as a major tourist site attractive to sightseers from both home and abroad.

Thank you for your attention. Hope to see you again.

Selected Tour Commentaries

SHAOLIN TEMPLE (II)

Ladies and gentlemen,

I'd like to take this opportunity to introduce myself to you all. (Introduction of yourself to the guests.) I am happy to have this opportunity to show you round the Shaolin Temple. I hope you will lend your kindly cooperation during this tour. Thank you in advance.

Why the Shaolin Temple is so popular? There are two reasons for this.

In the first place, it serves as the birthplace of Zen sect, a branch of Chinese Buddhism. A major branch of Buddhism, the Zen sect is an embodiment of local Chinese religions and Confucian doctrines that exerts widespread influence upon the Chinese culture. The Zen stands for deep meditation and the Zen sect advocates being serious to everything, thus the practice of Buddhism. The Zen sect pays attention to the result instead of means. It holds that everybody is Buddha-inclined and this is only shrouded by worldly ideas. As long as one is serious with each matter, the Buddhism is thus observed.

The way to practice Zen sect is to sit in meditation with one's face against the wall. It is widely believed that Bodhidharma, the founder of the Zen sect, had sat for nine years. As a result of this, his shadow was imprinted deep into a wall on the opposite.

Another reason for the popularity enjoyed by the Shaolin Temple lies in the martial arts, which enjoys a tradition of some 2,000

Shaolin Temple (II)

years. It is considered that the Shaoling Temple is one of the main birthplaces of martial arts. The Shaolin branch of Chinese boxing epitomized various schools prevalent in northern China and was praised widely by Chinese martial arts practitioners.

Bodhidharma developed a set of physical exercises to help his disciples to get rid of fatigue stemmed from prolonged sitting in meditation. After ages of development, a special branch of martial arts emerged.

The Shaolin Temple was first completed in 495, during the reign of Northern Wei Dynasty. In 527, Bodhidharma, the disciple of Sakyamuni of the 28th generation came here to practice Zen creed. In late Sui Dynasty, 13 monks who were good at club-wielding helped save the life of the soon-to-be emperor of the Tang Dynasty, Li Shimin. After his enthronement, Li conferred upon many titles, farmlands to the Temple and made it known far and near. During the Song and Ming dynasties, the Temple boasted 14,000 mu of farmland, more than 5,000 room-units of structures and over 2,000 residence monks. In late Qing Dynasty, the Temple began to decline. In 1928, a warlord set fire to the temple and damaged many buildings. Most of the architectures we are today visiting were rebuilt later.

Ladies and gentlemen, we are now approaching the scenic area of the Shaolin Temple. The Songshan Mountains we are seeing on the way consists of two hills, Mount Taishi and Mount Shaoshi. The Shaolin Temple is situated at the foot of Mount Shaoshi and covered by dense forests. Hence the name of Shaolin Temple. Broadly speaking, the Shaoling Temple refers to residence compound, pagodas, temples dedicated to the first founder and the second founder of Zen sect. Strictly speaking, this site consists of residence compound and pagodas to which we are going to pay a visit.

With the screening of a feature film concerning the Shaolin Temple a dozen years ago, this place of interest came to fame overnight. Tourists from home and abroad thronged here and a bian-

Selected Tour Commentaries

nual international festival featuring martial arts has been held. What is more, more than 30 schools offering martial arts lectures were founded and more than 10,000 students have graduated. Many of them come from other countries.

Well, here we are. Everybody please get off the coach.

We are now standing in front of Shanmen (mountain entrance) to the Temple. Looking up at the plaque hanging above the lintel, you will find the plaque bears three Chinese characters, Shaolin Si, or the name of the Temple. This is said to be handwritten by Emperor Kangxi of the Qing Dynasty. This work is very precious because the emperor seldom wrote.

This statue is dedicated to Maitreya, who was thought as the future successor to Buddha. It is one of the Buddhist teachings which says that one must keep to be optimistic in order to enjoy himself as well as happiness and longevity. This is the depositary of stone tablets, a symbol of interaction between the temple and the world.

It is said that there used to be an alley here. It was flanked by 18 wooden figures that could automatically fight with newcomers. Only those that were lucky enough to win the fight were eligible to become a monk. Those who also won the fight after long-time cultivation were allowed to graduate and practice Buddhism elsewhere.

This kind of tree is known as ginkgo. It has been here for thousands of years and has not born seeds yet. So it is also called as "Luohan (Arhat) tree".

The hall on the left is known as Hall of Demonstrating Hammer Movements. It shows some bodily movements of Shaolin boxing through clay figures. People used to say that one could master this kind of boxing in three minutes according to the statues.

This is the Hall of Heavenly Kings. These two imposing statues were dedicated to the Ferocious Gigantic guardians. The musical instruments in their hands symbolize good weather for the crops.

Now take a look at this stone tablet. It is the most valuable one of all the tablets this temple holds. Carved 1,200 years ago, it de-

Shaolin Temple (II)

picts how Emperor Taizong of the Tang Dynasty commended 13 monks who once helped save his life. The emperor is said to have autographed on the tablet.

The belfry and the Drum Tower were rebuilt in commemoration of the Temple's founding for 1,500 years. Enshrined on the ground floor of the belfry is a statue dedicated to Ksitigarbha, or Dizang in Chinese. He was the Bodhisattva that saved all the living creatures in Heaven and in Hell. He was believed to have possessed an unlimited amount of the best strains of seeds.

We are now approaching the major structure of the temple, Mahavira Hall, which serves as the center of Buddhist service. The hall contains statues dedicated to three famous figures of Buddhism, who are in control of three different worlds in terms of space and time. The one on the left was dedicated to Amitabha, the supreme ruler of Western Paradise. According to Buddhist sutras, this world is characterized by beautiful scenery and aroma as well as melodic music. The one on the right is the Bhaisajya-guru, founder of the so-called Eastern Pure Glazed World. It is said that people living there were free of all kinds of illnesses. The statue situated in the center is dedicated to Sakyamuni, the ruler of the present world of Saha. This is an imperfect world where people suffer from aging, illness, death and all kinds of hardship. Flanking these three statues are sculptures dedicated to 18 Arhats. The arhat is a rank title of the Buddhist hierarchy.

This piece of ironware weighs 1,300 jin (one jin equals half a kilogramme) and was cast during the reign of Emperor Wanli of the Ming Dynasty. It was used as a cooker. Since the temple once boasted as many as 2,000 monks, it was not uncommon that such a big pot was used.

The animal bearing the tablet is not a tortoise, but a Chinese mythical animal "bixi", who is said to be one of nine sons of the Dragon King and the one having the greatest strength. So there is no wonder that he is the right one to carry heavy stone tablets. Accord-

Selected Tour Commentaries

ing to the local tradition that the one who touches the animal will be free of worry and illness.

This structure is known as the Depositary of Buddhist Sutras. Rare books concerning secrets of martial arts were also safely kept here.

This room was a place where the abbots lived. Emperor Qianlong of the Qing Dynasty also lived here for some time in 1750, so this room was also known as the " Dragons's Court". This bronze statue was dedicated to Bodhidharma, the founding father of Zen sect. He traveled extensively before settling down in the temple. It is said he crossed the Yangtze River on a reed, with the help of the Guanyin Bodhisattva.

The Lixue (Standing in the Snow) Pavilion is the only structure that carries great importance. Once upon a time there lived a follower of Bodhidharma, Shenguang, who was eager to succeed his master. On a snowy night, he begged as usual with Bodhidharma outside, standing in the knee-high snow. The master set forward a prerequisite: he would not meet his demand unless it would snow in red flakes. Shenguang drew out the sword and cut off his left arm and stained the snowy ground. Bodhidharma was so moved that he passed his mantle, alms bowl and musical instruments on to Shenguang and gave him a Buddhist name of Huike. He was regarded as the second founder of the Zen sect. Emperor Qianlong wrote a phrase on a plaque in commemoration of this story.

Now we are going into the rearmost structure of the Shaolin Temple, Qianfo (One Thousand Buddhas) Hall. This hall was completed in the Ming Dynasty and the monks used to hone their boxing technique here. Erected there is a bronze statue dedicated to Vairochana, an incarnation of Sakyamuni. There stands on the wall a mural dealing with a scene of five Arhats in audience with Vairochana, a rare piece of folk artwork. This picture is composed of three layers dealing with mountains, clouds and roaring sea. The figures differ from each other and are vividly portrayed. Since lead

Shaolin Temple (II)

powder was used in the pigment, oxidation occurred and the color of some figures' face turned darker.

You might have noticed the deep hollows on the ground. They are 18 in total, which are worn by monks through longtime practice of standing position. The Shaolin school of Chinese boxing is a comprehensive way of martial arts, which embodies combat-orientated defensive as well as offensive skills. It is especially famous for the movement of the leg. In addition, this school attaches much importance to the application of appliances. It also emphasized the cultivation of breathing. Therefore, this school attained fame in China as well as in the world.

This structure we are visiting is known as Liuzu (Six Forerunners) Hall, where statues of five eminent Bodhisattvas, i. e., Mahasthamaprapta, Guanyin (Avalokitesvara), Manjusri, Samantabhadra and Ksitigarbha are enshrined. They are flanked by statues dedicated to six founders of Zen sect headed by Bodhidharma. Now I'd like to tell you an interesting story which is well known in China's Buddhist circle. Once upon a time there lived an eminent monk, known as Hongren, who was the fourth successor of the Zen sect. The aging monk was going to pass on his legacy to a follower who is clever enough. So he ordered his disciples to compose a poem to show their wisdom. His first follower Shenxiu wrote one which goes like this:

> My body is like a pipal,
> My heart is like the dressing table holding a mirror.
> I clean it constantly,
> In order to keep the dust away.

A little monk also wanted to have a try. So he dictated one like this:

> Pipal itself originally is not a tree,

Selected Tour Commentaries

While the mirror is not a table at all.
Since there is nothing around,
How can the dust fall?

The master appreciated this poem very much and passed on his mantle, alms bowl and belongings to this clever monk, then he became the fifth successor and was given the name of Huineng. Later, Huineng taught Zen sect in Nanhua (South China) Temple, Guangdong Province while his senior, Shenxiu, went on preaching in north China.

Ladies and gentlemen, here is China's largest group of ancient stupas, popularly known as Forest of Stupas, which number more than 240. The total number remains inexact to this day. This area has served as a cemetery which dates back to the Tang Dynasty. The dead monk's ashes used to be buried underground but a pagoda would be erected right above. The difference in shape and height just indicates the varying positions, popularity and support of disciples the deceased enjoyed when they were alive. What is more, all these pagodas are of one storey, because the Buddhism holds that odd number is the symbol of cleanness and bachelordom.

This is the only contemporary pagoda ever constructed in this area. It was dedicated to the last abbot, Shixingzheng. This one in peculiar shape belongs to Monk Xiaoshan of the Ming Dynasty. As a master of martial arts, he led the imperial army to fend off the Japanese invaders on southeastern coast. This is the tallest pagoda that was completed during the Song Dynasty. It was dedicated to a number of monks who had not attained great achievements or who had no disciples. Unlike other constructions, this pagoda has a door leading into it.

This derelict and cracked pagoda is the oldest of its kind. It was dedicated to Fawan, an eminent monk of the Tang Dynasty.

These pagodas provide precious evidences on brick-stone architecture, carving and sculpture, history of arts and religions. Now ev-

Shaolin Temple (II)

erybody has 20 minutes to move around at will. Please get on the coach on time.

Ladies and gentlemen, this is the end of our visit to the Shaolin Temple. Thank you for your cooperation. Hope to see you again here. Thank you.

Selected Tour Commentaries

THE THREE GORGES
OF THE YANGTZE RIVER

Ladies and gentlemen,

I am very glad to be your tour guide this time! Now the pleasure-boat is only 8 km away from the world-renowned Three Gorges of the Yangtze River.

In his poem "The Three Gorges", Chen Yi, a general of new China, writes: "How grand and magnificent the Three Gorges are! Only on board a ship can you really appreciate the beauty!" He outlined the features of the Three Gorges with one word "magnificent" and gave encouragement and impetus to the people to tour the amazing gorges.

Thanks to the magnificent landscape and gracefulness, the Three Gorges have turned out to be the world-renowned scenic spot. First of all, I'd like to give you a brief introduction to them before you enjoy them.

The Three Gorges are among the first ten most beautiful and famous places of interest and top the list of "the first 40 China tourist sites." They are also among the first key scenic spots selected by the state and one of the 35 best scenic spots in China. The Yangtze River is 6300 km long, next only to the Amazon River in South America and the Nile in Africa in the world. Its source traces to the highest snowy peak of Tanggula-Geladandong Mountain Ranges. However, in the time immemorial, the eastward-flowing Yangtze River had

The Three Gorges of the Yangtze River

three tributaries that flew in different directions. One of them flew east and emptied into the East Sea; another poured into the ancient Mediterranean Sea; the third flew south to the Northern Bay. The Yangtze River we see today is an old watershed that used to cut across the three rivers that ran east, south and west respectively.

The terrain of China in the past era was featured by " The terrain turned low from east to west", and the western part of the Yangtze River was a part of the Mediterranean Sea. A bay was near the eastern end of the Three Gorges. The "orogenesis" that happened 130 million years ago brought about the ever-increasing height of the earth's crust around the Three Gorges and the ancient Mediterranean sea retreated slowly from the western part of the Yangtze River. The eastern and western parts of the river ran westward and eastward respectively with the lump as the watershed. 75 million years ago, the ocean to the north of the Indian Ocean Plate was partially embedded into an oceanic trench of the Euro-Asian Continent. 54 million years ago, the Indian Ocean Plate collided with the Euro-Asian Continent and the slow elevation of the Qinghai-Tibet Plateau. As a result, the terrain was shaped with the west high and the east low and thus dammed the ancient Yangtze River's passage to the Red River. So the ancient Yangtze River had to join with young glacier rivers like the Tuotao River and the Tongtian River. With the continuous digging and erosion of the source, their fountainheads drew nearer and nearer. Due to the drastic hunch of the earth's crust many crevices were created. The vive water dug the earth year in and year out and finally the river blocked the Wushan Ranges. The river water continued to dig and cut its way out, and the river's bed got deeper and wider accordingly. In the end, in the passage from Fengjie of Chongqing and Yichang of Hubei Province the amazing Three Gorges took shape. The whole process took 1 million years or so.

The Three Gorges pass through the boundary between Chongqing and Hubei Province with a total length of 193 km long.

243

Selected Tour Commentaries

The Three Gorges include: the Qutang Gorge which features magnificence, the Wu Gorge which features serenity and beauty, and the Xiling Gorge which features numerous shoals and rapids.

(The boat entering Qutang Gorge)

Look! My friends, the marvelous gorge is just ahead.

This is the first gorge called the Qutang Gorge. The Yangtze River is partially stemmed by the Baidicheng Mountain and a bay of 1.6 sq. km is thus formed. It is very much like a weir and thus came the name "Qutang Gorge". It extends 8 km, starting from Baidicheng in the west and ending at Daixi Town in the east. At the mouth of the gorge there once stood a huge reef. This is the so-called "Yanyudui" which once blocked the throat of the Three Gorges and locked the current. With the ups and downs of the water, it sometimes looks like a horse and sometimes an elephant. "Yanyudui" once frightened the boatmen and visitors who had to pass by it. For many years, it was a big problem for the navigation. In 1958, workers removed this obstruction with explosives and since then the voyage through the Three Gorges has become safe and smooth.

[Introduction to Baidicheng (White Emperor City)]

The old construction complex on the mountain on our left ahead is the historical site of the Baidicheng. Baidicheng has a history of more than 1900 years. It is surrounded by water on three sides and mountains on one side. It lies 264 metres high above sea level. To the east of the gorge and the south of the river stands the 1415-metre-high Baiyan Mountain. And to the east of the gorge and north of the river erects the 1400-metre-high Chijia Mountain. These two mountains face each other and lock the river like a door. The magnificent Kuimen is just located here. It is the upper mouth of the Qutang section and is difficult for access.

According to historical records, during the reign of Wangmang in the West Han Dynasty, Gongsun Shu took possession of the land

244

The Three Gorges of the Yangtze River

of Sichuan area. He built a city here called Ziyang. There was a well in the city and white evaporation often rose up from the well like a flying white dragon. Gongsun Shu believed this was a good omen for him to ascend the throne in the future. He made a fuss about it and called himself "White Emperor" in 25 and renamed Ziyang as White Emperor City. In 36, Emperor Guangwu retrieved the lost land and Gongsun Shu got killed in the battle. The White Emperor City was destroyed to racks and ruins accordingly. Later on, people established the Temple of the White Emperor on the Baidi Mountain to commemorate Gongsun Shu for his accomplishment of administering Sichuan area.

Baidicheng is where Liu Bei entrusted his son to his Prime Minister Zhuge Liang on dying bed. Inside the City there is a palace called Mingliang Palace in which huge colored statues of Liu Bei, Zhang Fei, Guan Yu and Zhuge Liang are enshrined and worshiped; in "Tuogu Hall" the colored statues of 21 figures in the period of the Three Kingdoms are on display; and there is an "Observing Star Pavilion" where Zhuge Liang observed the positions and movements of stars for purpose of anticipating what would happen in the future. Statues of Zhuge Liang, his son Zhan and grandson Shang are enshrined in Wuhou Memorial Hall. In the exhibition halls on both sides of the Temple of White Emperor are collected over 80 stele inscriptions of Sui, Tang and other dynasties. The most valuable of all are two Sui steles. One was inscribed in 600 and the other in 602. The Record of Longshan Maintain Cemetery and Stupa of Jinlun Temple are inscribed respectively on these two steles. Sui steles not only record the first-hand information about hydrological data of the Yangtze River, but are of vital importance to studies of the history of Fengjie. Phoenix Stele is also called "the Stele of Three Kings", because inscribed on it are a phoenix, the king of birds, a phoenix tree, the king of trees, and the peony, the king of flowers. The most interesting and exciting stele is the stele in the shape of bamboo leaves. At first sight, it looks like three bamboo stems, but once you

245

Selected Tour Commentaries

give it a close look, you will find that it is a poem that praises the personality of bamboo for its endurance. The stele of 24-character poem written by Emperor Kangxi of Qing Dynasty is bound to rouse your keen interest.

Since time immemorial, Baidicheng has been of strategic importance for various kingdoms. The last ditch of Yiling Battle, one of the ten famous battles featuring the weak defeating the strong is right here. Kuifu to the west of the city has the site of Yong'an Palace where Liu Bei entrusted his Prime Minister with his son and the relics of the graveyard for Madam Gan, the Queen of Emperor Zhaolie. On both sides of the city there are deployments arranged by Zhuge Liang: water tactical deployment and land tactical deployment of troops. You can also find the site of the battlefield in which Li Zicheng and Zhang Xianzhong, leaders of the peasant uprising in the end of the Ming Dynasty, fought against the imperial army.

Baildicheng is a renowned "city of poetry". A lot of famous poets of all dynasties came here to appreciate the scenery and wrote poems. "Poet Immortal" Li Bai wrote an excellent poem "I Left Baildicheng in the Morning" and Premier Zhou Enlai calligraphed this poem and his calligraphic work is housed in the Temple of white Emperor; "Poet Sage" Du Fu stayed here for 2 years and wrote 437 poems which accounted for one third of all his existing poems. Liu Yuxi created a piece of poetry Bamboo Branches based on the folk song of Kuizhou area. In the spring of 1963, late Chairman Mao Zedong inspected the Three Gorges on board "Jiangxia". When the ship arrived at Baildicheng the sight stroke a chord in Mao's heart and he recited Li Bai's poem with high spirit: "I left Baildicheng in the morning and it took me just one day to cover 1000 li to get to Jiangling. Apes on both sides screeched here and there, and before you realise it the boat has already passed by 10,000 mountains."

Look ahead! You can enjoy the beauty to your heart's content because the scenic spots are numerous and miraculous here. There is a row of holes in the cliff of Baidi Mountain. It's said that the leader

The Three Gorges of the Yangtze River

of the peasant army Zhang Xianzhong conquered Baildicheng and guarded the mountains and all passes. The enemy blocked the river and cut off the water passage with heavy force. Zhang Xianzhong ordered his soldiers to fetch water through holes dug in the cliff. The enemy found that their tricks had been seen through and retreated reluctantly. The later generations call these holes "Stealing Water Holes". The two iron bars on the rock in front of "Stealing Water Holes" are the relics of "Pass-locking iron chains". In the past, iron chains could block the river. In this case the ships and boats could not pass. The water below the rock on which the iron bar is placed comes from the Caotang River. Go along the river for about 4 km and you will find yourself at the old residence of the great poet in the Tang Dynasty—Du Fu. Please look to the right side of the gorge. You can see a stalactite about 20 metres tall and 6 metres round. It is in the shape of a phoenix raising its neck and a stream of spring water flowing down slowly along the neck and thus comes the name "Phoenix drinking Spring Water". On the cliff in the air near "Phoenix" is the 'White-painted Wall." There are many inscriptions on it and you can see from these inscriptions the development of Chinese culture in the past. Look still upward and you will find a lot of and holes about the size of a bowl lined in the shape of the Chinese character "Zhi". They are the legendary "Meng Liang ladders" stretching from the river's bank to the top of the mountain. Under the rock not far from "Meng Liang ladders" is another stalactite. Please observe carefully and you will find that it looks like a monk hanging on the verge of the cliff shoulder over head. People call it "Hanging Monk Shoulder over Head". According to the legend, a monk purposely feigned a ghost to frighten people but his tricks were discovered by Meng Liang. Meng Liang then hung him up shoulder over head as a punishment. Still above the "monk" is a cave in the cliff called "Armour Cave". In 1958, two hanging coffins and other cultural relics were found in the cave. Please look at the left bank. "Fengxiang (Bellows) Gorge" is inscribed distinctively on the cliff.

Selected Tour Commentaries

According to textual research, the so-called "bellows" are hanging coffins of the Ba people in ancient times. And this mountain lane is the site of the ancient mountain road. People inscribed 8 Chinese characters to commemorate the builders of the road. That is "Seven Danger Gate". The interior of the cave is deep and winding and there are seven dangerous passes altogether. Therefore, it is called "Seven Danger Gate". Now please turn around and look at the southern bank. The limestone cave in the middle of the mountain is the mysterious "Golden Cave". Archaeologists excavated a lot of weapons, utensils and pink pictographs of ancient Ba people in the cave. This proves that this is the site of ancient Kingdom of Ba and thus has uncovered the mystery of the development of ancient Kingdom of Ba. Look upward along this mountain and you will find a huge stone erected there, towering against the sky. It looks like a giant rhino overlooking the far distance. People call it "Rhino Gazing at the Moon". My dear friends, the place ahead is Daixi County, also the end of Qutang Gorge. On the land where Daixi stream joins the Yangtze River is the site of the ancient Daixi people. This site dates back to 5000 years ago and was the settlement of the ancient people in the Neolithic Age of the matrilineal society.

(The boat entering the Wu Gorge)

The second gorge "Wu Gorge" is right ahead. The shape of Nanling Mountain is like the character "Wu", so the mountain gained its name. The gorge shared the same name accordingly. The whole gorge stretches 42 km from the Daning River in the west to the ferry of Badongguan.

(Visiting the Lesser Three Gorges)

Ladies and gentleman,

Attention, please! There is a city ahead to the north of the river. That is Wuxia, the seat of Wushan County. On the Gaoqiu Mountain 1 km northwest of Wuxia there is a taoist temple called

The Three Gorges of the Yangtze River

Gaotang Temple which enjoys a history of more than 1000 years.

The pleasure boat is anchoring at the wharf of Wuxia County and we're going to visit the Lesser Three Gorges of Ninghe River by "Liuye" Boat. This is Longmen Gorge with a length of 3 km. Look! Two lines of orderly square holes on the cliff are the sites of the ancient plank roadway. These two lines spread 400 km to Zhenping of Shaanxi Province and Zhuxi of Hubei Province. According to historical records, this plank roadway linked Qin, Shu and Ba Kingdoms and played an important role in the political, military, economic and cultural communications among them.

The gorge before us is the Bawu Gorge. It is 10 km in length. Look upward please! And now you can see the hanging coffins on the cliff. These coffins are about 300 metres high above the river. Archaeologists believed that these coffins were used for burying the dead or storing documents and archives. This gives supporting evidence that the ancient people had the customs and practice of "making good coffins with all they had" and "the higher the coffin hangs, the more filial the descendant is."

Now the "Liuye" boat is entering the Dicui Gorge, which is about 20 km long. Look! This is the Golden Monkey Mountain, and groups of wild monkeys are playing on the mountain. Local friends say that the number of wild monkeys is over 1000. Along the tributary on the right there are "Much Lesser Three Gorges," namely, the Sancheng Gorge, the Qinwang Gorge and the Changtan Gorge. When you pass through them, you will find yourselves very close to nature.

(Passing through the Wu Gorge)

Ladies and gentlemen,

Now the travel boat has entered the Wu Gorge. Twelve mountains stand on both sides of the Wu Gorge with six on either side. This constitutes the misty "Wu Gorge Gallery". Now please look at the left side. This is "Denglong Mountain" and it lies 15 km down

Selected Tour Commentaries

the lower reach of Wuxia County. And is 1215 metres high above sea level. It has six peaks which seem to wind their way upward as if they were lying dragons soaring towards the sky. Please look ahead now. This is "Shengquan Mountain" which is 1023 metres above sea level. On the top of the mountain the spring water is crystal clear and cold, and thus it got the name "Sacred Spring." In front of the mountain there is a white square rock. It looks as if a silver medal were fastened to the neck of a male lion, so it is also called " A lion with a silver Medal around Its Neck". And look far ahead, you will see Chaoyun Mountain which is 1324 metres above sea level. Whenever the sun rises, clouds on the top of the mountain seethe violently. And this is "Goddess Peak" which is the highest peak of all 12 peaks in this area. It is 30. km far from Wuxia County and 1112 metres above sea level. The Goddess is an independent natural stone column which stands 6.4 metres high like a gentle, slim and graceful maid on top of the peak. The story goes that Goddess is the incarnation of Yao Ji, the youngest daughter of the Queen Mother of Heaven. Yao Ji decided to live on earth after she helped Da Yu harness the turbulent river. She exposed herself to nature and gazed at the turbulent water in the river, navigating boats that passed through the gorges. Since Goddess embraces the sunrise and bids farewell to the sunset, the peak is also called "the Peak Looking over the Sunrays". In September 1965, on the very day when Premier Zhou Enlai accompanied a head of a certain foreign country here, the Goddess Peak unveiled her face and revealed her beauty distinctively, which is rare in September. Premier Zhou said wittily, "Due to the frequent fog and mist here, this Goddess seldom receives the mortal. Today, luckily, she received us in honor of your Majesty." That distinguished guest jumped with joy and said: "I saw her! I saw her!" now please look at the right. This is "The Flying Phoenix Peak", and it is 821 metres above sea level. The terrain of the peak is like a phoenix spreading its wings. In 676, a temple was built for the Goddess on the neck of the "phoenix", but now it is discarded. Behind the tem-

250

The Three Gorges of the Yangtze River

ple is a platform called "Lecturing Platform". And the peak ahead is "Green Screen Peak". It is 850 metres above sea level. On the peak trees are growing luxuriantly green like a verdant screen, thus is the name Green Screen Peak. The peak on the left is "Pine Trees Peak". This peak is 990 metres above sea level and the pine trees and cypress trees on it stand tall and straight, and the whole peak is covered with a carpet of green grass. Seen from distance, it looks like a round hat, so it is also named "Hat Box Peak". The peak in front of it is "Gathering Immortals Peak" about 995 metres above sea level. Seen for afar, the peak looks like an open scissors, so people also call it "Scissors Peak". The peak has many precipices and one of them is in the shape of stone stele. The ancient people inscribed 15 characters on it. As you can see, the inscriptions are bold and vigorous. This is also called "The Kongming Stele." On the top of the Gathering Immortals Peak there are jagged rocks of grotesque shapes like a whole set of tableware. It is said that after their gathering, the immortals left all there. The peak on your right is "Gathering Cranes Peak". It is 829 metres above sea level. Whenever the night comes, flocks of white cranes stand high on the top or hover over the peak. Hereby it gained the name. Just now we enjoyed the scenery of 6 peaks to the north of the river and 3 peaks to the south of the river. There are 3 other peaks hiding behind mountains to the south of the river out of our sight. Next time when you come to visit again I would like to accompany you to visit them on foot if you are interested in doing so.

Dear friends, the stream on our left is called Bianyu Stream. This is the boundary river between Chongqing and Hubei province. Inscribed on the rocks at the mouth are several characters "Wide Gap between Chu and Shu" (namely, Hubei and Sichuan).

This is the ferry of Badongguan and in front of it is the Shennong Stream. This stream traces to the southern side of the main peak of Shennongjia Mountains and runs from north to south and empties into the Yangtze River. It comprises 3 gullies: Mianzhu, Yingwu and Longchangdong. The Shennong Stream is famous for its

Selected Tour Commentaries

unique voyage: people drift to the Yangtze River by pea-shaped boat. The stream is full of twists and turns and the passage is also narrow, so this brings exciting experience to tourists going by pea-shaped boat.

Here we are! This is Shennong Stream. If you go rafting along the stream, you are supposed to get to the upstream by bus. You're expected to take care of each other, Safety is most important.

Look ahead, friends! Our pleasure boat is entering the western gate to Zigui of Yichang. This is Niukou and that is Shimen. They are also famous for perilous and swift rapids.

There comes the Xietan Shoal! We're now at the terrifying rapids.

The islet to the starboard of our boat is called "Liulaiguan". Whenever speaking of this islet, local people will tell you a story about Buddhas in Liulaiguan sitting back against back.

On the left is the old Zigui City. It takes after a huge gourd, so it is also called "Gourd City". Zigui is the hometown of Qu Yuan, a great patriotic poet in ancient China. In 1953, Qu Yuan, together with 3 other celebrated figures of other countries, were listed as the greatest cultural celebrities to be honored by the world.

This is the gate to the memorial temple for Qu Yuan and museum for Qu Yuan. The three characters "Qu Yuan Temple" were written by a famous writer Guo Moruo. Let's step forward. This is the bronze statue of Qu Yuan. It portrays that Qu Yuan was pondering with his head down and strolling in the wind. It is 3.92 metres tall and weighs 3 tons, making it one of the biggest bronze statues in China. Please look at both sides. These are eastern and western stele corridors. In the corridors erect 96 stone steles on which are inscriptions of 22 works of Qu Yuan such as Lisao and Jiuge. Besides, poems eulogizing him through different dynasties can also be found here. Let's walk upward. This is a two-storeyed exhibition hall in memory of Qu Yuan and it has two. One is an exhibition hall to commemorate Qu Yuan, the other is displaying unearthed cultural

252

The Three Gorges of the Yangtze River

relics in Zigui. Behind the hall is Qu Yuan's grave for his clothes.

If you happen to visit the Three Gorges during the Dragon Boat Festival or "Duanwu Festival", you will have the chance to watch the dragon boat competition set up in commemoration of Qu Yuan for his noble deeds, because he laid down his life for his country. Besides, you will enjoy the programs featuring gorge-and-river style, such as folk songs, boatman's work songs, I mean, these songs are sung to synchronize movements with one person leading.

(While the boat entering Xiling Gorge)

Now we start visiting the third gorge "Xiling Gorge". In Chinese "xi" stands for "west" while "ling" here stands for an ancient city "Yiling". It has been so named just because it lies to the west of Yiling (present-day Yichang). The gorge starts from Xiangxi County of Zigui in the west and ends at Nanjin Pass of Yichang in the east, and it is altogether 76 km long.

The stream on the left is called Xiangxi. Among the four ancient beauties in Chinese history, one is Wang Zhaojun, a virgin concubine of an emperor in the Western Han Dynasty. Her hometown - Zhaojun Village is at the source of Xiangxi Stream. In order to help the emperor establish a stable peaceful relationship with Xiongnu, a minority nationality at that time, Wang Zhaojun, with no regret, agreed to marry Chanyu, the leader of Xiongnu. Her noble deeds promoted cultural communications between Han people and Xiongnu people and brought harmony to both sides. Premier Zhou Enlai once praised her as "a figure that made contributions to the national solidarity of all ethnic groups". In commemoration of her, people restored her old residence, dressing table, purple bamboo garden, Queen well, Zhaojun platform and stele forests in Zhaojun Village.

Now our boat is entering "Gorge of Military Books and Sword". Look at the north side and what jumps into your eyes are books on the art of war and double-edged sword. The story goes that when Zhuge Liang entered Sichuan area, he hid books on the art of war

Selected Tour Commentaries

and double-edged sword in the cliff for brilliant offspring to reach for. Now we are out of this gorge and the shoal in front of us is Qingtan shoal. A number of rock collapses took place in this area through the ages. In 1029, a tremendous rock collapse cropped up and blocked the passage of the river for 21 years; in 1542, a mountain collapse took place, making the river running backward for over 50 km and blocking up the passage for the following 82 years; June 1985 saw another mountain slide which moved over 80 metres down to the Yangtze River, causing waves surging 36 metres high. Luckily, 1371 residents in the Qingtan Town below the cliffs were timely evacuated, but the town perished from the earth almost all of a sudden. Later on, a new town was built five km away from the gorge.

Look! That is the famous perilous Qingtan Shoal! In the old days lots of work songs sung by the boatmen in Qingtan area revealed the true picture of the hardship of the boatmen, such as "when you pull the boat onto the shoal, you find your skull knocked through; when you put the boat into the water, you can not tell whether you will be alive or dead"; "Sailing over the Qingtan Shoal, may Buddha and Heaven bless us all", and so on.

Along the river on the northern bank of Qingtan Shoal is "White Bone Tower". The inside of the tower is hollow. Two round openings are 2 metres above the ground. They were used as the passages for throwing in the corpses of victims from accidents in the Qingtan Shoal. From the middle of the Qing Dynasty to around 1949, numerous corpses had been piled up in the tower.

After the founding of New China, the navigators removed with thousands of tons of explosives the huge rocks which stood at the centre of the river and posed danger for thousands of years. From then on, boats and ships have been sailing safely and smoothly through the Three Gorges.

The gorge on our left is called "Gorge of Ox Liver and Horse Lungs". In 1900 under the reign of Emperor Guangxu, the English and German invading ships "Shutong" and "Ruisheng" intruded Xil-

The Three Gorges of the Yangtze River

ing Gorge under the cloak of "developing Sichuan area". They shot off a corner of "Horse Lungs". On this the famous writer Guo Moruo wrote, "Even the Gorge of Ox Liver and Horse Lungs cursed the aggressiveness of the invaders". This is a powerful condemnation of the imperialist's evil practice. The stream near the "Fairy Maiden Peak" on the right is called "Jiuwanxi". According to the legend, the great patriotic poet Qu Yuan planted a hundred mu of Jiuwan irises and orchids here. He also nurtured and educated the talented with intention of turning them into statesmen for the State of Chu.

Not far ahead is the Kongling Shoal. It starts from Jiuqunao and ends at Zhoujiatuo with a length of 2.5 km. The narrowest part in the north of the shoal is only five metres wide in dry season and it is also the shallowest part along the Three Gorges section of the river, with the record for the lowest water level only 3.1 metres. Qingtan Shoal and Xietan Shoal are famous for rapids, but "Qingtan and Xietan can not be called dangerous shoals if compared with Kongling, the real gate of hell". Kongling Shoal seems like a chessboard with rocks scattered all over. On the facade of one rock inscribes "Straight to me". Whenever a boat arrived here, it must sail towards this rock straightly if one wants to pass it without peril; otherwise, the boat would capsize and the people would get killed. For the last 100 years, numerous ships and boats have got capsized by striking rocks, including 7 ships such as "Ruisheng", "Fulai" and "Fuyuan". After liberation, these reefs and rocks were removed with explosives and the previous "gate of hell" has become a smooth pass.

(Introduction to the Three Gorges Project)

My friends, the construction site of the project of the Three Gorges is right ahead. The layer of the earth in this area is of hard granite and so this area is thought to be the most ideal place to construct a giant dam. The axis of the dam will cut off the Yangtze River right here. Please come closer and have a look. I'd like to give you some idea about this project first. On 3 April 1992, the 5th session of

Selected Tour Commentaries

the 7th National People's Congress passed The Resolution on Establishing the Project of the Three Gorges of the Yangtze River. Since then, the legislative procedure concerning this project has been completed and the project has entered the phase of implementation. On 14 December 1994, Premier Li Peng announced the starting of the project.

In the history of the Chinese nation, the harnessing of the Three Gorges could be traced back to time immemorial. In ancient times, there were beautiful legends on this topic, such as, the Goddess of Wushan Mountain assisted Da Yu to harness the river and the immortal bull in Xiling Gorge helped Da Yu to dig the Yangtze River. In modern time, Dr. Sun Yat-sen initiated the scheme of utilizing the hydroelectric potential of the Three Gorges. At first sight of them, an American geologist believed the Three Gorges had great waterpower potential. "Father of World's Geology" Muler and "Father of China's Geology" Li Siguang came to the Three Gorges for inspection respectively. As early as in 1946, experts from China and America gathered in Denver to study and design the project and ship locks. In July 1956, Chairman Mao Zedong swam across the Yangtze River and wrote a poem afterwards. In this famous poem, he depicted the blueprint of the project of the Three Gorges as "Erecting a stone wall in the west and cutting off the river in Wushan Mountain area with a high-rise dam above the river. Since the founding of New China, Mao Zedong, Zhou Enlai, Liu Shaoqi, Deng Xiaoping, Jiang Zemin, Li Peng, Qiao Shi, Li Riuihuan and other senior officials have come to the dam location of the project and construction site for inspection, planning and investigation.

According to the Three Gorges Project a concrete gravity dam is being built here. The dam is 1983 metres in length, while the total length of the top of the dam is 3035 metres. It is 185 metres high and has a storage capacity of 39.3 billion cubic metres while the normal storage water level is 175 metres. The anti-flood storage capacity will reach 22.15 billion cubic metres. The sand sorting capacity per sec-

The Three Gorges of the Yangtze River

ond is 2460 cubic metres. And the capacity for floodwater sluicing is 1.1 billion cubic metres per second. 26 generators are to be installed with a capacity of 700,000 kilowatts for each and the whole capacity of 18200,000 kilowatts. The annual generated energy will reach 84.7 billion kilowatt-hours (kwh). The passage construction on the left has an annual handling capacity of 50 million tons. The double-line locks of 5 levels can lift ships of over 10,000 tons. The single-line one level ship-lift can handle freighters or passenger ships of 3000 tons at high speed.

When completed, the reservoir will submerge arable land of 431,300 mu and about 1131,800 residents will be evacuated.

If calculated in terms of the pricing level in 1993, the total static investment of the project reached ¥95,646 billion, including ¥50,09 billion for pivot, ¥30,07 billion for emigrant settlement allowance and ¥15,3 billion for transmission project. Such a construction plan has been adopted, namely, first-class development; completion once and for all; storage of water at different phases and continuous evacuation. The time span for this project is 17 years. The whole process is divided into 3 phases: the first phase spanned 5 years and the river was dammed in 5 years from 1993 to 1997; the second phase will last 6 years, and by 2003 the first batch of power generators will be put into work and the permanent locks and ship lifts will be put into operation; the third phase will last another 6 years and by 2009 the whole three gorges project will be accomplished and 4 sets of generators will be put into practice annually.

A number of technical records of this project top the list of its kind in the world — the world's largest power station, the largest concrete, the largest navigation construction, the largest amount of cubic metres of earth and stone excavated, the largest amount of cubic metres of earth and stone stuffed, the largest amount of cubic metres of concrete used and the largest amount of metal structure installment.

After its completion, the project will play a vital role in anti-

Selected Tour Commentaries

flooding, power generation, navigation, cultivation, tourism, and purification of the ecological environment, evacuation for development, water transportation from South to North and water irrigation program. This is unparalleled among all the huge power stations in the world.

The Project of the Three Gorges is a great one that has attracted worldwide attention. It is also the greatest project since the building of the Great Wall and excavation of the Grand Canal in history. It is this project that opened a new era in history and will benefit the coming generations with the merits of this very generation.

Look! The scene on the construction site is really magnificent! These are self-unloading trucks of 45 tons, 77 tons and 140 tons. Those are giant forklift trucks and long-armed loading machine. Could you see the 80-metre-high cofferdam over there?

Please look at the hanging-cable bridge that spans the river! It is called Xiling Yangtze River Bridge and it is only 4.5 km away from the construction site of the project. The area north to the bridge is called Tietiaoshu, while the southern area called Datuo. The bridge project started in December 1993 and was completed in June 1996, with the total investment over ¥0.35 billion. The bridge is 1165,86 metres long, 18.4 metres wide and has a loading capacity of 290 tons. Its span is 900 metres and is reputed as "the first span in Shenzhou (namely, China)". The construction of this bridge has eased the busy transportation on both side of the project of the Three Gorges, ensured the passage of fleets of 10,000 tons and painted a colorful rainbow to the picture of the project of the Three Gorges.

Now our boat has entered Yellow Bull Gorge whose passage is like twisted intestines. People built a memorial hall for the Yellow Bull which was said to have helped Da Yu split the gorge. Later on, this memorial hall was renamed as the Temple of Yellow Bull and the Temple of Huangling. On the stele in front of the memorial hall is the inscription of the handwriting of Zhuge Liang. He once came here and recalled Da Yu who made great contributions in harnessing

258

The Three Gorges of the Yangtze River

the river and wrote down these words afterwards. That is the sago cycad planted by Zhuge Liang himself in front of the stele. 1983 saw the bloom of this sago cycad and this stirred up a sensation. Inside the temple there are a lot of stele inscriptions recording hydrological data about the Three Gorges in history. Among them there is one stele that writes as follows — "in 1870, floodwater deluged an inscribed board which is the symbol of the highest water level of the Three Gorges." All these historical records have provided an important hydro-geological basis for the construction of Gezhou Dam and the Project of the Three Gorges.

The northern bank of the roundabout ahead is Liantuo, the southern, Nantuo. In 1919, Li Siguang, Father of China's Geology, returned to motherland after acquiring a master degree at Birmingham University in England. In 1924, he led his students to make investigation into this area and defined the Sinian Genealogy in explicit and clear-cut terms. Geology of the Eastern Gorge of the Yangtze River and Its History, written by Li Siguang and his students, has enabled the research in this regard to take the lead in the world.

Ladies and gentlemen, our boat has passed through Nanjin Pass of Yichang, the eastern gate of the Three Gorges of the Yangtze River. The towering cliffs on both sides of Nanjin Pass form another natural strategic post and different kingdoms fought for it bitterly in history. Please look at the riverside area. Those places of interest are the Sanyou Cave, the White Horse Cave, Linfeng City, Platform of Drum-Striking for Zhang Fei and Pavilion of Supreme Happiness. The dam ahead is Gezhou Dam, the existing largest dam of the Yangtze River and a regulatory reservoir for the Project of the Three Gorges. The Construction of Gezhou Dam started on 30 December 1970 and was completed on 10 December 1988. Look! They are three locks and two power generation Factories. Those 27 holes are the locks of the outlet. That is the lock to soft sand. This is the dyke to control deposit. These are the main components of the Gezhou Dam. This dam is 2606.5 metres long and 70 metres high. The total

Selected Tour Commentaries

drainage area of the Yangtze River which the dam controls for the moment is 1 million squ. km, accounting for 55% of the total. The storage capacity of the reservoir is 1.58 billion cubic metres, 21 power generators are installed and the total installed capacity is 2.715 million kilowatts. The total investment amounted to ¥4.848 billion. The electricity generated here is transmitted to Central China and East of China and other areas through super-high-voltage power transmission lines and the dam has become one of the key energy bases in China. Since the first generator was installed in July 1981, the aggregate electricity turnout has reached 143 billion kwh by May 1994. The output value has scored ¥12 billion. A lot of foreign friends praised Gezhou Dam Project as "the pride of the Chinese people" and "the new Great Wall of the Chinese nation."

Dear friends, our boat will go through No.2 ship lock and it will take 50 minutes or so to pass it. Look! The lock gates of the upper reach have opened and the movable dual-purpose bridge is rising slowly to 18 metres high so that the ships and boats can pass safely. Now the boat is slowly entering the lock room. The lock room is 280 metres long and 34 metres wide. Ships of 10,000 tons can pass it without difficulty. Look there! The lock gates of the upper reach are closing slowly. The lock gates fit together perfectly and even a drop of water can not penetrate through. Tourists from home and abroad speak highly of this dam, some would say, "Miracle, it is really a miracle." Look! The lock gates of the lower reach are opening slowly. The two gates are 39.4 metres wide and 34 metres high; each weighs 600 tons, and the area is larger than two basketball courts. The control of both the lock gates and the valves is convenient and flexible. Now we're out of the lock room. The place we're going to is our destination city Yichang, the so-called "the Throat to the Three Gorges" and "the Throat between Chongqing and Hubei Province."

Friends, the magnificence of the Three Gorges never fails to strike a chord of feelings among the tourists. Many foreign guests

The Three Gorges of the Yangtze River

commended: "The Three Gorges of the Yangtze River are a wonder of the whole world. It is treasure bestowed by God". The ex-president of Singapore Lee said excitedly after his visit: "What amazing beauty the Three Gorges are! I would prefer to be a general manager of a Travel Agency of the Three Gorges when I resign some day."

Our boat will anchor at the wharf of Yichang harbour. And today you're supposed to be staying in Sanxia Hotel which is three-star-rated. We've booked air-tickets to Wuhan and Xi'an for you, so don't worry about that.

Three days' visit has conceived profound friendship between us and I will bear it in mind for life. On the point of saying goodbye, please let me, on behalf of all our crew members, extend all our best wishes to you, and I sincerely hope that you will enjoy the visit all the more in Wuhan and Xi'an!

Good-bye, dear friends!

Have a pleasant journey!

Selected Tour Commentaries

TEMPLE OF THE CHEN CLAN

Now we've come to the Temple of the Chen Clan. Please take your valuable articles with you and get off the bus to visit and appreciate the essence of Chinese architecture, which has stood for 100 years.

(Outside the gate)

My friends, this is the Temple of the Chen Clan. Construction of the temple began in 1890 and was completed 4 years later. The floor space of the main body is 6400 m^2 and is in the shape of Siheyuan, with a traditional Chinese architectural style. What is different between a Siheyuan and this temple is that the temple integrates 19 buildings, big and small, with several large siheyuan and adopts a strictly symmetrical layout. The central line is the axis, eastern and western palaces are built along the line and wing-rooms are constructed outside. It highlights striking features of clan temples and academies in South China. We often employ the following words to outline the whole constuction: "Shensanjin" "Guanwujian" "Jiutang" and "Liuyuan" "Jin" refers to the depth of the architecture. Inside the temple there are three rows of large halls; each is 80 metres long. They are tall, spacious, and imposing . Each row of halls is called one "Jin" so we have "three jin" or "Sanjin" "Jin" is a unit used by the ancient people to measure floor space, and "Guangwujian" means a floor space of 5 "jian." "Jiutang and Liuyuan" means that there are 9 halls and 6 courtyards. It is the most typical archi-

Temple of the Chen Clan

tectural complex, boasting the largest scale, and the most exquisite decorative techniques in folk architecture among all clan memorial buildings in Guangdong. It is famous for its rigorous symmetry, imposing outlook, exquisite ornament, magnificent style, and has won wide acclaim from visitors from all corners of the world. After visiting this memorial hall, the outstanding modern writer and poet Mr. Guo Moruo commended: "Wonderful workmanship can surpass nature, yet nature can never match workmanship; the wonder of architecture is created here, and it is better to enjoy its beauty than read only from books." Its elegance of ornamental technique shows forth in Mr. Guo's writing, and now let's see in person how it displays its beauty and elegance. Let's start our visit from outside the gate. Right now you can see that there is brick sculpture of figures on either brick wall of the gate. They depict two stories: one is the story of the Liangshan Mountain Gathering of the outlaws in a Chinese classic masterpiece, "All Men Are Brothers," and the other is a historical story, "Liu Qing Subdues Unruly Pony." (bringing the visitors to the sculpture of the latter one) This brick sculpture portrays a vivid picture of Liu Qing subduing an unruly pony. Liu Qing was a general of the Song Dynasty. At that time the neighboring country the Kingdom of Xixia eyed the Song Dynasty covetously and provoked the Song Dynasty under the pretext of subduing an unruly pony. General Liu Qing came to the fore and subdued the unruly horse with his wisdom and courage and nipped the problem in the bud. (Pointing to the brick) The man with firmly clenched and an awesome bearing is General Liu Qing. The subdued horse lies on the ground on its back. Many generals and are holding their breaths watching. The whole picture adopts the multi-tier technique and thus has a striking three-dimensional effect. The picture seems vivid and regular because many sculpting techniques are employed, such as sculpture, relief and piercing. By applying outstanding technique, the sculptor cut each line as tiny as a thread. Forty-odd figures are made true to life, as we can see here. In additon, the brick reliefs on

Selected Tour Commentaries

both sides, "One Hundred Birds worshipping the Phoenix" and "The Picture of Five Generations," make it all the more splendid. These kinds of brick sculptures are rare in Guangdong. They retain their glamour and splendour despite ages and exposure to weather.

(Turning to the stone lions in front of the gate)

In ancient times, families with distinguished social status would have a pair of stone lions placed in front of their residence. For one thing, it shows their high social status and noble origin; for another, it dispels wicked spirits. The one on the left is male, and the other on the right is female. Under the foot of the male lion is a stone ball symbolizing the power to unify the universe. Under the foot of the female is a cub, implying prosperous offspring. This pair of lions is no exception in terms of tradition. Yet in Cantonese's mind's eye they are above the other lions. Seen from their appearances, the male lion wears a smile while the female one is meek and lovely. They are more amiable than lions in the North. In an emotional sense, the cantonese deem them as sacred lions that can run against floods and preserve safety. A legend goes that 100 years ago, a deluge haunted the area of the Temple of the Chen Clan, and the people here could not bear the severe disaster. One day, growls of lions were heard from afar, and people saw two lions opening their mouths wide and swallowing all the floodwater. Then people were rescued at last. Since then, there have been no floods in this area. And the legend of "Stone growling to safeguard peace" has spread far and wide to this day. As you can see, the movable stone ball inside the lions' mouths imply that they can gulp down floodwater. People who come to the temple like to turn the stone balls for blessings. Please have a try.

(Coming to the stone drum in front of the gate)

Just now I mentioned that stone lions are symbols of a noble status. Can you find other stone carvings that play the same role of bestowing blessings? The high platforms on both sides of the gate? No,

Temple of the Chen Clan

they used to be the stages for performances on grand occasions. The relief drafts at the corner of the walls? I am afraid you're wrong again. They symbolize happiness and peace. This gertleman (lady) has it right. It's this pair of big drums.

In the past, it was a privilege to display stone drums in front of the gate: the size depended on social status. Whoever decorated their gates with stone drums in private against the concept of stratification would be considered ignorant of the laws of the court and would incur the death penalty. The Chen Clan, however, was not only entitled to furnish their gate with stone drums, but also had drum bases made as high as a man. Who knows why? (Vistitors are supposed to get the answer) Yes, that is right. It owed a lot to Chen Botao, who came in the imperial examination at national level, and therefore, this pair of stone drums would better glorify the Chen Clan than the stone lions did. The stone lions and stone drums are only two among the stone carvings in the Temple of Chen Clan. You can also see many other stone carvings on the buildings, such as stone columns, stone pillars, stone railings, stone slates, stone gates, stone platforms, stone chairs and stone fruit. Many techniques like sculpting, relief, carving and others are employed. The art of stone carving here is rated as the top of its kind.

Now let's enter the gate and have a look inside. Although nobody extends arm welcome to us today, two generals have looked forward to your coming already. (Now the tour guide distracts the visitors' eyes to the portraits on the gate) This is Qin Qiong, and this is Wei Chigong. They are not handsome, yet they do not show any intention towards your arrival. They made great accomplishments in establishing the Tang Dynasty and have stood guard for the peace and safety of Chen Family for over 100 years here. The story can be traced back to the Tang Dynasty 1000 years ago. It is said the Emperor of the Tang Dynasty Tai Zong or Emperor Li Shimin was Satan-possessed soon after he ascended to the throne. He heard ghosts wailing outside every night and he was too anxious to fall asleep. Fi-

Selected Tour Commentaries

nally he called in his ministers for solutions. Qin Qiong, the military general, said: "I have killed enemies like cutting melons and collected bodies like gathering ants in my life . So I would fear nothing in facing those ghosts. I would like to guard the palace outside the gate with Weichijingde (Weichi Gong)." Li Shimin was very pleased and approved this proposal on the spot. This move came to effect and nothing happened for several nights. Afterwards, the emperor ordered their images be portrayed and pasted on to the gate. They are wearing war robes, holding weapons with bows and arrows around their waists. Surprisingly, since then no evil spirits have haunted this palace. This story passed quickly and widely from mouth to mouth. Finally, it became known to all. To follow suit, people pasted the two generals' portraits on their own gates for peace and safety. From then on, the images of Qin Qiong and Weichi Gong have been the most popular gate-gods among the people. The two huge portraits of 4 metres high in the immemorial hall of Chen Family we see now are the mighty and imposing of images of the two gate. Both the red-faced Qi Qiong and black-faced Weichi Gong appear tall, powerful and awesome. The carving masters took the technique of line-drawing and heavy-coloring, effected striking colors and made the figures true to life. They deserve the reputation as the masterpieces of ancient colorpainting in China.

We will be seeing two similar frescos inside wing-rooms soon. One portrays the picture of a famous work *On Teng Wang Pavilion* written by Wang Bo, and the other portrays a famous poem, *A Feast of Peaches and Plums at Night,* written by the famous poet Li Bai in the Tang Dynasty. You may feast your eyes on them when we visit them later.

The Temple of Chen Clan was built with bricks and wood. Its brick sculpture is outstanding, and its wooden carving is even more vivid. It is reasonable to say that wherever you find wood in the temple, you will find magnificent wooden carving . Wooden carvings enjoy the largest number, the longest scale and the richest content of

Temple of the Chen Clan

carving in the temple. Please look upward, and you will see on the ceiling numerous figures, animals, landscapes and fruit. They were carved on every beam and each set of brackets on top of the columns, as well as on the eaves slates of over 1000 metres long. Some of them record historical storys, some tell folklore and some are landscapes of Guangzhou. We can say that all these words are a comprehensive expression of Cantonese wooden carving technique and exhibit the best of its kind. Let's take the carving on these four gates for example. They are one of the masterpieces. On each screen gate there are 3 wooden carvings: an upper picture, a middle one and a bottom one. The two upper ones are made with the technique of double-faced carving, and the bottom one is a relief. The carved part not only boasts exquisite and outstanding carving skills, but also allows ventilation and lighting. This adapts well to the moist climate of Canton. The rich content also expresses different meanings. (Explaining to the visitors from left to right) This is a picture scroll that depicts the fishermen enjoying themselves on the river after a day's work. As you can see, a net hangs high, the fisherman plays a musical instrument and sings to himself in a care-free manner; the mother caresses her child in her arms and watches children playing in the water with a smile on her face. The second picture is called Searching for a Plum in the Snow. In this picture the famous poet Meng Hao ran in the Tang Dynasty was going out to enjoy plum blossoms on a donkey on a snowy day. (Introducing the third picture) This picture describes a kind of folk dance called "Two Lions Fighting for an Embroidered Ball." It seems to have brought the people to a clamorous scene with drums and gongs striking. On top of this screen gate are carved independently 3 goats and 2 lions. Why did they carve them? In China, people regard November, December and January as 3 when the days are long and nights are short, so they are called Sanyang season, implying that the icy wonder has passed by and the new spring is approaching. "Goat" in Chinese shares the same pronunciation as "yang," and 3 goats refer to 3 months. "Tai"

Selected Tour Commentaries

in Chinese has the meaning of peace and safety, hence the picture got the name "Three Goats Open Tai." These 2 lions, one big, the other small, implies "Shaoshi" and "Taishi." The "lion" in Chinese shares the same pronuciation of "shi" in "Shaoshi" and "Taishi". In ancient times both "Shaoshi" and "Taishi" were official titles. "Taishi" was a powerful official in charge of military and political affairs in the royal court, and here it obviously refers to Chen Botao. "Shaoshi" refers to the offspring of the Chen Clan, who took minor posts under Chen Botao.

To express best wishes with homophones is one of the main expressions for the ornamental technique in the Temple of the Chen Clan. As you can see, each relief at the bottom of the screen gates follows this. (Introducing the first wood-carved screen gate) This carving is a Bajiao banana tree; under the tree there is a hen leading a group of chickens to search for food. The inscription means "making great fortunes to benefit generations to come." The big leaves of Bajiao banana trees symbolize the wealth of the Chen Clan, and the group of chickens symbolizes "generations of offspring filling the house." (About the second picture) The inscription for this picture means "With heaven and earth in the teapot, official posts and wealth come to the hand of Chen Family." You may wonder about the connections between the inscription and the teapot, wine vessel, phoenix, bat and unicorn carved in the picture. (Sparing some time for visitors to think this over before your explanation) In fact, "jue" in Chinese for the wine vessel shares the pronunciation of "jue" for the rank of nobility in Chinese, while "fu" for bat sounds he same as "fu" for happiness in Chinese. The teapot symbolizes the Chen Clan. Therefore, the whole picture means that the Chen Clan is small in a sense, yet it can hold the whole universe. As long as the descendants of the Chen Clan are and intelligent, they will gain titles and become something and enjoy blessings (phoenix), happiness (bat) and nobility (unicorn). The implication of this picture is not that explicit, but it fully demonstrates the ambition and ideal of the Chen Clan.

Temple of the Chen Clan

(Coming to the third and fourth screen gates)

Now I've got a question for all of you. Look at the two screen gates. One (the third) shows that smoke curls up in the air; the other depicts old, crooked bamboo. These two pictures form a Chinese character. Let's see who can get it first. (A question for visitors from Southeast Asia or Taiwan Province) It is the word for "longevity," and 5 bats are flying around. Each of them for one kind of happiness, namely, wealth, health, virtue, good luck, and longevity. This picture mainly highlights the implication of "five happinesses and ngevity." (pointing to the fourth picture) This picture forms a Chinese character "happiness" but is placed upside down with bamboo stalks. It means that fortune has fallen upon the Chen Clan. These two patterns both have the implication of "having fortune and longevity" and encourage the Chen Clan to be bold in making advances. Only in this way can they feel proud and elated like heroes and enjoy "continuous fortune and longevity" (the inscription of the third picture). Even if they are "great minds that mature slowly", they still can bring happiness and fortune to the Chen Clan (the inscription of the fourth picture). The content of the fourth pictures on the screen gates fully demonstrates the profound thoughts of the Chen Clan. The exquisite workmanship of wooden carving reflects the wisdom and intelligence of ancient laboring people. However, these are only a drop in the sea of the exquisite craftsmanship of wood carving in the Temple of the Chen Clan. On the 12 screen gates of Jiuxian Hall ahead as well as on the partition boards of the two halls on both sides, the Cantonese wood carving craftsmen exhibit a long corridor of Chinese historical stories. There are numerous stories and pictures to hear and see there.

(Entering the first "Jin" courtyard)

The architecture we'll see in this courtyard is also out of the common run. (introducing one by one with gestures) The well-built corridors on both sides don't join the 3 rows of palaces together, but divide the Academy into 6 courtyards. The hall in the front is the

Selected Tour Commentaries

main construction of the temple—Jiuxian Hall. Seen from outside, it is grand, imposing and magnificent. With low wingrooms serving as a foil, the main hall stands out more grand and magnificent. It was here that the Chen Clan held sacrifice ceremonies in spring and autumn and had discussions and gatherings at that time. What is worth mentioning here is that all the beams and sets of brackets on top of the columns of the whole hall were joined by wooden joggle joints instead of nails. A century has passed, but the hall still stands firm and beautiful. What is most attractive is the rich-color pottery and lime sculptures on the ridge of the roof. Classical stories of various kinds are included, and local landscapes, flowers, birds, fish, insects, figures, pavilions, platforms, buildings and attics can all be found here. It is really a feast for the eyes.

On the ridge of the roof, the top sculptures are pottery and the bottom, lime . The ridge runs 27 metres long and has a rich variety. It is simply a huge collection of three-dimentional series of stories, such as *Immortals celebrating the Birthday of the Heaven, Promotion of Official Posts, Eight Immortals Celebrating Birthday, Two Immortals called Harmony and Unification, Miss Ma Proposing Wine, and Qilin (a legendary animal) Sending a Son*. It is a world of stories and scenes, with more than 200 sculptured figures. All of them are of different appearances and postures and are true to life. You probably have already noticed the flying legendary turtle. It's tail sticks up high and two long barbels spread to the far end and make the whole ridge absolutely lifelike. Who knows why the turtle is placed here? ··· We can generalize the reason in four characters: *du zhan ao tou,* namely, standing alone on the head of the turtle. The story goes that in the past the candidate who got the first place in the imperial examination at the national level would stand on a stone step with a huge turtle carved on it, waiting for the emperor to receive him. The first successful candidate stood right on the head of the turtle, and hence the idiom came into being. The decoration of turtle here is not only to add uncommon grandeur to the temple, but also to express

Temple of the Chen Clan

the high expectations of ancestors of Chen Clan on the offspring to surpass Chen Botao, encouraging them to come first in the imperial examination so as to "stand alone on the head of the turtle."

Most of the pottery sculptures in this temple are made out of special craftsmanship of Shiwan. By taking the colors of yellow, green, sapphire blue, black and white as the main enamel glaze, the pottery sculptures are colorful and are thus considered one of the main ornamental workmanship of the architecture in this Temple.

Look! There is a monster on the vertical ridge. It takes the shape of a male lion with only one horn on its head. Its eyes are glaring at something and its ears are pricked up, its mouth is widely open and its tail sticks up, its hair standing on end. It occupies a commanding position and looks aggressive . This is the so-called unicorn lion, used to "subdue monsters with monsters" among the people to make sure that the country is prosperous and the people live in peace. It is also painted with heavy hues: red and green. Contrasting pleasingly with pottery sculptures on the ridge, stands another kind of architectural ornamental craftsmanship-lime sculpture. Works of this kind on various themes can be found on the bottom of the ridge, the roof, the corridor gates, the upper parts of the joint corridors and other places. They look rough when seen near and look true to life when seen from afar. The production process is also unique. Different from pottery sculptures, which can be baked first and then be installed to the needed places, the lime sculptures need to be made on the spot by the craftsmen to the requirement of themes and space and then be colored. In comparison with the pottery sculpture, the lime is not as durable, but it can bear weathering. Its splendid color, life-like shape make it still true to life and distinctive to this day. No one would expect that this particular artful cream is made of lime, grass paper and straw.

The two kinds of sculptures on the ridge are symbols of noble status for high officials and noblemen in ancient China. Of the Cantonese architectural craftsmanship, the ridge of the temple has the

Selected Tour Commentaries

largest scale and is made with the most exquisite technique. There are 11 such ridges with pottery sculptures and over 1800-metre lime sculpture construction in this temple. All above-mentioned make the temple the best of its kind in Guangdong.

(Climbing the flat roof in front of the Jiuxian Hall)

Dear friends, the workmanship on this ridge is magnificent and marvelous (pointing to the joined corridors on both sides), and the flower-belt-like joined corridors just feast our eyes and embrace profound meaning.

Then what does the flat roof we're standing on show us? Just the stone carved railings around? Or plates of "fruit" produced in Lingnan? Or the stage for opera performances on grand occasions? These are not the main purposes. We'll be lucky to see in this place the ornamental workmanship which was rare in ancient architecture in Guangdong. Even in the temple, there are no more places you can s ee such ornamentel craftsmanship. Let's see who has exceptional insight to find the rare treasure. (Now the tour guide should give visitors some time to search for it; it is easy to find) Excellent! That's the iron-cast painting embedded in the middle of the stone-carved railings. Its outstanding workmanship and rich and vivid designs not only reflect the advanced level of steel and iron-casting industry in ancient Buddha Hill area, but also embody the Chen Clan's ambition and aspiration for happy life: "*The Picture of Rice Ears and Carps*" expresses the wishes of "living at peace each year"; "*Lotus Flowers and Carps* expresses the aspiration of "having a hall filled with gold and jade"; "*Phoenix and Deer*" symbolizes "wealth and high rank"; "*Eagle and Bear*" symbolizes "heroes." The craftsmanship works are few but exquisite, the materials are rough but firm and durable. The iron-casting brings outstanding artflavor to the blueprint of the buildings of this temple.

(Coming to the last row of halls)

We've passed Jiuxian Hall and come to the back hall of the third

Temple of the Chen Clan

row of halls. This is where the ancestral tablets of the Chen Clan are placed and where were offered to their ancestors. On February 4th and August 4th each year, the Chen Clan would hold the spring and autumn sacrifice ceremonies here . On these two days, offerings on the altar table were abundant and people below the altar table are kneeling down and kowtowing. Slowly rising incense smoke accompanies each pious heart who is offering sacrifices and kneeling down to show respect to the thousands of tablets preserved here. There are "stresses" for the arrangements of the tablets. Those in the middle and on the upper shelf are for those Chen families who donated alarge amount of money to build this temple at that time; those beside the middle and on the bottom shelf are for those who made smaller contributions to build this memorial hall. Although thousands of tablets were burned during the Cultural Revolution, we still can imagine the large number of the tablets at that time from the huge shrine embedded in the wall for ancestral tablets.

(Diverting the visitors' attention with another family shrine)

Here displays a family shrine carved out of wood with golden paint. It exhibits far more than the shrine itself. It is a magnificent artistic treasure of wooden carving. The exquisite and superb craftsmanship, the magnificent and imposing decoration, the lifelike figures, the original conception, all make us overwhelmed with admiration.

(Bring the guests to the gods pavilion)

This is also a wooden carving treasure. It looks like a sedan chair but is not used for carrying people, it is similar to a shrine but is not used for preserving tablets. It is the gods pavilion used to enshrine deities. During the two sacrifice ceremonies in spring and autumn, people carried it in a procession along the street. When the gods pavilion is carried home, it implies that deities are welcome home and happiness will follow accordingly.

The gods pavilion can also be used to display the social status at

Selected Tour Commentaries

that time. As you can see, the gods pavilion has 4 levels from top to bottom in line with the social status. The upper 3 levels are connected by columns with golden dragon inscribed on them: the level with the dragon head has two characters which mean the imperial edict, and this surely refers to the "son of dragon" who is superior to the people; the level with the dragon body is for various civil and military officials who serve the emperor in the court; the level with the dragon tail is reserved for the local officials; on the bottom are carved the common people and servants. This is the whole implication of the gods pavilion.

You will enjoy different views at each pace in the temple, and the scene changes with your steps. The main seven decoration techniques are used for each design with its own profound meaning. Each figure has his own outstanding experience , each scene has a moving story behind it and each fine work reflects the outsanding workman ship of the Cantonese craftsmen. The temple is a treasure house of folk arts in Guangdong. There is too much to be seen in the temple, and time does not permit us to visit all the places. I have to say the visit today stops here. You can spend your free time enjoying the modern Cantonese handicrafts on display here to your heart's content. Every conceivable kind of carving can be found to feast your eyes, such as ivory carving, bone carving, horn carving, kernel carving, jade carving, stone carving, wooden carving , ink-stone carving, micro-carving, pottery, Cantonese embroidery, Zhu embroidery, paper cutting, lacquer ware and others. I see you on the bus in 20 minutes.

(Back on the bus)

Dear friends, what did you think of the Temple of the Chen Clan ?··· But now I'd like to return to the previous topic: What on earth are the seven architecture decoration arts of the temple? And why do we call it the museum of the folk craftsmanship in Guangdong? (Now the tour guide is expected to ask the visitors these two questions. You are supposed to let the guests answer just to activate

Temple of the Chen Clan

the mood of the guests and enliven the atmosphere on the bus) Now let's answer the first question together. The seven decoration arts are: brick sculpture, stone carving, color painting, wooden carving, pottery sculpture, lime sculpture and iron-casting. That is right. By employing these seven arts, the temple has become, in itself, a huge folk handicraft with elegant carving and fine works. It gives obvious to the social customs of late Qing Dynasty when the people aspired for elegance and exquisiteness as well as magnificence. As a crystallization of artistic wisdom and technique of the folk arts in Guangdong, the temple is deemed as a treasurable art legacy handed down from the ancient people. The masterpieces of various modern folk craftsmanship exhibited in the temple still make the good better. As early as in 1958, the temple became the place where the folk handiwork was collected, preserved, studied and displayed. Therefore, it is appropriate to name it the Museum of the Cantonese Folk Handicrafts." As early as the 1920s, a German scholar put the temple of the Chen Clan in the *Art of World Architecture;* a Japanese scholar regards it as the typical model for the architectural art in Lingnan area; a famous Chinese writer Mr. Guo Moruo praised it as a world where "Wonderful workmanship excels nature"; and now, this "bright pearl of architecture in Lingnan" is so grand and magnificent that it has become the pride of the Cantonese people. A number of foreign visitors are overwhelmed by its exquisite craftsmanship and extend praise to it.

My dear friends, the stories about the temple are numerous, its architeture is marvelous, yet our time here is too short to visit it all. I hope you can have the chance to come back to visit it again, to continue to listen to the stories and to see the parts you've not visited.

Good-bye, friends!

Have a nice trip!

275

Selected Tour Commentaries

STONE CARVINGS ON THE BAODING MOUNTAIN IN DAZU COUNTY

Dazu Stone Carvings are located in the county of Dazu in Chongqing municipality , about 120 km away from the city center of Chongqing. The carving work began in late Tang Dynasty and saw its heyday in the Song Dynasty. There are over 60,000 statues altogether and they are in 40 places of Dazu County. The statues on Mount Baoding and Mount Longgang (namely, Beishan Mountain) boast the most centralized collection, the largest scale and the most exquisite craftsmanship of all the places, and in 1961 this area was listed by the State Council as one of the first cultural heritage places under state protection.

14 km away from Dazu County, stone carvings on Mount Baoding were created from 1179 to 1249, or in the reigns of Emperor Chunxi to Emperor Chunyou in the South Song Dynasty. The person in charge was Zhao Zhifeng. Zhao Zhifeng was born in Xueliang township of Dazu County, several km away from Mount Baoding. He became a monk when he was five, and moved to the western part of Sichuan Province to learn Buddhism when he was 16. Then he returned home and had the Buddhism "Daochang" built under his care (Buddhism "Daochang" refers to the place where the Buddhist doctrine is publicized with images).

He dedicated his following 70 years to this course until he passed

276

Stone Carvings on the Baoding Mountain in Dazu County

away at the age of 90, when the forest of statues was completed at a preliminary level. The Buddha Bay we are seeing now is the major part of the stone carvings on Mount Baoding. This Buddhism "Daochang" also includes 12 other places and extends 2.5 km. The total mumber of the statues is over 10,000 and some of them are titanic and imposing with various dimensions. Since the planning was unified and the craftsmanship was consummate, there are few similarities between the statues. Moreover, the statues are each in connection with each other and are each in accordance with the Buddhism doctrine. "Almost the entire creed of this religion is included in one generation" (see the steel inscription in Dazu), and thus a Buddhism "Daochang" with a comprehensive, rigid creed and special features was formed. This is the only Buddhism *daochang* that houses huge stone carvings in China.

In an effort to build the Big Buddha Bay, Zhao Zhifeng built the Small Buddha Bay behind the Shengshou Temple. In terms of plastic arts , the Small Buddha Bay is the original copy of the big one. It is safe to say that the statues on Mount Baoding were carved as a result of the Buddhist scripts and the proposals by Zhao Zhifeng.

The introduction of Buddhism into China made the arts of Buddha stone carvings start to flourish gradually. The early-carved Buddha statues, such as those of Dunhuang and of Yungang carved during the North Wei Dynasty, were mostly influenced by the statue arts of Jian Tuoluo and Indian Buddhism, in terms of content , form and figure modeling. Up to the Sui and Tang dynasties, foreign influence lessened little by little. For instance, the modeling of the Tang Dynasty at the Longmen Grottoes was basically of the Chinese style. Dazu stone carvings are representatives of the later period of Chinese Buddhist history. The basic characteristics of the Buddha carvings during this period are that they reflect the earthly world, true life and a typical Chinese style. When the late Chinese leader Deng Xiaoping visited these stone carvings in 1986, he clicked his tongue with

Selected Tour Commentaries

admiration, saying that "These are completely of Chinese characteristics."

Now we'll give a brief introduction to some major enshrining grottoes and modeling arts here.

(Law-upholding Buddha statue)

No matter kind of sacred Buddhist place, they all have lawupholding deities built at the entrance. The Four diamond Kings in all Buddhist temples and monasteries are such deities.

The Dharma Protectors in this shrine (the second one) are different from those of other Buddhist sects. There are 9 altogether: the middle one is a Buddha , and the one above him is his incarnation. The deities on both sides of the Buddha are 8 Bodhisattvas, also called Eight Heavenly Dragons. You may feel perplexed to see that the Buddha and 8 Bodhisattvas are so terrifying and vicious. However, we know the Buddhist doctrine stresses deterrent forces. Therefore, they appear irritated in order to eliminate "evil obstacles" for the common people. People will encounter many obstacles subjectively and objectively in the process of enlightenment. Only when these obstacles are removed can they be enlightened as quickly as possible and finally elevate themselves to the level of Buddha.

(The carved image of six ways of Samsara)

The stone statues at the Baoding Mountain are carved to publicize the basic doctrine of Buddhism to the people in a vivid way, and the image is the first lesson. It starts with the outlook of life from the angle of Buddhism. The statues in this shrine (the third one) focus on "retributive justice" and "karma samsara" of buddhist doctrine. "Retributive justice" means that people will behave as long as they are alive. If their behaviour is beneficial to society and others, that is good, otherwise, bad. Good behaviolly will rewarded with blessings, and bad behaviour with punishments; if the reward is not forthcoming, it is because the time has not yet come when the time

Stone Carvings on the Baoding Mountain in Dazu County

comes, everyone gets his due reward or punishment. The so-called "karma samsara" refers to the fact that everything has its cause and effect. "If people want to know the cause of things today, they should look back to their former life; if they want to know the effect on their after life, they should examine today." So "retributive justice" and "karma samsara" can be mutually deducted.

The main statue in this shrine is called "Wuchang Giant Ghost" and is about 6.6 metres tall. According to Buddhism, tens of thousands of things created in the world are composed of four elements: earth, wind, water and fire. They are called "Sida" in Chinese. Tens of thousands of things are created for different reasons, and are formed with the combinations of various conditions. Buddhists call it the "combination of cause and luck." If cause and luck are combined and compatible, it is "to be." If not, it is "not to be." All things change and have their beginnings and endings. This is known as "Wuchang" impermanence or "Kong" (empty); that is, "everything is changing, and the sensuous world is illusory." The "Wuchang Giant Ghost" carries a big wheel of 2.7 meters in diameter with two arms. The wheel actually is a miniature of the "sea of bitterness," or "the earthly world." There is one man sitting at the center of the wheel. He stands for the people who practise Buddhism. Six rays of light are coming from the center of his heart and divide the wheel into six parts. This implies that "the source of all things created are in the heart and everything is created by the heart." To put it in a plain way, thought has control over action. There are small circles inside the rays, and inside the circles are Buddhas or Bodhisattvas. This means people all have Buddhism in their minds, and all have possibilities of becoming Buddhas. Under the person practising Buddhism there are 3 animals: a pig, symbolizing avarice; a snake, symbolizing vice and envy; and a pigeon, symbolizing stupidity. Buddhists call avarice, vice and envy and stupidity "three evil traits." Owing to the influence of these three evil traits, people's sense of Buddhism will be blocked or destroyed, and will do evil and incur punishment

Selected Tour Commentaries

in return. In the end, people will fall to the 3 lower levels of incarnation: animal incarnation, hell incarnation, and hungry incarnation. If people don't accept or can avoid the influence of these 3 evil traits, they will do good and be rewarded. In the end, they will enter the 3 upper incarnations: human incarnation, heaven incarnation and God of War incarnation. Even if they enter the 3 upper incarnations, people are still not free from sufferings or the samsara. The aim of Buddhism is to lift people out of these three incarnations of rebirth and avoid the samsara. That calls for further practice of asceticism: "learn diligently the Buddhist doctrine, keep a quiet mind and cultivate the mind so as to perceive both the past and future; eliminate avarice, vice, envy and stupidity," and thoroughly get rid of and sever aspirations for material gains. Four sentences are inscribed on both sides of this set of statues. The general idea is as follows: "There are various kinds of people in the world, and they are avaricious about material gains and find themselves degenerated. Please look at the Buddhas above the earthly world. They used to be ordinary people in the world." With excellent images and words, it is clear from a glance that the earthly world pressures you with an endless "sea of bitterness." How do you get rid of it? What you do is follow Buddhism.

(Three Saints of Avatamsake School)

The statues in the 5th shrine are grand, imposing and enjoy outstandin gcraftsmanship. The average height is 8.2 metres and the width 14.5 metres. This group covers an area of about $120m^2$. The Buddha statue is 7 metres tall; his shoulders are 2.9 metres wide and his chest is 1.4 metres thick. The Buddha statue inclines and protrudes out of the cliff about 4 metres. It is extremely difficult to carve such Buddha statues, to say the least.

The statue in the middle of the three is Avairocana, and is also called the Buddha of unmeasurable logevity and light. The other two on both sides are his underling Pushan Samantabhadra and Manjusri.

Stone Carvings on the Baoding Mountain in Dazu County

According to the Xian Sect, Manjusri should be on the left and Pushan on the right, but the Mi Sect arranged them to the contrary. Over the head of Avairocana are two rays of light. This is an important characteristic of stone carving in line with the Mi Sect.

This shrine is outstandingly successful in terms of its artistic effect. From the angle of modeling the statues slope 2 metres from the crag. And when you look upward, you do not have the sense of imbalance of the carving proportion. The Buddha looks downward and meets the eyes of the visitors. This demonstrates the benevolence of the Buddha: solemn but kind while looking over the common people, to show his concern for them. Judging by the size, each statue is over tens of tons in weight. Yet wrinkles on the swlpted kasaya are bold and unconstrained, making it smooth and imposing and giving us an impression of silk-made quality. It is not exaggerating to say that the kasaya seems to be just out of the water and exposed against the wind. This again sets off the outstanding making of Buddhas and Bodhisattvas. As for the carving techniques, the wrinkles on kasaya are both realistic and vivid. They were carved with an exquisite out line. In terms of mechanics the hanging arm of Manjusri is 2 metres away from the torso and his hand holds a pagoda about 1. 8 metres high and over 4 00 kg. The pagoda has been there for more than 800 years and Manjusri has never moved his hand for a rest, with the pagoda remaining where it was. What sustains the heavy weight? The kasaya of course. The kasaya comes down from the shoulders to the elbows like an opened bow and props up Manjusri's hand in this way. The gravity falls down along the kasaya into the deep crags. Just like the arch-bridge, which draws the pressure to the bridge piers, this tremendously strengthens the firmness of statue. The same is true of the hand of Bodhisattva Pushan, which holds a Jingang pagoda. All of the three statues incline forward and there is no perspective leek at all when you look upward in front of them. The proportions are very coordinated. All these attainments owe a lot to the experiences of carving through dynasties. These statues reach a new

Selected Tour Commentaries

artistical and scientifical height.

(Avalokitesvara with thousand arms)

This is a very famous statue on Mount Baoding. According to the Buddhist doctrine, Avalokitesvara (Goddess of Mercy) can relieve the people of all sufferings, that is, Avalokitesvara is an Almighty Bodhisattva. The Mi Sect built the Avalokitesvara with a thousand arms to show that she has unconstrained power and can save the ordinary people. There is one eye in each hand. It implies that she looks on the whole world, has eyes sharp enough to perceive the minutest detail and has supreme wisdom.

This shrine (the 8th one) is 7.20 metres high, and the statue is 12.50 metres wide, covering an area of $88m^2$. Avalokitesvara is 3 metres tall and behind the statue there are 1007 arms stretching like the feathers of a peacok. The gestures are of various kinds and there is no similarity between any two. Each hand has one eye and holds a musical instrument used in a Buddhist mass. It is gilded all over and stands magnificent, making people dazzled and overwhelmed by the grandeur. According to the creed of Buddhism, Avalokitesvara with 8 hands and more than 8 hands can be called Avalokitesvara with a thousand hands. But there is no other Avalokitesvara under the sun with more hands than the one at Baoding Mountain that covers an area of $88m^2$. In the past, people in Sichuan Province said that they went to worship on Mount Ermei and Mount Baoding separately. Th ey went to worship on Baoding just to pay homage to the Goddess of Mercy with a thousand hands . In the past thousands of devotees covered tens or hundreds of km to come here to burn incense and pray for good luck.

In terms of art, the style of feathers opening on a peacock was employed in the arrangement of these 1000 hands. They lie layer upon layer in order but not in a dull manner. At first sight, people will think they are beyond enumeration. This is much wiser than a regular arrangement, such as 100 hands a row and 1000 hands ten rows.

Stone Carvings on the Baoding Mountain in Dazu County

In this way this statue has achieved an endless artistic effect. The modeling of hands is also marvelous. According to the doctrine of Buddhism, the Bodhisattva has 32 images, soft and gentle fingers and plump soles. These fingers are slender and tender like those of beauties. Many female dancers come here to observe the beautiful hands of Avalokitesvara and then imitate their gestures back on the stage. This, of course, brings about good artistic effects.

There are over 1000 instruments and articles in Avalokitesvara's hands, including musical instruments in the Buddhist mass and daily necessities of the common people. This provides an abundant basis for the study of social life in the Song Dynasty. There is a vertical eye on Avalokitesvara's forehead, which is unique to the Mi Sect rather than to the Xian Sect of Buddhism. This eye can see through the mystery of people's minds and the future. We often say that someone has exceptional insight, and this insight refers to this eye.

(Nirvana of Sakyamuni)

The statue in front of us now (the eleventh shrine) occupies the most prominent position. The whole scene is 31 metres long in order to highlight the Nirvana of Sakyamuni. Since the big Buddha statue is lying down, people also call it "Reclining Buddha." However, there is no such an expression in Buddhism, and it should be called, accor ding to the doctrine, the image of the Nirvana of Sakyamuni. Nirvana is the highest spiritual plane of Buddhism. It does not refer to death, but a state in which Buddha has no aspiration for the world, keeps optimistic and quiet and stands aloof from the matter of life and death.

The statue is in full conformity with religious rites. As recorded in the scripts of Nirvana, Sakyamuni passed away between two spinulose trees, so this scene is called "sacred traces of double spinulose trees." When he ched nirvana, he lay on the right with his head towards the north and his face towards the west. Before nirvana, his disciples sprouted from underground to listen to his last lecturing.

Selected Tour Commentaries

These half statues (altogether 14) are all his disciples, who arose from the earth. The one in the middle is an emperor, which shows that even the emperor came to extend condolences to Sakyamuni at his nirvana. The statue of Sakyamuni keeps his composure and solemnity. His vertical eye is half closed as if he was wide awake. This demonstrats the ideal state of nirvana wherethere is no distinction between life and death. But in the frescos in the Dunhuang Grottoes, the earth shook, trees fell down and houses collapsed; his disciples were so sad that they cut open their bellies and wished to die too. If the statues were arranged in this way, however nirvana could not justify itself: since nirvana is the highest state and the highest ideal, why is the scene so horrifying? Buddhists also felt the self-contradiction in this regard and gradually changed the statues in later periods to the atmosphere seen today: solemn, tranquil and grand.

The sculptors were very wise in their artistic arrangement: there was no problem carving a 31-metre-long Buddha, which is not small. But if the 31 -metre-long statue was placed in the 600-metre-long Big Buddha Bay, it would be less magnificent. Therefore the sculptors carved a Buddha with the proportion of 60 metres and left half of the statue (Below legs) in the rocks. At the same time, a spinulose tree was removed to the front of the leg from near the head. Thus, it highlights the theme and leaves much room for imagination. The whole picture features the following: the small sets off the big, the vertical breaks the horizontal , the rough contrasts with the exquisite, the head and crown are made with care and precision while the clothing of Buddha are carved with bold and resolute skills … all the above demonstrates the skillful and supreme carving craftsmanship of ancient artisans in China. The pictures of "Sakyamuni Was Born" and "Nine Dragons Bathe the Prince" beside the statue give impetus to people to reminisce the life of Buddha. And the smart design that let the water set from the pond above the Big Buddha Bay and the rainwater in summer flow out through the mouth of the dragons enables the statues to remain almost intact through 800-

Stone Carvings on the Baoding Mountain in Dazu County

year exposure to weathering. This is a marvelous accomplishment in Big Buddha Bay.

(Statues of loving kindness of parents)

Among the stone carvings in Dazu County, this shrine (No. 15 shrine) preserves the statues that have Chinese, local and earthly features of life. Every visitor can find a trace of his own here. The figures , the events, the clothing and the articles and instruments are all typical of the Sichuan style. Carvings here are completely Chinese-style sculpture art.

The whole shrine is divided into ten groups of statues, including "In the family way," "Suffering in labor," "Washing naps," "Moving the baby to place while the mother lies in the wetted bed," and "Missing sons and daughters when they are far away." All these exhibit the matchless loving kindness of parents towards their children. Each group has both images and words which bring out the best in each other. The words for the last group go like this: "Parents of 100 years old still worry about sons of 80 years old; even when they die, their spirits still show concern for them··· " This vividly demonstrates the troubles and pains of parents in bringing up their children and makes people examine their own conscience and then be as filial as they can. Buddhism does not stress filial duty at all, while the ethics and morality in China both place filial duty above all else, and assert that "filial duty is the best of all virtues" and "seeks loyal ministers from filial sons." Confucianism and Taoism are against Buddhism mainly because they criticize it for its ignorance of loyalty and filial duty. If Buddhism intends to become wide-spread and gain more believers, it must transform itself. The Buddhism we see here is a transformed one, or we may call it "external Buddhism with internal Confucianism."

The style of the statues in this shrine is impressive. It seemed to be in the nature of those unknown artisans to display life through the statues here. Visitors in front of them 800 years later feel that they

Selected Tour Commentaries

are not worshipping Buddhas here but enjoying images that exhibit their own family life. The mother makes dry room for her baby while she herself lies in the wetted place; the senile and aged couple who see their son off seem to be reluctant to say good-bye, though they have walked a long way. All of the images a removing and instructive. The big characters inscribed on the stone, "few are aware of others' gratitude while many are ungrateful," have shocked many sons and daughters who have seen these words.

The gap between deities and human beings is narrowed here. In view of this, we'd like to say that the stone carving statues in Dazu County are not only deity statues, but also human statues, the statues of out-and-out Chinese, and Sichuanese in particular.

(Carvings of the hell)

The statues in this shrine (No. 20 shrine) cover a length of 30 metres and there over 100 figures of different personalities are carved here. This is the earliest, largest carving of hell, with the most comprehensive content in China at present. The picture of the hell created by a famous ancient painter, Wu Daozi, has only been described in historical documents, but the real work has not been found yet. The picture of the hell preserved in the Paris museum is reported to be painted by Wu Daozi; however according to the result of textual research by experts, it is not an original but a copy made by later generations. Thus, it is safe to say that the work of the Song Dynasty in this shrine is the earliest of its kind.

The 18th hell is actually a distorted reflection of society. Those unknowns sculptors were very adept at creating figures out of real life in terms of displaying the personalities of the images of their works. Most of the figures here can only be found in the earthly world , such as the smart errand boy, the worldly officials in the yamen, the meek and simple maid in mansions, and the sots of various kinds in the picture of swearing off drinking.

The statue of "the lady raising chickens" in the hell of knife

Stone Carvings on the Baoding Mountain in Dazu County

ships is the supreme work among Dazu stone carvings.

At sunrise a country woman opens the chicken cage. Two chickens are having a "tug-of-war" for an earthworm. Because the chicken cage is opened a little on one side and the feet of the chickens block the opening, the small chicken has no way out and tries its best to break through by pecking the adult chickens' feet. The peasant woman is lost in deep thought while her two hands are put on the cage. It is a typical picture of the"Happiness of raising chickens."

According to the creed of Buddhism, one kills go to hell if one will the chickens he raises. This peasant woman may think of the saying "If I do not go to hell, who else will go?" and sustain the heavy family burden with such spirit, or she may be thinking that she can make some money through raising chickens and thus she is comforted, or she may feel that with all hardships life is still hard to part with when she sees the living picture of the chickens ··· All is unknown and left for the visitors to guess and imagine.

The theory of Chinese ancient arts says that it is better for an art work " to please people than to surprise people, but to make people think is even better than pleasing people." The excellent works of art should rouse people, seek eternity through temporary description and extend time and space for visitors. "The lady raising chickens" is such a work of art. 800 years have passed, but tens of thousands of visitors from home and abroad still often stop in front of this mid-aged peasant woman and bury themselves in thought, unable to tear themselves away from it.

Among the carvings of the hell, all statues created are ugly and vicious except this peasant woman, who appears healthy, beautiful and amiable. Many visitors feel confused about this. Actually there is no mystery in it at all. All of the unknown artisans who made the statues at Mount Baoding came from the vast countryside. This peasant woman is probable the sculptor's wife or his mother; how could he make his relative ugly and vicious? The religious discipline gives way to human feelings here. This is the victory of art and the awak-

Selected Tour Commentaries

ening of humanity!

Perhaps owing to the intrusion of the army sent by the Yuan regime into Sichuan Province, parts of the last ten Arhats were left unfinished. The Chinese history books written in biographical style have never recorded those unknown who have won world acclaim for China's sculpture art except for a few names like Yang Huizhi; still worse, no books on sculpture techniques have been written and passed down. The unfinished works on Mount Baoding are like a wordless book, telling later generations how do quarrying, how to make rough works and then polish them with care and precision. Anyway, they demonstrate the whole production process of these stone statues. History is merciful in this sense, after all.

[Yuanjue (Full Enlightenment) Buddhism *daochang*]

This shrine (No. 29) is the best of the stone carving art on Mount Baoding. The inside of this grotto is rectangular. It is 6.02 metres high, 9.55 metres wide and 12.13 metres long. The main statues are three Buddhas, and on both sides of them are 12 Yuanjue Bodhisattvas. All western visitors who've come here feel amazed by the exquisiteness of the statues in this grotto. They agree that if these statues were put together with the first-class sculpture works in the world, they would not be outshined. Now let's focus our attention on the artistic achievements of this grotto.

First of all, sculptors were adept in creating a typical environment.

All statues on Mount Baoding were carved on the surfaces of cliffs except those at Yuanjue Buddhism daochang, which was in the form of a grotto. The grotto is not natural, but cut in a huge stone. It employs symmetry to form a hall and thus creates a grand and solemn atmosphere, making it the place for Buddhist publicity.

Sculptors employed many techniques to create the sense of mystery in this grotto . (Buddhas will ask those who practise Buddhism about their knowledge of the creed and their behavior; if the Bud-

Stone Carvings on the Baoding Mountain in Dazu County

dhas feel that they've done enough, then th ey will become Buddhas, too; therefore, this atmosphere is required here) Let's take the light for instance. As the paved path inside goes deeper, the light gets dimmer and dimmer. When you enter the grotto, your eyesight is indistinct for your eyes have not adapted to the surroundings. When you stay longer and your eyes have adapted to the darkness , your eyesight becomes more and more distinct and statues emerge in an endless stream. This conforms to the creed that "the light gets brighter when you go closer to Buddhas." There is an opened window in the front of the grotto and rays of light fall upon Buddhas who examine believers. This is like the spotlight on the modern stage: the attention of the visitors inside is shifted to these Buddhas. With the movement of the light, visitors can have a closer look. Thanks to the narrow entrance of the grotto, there is a difference of temperature inside and outside the grotto. It is cool in the summer and warm in the winter in the grotto. This is also in line with the Buddhist saying "when you stay with Buddhas, you feel cool in the summer and warm in the winter." Attention was also paid to the acoustic design. As long as there is a little sound in the grotto, it will be echoed endlessly. This brings you a sense of peace and quietness in the Buddhist shrine.

Secondly, the design is prudent and thorough and the construction is precise; the craftsmanship is comprehensive and exquisite.

This grotto has a complex structure and there is a multitude of statues. Yet all stones are original instead of being carried from outside. It is pretty hard to this without thorough plans and careful construction. In terms of technique, the statues in this grotto are an exhibition of the collection of the best sculptures. The stones are coarse grit, yet the ornamental crowns worn by the 12 Yuanjue Bohissattvas are carved with superb workmanship and pierced to the point that light can penetrate all four sides. The thinnest part is even thinner than a little finger, and still they remain intact after a history of 800-some years. As to the clothing of these Buddhas, they have strong

Selected Tour Commentaries

sense of real things and look like satin. Even the altar tables in front of the Buddhas look like wooden ones at first sight. A lot of people doubt that they are made of stones, and the doubt will be dispelled only after they knock at them with their own hands. The background for Buddhas and Bohissattvas is decorated with mountains, rivers, buildings, platforms, bir ds, animals, etc. This indicates that it is the earthly world. The background is bold and unconstrained while the figures are clean and tidy; the altar tables are of simplicity. In the past people said that China's stone carving saw its flourishing in the Tang Dynasty and declining in the Song dynasty and this was nearly the final conclusion. Yet the existence of these Dazu stone carvings has changed this view and corrected it as "flourishing in the Tang and Song dynasties." Thirdly, 90% of the statues in this grotto remain intact . It is rare in China that statues could be preserved so well over 800 years. Due to various reasons, there has never appeared large-scale stone carving in China since the Southern Song Dynasty. Therefore, this Yuanjue grotto with exquisites statues seems to put an exact end to China's stone carving of Buddhism. However, if we take the leaping lion outside the grotto as a "punctuation mark," it seems as if a big question mark were left to us. The ancient people said: "the future generations see us just the same way we see the past ones." While we feel proud for the rare art treasure created by our ancestors, what will we offer to our offspring for them to be proud of? This is a question that each Chinese should and must answer.

Probably this is the enlightenment we get from the visit to these Dazu stone car vings.

THE LI RIVER

Dear friends,

welcome on board for cruising the beautiful Li River. Our boat is going to leave Zhujiang port, which lies at the foot of the Bat Hill and at the bank of the Bamboo River. The port is 22km away from Guilin City proper, and is mainly used for foreign guests. Now, let me give you a brief introduction to the Li River.

Li River belongs to the Zhu River system and originates from Mao'er Mountain in Xing'an County north of Guilin City, which is 88km from here. The peak of Mao'er is the highest peak in the Yuecheng Mountain Range with an elevation of 2,238 meters, the highest peak in middle southern part of China. The streams from Mao'er peak gather into the Li River. There is still a canal called Lingqu canal dug during the time of the First Emperor Qinshihuang more than 2,000 years ago as the first canal in Chinese history . The canal connects the Li River and the Xiang River in Hunan Province. The latter belongs to the Yangtze River system. However the Xiang River has a unique feature in terms of general topography of China. As we all know, most rivers in China flow from west to east, because the western part is generally high than the eastern part. The exception is the Xiang River, which flows from the north to the south. The name of the Li River probably comes from "Xiang-Li", literally meaning "going to different directions". Another explanation suggests that "Li" means "clear" which is perhaps the best explanation

291

Selected Tour Commentaries

of the Li River.

The river once played an important role in Chinese history after the Lingqu Canal was dug. It connected central and southern China, and had great impact on political, economic, cultural and military affairs of Guilin and the southwestern part of China at large. The canal also facilitated the unification of China by the Qin Empire. The Li River comes from Xing'an County and goes through Guilin, Yangshou, Pingle County, and Wuzhou where it pours into the Xi River. The river has a total length of 437 km. The Li River which generally we call refers to the part from Guilin to Yangshuo with a total distance of 83 km.

For more than 2,000 years this area-now home to three million people-has been a magnet for poets and painters, soldiers and sailors, missionaries and monks. There are cities in China far better for food, and others more famous for culture, but when you're looking for landscape-that classical scenery of Chinese scroll paintings, I think you have found out Guilin is your place.

Nowhere else in China so enamors visitors as the dreamy landscape in this part. It is a forest of beautiful humpbacked peaks which top over the blue water. Like a vision from Chinese scroll paintings, the 100-km stretch of the Li River is called a 100-km art gallery. The celebrated Tang dynasty poet Han Yu once described the beautiful landscape over a millennium ago "the river forms a green silk belt, the mountains are like blue jade hairpins." Someone else described the scenery as "Thousands of peaks stand around, one river circles the city." Contemporary poet He Jingzhi wrote with enthusiasm in his poem Ode to Guilin:

Oh, the God of cloud.
The fairy of fog,
Come from the mountains of Guilin
The depth of affection
The beauty of dream

The Li River

Come from the water of the Li River.

My dear friends, the Li River is welcoming you. I hope you will enjoy the first leg of your boat trip.

The Bamboo River

(Biyadanxin)

A green hill with a red cliff called Biya (red cliff) seems to block our way. It stands on the left bank of the river, You can see the reflection of this 30 meters high cliff in the clear water that flows slowly at its foot. It seems that the flowing water is trying to tell you a moving love story.

Once upon a time, a girl called Guihua lived north of the cliff and a young man named A'niu did farming in the south. Their love songs echo between the cliff day after day. They got to know each other through the songs and fell in love with each other desperately. But the towering Biya cliff prevented them from meeting each other. They discussed cross the river that they would build a road connecting their villages and as soon as the road was finished they would get married. Guihua and A'niu started to chisel a road on the cliff, one from the north to the south, one from the south to the north. They had worked very hard for 3 years. Their blood tinged the cliff. Many villagers were so deeply moved by their loyal love that they all joined them to build the road. When the work was almost over, a huge stone from the cliff fell onto A'niu and killed him. When Guihua saw that she was totally immersed in sorrow and jumped off the cliff. The villagers built the Hall of Biya to commemorate the loyal lovers. It's a pity that the hall did not exist any more due to the long time damage by wind and rain. However, there are still some steles left for us to get to know that. It is said that if you sit on a rock on a moon lit evening, you could hear clearly the calls "A'niu! Guihua!" from the Li River. A'niu, Guihua.

Selected Tour Commentaries

(The Bat Hill)

Now we can see the river rush to the steep Bat Hill with speed. The 2 peaks in front with flat yellow cliffs look like 2 flying bats. The 9 peaks on the right look like 9 cattle plowing the land. The 5 peaks on the left look like 5 running horses. If you look carefully, you will find out that the 2 peaks ahead look like 2 lions playing with an embroidered ball and looking around the 3 islets. There is a local folk song depicting the scenery "9 cattle look like 3 islets, the river flows on both sides, 5 horses running across the river, and 2 lions play with an embroidered ball."

(The Yellow Cow Gorge)

The Yellow Cow Gorge is the No. 1 gorge along the Li River. A battalion of limestone peaks rising abruptly from the plain is what makes the scenery along the Li River so special. These karst formations, thrust up from a limestone seabed hundreds of millions of years ago, dominate the surrounding countryside, rank after rank in ever hazier hues until they shimmer teasingly on the horizon. The Li River winds among them, carrying the narrow bamboo rafts of fishermen who use cormorants to catch their fish: they are the small, straw-hatted figures in the scroll in real life, their boats are the little black brush strokes in the scroll. So the trip down the river through these scenes of timeless grandeur is the highlight of every visit to Guilin.

(Dragons Playing Water)

There are several stalactite poles hanging on the left cliff. They twist like huge dragons drinking water from the river. Parts of their bodies were hidden in the cliff. During spring and summer seasons, when the water in the river raises, the dragons' heads sticking out over the river will spout water. Legend has it that these dragons were sent by the God of Heaven to collect the fragrance of osmanthus flowers long time ago. The slopes of the mountain were full of os-

The Li River

manthus flowers, the fragrance of which rose up to the heavenly palace. The fairy Chang Eh living in the moon was attracted and wanted to come down to the earth. The God of Heaven was so angry about it that he sent several dragons to Guilin to absorb all the fragrance and take it back to heaven. Out of his expectation, however, the dragons themselves were attracted by the beautiful scenery of the place. In stead of taking back the fragrance to the heaven, the dragons brought rains into a pool called the Fragrance Pool. The osmanthus trees growing on both banks of the Li River were irrigated with the water from the pool and they became even more exuberant. In August the fragrance of osmanthus flowers will cover both banks of the river. No wonder this place is called Guilin (whose literal meaning is "osmanthus forest").

(Yearning for Husband Rock)

On the left slope stands a piece of rock in the shape of a young wife with a child on her back. She is expecting her husband to return. It is the famous "Wangfu (Yearning for Husband) Rock" on the Li River. There is a story about a peasant family living here long time ago. The husband worked in the field and the wife worked at home. They lived a happy life as what was described by the East Jin Dynasty poet Tao Yuanming. But one day, a war broke their peaceful life. The husband was conscripted, leaving his wife and a young child at home. The husband failed to return home when the promised 3 years had pasted. Then five years passed. Day after day, the wife went to the hillside with her child on her back to wait for her husband.

At last, she saw her husband stumbling toward her. The wife was so overwhelmed with happiness that she turned into a piece of stone. When the husband saw what happened to his wife, he became hopeless and also turned into a stone. From then on, the peak was called Yearning for Husband Rock. Almost every hill along the Li River has an interesting story or legend showing the local people's at-

Selected Tour Commentaries

titude towards life.

Caoping Scenic Spot

If we compare the Li River cruise to a fascinating musical movement, the part from Zhujiang to Caoping is the overture of the movement; from Caoping to Yangti is the development of the movement; from Yangti to Xingping, the climax of the movement; from Xingping to Yangshuo, the conclusion of the movement.

Caoping is covered with green meadow and beautiful field. There is a village called Caoping Village on the left. It is surrounded by mountains on 3 sides while facing river on one side. The 5,000 villagers are mostly Hui nationality. Caoping Village is located in the middle of the Li River. It was very backward in the past because of the inconvenience of transportation.

With the help of the people's government, the diligent villagers built a road. As electricity, water and postal service have been supplied, Caoping villagers are catching up with modern society. Before long, Caoping will develop into the most charming scenic spot on the Li River. The combination of natural scenery and folk culture will be very attractive to the tourists. In April each year, the snow-white plum flowers covered this area. Several months later, the trees will bear ripening plum fruits. Tourists can visit a cavern by bamboo raft. They can also walk in the underground river under the Anji Hill, and enjoy the poem chanting, the music and the dancing shows in the cavern.

(Guanyan Cavern)

The mountain in front looks like a golden crown of the Han Dynasty, so comes the name the Crown Hill. There is a grotto called Guanyan Grotto at the foot of the hill. It is the exit of an underground river which has a different source from the Li River. The water flowing out of the underground river is usually clearer than

The Li River

that of the Li River. It rises and falls at the same time as the Li River. Some people had tried to look for its source. But all the attempts failed because of the complex terrain in the deep and dark cavern. In 1987 British Royal Diving Team cooperated with Chinese Geological and Hydrological Investigation Team to probe the underground river. They dived 24 meters underwater and find that the fish there was more than one meter long. But they still failed to discover the source of the underground river, which remains a mystery of the Li River.

As poet Cai Wen of the Ming Dynasty wrote: "The deep cavern opens with clear water, beautiful stones pile like clouds, one stream of water comes out of it, no one knows where it rose

Look, the zigzagging mountain trailing over there leads to another mysterious cavern. The part that has been probed is 12km deep, 3km of it is open to the public. The cavern is filled with strangely shaped rocks, waterfalls, and tinkling water. The cavern was facilitated with high-tech equipment. The facilities include a small railway, pleasure boats and computer-controlled lights and sounds. Please follow me and enjoy the poetic scene in the cavern.

(The Xiu Hill)

Look the colorful cliff in the front. It looks like a huge piece of silk embroidery with the design of pearl tower and 8 immortals passing the sea. That's why the hill is called Xiu (embroidery) Hill. There are also 2 caverns in the cliff over there. They appear no special for their exterior, but you will be impressed by the unique scenes inside. Many stalactite and stalagmite look like fruits and vegetables, others like birds and beasts. It is true that every hill in Guilin has a cavern, and every cavern has unique features.

(The One-side Ferry)

Some people claim that the cliffs in Guilin are works of immortals. Though not believable, it is a way to express their impression of the stunning scenes of Guilin. Look, the hill on this side looks as if it

Selected Tour Commentaries

were cut by a magic axe. That is a legendary ferry called "The One side Ferry" under the cliff. The hill trail was cut short by the precipitous cliff, so the ferryboat only goes forth and back along one side of the riverbank. This is really a unique thing on the Li River. Because of the inconvenience of transportation, local people who only depended on fishing and farming lived poor lives. After the new China was founded, roads were built on both side of the river. As the economy develops, the living standard of the villagers has been greatly improved. The village in the front is called Taoyuan Village though it is not the secluded life described in Tao Yuanming' article, it has similar rustic surroundings free from outside influence. There are lines of blue-roofed houses hiding behind the bamboo groves. Traces of smokes from kitchen chimneys curling upwards before the setting sun. The shepherd would play flute to a fisherman's song at dusk. What a picturesque village for a leisurely country life!

The Li River, Caoping in particular, is rich in fish and shrimps. You are welcome to try the four most famous dishes of the Li River: the steamed Li River fish, fried shrimps, stir-fried river snails, and stewed fish with Huai Hill wolfberry.

(Millstone Turned by the Immortal)

The hill on the left ahead looks very much like a crawling seal just coming out of the Li River. It is looking up at the beautiful sky. So the scene is called " the seal observing sky." Figuratively speaking, the Li River is like a 100-km gallery with a collection of every precious thing in the world. There are images of precious flowers, birds and beasts which require your rich imagination to recognize them. The interesting thing about the scenery is that the more you imagine, the more the rocks resemble the things in your mind. If you don't think about it, it's just a piece of plain stone.

Behind the Seal Hill is a lower hill, on top of which lies a piece of stone on the other one. It looks like a stone mill in the countryside. You can also see a man working hard to turn the mill. It is said

The Li River

that rice milled there will come out from the hole at the foot of the Seal Hill. Thanks to the endless rice coming out the hole as a result of the hard work of the immortal, such a lovely seal could feed itself and grow to such a big size. This scene is called "Mill being Turned by the Immortal."

(Painting Brush Hill)

On the right riverbank, a hill named the Painting Brush Hill juts straight up from the ground with a pointed tip like a Chinese writing brush. Chinese brush has always been used for painting and calligraphy. Its size varies a great deal. This is the largest brush produced by nature to paint the picturesque Li River. It will continue to paint more beautiful Guilin scenery and happy life using the huge brush.

(Shoals of Gong & Drum and Mandarin Ducks)

The winding Li River has many bends and shoals. There are altogether 360.5 bends and 360.5 shoals on the 83-km stretch from Guilin to Yangshuo. The water flowing from the shallow part of the shoals produces sounds like music from heaven. This music of the Li River would bring people into a reverie as if they were in a fairyland. Let's look at the two huge stones on the left riverbank. They are called Gong and Drum Stones since one looks like a gong, the other looks like a drum. There are two stone pillars on the right bank resembling a gang hammer and a drumstick. When riverboat passes the place, people on board sometimes could hear the tinkling sounds of gang and drum. If you listen carefully, you can probably hear the singing of a couple of mandarin ducks. "The heaven may not have this music, you can only hear it on the Li River".

Yangdi

Our boat is going to arrive at Yangdi. The stretch of river from Yangdi to Xingping is the most excellent part of our cruise. It is the

Selected Tour Commentaries

climax of the musical movement we are enjoying.

There is a small town called Yangdi hidden in the bamboo forest. The two hills behind the town are at the same size and height. They are just like a goat hoof hanging upside down. So comes the name of the hill and the homophonic name "Yangdi" for the village. The road leading to Guilin from Yangdi is 59 km long. During the dry season each year, tourists would get on board here for the boat trip.

"Yangdi Green Bamboo" is one of the famous scenic spots of the Li River. The scenery is like one scroll of traditional Chinese painting with blue river blocked by green hills, and groves of bamboo growing on the riverbank. Traces of smokes rising from a few farmer houses mixed with the mist that created a mysterious atmosphere. The green bamboo groves on both sides of the river are waving to us in the light wind. They are the incarnation of the diligent and brilliant local people. The people along the Li River love the bamboo very much for its various uses. For example, bamboo shoots are the material for their favorite dishes. Bamboo is also the material for many beautiful handicrafts. The evergreen bamboo of Yangdi adds much vitality to the scenery.

(The Carp Tapestry)

There are some strange stripes with bright colors on the cliff resembling a huge carp swimming upside. It is called carp tapestry. The deep pool at the foot of the cliff is called "The Carp Pool". The story goes that the huge carp is the king carp in "The Deep Pool". He often heard people talking about the beauty of the Li River. One day, it was caught by the stalactites on the cliff when it jumped out of the water. It was so fascinated by the beautiful scenery that it did not even notice the problem until it was ready to get back to the pool at the sunset. Unfortunately, it failed to free itself, no matter how hard it tried. If you look at that more carefully, you may find that it is still blowing its gill.

The Li River

Child Worshipping Guanyin (Avalokitesvara)

In Chinese Buddhist stories, Guanyin is the Mother Buddha or Goddess of Mercy. People pray for blessings from Guanyin when they are in difficulties. There are a variety of images of Guanyin in Chinese painting, sculpture and porcelain. You can also find Guanyin in the Li River.

On the left there is one group of peaks. Some have round tops and some have point tops in shapes of lotus flowers. The high peak over there looks just like a Guanyin sitting on the lotus. The lower peak at the foot of the lotus peak looks like a child saluting Guanyin. Dear friends, if you want to ask Guanyin for blessing, you can pray in your mind for that. It is said that this Guanyin is very efficacious.

(The Immortal on Guard)

The hill on the right looks like an elderly immortal in a robe standing by straight on the riverside. On the one hand, he is there to welcome us. On the other hand, he is responsible for guarding the Li River. As we know, the beauty of the Li River comes from its wonderful natural landscape. The immortal is quite vigilant in guarding the beauty of the Li River.

(The Stone Waves)

There are miles of brown rocks like waves over there. It is especially hard to tell the stone waves and real waves apart on a moonlit evening. You can find scenes similar to that at the seaside.

The small village on the left riverbank is named after the Stone Waves. There are many small hills surrounding the village. The most distinctive are the five hills to the north of the village. They are connected in the manner of five fingers. There is a small piece of rock like a lion climbing on the fingers. It is said that the rock looks like a bear lying on the back to bathe the sunshine.

(The Apple Hill)

Look at the big and round hill in the front. It looks like an apple with a dent at the round place. It is said to be the world largest

Selected Tour Commentaries

apple weighing 360 million tons. It is a pity that the tip of the apple is missing. People say that once it had a tip. But it was broken when someone tried to pick it up. The apple is still growing with each day. There is also a god safeguarding the apple. The magic apple of the Li River will be brightly shining at sunset.

(The Eight Immortals Peak)

On the upper right, the steep peaks and flowing clouds create a mysterious atmosphere. The eight peaks over there are eight immortals in a famous Chinese fairytale. The immortals originally lived in Penglai, Shandong Province. Why were they here then? It is said that, the eight immortals were once on a journey together and came to Guilin. They were attracted so much by the beauty of the place that they decided to stay. So the scene is named " The Visiting Eight Immortals".

(The Nine-Horse Painting Hill)

The huge cliff in front with rich colors look like an enormous piece of Chinese landscape painting. If you have a close look at the cliff, you will be surprised to find out that it is in fact a painting of herding horses.

There is a big white horse heading right on top of the cliff. Under the mouth of the white horse is the head of a black horse with sharp ears. On the right back of the white horse is a small black horse with distinctive figure. There is a big horse head under the belly of the white horse with a black grotto as its eye. On the cliff, actually there are quite a number of horses, "nine" in Chinese culture in fact means many. Where did all these horses come from? Legend has it that it was the monkey king who freed all the horses in heaven just because he was unhappy with his appointment as the official in charge of horse herds appointed by the Jade Emperor of Heaven. When the horses in the heaven came to this place, they were so fascinated by the beauty and luxuriant grass that they leave the shades

The Li River

behind them. Another story goes that there was a painter who saw the beauty of shades on the cliff, and decided to paint them. Yet the changing shades made it impossible for the painter to depict them. The poor painter, however, did not give up easily. He painted and painted until he was turned into a stone one day. If you look back, you will see him still standing on that hill. A folk song about the horses goes like this, "Herdsman, how many heavenly horses can you count? If you recognize seven, you will win second in palace examination. If you recognize nine, you will take the first place."

(The Lion Looking at Nine Horses)

There is a hill with round top and yellow cliff at the foot of the hill. The whole hill looks like a lion, with the top being the head of the lion. There is a yellow triangle-shaped mouth on its head. Its smiling eyes are looking back to us. The scene is called "The Smiling Lion Welcoming Guests from All Over the World," or "The Lion Looking back at the Nine Horses."

On the left of the lion, there is a black horse heading right. If you look carefully, you will find out a white saddle on its back. It is said that this horse was one of the nine horses and was left behind the others for it was running slowly. The famous Chinese writer Guo Moruo once visited the Li River, but he could only find out eight horses at the Nine Horses Painting Hill. When the boat arrived at this place, he suddenly realized that the ninth one was left here.

(The Monkey Eating Watermelon)

You may have heard of the story of Monkey King. He is now shepherding a herd of horses on the heaven. He is happy to know that we are visiting this beautiful place. So he sends one of his grandsons to welcome us with fruits from the heaven.

A stone looking like a little monkey embracing a watermelon with its hands stands on the slope of the mountain. The little monkey is now secretly eating in the watermelon with gusto would not like to

Selected Tour Commentaries

do its duty well. Well, we'd better not tell of him, for every child is gluttonous after all.

(The Bear Observing the Sky)

Now let's look at the lovely bear who is observing the sky. The hill besides the bamboo forest on your left looks like a bear with limbs in the air. It is watching the passing clouds in the blue sky.

Our boat has made a big turn. This time you can find out that the upper lip of the bear seems like the head of a tortoise having reached the top of the hill. So this picture is also depicted as "the Tortoise Climbing the Hill."

We have seen many groves of bamboo on the riverbank. The evergreen bamboo brings a lot of vitality to the Li River. The branches of the bamboo resemble the tails of phoenix. So comes the name phoenix tail bamboo. The charming scenery over there attracts a lot of painters, photographers and filmmakers.

(The Reflection of Yellow Cloth)

The Yellow Cloth refers to the colourful stripes of the hill over there. We can see the beautiful reflection in the water. Thus the name of the scene. There stand seven hills on the riverbank. The story goes that the seven fairies were so enchanted by the beautiful Li River that they turned themselves into hills to stay there forever. As described by an ancient poem, the river becomes clearer in Xing'an, many green hills are immerged under the water, above which the boat is moving. There is a saying that the immortals would prefer to becoming local residents of Guilin living the immortal life up in heaven.

(The Camel Passing the River)

There are 3 hills connecting each other and they look like a big camel. The camel seems ready to walk across the river. So the scene is called the camel passing the river.

The Li River

Xingping

Our boat is entering Xingping. This beautiful place has attracted many writers in the past years. Many pictures which were taken at this place have won prizes in world competitions. Xingping is the highlight of the Li River Cruise. The river pass around the hills and farmer houses are scattered throughout the bamboo groves on the bank. This is the famous 8 scenes of Xingping. Xingping is representative of the exquisite and changeable beauty of the Li River. The tranquil hills contrast the flowing water. The clear hills in front stand out of the background of the misty hills. The scenery changes at different seasons in a year, even at different times in a day. One can hardly see the whole scenery in a short time. The famous painter Xu Beihong had once lived here for 2 years just attempting to paint the attractive landscape.

The hills in front line up to welcome us. Among them, the left ones are called Buddhist Hill, Chaohu Hill and Five Fingers Hill respectively. The hills on the right are like lotus flowers coming out of the river.

The small town before us is called Xingping town. With a history of more than 1,300 years it is one of the 4 well-known ancient towns in Guangxi Province. More than 1,000 years ago it already got a county town in the year of 590. Xingping is like a fairyland along the bank of the Li River.

There is a cavern called the Lotus Flower Cave 4km away from here. It is famous for the 108 lotus flower-shaped stalactites in the cavern. 108 is a special number in Chinese culture. There are 108 generals in the Chinese classic "Water Margin". The traditional Chinese fiction normally has 108 chapters. It happens that there are 108 lotus flower-shaped stalactites in the Lotus Flower Cave. Are there any connections among them? Or is it just a coincidence of nature and culture? This mysterious question needs to be resolved by people

305

Selected Tour Commentaries

after us.

(The Tryst of a Monk and a Nun)

Look back, you can see 2 hills connected with each other. The hill on the left is wide with a round top and looks like a monk. The other one on the right is like a slim nun. It seems that they are having love talks, hence the name of the "tryst of a monk and a nun".

(Beauty Looking into a Mirror)

The girls living at both sides of the Li River are beautiful, due to the beauty of the hills and river. There is a hill on the right with round top and big bottom. The whole hill is in the shape of a beautiful girl. The round top is the head on which there is a piece of colorful cliff like the face of the girl. The appearance of the lovely girl is just like a young girl of the Zhuang nationality. The local people call the hill the Beauty Hill. There is a small round hill in the shape of an ancient copper mirror besides her. It seems that the girl is doing the make-up with the mirror.

(The Beauty of Field Snail)

The hill on the right with sharp top and round bottom is about 160 meters in elevation. The hill is like a big field snail. Legend has it that it was turned from a beautiful fairy. The local people call it Lady Snail. The clever fairy came to the earth secretly when she was tired of the monotonous life in the heaven. She was so much attracted by the beautiful scenery of Xingping that she decided to settle here. She taught Xingping people to weave and Xingping girls to sing. The cloth she weaved was as beautiful as the cloud in the sky. The song she sang attracted hundreds of birds to sing with her. Her action angered the God of heaven. She was turned into a field snail as a punishment. From then on, there is a Field Snail in Xingping. The local people built a temple to commemorate her. This scene is called " Beauty of Field Snail." People wish that the youth and beau-

306

The Li River

ty of Lady Snail would remain forever.

(Carp on Shuojiang)

The long hill looks like a carp heading right. The peaks of the hill appear like a fish. Several smaller peaks form its fins which also look like a lovely Pekinese. For this largest carp ever found in the world nobody knows how to weigh it, I think.

There are 4 features of the Li River: strangely-shaped green hills, clear water, unique caves and beautiful jagged peaks. There are also 4 beauties like waterfall, springs, shoals and bamboo. The Li River still has other four characteristics: grotesquerie of ancient banyan trees, uniqueness of the Painting Hill, mystery of Guanyan Cavern, charm of the One Side-going Ferry.

We have seen rustic beauty on both sides of the river. It is like a symphony, the village being its notes and forests its movements. I believe the beauty of the Li River will give you deep impression.

Yangshuo

(The Huge Dragon Welcoming Guests)

Our boat is entering Yangshuo. There is a high hill like a huge dragon's head. It seems that it is saying, "Hello, friends, welcome to Yangshuo." Yangshuo is an ancient town with a history of more than 2,000 years. Yangshuo has received millions of guests from all over the world in the past several decades. In the ancient time, there was a poem comparing the beauty of two other places with the beauty of Yangshuo. The following is its main idea:

When Tao Yuanming was the county magistrate of Pengze, he wrote about the beauty of the rustic life in Peach Flower Valley; the Heyang County magistrate Panyue ordered all the households in the county to plant flowers to beautify the place. But the beauty of these two places could in no way compete with the charm of Yangshuo as people here live among the lotus flower peaks.

Selected Tour Commentaries

(The Lotus Flower Peaks)

The town of Yangshuo is located at the center of a big lotus flower. The hill in front is called Lotus Bud Hill. You will see the beauty of hills and rivers if you climb up to the top of the hill. Every year, in early autumn, both water and sky are very clear. The whole hill and the cloud reflect on the broad river. Lotus Bud Hill is just like an opening lotus flower coming out of the water.

(The Stone Carving)

There are many stone carvings on the Lotus Bud Hill. The cursive script "Dai" in Chinese character written during the reign of the Emperor Guangxu in the Qing Dynasty adds much charm to the hill. The character "Dai" is called one word poem because of the hinted meaning in it. A writer paraphrased this one-word poem as," The beauty has no equals in the world, a young man should strove for the best." Dear friends, what comes into your mind about this word? By appreciating this word, we can conclude that the beauty of the Li River is too wonderful for words.

Dear friends, we are coming to the end of our cruise. Thank you for your support to our work. Please give your valuable comments and advice for our improvement. Hope to see you and your friends come again.

THE STONE FOREST

(On the way from Kunming to the Stone Forest)
Ladies and gentlemen,

We are now going to pay a visit to the Stone Forest as well as to the homes of local people of the Yi nationality. The highway we are traveling along was the first high-grade highway ever constructed in Yunnan Province, opened to traffic in 1991 and is 120 kilometers in length. We will travel 83 kilometers before we reach our destination.

This highway is also known as the Red Road, which was also used to be called Silk Road of the Southwest that once linked ancient China with places as far away as the Arabian Peninsula. It is also nicknamed the Road of Jade, because it links Myanmar, or the Kingdom of Jade, and Yunnan, known as the Place of Jade Assemblages. What is more, this highway is also called the Road of Black and White, symbolizing the fight against drugs, and Road of Gold and Aroma. Yunnan is famous for its gold, silver reserves and spices. As the legend has it, Emperor Hanwu of Han Dynasty dreamt of colorful clouds in southwest China, which was considered as an auspicious omen, hence the name for this vast territory of 394, 000 square kilometers. Unique in climate, ethnic nationalities, resources, tourism, science and technology as well as geology, this province is rich in natural scenes as well as in human and cultural wonders, famous for a variety of flora and fauna, nonferrous metals, costumes and travel scenes. The Stone Forest serves as an epito-

Selected Tour Commentaries

me of the province on the southwestern border.

(The Stone Forest in Lunan County)

Lunan stands for a place strewn with black rocks in the language spoken by local people of the Sani Nationality. This county is densely populated by Sani people and covers a space of 1,725 square kilometers. 62 percent of this hilly territory is limestone, which makes this county famous far and near. Lunan boasts some 154 picturesque scenes, among which seven are the most famous.

Of all these places of interest, the Stone Forest is the most famous. It features the major and minor Stone Forests with stones in different sizes, shapes and colors. Dotted with stone paths, corridors, bridges, portals, pillars and caves everywhere, this group of exotic rocks has drawn wide admiration from famous politicians, scholars, writers and experts from home and abroad.

The scientists found that the Lunan area used to be a vast ocean during the Proterozoic Era (600 million years ago) and Archaeozoic Era (350 million years ago). With large-scale sea erosion and earth warping, a layer of 1,000 to 2,000 meters piled up. During the late Carboniferous period (320 million years ago), the sea receded and gave way to gigantic seas of mountains.

In this way the Stone Forest came into being.

The Stone Forest is characterized by Karst topography, which is named after the Karst Plateau between the former Yugoslavia and Italy. In every way it ranks above all the similar territories in the world, and is thus known as the Number One Wonder in the World.

(Kunming-Yuxi Highway)

This is the second high-grade highway in Yunnan Province. The famous Chinese navigator Zheng He of the Ming Dynasty, and the composer of the national anthem of the People's Republic of China, Nie Er and a number of renowned local doctors and figures once lived along this road. A number of ancient animal fossils can also be

310

The Stone Forest

found by the road. Fossils of China's most remote society, Yuanmou Man (lived more than 1.7 million years ago), China's earliest pithecanthropus, Romapithecus (lived more than eight million to 15 million years ago), Lufengosaurus, which lived more than 200 million years ago and a species of worm dating back to 570 million years ago were found. It can be said that Yunnan is the cradle of living creatures of the earth.

(Yunnan-Vietnam Railway)

[At the junction of Yunnan-Vietnam, Nanning-Kunming and Anlong-Shilin (The Stone Forest) railways] China's first railway linking with other countries is the Yunnan-Vietnam Railway, which is 855 kilometers in length and was completed by the French imperialists between 1904 and 1910. France made an annual profit exceeding ten million francs from running this railway. Local people and Chinese students studying in Japan launched several major protests.

[At the head of the Zhujiang (Pearl) River]

This is the Nanpan River, the upstream reach of the Zhujiang River and China's third longest river, which originates in the Maxiong Mountain in Qujing, Yunnan Province. The source is actually a small pond in the Cixiong Cavern.

(Yunnan-Vietnam Railway)

This railway is built with the blood, sweat and bones of Chinese laborers. The construction lasted for seven years and involved no less than 300,000 laborers from across China. More than 70,000 Chinese laborers died from the hard work and maltreatment. It is said that with each sleeper laid, a laborer would die.

(Local people of the Sani Nationality)

(At the welcome signpost) The Sani people are aboriginal to the Stone Forest. They use 1,200 characters to pass down long cultural and folklore traditions. Among those, the lyric of Ashima is the most famous, and was rendered into some 20 languages including

Selected Tour Commentaries

Chinese, English, French and German, etc,. In Japan alone, there are three editions that have appeared in print.

The Sani people are a subdivision of the Yi Nationality. The Yi people rank first in 26 minority nationalites of the province, with 4. 1 milllion, or 11 percent of the province's total population (1996). The Yi people have the tiger as their totem, use a 10-month solar almanac and observe the world's sole festival of fire, the Torch Festival. They also pay sincere respects to the stone.

The Sani people are famous for their bravery and hard work. They are hospitable and attach major importance to education and martial arts. The intellectuals enjoy supreme privileges among the populace. The Sani people start to learn wrestling in childhood.

On the other hand, the Sani people are also good at singing and dancing. Mastering these skills is a must for everyone, with young unmarried people in particular. This has drawn high praise from prominent scholars of China. A number of Sani songs and dances as well as feature films adopted from the local lyrics have won awards on many important occasions.

The wedding ceremony is noteworthy. Young people can choose their sweet hearts or make wedding arrangements at their own will. The engagement and wedding are inevitably accompanied by wine. To take the bride back home, the bridegroom must answer questions from his would-be parents-in-law with songs. Then the bridegroom and his escorts are allowed in to take back the bride. A friendly broil and fight will ensue. Then, the participants and onlookers will drink wine, sing folk songs and dance throughout the night.

(The Stone Forest and the Sani people)

The Stone Forest is not only famous for its natural beauty, but is also renowned for attractions in many respects. The Lunan County is characterized by Karst topography, dancing and singing, wrestling, painting and tobacco. It is also famous for apples, pigs, coal and green manure. In 1995, the county's annual revenue totaled nearly

The Stone Forest

81 million Renminbi yuan.

Like a forest, the Stone Forest can help moderate the temperature. Characterized by a low-latitude plateau monsoon climate, the average temperature is 15.3 degrees Celcius, with an annual rainfall of 960 millimeters. With this, it was rated by the United Nations as one of the areas with the cleanest air through field measurement. Therefore, visitors from home and abroad stream into this place of special interest.

(At the crossroads of the Stone Forest)

Over there is located a village where people of Han and Yi nationalities are populated densely. Proceeding northward will bring us to a place where two precious tablets have been on display since 1961, when the site was listed by the government as a key place of interest under meticulous protection. Traveling southward for some 30 kilometers will take us to one of the largest cataracts in southwest China, the Big Plunge Basin. Proceeding further southward will bring us to the hometowns of some famous ancient and contemporary Chinese scholars.

(By the Lufangtang Reservoir)

On the surface of the rocks on the other side of this reservoir, there are numerous marks from whips, which are said to have been left by Jinfen Ruoga, a mythical Sani super-hero. As the legend has it he drove mountains of rocks to the riverside to dam up a flooding river. The rocks refused to move any further when the cocks crowed at dawn. When every effort failed, he turned himself into a gigantic rock and eventually succeeded.

(In the Major Stone Forest)

(On the northern shore of the Stone Forest Lake)At the suggestion of the late premier Zhou Enlai and his aid Chen Yi, a small pond was widened and deepened to become this beautiful lake. On

Selected Tour Commentaries

the eastern shore and under the leafy cover of trees lies the Stone Forest Guest-house, which provides performances involving aborigine songs and dances. We will park in the front of the structure. (On the eastern shore) Over there is a village known as Wukeshu (Five Trees) Village; in it live people of Yi nationality.

This lake is also known as the Guanyin (Avalokitesvara) Lake. As legend has it, there used to be a young couple who survived the flood in a wooden bath tub in the remote area. They then gave birth to generations of Sani people. As the sea began to recede, they stuffed the two deep holes in the depth of the sea with golden and silver sticks in cooperation with the Dragon King's youngest daughter. The Sani people said that this girl is turned by Avalokitesvara

(A street with Sani characteristics)

The Sani women are good at embroidery. Sani embroidery enjoys a long history dating back to the Ming and Qing dynasties, which is characterized by rich and irregular patterns. In 1992, a fine piece of embroidery entitled The Shepherd Returns from the Stone Forest was presented to be kept by the United Nations. Two years later, another work won a grand prize at the Mongolian International Commodity Fair.

The Sani women can bargain in foreign languages with international tourists. This street is one of the five famous streets featuring ethnic ways of life in the province.

(On the shore of the Lion Pond)

This pond features lion-shaped rocks in and by the pond. On top of the rocky hill, there is a structure known as the Lion Pavilion. Prominent figures of China and abroad have paid frequent visits to this scene. Tourists will enjoy a diversified and beautiful view here, overlooking the skyline of the stony topography. As early as in 300 BC, the Stone Forest was first mentioned by Qu Yuan, a prominent Chinese poet. It was also admired by Marco Polo, the Italian travel-

The Stone Forest

er and other famous tourists from home and abroad. During the reign of Ming emperors, this site was made a famous spot of interest.

In 1982, it was formally listed by the state as national area of scenery.

(At the scene of a Black Buffalo Plays with Water)

It is said that this scene has something to do with an ancient story. A teenager shepherd lost a black buffalo under his care during a thunder storm. When he eventually found it, the animal had already turned into a rock. However, it showed the way to an orchard of plums. Therefore, the Stone Forest was also known in ancient times as the Orchard of Plums.

(In the front of Zhu De's Inscription)

(On the surface of a huge rock between the Osmanthus Garden and the Natural Stage) The inscription imprinted on this rock is written by Zhu De, the late chairman of the Standing Committee, National People's Congress of China, in June 1962 when he paid a visit to frontiers. It means: "Numerous peaks stand imposingly and are covered in woods."

(Before the Wonderful Scenery of the Stone Forest)

This is the most typical scene of this scenic spot, a must for every tourist. This scene is characterized by groups of imposing rocks and numerous inscriptions in relief.

(Under the scene known as In Imminent Peril)

This is the most dangerous place of the Stone Forest. Everybody should hold his breath or the huge stone overhead will drop. This hanging stone has been here for some three million years and underwent many thunders and severe earthquakes. The cause remains a myth.

Selected Tour Commentaries

(By the Jade Pond near the Sword-shaped Peaks)

This is the deepest place of the Stone Forest. As a legend has it, Aoyama, a man of unusual strength, was locked in fierce fight with God. Out there lies an aquatic corridor.

(In the Narrowest Pass)

This is the narrowest pass of the Stone Forest, which is 30 centimeters at the narrowest. People believe that after passing along this opening, all good wishes will become true.

(By the scene of Two Birds feeding Each Other)

This scene was likened to love between the old and the young and is considered as a monument to this.

(By the scene of Tortoise of Thousands Years Old)

The Sani people believe that when seeing this tortoise-shaped rock, their wishes will come true. Touching it will make people enjoy longevity. Why not touch it?

(By the Stony Bell)

This was thought as the treasure bequeathed by the Goddess of Happiness, Zhuobishi.

(In the Natural Singing Room)

This place makes your voice more pleasant. Everybody can have a try.

(In the Pavilion for Admiring the Peaks)

This is one of the most spectacular scenes of the Stone Forest. We will see numberless peaks against impressive skylines. Hence the title of Stone Forest. Over there is a phoenix-shaped rock. It is tidying up its plumage.

316

The Stone Forest

(In the Deep Valley)

This is one more scene famous for its dangerous position, known as the Flying Stone. This gully is said to be the path opened up by Brother A Hei, the legendary sweetheart of the beautiful heroine, Ashima, with his gigantic bow.

(Outer Stone Forest)

This is a scenic area that is much larger than the combined major and minor Stone Forests. It covers an area of tens of kilometers in circumference.

(On top of the Stone for Waiting the Husband)

Legend has it that a beautiful Sani bride, who went by the name of A Xiu, used to step on it, waiting for her husband's return from service.

(By the Mother and Son on Travel)

This scene is based on a legend involving a couple and their son in travel.

(On the Old Circular Wrestling Ground)

On each Festival of Torch which falls on June 24th of the Chinese lunar year, the Sani people stage wrestling, buffalo fighting and other important activities to celebrate. Legend has it that on this day in ancient times, knife-wielding villagers from 99 villages and thousands of torch-bearing cattle and sheep stormed a fortress held by an evil lord, and set the captives free. Hence the observing of this festival.

It is also noteworthy that the Sani people based their lives on a 10-month solar calendar, which depends on the movement of sun and of the Big Dipper. This was rated by contemporary scientists as a great law. This year's Festival of Torch falls on ---. I strongly suggest that you come back again then. You will enjoy yourselves for sure.

Selected Tour Commentaries

On that day in the evening, bonfires will be made and visitors and local villagers will dance to the accompaniment of aborigine stringed instruments.

(In the front of frescos painted by ancient people of the Yi nationality)

This is a 18-meter-tall fresco painted on a huge stone. The lower part of the painting is part of the Sani hieroglyphics, which depicts ancient social life, worship of reproduction and warfare from Han to Qing dynasties.

The Sani people are also good at drawing. China's National Gallery of Fine Arts has collected 30-strong pieces of paintings drawn by local peasants.

(Atop the Sentry Hill)

This is the tallest peak of the whole scenic area. In 1857, a large-scale rebellion broke out amongst the Yi people in support of the Taiping Revolution. This was where the rebels stood sentry. Later, the Yi people also rose in arms against the reactionaries.

(In the Minor Stone Forest)

Unlike the scenes of Major Stone Forest, the scenery of Minor Stone Forest is characterized by smaller and less imposing peaks and rocks. Many Chinese films and TV dramas were filmed here.

(Atop the Stone for Admiring the Plum)

The poem inscribed on the stone was written by the late Chairman Mao Zedong. Other leaders of Vietnam, Indonesia and Malaysia have also paid visits to the stone.

(At the foot of Ashima)

This scene was named after a legend passed down by the Sani people for generations. This was among the most popular folk stories

318

The Stone Forest

in China. Time was when there lived a beautiful girl in a place called Azhuodi. Known as Ashima, which stands for gold-like beauty, she fell in love with Brother A Hei, a brave hunter and famous wrestler. As A Hei was out shepherding the flock in a winter, a local landlord named Rebubala took Ashima hostage. A Hei rushed back home and won back his sweetheart through song-singing and wrestling. However, the triumphant couple was swept apart midway home by flood water that was caused by Rebubala and evil deities. When the flood receded, the beautiful girl turned into this rock. It is said that on the night of each Festival of Torch, she will quietly visit her parents, her husband and siblings under the cover of darkness. This tale is the embodiment of the ethnic culture of the Sani people. It takes the central stage of the culture of Stone Forest.

The Sani people believe that Ashima will bring happiness, longevity and love to every visitor. Ladies and gentlemen, now come receive her blessings in order to lead a better and sweeter life!

Li Weihong
(The Ashima Travel Service of Yunnan Province)

Selected Tour Commentaries

HUANGGUOSHU WATERFALL

Ladies and gentlemen,

Today we are going to pay a visit to the Huangguoshu Waterfall, the largest of its kind in China as well as one of the largest in the world. It was rated by the State Council as one of China's major places of interest.

This spot is located on the Baishui (White Water) Stream, a tributary of Dabang River stretching through the border of Zhenning and Guanling counties, and is 137 kilometers to the southwest of Guiyang, provincial capital of Guizhou. It is a one-hour-and-a-half drive from Guiyang to this waterfall.

Here we are. This is the world-renowned Huangguoshu Waterfall.

This waterfall is 68 meters tall and 81 meters wide. It is characterized by thunderous roars and heavy mist. The mist can stretch several hundreds meters and often enshrouds nearby farmers' houses and fairs. In winter and spring, the water flows light like satin hanging down; at this many famous Chinese travellers and scholars have marveled. A famous calligrapher of Qing Dynasty, Yan Yinliang, once likened it to naturally grown cotton.

Now we proceed to a place where the flow sinks into the Xiniu (Rhino) Pond. As legend has it a heavenly rhino hid itself underneath the water, enshrouding the pond in a veil of myth. You can enjoy a beautiful view when standing by the pond at 10 AM or 4 PM

320

Huangguoshu Waterfall

on a sunny day: amidst the mist and fog, a colorful rainbow will rise from the deep of the pond.

According to legend, there used to be a large orchard by the waterfall where pomelo, or "huangguo" in the local dialect, were grown. Hence the name of Huangguoshu Waterfall.

Unlike waterfalls in other countries, this cataract is unique in that it is the largest waterfall found in a background of Karst topography. It features a number of scenes on the ground and in the water, among which the Water Curtain Cavern is the most miraculous.

Ladies and gentlemen, we will first of all tour the Water Curtain Cavern before paying a visit to the Xiniu Pond.

Here we are. The Water Curtain Cavern is 134 meters long and consists of 6 caverns, 6 halls, 3 fountains and 6 passageways. A scene from the Chinese TV drama Monkey King was shot in the cave.

This is the No. One Cavern, which is the lowest in its level, or 40 meters above the surface of the Xiniu Pond. It is about a dozen meters in width and is constantly curtained by the waterfall in the very front. High above in midair in the front of this cavern, there hangs a group of calcific rocks, known as the Miniature Garden. The surfaces of the rocks are covered with aquatic plants and colorful flowers in blossom.

This is the No. Two Cavern, which is only 4 meters away from the No. One. Known as the Crystal Palace, this scene constitutes the heart of the Water Curtain Cavern, which is 11 meters long, 9 meters tall and 3 meters wide. By the path there is a fountain which flows all year round. On top of the cave hang numerous stalactites taking the shape of bells, and straws with different colors. It also features rocks in the shape of mantles and curtains; all these add to the beautiful scenes of the Water Curtain Cavern.

The No. Three Cavern protrudes outward, making it look like a balcony. This cavern is one meter in height and three meters in length, and railed off from the outside. Visitors can feel the cataract

321

Selected Tour Commentaries

with their hands against the railing, therefore this scene is also called the Balcony for Feeling the Cataract. Different from other waterfalls in other countries, this cataract is touchable-this is the special characteristic of the Huangguoshu Waterfall.

Walking down 22 steps from the Fifth Cavern will bring us to the Sixth Cavern, a rectangular hall. Being 10 meters long, two meters wide and six meters tall, this hall joins the exit and is covered by the cataract. When the flow is low, people can enjoy a mirage-like view of the rocky cottages and newly built hotels. People can also overlook the deep pond and appreciate the beautiful sunset. This is one more characteristic of this famous cataract.

Professor Ford, the president of International Cave Association once commented: "The Water Curtain Cavern is the most beautiful cave in the world. This is the best-preserved cave I have ever seen."

Ladies and gentlemen, now we are going to visit a chain of scenes of Xiniu Pond. The cataract consists of a chain of drops and ponds downstream. The biggest of its kind, the Xiniu Pond is 17.7 meters in depth and is constantly shrouded by a thin veil of mist and watery fog. With the reflection of sunshine, a spectacular rainbow emerges midair in mid-morning and afternoon, so the ancient travelers used to liken this scene to Morning or Evening Glow against the snowy glow.

The Huangguoshu Waterfall formed with the help of water erosion. With the constant erosion upstream, the Karst riverbed widened and deepened, thus forming quite a few cataracts, sinkholes and underground flows. With the constant enlarging of the underground rivers and caverns, chains of upright caves and caverns were formed and then collapsed. In the end, the Huangguoshu Waterfall and steep riverside bluffs downstream emerged. This was the work done by the powerful force of Mother Nature.

According to regular statistics provided by Chinese engineers, the Xiniu Pond is capable of absorbing energy carried by the flow and will not enlarge further in the foreseeable future.

Huangguoshu Waterfall

Seeing this wonderful waterfall is a rewarding experience. I hope it will leave you with deep impression and I also hope you will introduce it to other potential visitors. This scenery belongs to the world as well as to China.

Selected Tour Commentaries

THE POTALA PALACE

Ladies and gentlemen,

Welcome to Lhasa of China. I am sure that you will enjoy the unique sights and culture of the Tibetan Autonomous Region. Today I will show you around the world-renowned Potala Palace.

(About Potala)

In Tibetan, "potala" stands for "Potalaka." It is said that followers of Lamaism thought the Red Hill was so beautiful and picturesque that it equaled the Potalaka, which Avalokitesvara Bodhisattva used as his abode. Hence the name of the magnificent structure built on top of the hill.

The Potala Palace serves as an embodiment of palaces and monasteries. Its foundation is situated at the foot of the Red Hill and the structure stretches along the elevating slope upwards to the hilltop. The main structure consists of 13 stories and is 113 meters in height, and it covers a floor space of 120,000 square meters. It overlooks Lhasa, the capital city of Tibetan Autonomous Region, and provides a grand and lofty, as well as marvelous view.

It is widely thought the Palace was originally completed in the seventh century during the reign of Songtsan Ganbo, who was then the monarch of the Tubo Kingdom in Tibet. The structure consists of 1,000 room-units and was linked up by elevated passageways. Outside the Eastern Palatial Gate, there was a brick-laid racing court

The Potala Palace

which was 18 zhang (one zhang equals 3.3333 meters) by 300 zhang. The whole structure was ruined by thunder and war and remained desolate for a long time.

In 1645, the Fifth Dalai Lama came to power with the help of a Mongolian chief. To consolidate the feudal serfdom and to further exert his political power, the Dalai Lama ordered that the Potala Palace be rebuilt. Aside from the remaining structure built during the reign of Songtsan Ganbo, the White Hall was constructed on each side of it. From then on the Potala Palace has served as a residence as well as political center for successors of the Dalai Lama. Later, reconstruction and additional work were conducted on many occasions and the Red Hall and Sacred Pagoda were added to the scene. In this way, the supreme power and powerful military prowess enjoyed by slaveholders were demonstrated.

The palatial construction of Potala Palace falls into four parts: the Red Hall and White Hall on top of the Red Hill, and the Dragon King's Pond behind the Hill, as well as "Snow" at the foot of it.

The Red Hall is situated at the top of the Red Hill, which houses sacred pagodas dedicated to successive lines of the Dalai Lama and various smaller family halls for worshipping Buddha. It is considered the very center of Buddhism as well as of the universe.

Flanking the Red Hall is an extensive building known as White Hall, which features palatial halls, grand meditation rooms, Gaxag, or local government institutions and Lamaist study halls. Located uppermost, the Sunshine Hall has served as the Dalai Lama's residence. In rear of the Potala Palace, there lies a garden known as Dragon King Pond, which is three kilometers in circumference. In the center of the lake there lies an islet where the Dragon King Palace and the Elephant Cell are built. The "Snow" is situated at the foot of the Red Hill, and houses Gaxag's prisons, a sutra press, workshops and stables. The whole group of buildings is enclosed by walls and guarded by pillboxes.

According to Lamaist doctrine, there exist three major realms,

Selected Tour Commentaries

i. e., desire, form and the formless. The construction of the Potala Palace was based on this, using the Red Hall, White Hall and the "Snow" to respectively embody the realms. What is more, the Buddhist doctrine was demonstrated to the full through extreme expansion of the floor space and stark contrast of layout.

Next, I will expound on this in terms of individual spots of interest.

(Blank Stele)

This tablet was dedicated to the completion of the Potala Palace. The Fifth Dalai Lama moved from Zhebang Temple to the White Hall in 1653, when the main building of the Palace was completed. In the eighth year after his death, a regent demolished part of the old houses between the Eastern and Western White hall, and built instead the Red Hall and the Sacred Pagoda to house the dead Dalai Lama's body. To do this, more than 7,000 artisans were levied and a total of 2. 134 million taels of silver were spent. Emperor Kangxi of the Qing Dynasty also sent 114 artisans of Han and Manchu nationalities to help. The project was completed in 1693. In that year a grand gala was held and this stele was erected in front of the Palace.

(Deyang Palace and Dasongkuo Hall)

Let's first of all pay a visit to Deyang Palace and Dasongkuo Hall (proceeding along four sections of pebble path and reaching the Eastern Gate). On each side of the gate are paintings illustrating Four Vajras, or heavenly guardians. In the front there is a tunnel in the court wall, which is four meters thick. Looking up, you will see two giant drums which were used to give time.

(In the middle of the slope there is a huge platform) This is the Deyang Palace, which is more than 70 meters above the ground and covers a total floor space of 7,600 square meters. This platform was rammed into with an indigenous soil and is marvelously smooth. It was reserved for the Dalai Lama and high-ranking Lamaite as well as

326

The Potala Palace

lay officials to enjoy music, dance, Tibetan drama and sorcerer's dance in a trance on major occasions. (Ascending the staircase on the western side of the Deyang Palace) This is the covered passageway of Dasongkuo Hall, which leads to every hall. On the wall there are ancient frescos. (On either side of Western Gate) This is a painting dedicated to the Four Heavenly Guardians. Buddhism advocates that these guardians are entrusted with the duty to protect mountains, rivers, forests and land in Four Continents. (On the southern wall) This is the edict by the Fifth Dalai Lama to make Sangjie Jiacuo a governor regent, which ordered all Tibetan lamas and lay people to come under his rule. On the eastern and northern sides are paintings depicting the marriage of a Tibetan ruler with a princess from Tang Dynasty. The story is like this: the Tibetan ruler, whose name is Songtsan Ganbo, sent an envoy to the court of Tang Dynasty in Chang'an (today's Xi'an in Shaanxi Province) to seek marriage with a Tang princess. The envoy carried with him bountiful amounts of betrothal gifts, i.e., 5,000 taels of gold and a variety of pearls and gems. Emperor Taizong agreed and decided to marry his daughter, Princess Wencheng off to the Tibetan monarch. Upon the princess' arrival in Lhasa, Songtsan Ganbo met her in person at the head of the Yarlung Zangbo River. A large number of artisans, grain seeds and cattle were also brought along by the princess. Later, advanced production technology, such as the making of silk, wine, paper and ink that were enjoyed by the Han people was gradually introduced to Tibet.

The frescos on the walls of Dasongkuo Hall were classified as Tibetan artwork dating from an early period. This type of work was subject to influences by Buddhist frescos in Nepal, India and central China and is characterized by exotic style. This was proved by paintings in many Tibetan structures.

(Cuoqin Hall and the Sunshine Hall)

Cuoqin Hall, or the Eastern Hall, was completed in 1645. The

Selected Tour Commentaries

biggest hall within the White Hall and supported by 45 huge pillars, it can house more than 500 lamas at a time. It was in this hall where the Dalai Lama ascended the throne and attended to political affairs as well as participated in other eventful religious and political activities.

(On the northern part of the Hall) This is the Dalai Lama's throne. Above it hangs a huge plaque that bears an inscription - "To vitalize and pacify the frontier," which was thought as a handwritten work by Emperor Tongzhi of the Qing Dynasty. (On the eastern wall of the Hall) The fresco on this wall depicts yet another marriage between a Tibetan ruler and a Tang princess.

Before 1642, all the four successive Dalai Lamas had served as religious leaders of the Yellow Sect of Lamaism instead of as the head of Gaxag regime. In 1643, the Fifth Dalai Lama came to power owing to the help of a Mongolian chief. Ten years later, Emperor Shizu of the Qing Dynasty conferred upon him the official title of Dalai Lama. This title became known to the public thanks to the publicity given by the Qing monarchs.

Another title that shares equal status is Bainqen Erdeni. This title was reserved for the reincarnation of the most eminent Living Buddha of the Gelu School, a sect of Lamaism. He has been widely considered as the reincarnation of Amita, or Buddha of the Infinite Light. "Bain" is an abbreviation in Sanskrit, which stands for scholar. "Qen" means grand in Tibetan. So this title stands for "grand scholar" in English. In 1645, the fourth disciple of Tsong Kha-pa, founder of the Yellow Sect, was entitled as the Bainqen Bokdo and the western Tibet was put under his rule that based itself in the Zhaxi Lhunbo Temple. "Bokdo" refers to a wise and brave figure in Mongolian. In 1713, Emperor Kangxi of the Qing Dynasty conferred upon Luosang Yixi the title of Bainqen Erdeni, and thus consolidated his dominant role in Gelu School of Lamaism. The late three leaders of the school were also admitted posthumously. From then on, all events involving the reincarnation of Bainqen Erdeni would invari-

The Potala Palace

ably be approved by the central government. This has lasted for ages.

(Ascending the third floor on top of the White Hall) These are two suites of residence for the Dalai Lama. Sunshine slips through the window all year round, hence the name of the Sunshine Hall. Each year, the 13th Dalai Lama would move from the summer palace of Norbu Lingka Park to this hall, so the Potala Palace also served as the winter palace for him. The hall is characterized by colorful decor, colored pillars, gilt bed and jade utensils. The rooms on either side were reserved respectively for the 13th and 14th Dalai Lamas.

There is a striking contrast in terms of architectural style. Judging by the external shape, the Potala Palace was constructed on an ascending hill. A spatial grandeur and loftiness was thus created. In this way, the supreme authority enjoyed by the ruling elite and the unfathomableness of Buddhism were demonstrated to the full.

The majority of interior rooms, however, are narrowly partitioned, and are linked by poky and winding corridors, low passageways and steep staircases. The layout of the Potala Palace is thought of as an illustration of Buddhism. It appeals to people with its imposing architecture and meticulous details, while narrow and tortuous passageways serve as synonyms for Buddhism practices. All the windows are extremely narrow and can only let in a little sunshine. Coupled with ever lit numerous oil lamps, a mystic, hallow, unreal and quiet atmosphere dominates the scene. 13 rows of narrow and trapezoid windows were set on the facade of the Potala Palace, which is more than 300 meters wide and 100 meters high.

(The Red Hall)

The Sacred Pagoda halls and various meditation halls constitute the centerpiece of the Red Hall. A total of eight sacred pagodas dedicated to generations of Dalai Lamas are housed inside. The largest and the earliest is the one dedicated to the Fifth Dalai Lama. Com-

Selected Tour Commentaries

pleted in 1690 and 14.85 meters in height, this three-storey pagoda consists of a pedestal, a main body and the top. The specifically preserved body of the Dalai Lama was enshrined inside. The overall surface of the pagoda was coated with gold and inlaid with pearls and gems. To achieve this, more than 110,000 taels of gold and some 1,500 diamonds, rubies, emeralds, true jades, pearls and agates were applied. Sixipingcuo, or the Western Hall used to be the Fifth Dalai Lama's memorial hall. Supported by 50 huge pillars and covering a floor space of 680 square meters, it is the largest hall in the Red Hall. A plaque bearing Emperor Qianlong's dedicatory inscription hangs above and takes the dominant place of the structure. In the center is the throne reserved for the Fifth Dalai Lama, and frescos on sidewalls depict the whole life of him.

One piece on the eastern wall deserves close study. This work deals with Emperor Shunzhi's receiving of the Fifth Dalai Lama in Beijing in 1652. The Emperor, who sits up straight and puts his hands on knees and casts a kindly look, listens, thinking attentively. The Fifth Dalai Lama was giving a lecture on Buddhism. He sits cross-legged on an altar, his head hanging and looking inwardly.

(There is a pair of canopies on display inside) This pair is a rare treasure of the Potala Palace. Whenever the Dalai Lama ascends the throne or attends to political affairs, this pair of canopies would be hung in the hall. It is said that to weave the canopies, Emperor Kangxi specifically built a workshop and the whole work took a year to complete. Then, he sent an envoy with the canopies to Tibet. On all sides of the hall are side halls. Situated on the northern side is a hall that houses statues dedicated to Sakyamuni, successive Dalai Lamas, Buddhas of the three periods, Bhaisajyaguru Buddha, and a sacred pagoda for the 11th Dalai Lama.

"Gangyur," a set of precious Buddhist sutras printed in Tibetan, is niched on bookshelves. It was presented by Emperor Yongzheng as a reward. (On the eastern side of the hall) This is the Hall of Buddhist Passage, which enshrines a bronze statue dedicated to Tsong

330

The Potala Palace

Kha-pa as well as some 70 statues for eminent lamas of the Gelu and Gadang Schools. (On the southern side) This is the hall that is dedicated to Padma-Sambhava, the founder of Ningma School (Red Sect). A number of statues are enshrined inside.

(At the west end and the back of the Red Hall) This is the Sacred Pagoda Hall dedicated to the 13th Dalai Lama. It was built between 1933-6 and features three storeys and is 14 meters in height. It was coated with 590 kilograms of gold foil and inlaid with pearls and gems. It is one of the most valuable sacred pagodas of the eight such structures. (On the third floor there are many frescos) These frescos deal with the life of the 13th Dalai Lama, including his reception by Empress Dowager Cixi and Emperor Guangxu in Beijing in 1908.

(Qoigyal Zhubpug and Pagba Lhakang Chapels)

These two chapels are the only remaining architectures dating from the Tubo Kingdom, or ancient Tibet.

The Qoigyal Zhubpug Chapel was completed in the seventh century and is one of the oldest buildings of the Potala Palace. Inside, statues dedicated to Songtsan Gambo and his wife, Princess Wencheng, and a Nepalese princess, as well as courtiers were kept. They are precious artworks made during the early Tibetan history. The chapel is 3.7 meters in height, and was originally supported by two carved pillars. Later on, another nine pillars were added to further buttress the beams and the roof.

(Ascending yet another floor) This is the Pagba Lhakang Chapel. The original features of it are no longer clear due to renovations on many occasions. Dipamkara, the major Buddha that is worshipped in Potala Palace, is enshrined here. Statues that are dedicated to the Dalai Lamas, Tsong Kha-pa and stones bearing footprints of Padma-sambhava, Tsong Kha-pa as well as a teenager, and the 12th Dalai Lama are on display in showcases around the room. In the forefront hangs a plaque bearing the handwritten dedicatory inscription by Emperor Tongzhi of the Qing Dynasty.

Selected Tour Commentaries

(Sasonglangjie and Qimeigandan)

We now have come to the uppermost hall of the Potala Palace, where a painting and a memorial tablet dedicated to Emperor Qianlong are kept. Starting from the Seventh Dalai Lama, his successors would pay their homage to the Emperor in front of the memorial tablet. (Arriving at Qimeigandan) This hall was completed in 1690 and served as the meditation room for the Sixth Dalai Lama. He was a prominent figure in the Tibetan history. Clever in his childhood, this eminent lama used to be a disciple of the Fifth Bainqen Lama and was well educated in astronomy, medicine and literature. He was sent on exile in northwest China as well as in India and Nepal at the age of 25 and suffered a lot. A love poem he wrote was rendered into English, French, Russian, Japanese and Indian.

(Adieu to Potala Palace)

To sum up, the Potala Palace serves as a material demonstration of Buddhist doctrine. It applies all kinds of artistic means to illustrate the power of the Buddhism and encourages people to follow suit.

In terms of architectural style, the Potala Palace is characterized by traditional Tibetan features and structures of stone and wood. What is more, in its architecture, the style of the Han nationality can be seen through beams, brackets, the gilt rooftop and the covered ceiling. It is a perfect embodiment of the wisdom and labor on the part of Tibetan and Han people.

The Potala Palace was listed by the State Council as a major site to come under protection of the local government in 1961. Each year, the government would set aside funds for its renovation. Since 1989, a five-year historical renovation work had been carried out that involved more than 53 million Renminbi. More than 150 specialists and technicians from some 10 provinces and regions have taken part in it. The Potala Palace has also been inscribed on the World Heritage. List by UNESCO.

Ladies and gentlemen, now our tour to the Potala Palace is

The Potala Palace

drawing to a conclusion. I hope my explanations were helpful for your better understanding of the Potala Palace. Welcome back in the future.

XI'AN MUSEUM OF STELE FOREST

Ladies and gentlemen,

Welcome to the Xi'an Museum of Stele Forest.

To begin with, I'd like to make a brief introduction to the origin of this point of interests.

Xi'an used to be the capital city of Qin, Han, Sui and Tang dynasties. As a result of this, its economy and culture were developed to a rather high level. A large number of famous steles that were the hallmark of the Confucian school, such as "Kaicheng Stone Scriptures" and "Shitai Inscription on Filial Piety," came into being in this period.

In 904, the Tang imperial court moved from Chang'an (today's Xi'an) to Luoyang and the defenders drew back to the inner city, thus deserting many precious steles in the suburb. Later, somebody moved them elsewhere.

In 1087 during the Northern Song Dynasty, a local governor moved these deserted stone steles to where today's Forest of Steles is. The foundation of Xi'an Stele Forests was thus laid. Later on, refurbishment and additions were carried out on several occasions. It is noteworthy that in 1588 during the Ming Dynasty, a local governor renovated 40 broken steles of "Kaicheng Stone Scriptures" that suffered during an early earthquake, and added another 96 stone tablets and placed them beside the original ones.

In 1664 during the Qing Dynasty, a Shaanxi provincial governor

Xi'an Museum of Stele Forest

added another 114 steles using the original calligraphic and inscription style. With this being done, all fundamental Confucian classics were carved in stone tablets and the Stele Forests gained nationwide fame.

During the reign of the Emperor Qianlong of Qing Dynasty, a scholar-turned provincial governor oversaw a large-scale renovation and research work. He also set guards for protection of the site.

In 1936, a local committee was formed to carry out a renovation project of the Stele Forests and a thorough face-lift ensued. In 1944, the Historical Museum of Shaanxi Province was founded and became responsible for the administration of the Stele Forests.

After the founding of the People' Republic, the central and local governments alike have attached great importance to the protection and development of the site.

In 1952, the government earmarked special funds for a related project. And three years later, the Shaanxi Provincial Museum came into being. In 1961, the Stele Forest joined the list of cultural relics that come under state protection. In 1979, the museum was further reinforced as a precaution against a potential earthquake. And in 1982 again, the Seventh Exhibition Room was added.

The 900th anniversary of the founding of the Stele Forest fell in 1987. The stele Forest covers a total floor space of 32,000 square meters, among which 6,000 square meters go to the exhibition rooms. The exhibition area of steles covers an area of 3,000 square meters, which consists of seven exhibition rooms, six covered corridors and one tablet pavilion. The museum houses more than 2,000 steles, half of which put in display. In 1992, the newer Historical Museum of Shaanxi Province was completed and was separated from the original one in the site of Stele Forest. The following year, the Xi'an Museum of Stele Forests was formally founded.

The major pavilion housing the famous "Shitai Inscription on Filial Piety" was placed on the central axis that runs through the buildings. A plaque bearing " Stele Forest" hangs on the facade. In-

Selected Tour Commentaries

side the structure there is the tablet bearing the Shitai Inscription on Filial Piety. The earliest of its kind on display in the Stele Forest, it consists of four huge and tall pieces of stone and takes the shape of a square. It deals with a dialogue between China's great ancient philosopher Confucius and one of his disciples. They exchanged their viewpoints on filial piety. The inscription was handwritten by Emperor Li Longji of the Tang Dynasty. It is believed that the monarch hoped to achieve harmony amongst all his subjects through the erection of the stele. This precious piece of stonework was highly appreciated for its historical and artistic values.

The exhibition compound features seven rooms that are dedicated to steles on various subjects, rubbings as well as historical records. The exhibits deal with history, science, politics and everyday life literature.

Now we enter the No. 1 Exhibition Room. This room is reserved exclusively for the Kaicheng Stone Scriptures. Named after the reign mark of Emperor Wenzong of the Tang Dynasty and serving as the brainchild of the prime minister, the whole project took seven years to complete. In the end, the 12 complete classical Confucian works that totaled more than 650,000 Chinese characters were inscribed on 114 tablets. In 1664 during the reign of Emperor Kangxi of Qing Dynasty, another 13 classical Confucian works were inscribed. In the Tang Dynasty when typography was not yet invented, this set of stone inscriptions contributed to the preservation, publicity and collation of the classics in feudal times.

The No. 2 Exhibition Room features tablets dating from the Tang Dynasty, and serves as one of the most complete calligraphic treasure houses.

Situated at the southern tip of the row on the west is the tablet that tells how Nestorianism was introduced to China in 635 during the Tang Dynasty. According to it, Emperor Taizong sent his prime minister to meet a visiting Nestorian at the suburb of the capital city of Chang'an. Nestorianism enjoyed prominence for 150 years during the Tang Dynasty, but this is the only historical testimony that was left behind. It was excavated in 1623, and moved to the present site in 1903.

Located on the western and northern sides of this tablet are two tablets bearing calligraphic works by two famous Tang calligraphers. One of the calligraphers is Ouyang Xun (557-641), a prominent figure famous for his calligraphic prowess in the early Tang Dynasty. He was rated as one of the four most famous calligraphers who were well versed in regular script in early Tang period. The other work was written by his son, Ouyang Tong, also an eminent calligrapher. It was erected in 663 and tells of a story about a famous Buddhist.

Northwest to the stone tablet bearing inscriptions written by the junior calligrapher is a tablet that bears a calligraphic work by Chu Suiliang (596-659), another famous calligrapher in the early Tang Dynasty, as well as an inscription in Sanskrit. He was regarded as one of the four most famous calligraphers who were well versed in regular script in the early Tang Dynasty.

At the southern tip of the first row on the east, there is a tablet known as Duobaota Stele. It was written by Yan Zhenqing (709-785), a great calligrapher in the heyday of the Tang Dynasty, and was erected in 752, when he was 44 years of age. He was famous for developing an official script that has left a tremendous influence upon calligraphic circle in later years. There is one more stele bearing one of his works nearby.

Further northward, there stands a tablet bearing a calligraphic work by Xu Hao (703-782), a contemporary of Yan Zhenqing, that deals with Buddhist exchanges between China, India and Japan during the Tang Dynasty. Right behind this tablet, is the stone stele that bears a piece of work written by Liu Gongquan (778-865), another famous calligrapher of the Tang Dynasty. He was well known for the mould of the official script style. This piece concerns the life of an eminent local Buddhist monk. It has served as a model for anyone who is about to study his style.

Selected Tour Commentaries

To the south of this stonework stands a stele that bears memorial articles written by Tang monarchs in the style of Wang Xizhi (321-379), an eminent calligrapher of the Eastern Jin Dynasty who was well versed in running script. To gather Wang's work for the inscription project, a hefty reward was offered. The project lasted for 24 years before it came to the conclusion. Wang was widely considered as the sage of China's calligraphy.

In addition, this room also displays other styles of work. It is the showpiece of Tang calligraphic works and serves as the central part of the Stele Forest. The exhibits in the No. 3 Exhibition Room features calligraphic pieces between Han the and Qing dynasties in various styles.

The first and the second tablets in the southeastern part of the room were written by a Buddhist monk in 999, or during the Song Dynasty. Radicals and basic structural components of Chinese character in the form of seal characters were carved in the stele. They serve as a model of seal style.

The first stele standing at the southern tip of the second row on the east is known as "Xiping Shi Jing" and deals with events in remote times. It was erected during the reign of Emperor Lingdi of the Eastern Han Dynasty (24-220). As the majority of the inscription wore out, only 461 characters remained.

The third tablet in the same row is known as "Cao Quan Stele" and was erected in 185 during the Eastern Han Dynasty. This tablet is characterized by its headless and square shape. It was excavated during the Ming Dynasty (1368-1644) and relocated to the present site in 1957. The tablet serves as a eulogy dedicated to a local magistrate. It was written in official script, serving as a precious model of calligraphy.

The fifth tablet serves as yet another model of official script. It was the handwritten work by a local magistrate in praise of Cang Ji, the legendary figure who was believed to have invented the Chinese character. There are other rare steles bearing calligraphic master-

Xi'an Museum of Stele Forest

pieces by prominent calligraphers.

The first stele of the fourth row bears an inscription written by Zhao Ji, an emperor of the Song Dynasty (960-1279). It deals with educational systems, regulations and a selection of the talented during that period. The emperor was well versed in calligraphy and painting techniques.

The majority of steles standing on the west feature are in running script by famous calligraphers in the Tang Dynasty. To sum up, we can have a glimpse of the transition from the Han to Song dynasties in terms of calligraphic trends in the room. We can also understand the changes of stele traditions.

Many square-shaped tombstones are also on display in the third and fourth exhibition rooms. They hold clues to the official and administrative system, geology, events, customs, literature and arts, so these are to some extent more valuable than steles themselves. Some of them are calligraphic work by famous hands. The fourth room holds steles bearing famous poems, articles and statuary by line carving, which originated between Song and Qing dynasties.

The first tablet in the first row on the east is a composite stonework that features five square steles bearing a 115-character calligraphic work by Huang Tingjian (1045-1105), a famous calligrapher of the Song Dynasty. The second tablet is inscribed by Su Shi (1037-1101), a great writer and a renowned calligrapher. Unfortunately, the tablet wore out due to longtime weathering. To the back of it lies another tablet that bears a poem written by Mi Fu (1051-1107), his contemporary with equal literary achievements. Su Shi, Huang Tingjian, Mi Fu and Cai Xiang were the four greatest calligraphers of the Song Dynasty.

In the Yuan Dynasty that followed the collapse of the Song Dynasty, there emerged another famous calligrapher who went by the name of Zhao Mengfu (1254-1332). There is one tablet bearing a piece of his penmanship in the back of that dedicated to Mi Fu. He has another piece of work that is on display in the Sixth Exhibition

Selected Tour Commentaries

Room.

The Fourth Exhibition Room is famous for line carvings on display. The exhibits include a double-line carving depicting a famous painter of the Song Dynasty, two works of the Ming Dynasty concerning Bodhidharma's medication and his crossing of the Yangtze River, a carving originated in the Qing Dynasty depicting a famous ancient general and other precious works. All these are invaluable historical records bearing testimony to geography, architecture and places of interests in ancient China.

This is the Fifth Exhibition Room of the Stele Forest. The majority of the stone tablets that are on display are that of the Qing Dynasty. In the eastern row close to the main entrance stand two steles that bear handwritten works by Emperor Kangxi.

In the third row on the west, there stands a stone tablet known as "Yishan Stone Inscription." It was written in little seal by Li Si, the prime minister of the Qin Dynasty, and erected in 219 BC when Emperor Qinshihuang, the founding father of the Qin Dynasty, ascended Zouyi Mountain on an inspection tour. It was the first of its kind erected on the tour. The stele features 223 characters and was dedicated to his achievement the abolishing the enfeoffment system and establishing the prefecture and country system. In 993 during the Song Dynasty, a newer one was erected in the same site.

In the second and third rows on the east, there are some steles erected during the Qing Dynasty featuring philosophical maxims. In addition, other pieces of stonework are put on display in this room; they are mainly dedicated to the renovation projects of Buddhist monasteries and cities, irrigation systems and running of schools.

Here is the Sixth Exhibition Room. The majority of the exhibits here are dedicated to poems and verses of the Qing Dynasty, with a minority of them bearing literary works of the Yuan and Ming dynasties. Among these the famous items are: calligraphic works by Zhao Mengfu (in Yuan Dynasty), Dong Qichang (in Ming Dynasty), Emperor Kangxi of the Qing Dynasty as well as Lin Zexu, a prominent anti-opium Qing official. The stone inscription by Lin Zexu was written in running script in 1842, which was a rare piece amongst works by the late Qing calligraphers. As with the Fifth Exhibition Room, there are some tablets that are dedicated to famous maxims in this room, too.

The Seventh Exhibition Room is widely known as a smaller Stele Forest with the greater Stele Forest since it houses a famous set of rubbings dating from 992 in the Song Dynasty. Emperor Taizong ordered a famous calligrapher to create a facsimile of precious of works by generations of imperial rulers, high ranking courtiers and famous calligraphers that the royal court collected, and the rubbings were presented to court officials for collection. The exhibits on display here were facsimiles inscribed on 145 stone tablets. They were arranged in two rows.

This room is particular in that it serves as a treasure house of masterpieces of calligraphy originating from various times. It also serves as a living example of China's calligraphy as well as the development of stone carving. It certainly serves as a rich source for calligraphy researchers and lovers alike.

To sum up, the Xi'an Museum of Stele Forest serves as a forest of tablets, calligraphy and China's ancient cultural traditions. It bears an everlasting testimony to the cultural hallmark of China.

With this our visit draws to a conclusion. Hope you have enjoyed the visit here. Goodbye and good luck.

Selected Tour Commentaries

HISTORY MUSEUM OF SHAANXI PROVINCE

Ladies and gentlemen,

Welcome to the History Museum of Shaanxi Province. Situated northwest to the famous Greater Wild Goose Pagoda in the provincial capital of Xi'an, it is China's first large-scale national museum that boasts modern facilities.

The construction of the museum started in 1983 at the will of the late premier Zhou Enlai. The project was completed and open to business on June 20, 1991. The whole facility covers a total floor space of 65,000 square meters, with 55,600 square meters of building area. The exhibition route totals 2,100 meters. The architectural complex features construction style prevalent during the Tang Dynasty, i.e. there are lofty buildings on four corners while the palaces and halls are situated in the center. Judging by appearance, this museum is magnificent as well as grand, and serves as a fine embodiment of ancient construction style with modern technologies. It can be considered as a reflection of national traditions, local characteristics and modern trends.

The province of Shaanxi has served as the national capital of 12 feudal dynasties such as Zhou, Qin, Han, Tang, etc. It is also rich in underground cultural relics. After its founding, the Historical Museum of Shaanxi Province put on display more than 370,000 pieces of rare relics that were unearthed in the province. Among these are the

History Museum of Shaanxi Province

bronze wares, pottery figurines, gold and silver articles, as well as tomb frescos dating from Tang Dynasty. The majority of them serve as ingenious national treasures of China.

This museum has been drawing constant visitors from China and abroad with its quality exhibits, beautiful environs and special attractions. The party general secretary and China's president Jiang Zemin, premier Zhu Rongji and 40 other national and Communist Party leaders, as well as some 400,000 international visitors have paid their visits to the museum. In addition, more than 40 foreign heads of state and government leaders including Japanese emperor have also visited this comprehensive museum.

China's president Jiang Zemin, French president Jacques Chirac as well as other Chinese and foreign leaders have written dedications calling for better protection of the national treasure trove and heaping praises on the wisdom of the Chinese people.

Since the completion of the museum, a total of three million people have paid their visit to it, making it one of the major showpieces of patriotic education and cultural exchanges between China and world.

The Historical Museum of Shaanxi Province is rich in cultural relics. The plaque of the museum is copied after calligraphic works by Guo Moruo, a famous modern writer, poet, historian, calligrapher as well as a renowned statesman in China. The gigantic rock lying in the fountain on the facade of the main building is taken from an ancient lake dating back to the Han Dynasty. The horse statues standing on either side of the main gate were cut 1,119 years ago in the Tang Dynasty. They reflect the culture of the Tang Dynasty.

This is the Hall of Preface, which presents three pieces of giant pictures and one stone lion. These pictures of the Yellow River and Loess Plateau show the long traditions enjoyed by the Chinese while the stone lion, lying in the center, came from an ancient tomb dating from Tang Dynasty. It was carved in 670 from a giant monolith and is 3.5 meters tall, three meters long and 1.2 meters wide. It is a reflection of fundamental historical and cultural styles prevalent in Shaanxi Province.

Now I will guide you through the exhibition section of the ancient history of the province, a time span of more than one million years. This section is composed of three exhibition halls in seven sections, covering a total area of 6,000 meters and featuring 3,000 chosen rare articles of cultural relics.

This is the Pre-Historical Exhibition Room that spans from 1.15 million years BC to 21-century BC. These are fossilized skulls of Lantian Man (1.15 million years ago) and Dali Man (more than 100,000 years ago). It is significant that the Lantian Man was the earliest homos erectus in the northern hemisphere. This skull is believed to be from a 30-something female, with a brain capacity of roughly 780 milliliters. Also on display are stone implements used by them. Though primitive, these tools enjoyed a significant place in the human tool development. Dali Man belonged to a newer phase of human development, or homo sapiens. The tools were also classified as chipped stone type. All the above-mentioned exhibits belong to the Palaeolithic Age.

There are quite a few pieces of cultural relics dating from the Neolithic Age that have been found in Shaanxi Province, e.g., ground stone tools originated from Laoguantai Culture of Huanxian County, which dates from 8,000 years ago.

The Neo- and Palaeolithic ages are differentiated by four major markers, i.e., polished and smooth stone tools, pottery making, settlement and primitive agriculture.

Bountiful pieces of cultural relics of Laoguantai, Yangshao and Longshan cultures can also be found in showcases here. The tools on display here show that our forebearers no longer depended solely on gathering and hunting, but began to resort to slash-and-burn cultivation.

The Laoguantai Man managed to make and use pottery. The appearance of pottery marks the first time that man turned natural material into another with the application of fire. The Banpo Man of the Yangshao Culture made finer pottery with fish and deer designs on it. They were also able to make pottery figurines, xun's (an ancient egg-shaped, holed wind instrument), and the forebearers of characters—carved signs. The invention of pottery served to provide man with boiling and steaming utensils and thus drastically improved their living standards. These polished bone arrowheads, fishhooks, awls, and needles that are on display here serve as a reflection of organizational abilities that the female chiefs of Banpo Culture boasted.

The black pottery items on display in showpieces here belong to the Longshan Culture, or 4,900-4,000 years ago during the patrilineal society. Lying on the bank of Weihe River, this site of cultural relics is characterized by the appearance of steaming-boiling utensils and wine vessels. A total of 81 stone knives were excavated. The drastic increase of stone knives serves as a sign of transition from slash-and-burn cultivation to hoe-based agriculture.

This is a huge picture about the Huangdi (Yellow Emperor) Mausoleum. He was one of the earliest Chinese emperors in remote times. The two emperors Huangdi and Yandi have contributed a lot to the improvement of everyday life and agriculture. With their contribution, China entered the ancient period of civilization and thus heralded the new era of the 5,000 years of civilization.

The Huangdi Mausoleum is situated on the Beiqiao Hill of Huangling County. A renovation project is now underway to reflect through its architectural style the building trends prevalent in the Han Dynasty.

The Second Exhibition Section

Zhou (21st century BC to 770 BC)

The early history of Chinese civilization started from the 21st century BC and involved three dynasties of Xia, Shang and Zhou. The exhibits originating from Zhou on display here do not actually refer to the Zhou Dynasty taught in textbooks. It refers to the Zhou Nationality, Zhou Fang Country and the Western Zhou Dynasty.

The people of Zhou were descendants of Hou Ji, or the King of Cereals. The cultural remains of this period are classified by archeologists as the Former Zhou Culture.

After several hundred years of development, the Zhou people gradually settled down and established an official system in the 16th century where today's Fufeng and Qishan counties lie. Confronted by the powerful presence of the Zhou people, the Shang Dynasty was forced to recognize the tribe and conferred the title of chief to all dukes and princes upon it. The exhibits on display here are known as the earliest construction materials in China, i. e., nailed tiles and hollow hammering blocks. Being light, soundproof and thermal insulating, the latter are still in use today.

The Western Zhou Dynasty ranked as the third largest country in Chinese history and was characterized by slave society. It also boasted a high-level economic development of the slave society. Since the Western Zhou Dynasty made Xi'an its capital, thus placing the city as the center of China's politics, economy and culture, it shared a major position in the history of world's civilizations.

The Western Zhou Dynasty (11th century BC-770 BC) served as the peak time of China's Bronze Culture. Since the capital was founded in Shaanxi Province, this province enjoyed a relatively more advanced bronze casting industry. This province is characterized by a large number of various beautifully crafted pieces of bronze wares that were unearthed. In nearly 40 years to date, more than 3,000 articles of bronze ware were unearthed in the province while this museum collected 2,000 articles of them. It is noteworthy to say that many of the articles bear inscriptions that deal with wars, reward of arable land and commercial transactions. These inscriptions serve both as valuable historical records as well as masterpieces of calligraphy.

"Ding," a cooking tripod with two loop handles and three legs that was originally used for cooking pork, beef and mutton, became a symbol of power and hierarchy with the development of an official system. In burials, the number of dings that were put into use was also strictly restricted. The emperors were entitled to nine dings and eight guis (a cooking vessel with three hollow legs), while the dukes and princes were entitled to seven dings and six guis.

The Third Exhibiton Section

Qin Dynasty (770 BC-206 BC):

The historical and cultural traditions of Shaanxi Province are characterized by achievements that were attained by people of the Qin Dynasty. During the Warring States Period, the Qin State made Yong (today's Fengxiang County) its capital city. The bronze construction materials and eaves tiles on display here belonged to this period and served as a reflection of the kingdom's ambition. A giant coffin and 166 skeletons of sacrificed men excavated in the southern suburbs of Yong bore a terrifying testimony to the cruelty of the sacrificial system in the early Qin Dynasty.

The Warring States Period (475-221 BC):

This period served as the beginning of the feudal society in China. It was characterized by large number of talents, freedom of artistic creation, widespread application of iron agricultural tools as well as some large-scale irrigation works in the Qin State. This showed that this state attached great importance to agriculture and that the whole society was based on the agricultural activities. For example, the construction of Zhenguo Canal linked the Jing River and northern Luo River and totaled 150 kilometers in length. With this, some four million arable pieces of land in the northern Shaanxi Province were irrigated and the yield increased from 35 kilograms per mu to 120 kilograms, laying a sound economic foundation for the unification of China by the Qin State.

Selected Tour Commentaries

After a reform drive led by Shangyang, the prime minister under Duke Xiaogong of the Qin State, the capital was relocated in Xianyang. With the rapid development of production and the introduction of standardized production of arms, the weaponry used by Qin armed forces was updated constantly. This bronze sword, although buried underground for more than 2,000 years, is still sharp enough to cut through 18 pieces of paper. It is found that the surface of the weapon was plated with a two-micro-thin coat of chrome-saline oxide. Considering the technology of chrome plating was not invented by the German and American engineers in the West until the 30s, this is especially important and significant.

The crossbow used to be the most advanced weapon in the cold-arm period before the advent of gunpowder. This kind of crossbow was capable of shooting 100-gram king-sized arrowheads with a kill radius of 900 meters. China developed this kind of weaponry 15 centuries earlier than the Europeans.

The terra-cotta warriors on display here were among the first batch that were excavated from the No.1 Pit of the terra-cotta warrior site. Swords, spears and bronze weaponry were also unearthed. In 221 BC the First Emperor of the Qin Dynasty, with powerful armed forces, brave soldiers and sharp arms and by applying a strategy of befriending distant states while attacking those nearby, took only ten years before he unified China and set up the first centralized authoritarian regime in China. This system exerted a tremendous influence upon China's history.

In addition to constructing the terra-cotta warriors site—which was widely believed to be the eighth wonder in the world, and the building of the grand Great Wall, the First Emperor also abolished the enfeoffment system, unified and standardized characters, weights and measures, monetary units and the width of axles. He also built a network of highways that radiated from the capital of Xianyang in all directions.

The relics in the showcases bear testimony to these historical facts: this is the stone weighing apparatus that was widely used during the Qin Dynasty; a circular coin with a square hole in the center, known as Ban Liang Coin, was put into circulation across the country. This kind of coin was used by the populace for more than 2,000 years.

In December 1980, two sets of painted bronze chariots and horses were excavated in the vicinity of the First Emperor's mausoleum. They were cast at a 1:2 scale and are rated as top-grade in terms of shape, grade, decoration, construction and harnesses. This discovery provides valuable and precious records to the research of the ancient chariot system and the emperor's usage of chariots.

The First Emperor of the Qin Dynasty also accepted the land ownership, and thus promoted the development of Chinese history. In the meantime however, he was very harsh towards the common people, carrying out very strict laws and punishment and levying heavy taxes. His son, who went by the name of Hu Hai, was even crueler, leading to China's first peasant revolt that overthrew the regime.

The Fourth Exhibition Section of No.2 Exhibition Room

Western Han (202 BC-8 AD)
New Mang (8-23 AD)

The Han Dynasty is known in Chinese history as a feudal dynasty that was characterized by an ever-powerful and prosperous state, exerting everlasting influence upon later dynasties and contributing to the formation of the Han nationality. Nowadays many countries in the world refer to the people and culture of China as "Han,".

The first exhibit that we will see in the Fourth Exhibition Section is this gilt bronze "zhong," a weighing apparatus prevalent in ancient China, which served as a symbol of prosperity and richness. Liu Bang, the founding father of the Han Dynasty, located the capital city on the bank of Wei River. It was 36 kilometers in circumference, nearly two times that of Rome.

The Han Dynasty was famous for well-developed metallurgy, iron casting, salt and jade carving. This is a stone mill, the first of its kind in China and most probably in the world. It revolutionized people's way of eating.

This color painted bronze lamp decorated with mackerel was vividly shaped and exquisitely made. The direction of the light is adjustable, the fume and dust can also be absorbed into the body of the goose, thus dissolving them with water to purify the air. It can also be taken apart for cleaning.

This gilt and silver incense burner was excavated in May 1981 and was fairly well preserved. It belonged to Princess Xinyang, the elder sister of Emperor Wudi of the Han Dynasty. It was rated as a piece of national treasure that this museum collects.

This seal made from a white jade may belong to the famous empress Lu Hou. It was especially precious considering the fact that few artifacts that belonged to her were left behind.

The agriculture in the Western Han Dynasty enjoyed a giant leap forward thanks to the introduction of the ox into cultivation, wide use of iron tools, building of irrigation works and improvement of cultivation technologies, as well as an effort the state made to lighten the burden on peasants. This can be reflected by the excavation of a large number of pottery utensils that held grains in them as well as stout cattle and poultry.

The Han Dynasty was also known for its scientific and technological achievements in arithmetic, papermaking, anaesthesia and the invention of a seismograph, leaving a profound influence upon the development of science and technology in China as well as in the world.

This arithmetic method conducted by ivories is of the decimal system. The excavation of the paper made at Baqiao in the Western Han Dynasty made China's history of papermaking 150 years longer.

History Museum of Shaanxi Province

Papermaking is one of the four major inventions that originated in China in ancient times. The other three are: gunpowder, the compass and printing.

These horses of fine breed were introduced from the west when Zhang Qian, an imperial envoy, was sent on a visit to the outlying countries in the west by Emperor Wudi of the Han Dynasty in 138 BC and 119 BC . This visit opened up the famous Silk Road that started from Chang'an and ran through the Euro-Asian continent, contributing to the economic and cultural exchanges between China and the Western world. By then Chang'an had already become a center for international exchanges in Asia.

Fragments of silk also were found along the Silk Road, a fact that reflected a great importance being attached to the sericulture. The dynasty saw the introduction of a variety of silk fabrics such as damask, monochromatic and multi-colored figured silk, as well as wool and linen fabric.

There is also a separate showpiece of terra-cotta warriors dating from the Han Dynasty in the Exhibition Room. The 46 pottery figurines were selected from 3,000 sarificial objects in an attendant tomb of Emperor Gaozu in 1956. They were vividly portrayed and complete with color painting all over. The garment, armor, weaponry and hairstyles were depicted in meticulous detail. A fairly large amount of the terra-cotta warriors were cavalrymen, showing that mounted troops then were a separate arm of services.

The Han Dynasty also boasted a famous physician, Zhang Zhongjing, and an eminent surgeon, Hua Tuo in the medical field. In literary circle, the Han Dynasty is known for the Han verses and poems in the Yuefu style as well as Shi Ji, a famous chronicle of major events that occurred in China's history.

In late Western Han Dynasty, Buddhism was introduced to China. During the Eastern Han Dynasty, the Confucian doctrine was made orthodox, which left an indelible mark upon China's ideological heritage.

Selected Tour Commentaries

The Fifth Exhibition Section of the Second Exhibition Room

Northern Wei and Northern, Southern Dynasties (220-581)

The period started with the establishment of the Northern Wei Kingdom and ended with the unification by the Sui Dynasty, and spanned a period of 300-odd years. This period was marked as a restless and unsafe age, which resulted from the collapse of the centralized country, social unrest and the southbound move of ethnic groups. As a result, a national blend of nationalities took place that centered in today's Shaanxi Province. This has laid a foundation for the massive development that served as the hallmark of the Sui and Tang dynasties, as well as the turning point for the Chinese people.

This period is characterized by clear-cut features of the military and locale. The bronze cross-bow and triangular spurs on display here were found in an ancient battlefield.

This polyhedron seal features 24 sides, including 16 squares and eight triangles. All sides of the 14 squares bear inscriptions. The owner of this precious seal was Dugu Xin, one of the nobles of the Xianbei nationality in Western Wei Kingdom. All of his three daughters were married off to three emperors in three separate kingdoms or dynasties. In this sense he can be called the most prominent father-in-law in ancient China.

During this period a large number of people of ethnic nationalities moved to Shaanxi and settled down here. As a result, many of today's surnames are derived from ethnic groups. You can have a glimpse of this development from this chart here.

This statue of an armored horse with riding musicians was introduced from Persia. It is reminiscent of life on steppe.

At the same time, Buddhism saw a dramatic development in this area. Many of the Buddhist statues on display here reflect this fact. What is more, calligraphy, stone carving, frescos and poems were also in full swing.

The Sixth Exhibition Section of the Second Exhibition Room

The Sui and Tang dynasties (581-907)

China's feudal society saw a booming and prosperous time during the Sui and Tang dynasties. The Sui Dynasty was founded by Emperor Yang Jian in 581. In 589, he overthrew the Chen Dynasty and unified China, thus ushering in the second largest unified and prosperous period in China's history.

This period was characterized by a stable state, a relatively lighter burden levied on the populace and a booming economy. A ruling regime consisted of three provinces and six ministries as well as an imperial examination system. A famous canal that ran from Beijing to Hangzhou was also cut. The famous Zhaozhou Bridge and Daxing City were completed by ingenious engineers. A printing technique applying cut blocks was invented during the reign of Sui emperors.

The Tang Dynasty (618-907)

This dynasty was founded by Li Yuan. The founding emperor was later succeeded by his son, Li Shimin, known as Emperor Taizong. The junior emperor used to be a prominent politician in ancient China in that he was industrious to attend political affairs, gave full play to talents, reduced taxes on people and went to all lengths to develop the economy. The dynasty was also known for the appearance of the sole female emperor in China's history. This prominent female, who went by the name of Wu Zetian, inherited the political stratum from Li Shimin and further consolidated the foundations of the Tang Dynasty.

During the reign of Emperor Xuanzong, this dynasty was in its heyday in terms of political and economic development. China then was characterized by an expansive territory, rich resources, a large number of talented people and the harmonious coexistence of people of all nationalities. Diplomatic, religious and cultural exchanges between China and the outside world were carried out. According to archeological discoveries, objects of the Tang Dynasty were found as far as Europe and Africa.

The Chang'an City during the Tang Dynasty was constructed on the basis of Daxing City of the Sui Dynasty. It was 35 kilometers in circumference and covered a total area of 84 square kilometers, 2.4 times larger than the city in the Han Dynasty, seven times that of Byzantine, capital of Eastern Roman Empire, and six times that of Bagdad. It was even 9.3 fold larger than that during the Ming Dynasty. The city consisted of a palace compound, imperial compound and outer city. The central axis that ran through the city was known as Scarlet Bird Avenue, which was 155 meters in width. A section of it was even as wide as 440 meters, probably the widest street in the world. On the basis of this, the city was divided by 11 longitudinal avenues and 14 streets. In all, the whole city featured 108 sections, or fang. This checkerboard-shaped layout exerted a profound and lasting influence upon later dynasties and was copied by some Asian countries such as Japan and Korea for their city design.

To facilitate the development of industries and commerce, two areas in the city were set up as markets (an equivalent of two fangs each), where 8,000-12,000 stores or stalls were installed. All year round, the markets remained brisk with business activities. In addition, many artisans that specialized in silk-weaving, printing and dying, gold and silver ware, porcelain, tri-colored glazing of pottery, and bronze mirrors plied their trades in the markets. Many of the rare precious articles that are on display here were probably made by them.

A fair amount of exhibits in this exhibition come from an excavation in the southern suburbs of Xi'an in October 1970, such as a gilt octagonal silver cup decorated with designs of western musicians, an agate cup with a beast-shaped top, gold and silver coins from Japan and the Eastern Roman Empire, pottery and porcelain figurines. All these bear testimony to a friendly relationship that was shaped between China and other countries.

The tri-colored glazed pottery ware was mainly excavated in Xi'an and Luoyang, and the amount is extremely limited. A variety of everyday utensils and statues of fine horses, camels, court ladies, and officials can be seen here. The craftsmanship is especially superb.

It was during the Sui and Tang dynasties that a splendid civilization was formed and consolidated, and this led to the peak of a feudal culture. Since the Song and Yuan dynasties, the political, economic and cultural center has gradually shifted from Shaanxi to south China, and local culture has slipped on a decline. Such appealing handicrafts can no longer be found in the province.

So much for our visit to the Historical Museum of Shaanxi Province. Hope every one of you have had a good grasp of what the museum presents and exhibits

Selected Tour Commentaries

TERRA-COTTA ARMY MUSEUM

Distinguished ladies and gentlemen,

Today, we will pay a visit to the Terra-cotta Army Museum. This museum is situated 35 kilometers east of Xi'an, and is a 50-minute drive from downtown city to the museum. It was first opened to public on October 1, 1979. Since then millions of visitors, including heads of state and party leaders of China and abroad, have visited this human wonder and heaped praise upon it.

Before we start to see the stunning scene of the terra-cotta army, I'd like to say something about Yingzheng, or the First Emperor of the Qin Dynasty, as he was closely associated with this amazing site.

Born in 259 BC, Yingzheng ascended throne when he was 13 years old. According to succession tradition, however, he was not eligible to attend personally to state affairs until he was 22 years old. So, it was the empress dowager, the prime minister and the head eunuch who wielded power behind the screen. In 238 BC, Yingzheng, who just reached 22 years of age then, paid a visit to the old capital for the coronation ceremony. Lao Ai, the head eunuch, laid an ambush for him on his way back home in a bid to kill him. However, the new king detected the plot and defeated him and brought him to justice. Then, he sent the prime minister into exile to consolidate his rule.

To further boost his power, Yingzheng promoted a number of

talented and competent civil servants and generals. In order to unify the greater China, he laid down a military strategy of befriending distant states while attacking those nearby. Starting in 230 BC, he set out on this goal. By 221 BC, he defeated six countries in less than ten years, concluding the chaos of more than 500 years known as the Warring States Period. By this time, China's first-ever centralized feudal power was founded and laid a solid basis for the rapid development of economy, politics, ideology and culture.

From then on, Yingzheng called himself the First Emperor in the belief that his descendants would pass down his regime from generation to generation. To achieve this, he shook up the civil system in three areas: firstly, he was responsible for the promotion and demotion of officials at all levels; secondly, he abolished the enfeoffment system and set up a system of prefectures and counties; and thirdly, he uniformized the legal system, writing characters, currency and weighing apparatus as well as measures. He also commissioned a large number of laborers to pave high-grade carriageways to facilitate the economic and cultural exchanges. In addition, he built on old foundations the Great Wall that snaked from Lintao in Gansu Province in the west to Jieshi in Liaodong Peninsula in the east, and thus thwarted harassment by the northern nomadic groups.

Like other monarchs in Chinese history, the First Emperor of the Qin Dynasty built his own grand and luxurious mausoleum. He ordered the construction when he came to power at the age of 13. This imperial mausoleum was originally 120 meters tall and 2,000 meters in circumference. Now it is still 76 meters tall and 400 meters in circumference. The memorial park on the ground can be deemed as a miniature capital, since the First Emperor truthfully copied the layout of Xianyang, the capital city. There used to be a palace compound in the northwestern part and a fishpond in the northeastern corner. In the outer compound there was a quarry pit in the northwest and a graveyard in the west. According to historical records, the country boasted a population of 20 million, among which seven

Selected Tour Commentaries

million were able-bodied laborers. To construct the mausoleum, more than 700,000 people were conscripted.

The mausoleum of the First Emperor can be likened to a gigantic group of underground palaces. The ceiling is said to be decorated with a map of constellations; the stars were made with a variety of glistening pearls and gems. On the ground lie Chinese territory and mercury-filled rivers, lakes and seas. An audience hall was also built. To keep the thieves away, automatic bows were installed on each door leading to the grave.

In order to enjoy himself in the nether world, the First Emperor moved almost all his belongings with him and buried some court ladies alive. In order to keep secrets from being disclosed, he also buried alive all the artisans who were involved in building the mausoleum. This is the No. 1 pit of the terra-cotta army. They were found in March 1974 when local peasants were sinking wells in the countryside. They reported their finding to the administration of cultural relics. As a result, a total of three pits were found. They were believed to be attendant tombs of the First Emperor's mausoleum.

A prolonged and hard excavation drive was launched. Five years of hard work resulted in a gigantic and well-structured museum that was built above the underground artifacts. The No. 1 pit was open to the public in October 1979. On the World Tourim Day that fell on September 27 1989, the No. 3 pit was completed and opened up. A marble structure was also built in November 1994 on the No. 2 pit. Further excavation work is still being carried out.

The No. 1 pit is characterized by its sheer size. It is 230 meters long and 62 meters wide, and covers a total area of 14,260 square meters. On the east end there stand three rows of terra-cotta warriors who face east. Numbering a total of 210, they were meant to serve as the vanguards. Behind them are the main force in 38 columns and were positioned in 11 tunnels. The ground of the tunnels were laid with black bricks and the wooden roofs were supported by pillars. The roof was covered by an impressed mat that was to be

Terra-cotta Army Museum

topped by soil. Each tunnel is five meters deep from the surface. On the south, north and west sides of the tunnels, there stand rows of warriors who face outward. More than 1,000 pottery figures have now been unearthed from this pit. It is estimated that more than 6,000 terra-cotta soldiers will eventually be exhumed when the project is completed.

This is the No.2 pit, an L-shaped phalanx of charioteers, cavalrymen and infantrymen. It is estimated that more than 1,000 pottery soldiers, 500 chariots and saddled horses will be excavated at last. This pit covers an area of 6,000 square meters. It features a small phalanx in the east featuring 334 bowmen. The southern part of the pit features a phalanx of 64 chariots in eight rows. In the center there are 19 chariots and armless soldiers. The northern end of the pit features a number of chariots and cavalrymen.

Now we have come to the No.3 pit, which is located 25 meters to the west of the No.2 pit. It was discovered in 1976 and is M-shaped, covering a space of 520 square meters. Only one chariot and 64 pottery warriors were unearthed here. They stand in pairs armed with "shu," an ancient weapon made of bamboo. Archaeologists believe that this pit was meant as a commander post.

Archaeologists share the view that more than 8,000 terra-cotta warriors will be exhumed when all three pits are cleared. These warriors are different from each other in their complexions and postures, as all of them were copied after soldiers and commanders of the palace guards in real life. Visitors can tell if they were cavalrymen, infantrymen or bowmen judging by their uniforms and postures. The heights of the figures vary from 1.7 meters to 1.9 meters, and the weights from 100-odd kilogrammes to 300 kilogrammes.

The terra-cotta horses exhumed from the site were meant to be bred in northwest China. They are 1.5 meters tall and two meters long. They were kilned in parts and then were put together. The ears are pricked up and the postures graceful. This shows that the Qin people were especially good at breeding horses.

Selected Tour Commentaries

Why did the First Emperor decided to kiln so many pottery warriors and horses? And how were they made? The records showed that he originally wanted 4,000 teenaged boys and girls to be buried alive when he passed away, and he ordered Li Si, his prime minister, to carry this out. Fearing that this would lead to civil revolt, Li Si suggested life-sized terra-cotta warriors and horses be kilned instead. The emperor accepted this advice and ordered that the project be accomplished copying his 8,000 palace guards. The artisans went to great lengths to meet the demand. Initially, the products were overburned. Later, an artisan happened to work out a special technique of kilning the unfinished work seperately before piecing them together. In this way, some 8,000-pottery warriors were made.

The majority of the weaponry that these warriors held is made from copper and tin in addition to 13 other rare metals. To guard from rust, the Qin people plated the surface of arms with a coat of chrome-saline oxide, much earlier than today's technique that was invented by the Germans in the 30s. The crossbows came in three sizes. The most powerful of them could hit targets some 600 meters away.

The two sets of bronze chariots and drawing horses on show here are excavated in a site 18 meters to the west of the main mausoleum in 1980. Each of the chariots is drawn by a team of four horses. The chariots, horses and figures were cast at a scale of 1:2. The chariots were decorated with 1,720 pieces of gold and silver ornaments, weighing a total of seven kilograms. These artifacts provide us with precious historical and scientific clues to the carriage system, metallurgic attainments and craftsmanship of the Qin Dynasty.

It is now over 2,000 years since the death of the First Emperor. However, his unprecedented achievements and the existing terra-cotta warriors as well as horses leave much thought to us. We can centainly learn a lot from the visit to this wonderful spot of interest.

HEAVENLY LAKE IN XINJIANG

Ladies and gentlemen,

Welcome to the Xinjiang Uygur Autonomous Region. Situated in the heartland of the Euro-Asian continent, this region is characterized by large expanses of territory, numerous ancient cultural and scenic spots, and a multitude of ethnic people of nationalities as well as a variety of interesting social customs. But today, I will show you around the Heavenly Lake that is cuddled in the Tianshan Mountains.

Situated on the slope of Mount Bogda, 110 kilometers to the east of Urumqi, the capital city of the Region, the Heavenly Lake is less than a three hour drive from Urumqi. The Tianshan Mountains cover a vast expanse of hilly areas. They are 1,700 kilometers in length and 300 kilometers in width, roughly one quarter of the whole territory of this northwestern autonomous region. These east-west mountains originate from the Pamirs and lie in the center of Xinjiang, dividing the territory into two, with two basins of Tarim and Junggur on each side. Characterized by steepness and natural grandeur, this huge group of mountains is widely seen as the symbol of Xinjiang.

The Tianshan Mountains were first mentioned in the chronological works of the Warring States Period. In later dynasties, various names were applied to them. In a time span of over 2,000 years, this group of steep and snaking mountains and peaks have witnessed a large number of historical events, including various exchanges between China's central government and its neighboring countries in the west. They also bear testimony to the emerging of the world-famous Silk Road.

Now we arrive at the foot of the famous natural wonderwork. Featuring snow- and ice-covered hills, valleys, glaciers, luxuriant vegetation and fresh open air, the Tianshan Mountains stand more than 4,000 meters above sea level. They are topped by Mount Bogda, which is 5,445 meters high and looks as if it were a natural guard for the capital city of Urumqi. The snow and ice serve as a natural reservoir that nurture the farming of the autonomous region. Owing to this, local farmers in the region successfully grow wheat, regardless that the average rainfall is less than 150 millimeters. Water found in the glaciers is used for wine brewing and is also packaged as mineral water for drink.

The climate of the Tianshan Mountains is characterized by a variety of types. With the ascending topography, the temperature decreases and a clearcut zoning of vegetation appears. In areas where the altitude is 1,600 meters below the sea level, a steppe type prevails. In areas where the altitude is between 1,600 and 2,800 meters, a combined climate type of steppe and forest dominates. In areas that stand 2,800 and 4,000 meters above sea level, an alpine-meadow climate exists.

These mountains are also rich in forest resources. This area boasts two million hectares of forested land and more than 100 million cubic meters of timber. Dragon spruce is the dominant species. Siberian larch, birch and other rare trees grow as well.

Luxuriant vegetation can be found in the valleys deep in the mountains. As many as 60 species of grass, including medicinal herbs, grow in vast expanses. Droves of wild animals including Mongolian gazelles and red deer roam around. Brown bears, wild hogs, roe deer, argali, snow leopards, lynxs and swans can also be found.

Xinjiang Uygur Autonomous Region also serves as a home to

Heavenly Lake in Xinjiang

people of 47 ethnic groups such as Uygur, Kazak and Mogolian. The Kazak people mainly live in the picturesque tourist area of Heavenly Lake. Living a nomadic life, the Kazak herdsman dwell in white-colored yurts. This way of life was first mentioned in a poem written in the Han Dynasty, and this show that the Kazaks have led this life for at least 2,000 years. A typical yurt is composed of wall-like felt, supporting poles, ceilings, felt rug and the door, which is easy to assemble and dismantle. It can shield against heat in the daylight and chill at night. There is an opening of 0.33 meters in diameter on the ceiling to let in the light.

Now let's pay a visit to the yurt. The Kazaks are easy to tell from the costumes they wear. A typical Kazak girl or young women puts on a long and pleated dress that has floral designs on the sleeves. On the outside she dons a leather robe buttoning down the front, and a multi-colored cone-shaped headgear that is decorated with owl plumage. A young man wears a white-colored and lace-trimmed cotton shirt inside and leather robe outside. Men also wear a wide and long cotton belt around their waists to shield from wind. They invariably carry with them a knife on the right side of the belt. The majority of costumes are homemade by themselves.

The Kazaks are Moslems. Pork is a strict taboo. The aged people will be given priority when entering the yurt; visitors are supposed to sit on the rug instead of the host's bed. Visitors should accept the host's treat even if they do not feel like food or drink. They should wash their hands before and after the meal.

Tea with milk is an everyday drink that is widely enjoyed by the Kazaks. It is made of brick tea, fresh milk and salt. The drink contains aromatic oil that helps in digestion and refreshing. Kazaks enjoy a fermented and baked flour pancake as their staple food. Known as "nang," this food is prepared in a round frying pan. Specially fried rice is also widely enjoyed by the Kazak people. It is prepared with fresh mutton, carrot, onion, vegetable oil, lamb oil and rice. Many herdsmen also enjoy boiled mutton. This course is served with a

Selected Tour Commentaries

knife, and the guest can help himself with his own hands as well.

Proceeding forward again, we will finally arrive at the Heavenly Lake. The first sight of the wonder is the Stone Entrance, or one of the eight wonders of the Heavenly Lake tourist area. This scene features precipitous cliffs and deep gorges with roaring waters flowing between.

On the west, the visitors will see a pool of clear and tranquil water, which is known as Western Minor Heavenly Lake. Termed as Dragon's Pool Reflecting the Bright Moon, it is one of the eight wonders in this area.

Proceeding along the zigzagging path, we will at last reach the lake proper. The Heavenly Lake is shaped like a crescent. It is 3,400 meters long and 1,500 meters wide, and covers a space of 4.9 square kilometers. Standing 1,980 meters above sea level, this lake is 40 meters deep on average, with the deepest reaching 105 meters.

The Heavenly Lake is a moraine by nature. Splendid peaks and glaciers were developed some 200,000 years ago. As a result of prolonged scouring and wearing off of the glaciers, a gigantic pit was formed. Later, the climate turned warmer, glaciers receded and a large amount of gravel accumulated, resulting in huge terminal moraines. In the end, the Heavenly Lake took shape. Since remote times, quite a few of myths and legends circulated concerning the beautiful scenery.

Standing by the clear lake, visitors can admire another three wonders of the area.

On the northern bank of the lake stands an old elm, which is the only tree by the water. It is termed the "Magic Needle that Tranquilizes the Ocean." On the southeast, people will see the snow-covered Mount Bogda. In the bright sunlight, the three main peaks shine and glisten. This scene is known as "Appreciating Snow on the Southern Hills."

In addition, people can also see the sunrise amidst vapors and mists. This is known as "First Rays on Seas of Mountains." Visitors

Heavenly Lake in Xinjiang

can also enjoy different yet beautiful views in the afternoon and at dusk.

Proceeding further westward, there stand three huge rocks in deep valleys some 4,000 meters away. These rocks are 2,718 meters above the sea level and resemble three candles in a row, hence the name of "Three Stones that Support the Sky." In the olden times, the Taoist priests that lived in the mountains used to hang lamps atop the huge stones as a sign of peace and stability. Therefore, these stones are also known as the "Lamppost Hills."

Still, there is one more scene known as "Viewing Pines on the Western Slope." Visitors can enjoy the beautiful forests of countless dragon spruces. Wild mushrooms can also be gathered in the woods. At last, in the downstream of the Heavenly Lake, there is a running and roaring cataract that is known as "Soaring Cataract and Suspending Fountains." The pool at the foot of the cataract is known as Eastern Minor Heavenly Lake.

Now I'd like to tell you something more about the lifestyle of the Kazaks. The Kazaks are music lovers, and fine horses and songs are likened as wings for them. Many of them pluck "dongbula," a string instrument, and sing songs on horseback. There are lyricists who sing folk songs and ballads for a living. On each summer, a number of competitions are held and rewards are offered for prize-winning lyricists. Each competition will last about seven to ten days.

The Kazaks are also fond of a dynamic dance that is rich in nomadic characteristics. They usually dance to the accompaniment of dongbulas. Corban and Rozah are the most important eventful festivals for the Kazaks. On these occasions they are duty-bound to pay visits to friends and relatives. What is more, on each Spring Equinox, the Kazak people celebrate it as their New Year's Day. A special meal that is a blend of mutton, cheese and cereal will be prepared.

The Kazaks, both men and women, are good horse riders. On major festivals a variety of equestrian competitions are held. Marks-

Selected Tour Commentaries

manship and wrestling contests that are carried out on horseback are also held.

With this our visit to the Heavenly Lake and the accompanying tourist wonders draws to a conclusion. I hope this will leave you with a rewarding and lasting impression. Thank you all.

责任编辑:程伟进 赵翔翔
责任印制:李崇宝

国书在版编目(CIP)数据

走遍中国:中国优秀导游词精选 = Touring China: Selected tour Commentaries:英文/国家旅游局编:王军等译. — 北京:中国旅游出版社,2000.8
ISBN 7-5032-1757-X

Ⅰ.走… Ⅱ.①国…②王… Ⅲ.旅游指南-中国-英文 Ⅳ.K928.9

中国版本图书馆 CIP 数据核字(2000)第 68324 号

书　名	Touring China: Selected tour Commentaries
编　著	国家旅游局
译　者	王　军　等
出版发行	中国旅游出版社
	(北京建内大街甲9号　邮编 100005)
印　刷	北京 1201 印刷厂
版　次	2000 年 8 月第 1 版
	2000 年 8 月第 1 次印刷
开　本	787×1092 毫米　1/32
印　张	11.75
字　数	395 千字
印　数	1—10000 册
定　价	28.00 元

·如发现图书残缺请直接与我社发行部联系调换
(电话:010-65201174)